D0734381

Field Guide to the Birds of North America

Third Edition

Third
Edition

Field Guide to the

Birds
of North America

NATIONAL
GEOGRAPHIC

WASHINGTON, D.C.

Contents

Library of Congress CIP data appears on page 476.

Introduction

North America enjoys an abundance of bird life. More than 900 species of birds breed here, or visit the continent regularly, or drop in occasionally. This is a daunting number for a newcomer to birdwatching—today more frequently called birding—who is merely trying to identify a stranger at the feeder. But no one person, not even the most persistent birder, has seen all these birds. Many species are found only in certain regions or specialized habitats, and some are extremely rare in North America.

Birding is a challenging endeavor that engages millions of people. The challenge lies not only in finding birds but also in accurately identifying each bird seen, and this requires both preparation and experience. But birding is also an egalitarian activity in which an informed amateur has as good a chance as a trained professional to sight an elusive species and make a valuable contribution to our knowledge of North American birds.

For every level of interest, the field guide is an indispensable tool. The first place to use it is at home. Leaf through it often to become familiar with the wonderful variety of birds that inhabit or visit our continent.

What's New in This Edition

This third edition of the *Field Guide to the Birds of North America* differs in a number of significant ways from the previous editions. To begin with, its organization has been revised to follow more closely the sequence found in the *Check-list of North American Birds* (7th edition, 1998) of the American Ornithologists' Union (A.O.U.). The A.O.U. Check-list arranges species according to their presumed natural and evolutionary relationships and is widely followed by most ornithologists and birding communities in North and Middle America. The Check-list (and its biennial supplements) is also considered the authority for scientific and common names. Many names have been changed in recent A.O.U. decisions. These changes are incorporated in this third edition and are cross-referenced in the index under the old, second-edition names. Many birds formerly regarded as subspecies, for example, are now raised to full species status. The Scrub Jay was formerly considered a single species, but is presently split into three seperate species. So the listing for the former Scrub Jay refers you to three new entries: Florida, Island, and Western Scrub-Jays.

Altogether, the third edition offers some 80 additional species, all illustrated, that represent, besides split species, either newly established populations, such as the Shiny Cowbird, or new accidental visitors, such as the Variegated Flycatcher. It adds established exotic species such as Orange Bishop and numerous parrots. Some 35 new plates incorporate the new species, add diagnostic features or new plumages for existing species, or correct misleading features from the previous editions.

Also, a few exotics whose introductions failed have been

Island Scrub-Jay

Shiny Cowbird

Variegated
Flycatcher

deleted. These include Red-legged Partridge, Japanese Quail, Black Francolin, Java Sparrow, and some of the exotic waterfowl. And Solander's Petrel and Cuban Emerald were deleted because of identification problems in the original sightings.

Each existing text account and range map in this third edition has been revised to bring it up to date with current knowledge obtained from experts in the field. For greater clarity in reading the maps, an orange color has been substituted for the yellow that originally depicted breeding range. All these changes make the *Field Guide to the Birds of North America* one of the most comprehensive and accurate guides available.

Species Selection

This guide includes all species known to breed in North America–defined here as the land extending northward from the northern border of Mexico, plus adjacent islands and seas within about two hundred miles of the coast. Also included are species that breed in Mexico or Central America or on other continents but are seen in North America when they spend the winter here or pass through on regular migration routes.

For those accidental visitors that are seen in North America only when they wander off course or are blown in by storms, our standard generally requires that they have been seen at least three times in the past two decades or five times in this century. A few species, such as the Asian Brown Flycatcher, that do not yet meet this standard are nevertheless included because of a strong likelihood that they will be seen again, especially if knowledgeable watchers are looking for them.

Orange Bishop

Many exotic species—birds from other continents that have been introduced into North America mainly as game, park, or cage birds—are now seen in the wild. Those that have become locally established, such as the Orange Bishop, are included. A few, such as the European Starling, now occur continent-wide.

Families

Scientists organize species of animals into family groups that share certain structural characteristics. Among the birds, some families encompass more than a hundred members; others have only one. Characteristics within a family are often helpful in identifying birds in the field. Take the members of the Picidae family (page 274), for example. Strong, sharp bills, strong claws, and short legs are among the features that make them easily recognized as woodpeckers. Their family resemblance narrows down the list of possible identifications to a manageable number.

Thus, it pays to become familiar with the brief family descriptions at the beginning of each group in this field guide for information applicable to all members of the family. You will also find within some family sections a description of smaller groups such as the sapsuckers, four woodpecker species (three shown here) that share some unique traits.

Sapsuckers: Yellow-bellied, Williamson's, Red-breasted *daggetti*

Scientific Names

Each bird species has a two-part Latin scientific name. The first part, always capitalized, indicates the genus, a group of closely related species more narrowly defined than that of the family. Nine members of the family Picidae are placed in the genus *Picoides.* Together with the second part of the name, not capitalized, this identifies the species. *Picoides pubescens* is the name of one specific kind of woodpecker, commonly known as the Downy Woodpecker. *Picoides tridactylus,* or *P. tridactylus* for short, is the Three-toed Woodpecker. It is a feature of scientific nomenclature that no two species share the same two-part scientific name, or binomial.

Species are sometimes further divided into subspecies, when populations in different geographical regions show recognizable differences. Each subspecies, or race, bears a third scientific name, or trinomial. Out of eight subspecies worldwide of Three-toed Woodpecker, three are found in North America. *Picoides tridactylus bacatus (P. t. bacatus)* identifies the dark-backed subspecies of the Three-toed Woodpecker that inhabits eastern North America. *P. t. dorsalis* is the paler backed race of the same woodpecker found in the Rockies. *P. t. fasciatus* is an intermediate subspecies found from Alaska to the northwest.

Three-toed Woodpeckers: *fasciatus, dorsalis, bacatus*

If the third part of a scientific name is the same as the second, the subspecies in question is the *nominate* race. The race that was originally described becomes the nominate race when one or more subspecies are subsequently named. It serves as a kind of benchmark in describing other races of the same species. Thus, among the woodpeckers known as sapsuckers, *Sphyrapicus ruber ruber* is the nominate race of the Red-breasted Sapsucker, found in the northern part of this species' range. It was described earlier than the more southerly race of Red-breasted, which carries the scientific name *Sphyrapicus ruber daggetti.*

family	Woodpeckers	Picidae
genus	Sapsuckers	***Sphyrapicus***
species	Red-breasted Sapsucker	*Sphyrapicus **ruber***
subspecies or **race**	Red-breasted Sapsucker (southern subspecies)	*Sphyrapicus ruber **daggetti***
nominate race	Red-breasted Sapsucker (northern subspecies)	*Sphyrapicus ruber **ruber***

Latin names are used in this book for learning and clarity. As a rule, we have tried to illustrate or describe the extremes of variations that look distinctly different from other races of the same species. For example, of the more than 20 races of Horned Lark in North America, we show the most typical and also the extremes within the species.

How to Identify Birds

You catch a momentary glimpse of a bird in a bush. From the flash of red and the hint of a crest that register in your brain, you know immediately that it was a male Northern Cardinal. This identification was easy, because the male cardinal is the only crested, all-red bird found in North America. The bird's color and crest, then, served as the primary field marks in the identification of this particular bird, and a flash was all it took to identify this common and distinctive species. *Field marks*—a bird's physical aspects—are the clues by which birds are identified. Field marks include plumage, or the bird's overall feathering, as well as the shape of the body and its individual parts, and any actual markings such as bars, bands, spots, and rings. A field mark can be as obvious as the Northern Cardinal's color or the Killdeer's double breast bands (page 156), or as subtle as the difference in head shape between Greater and Lesser Scaup, a much more reliable field mark than head color. Some field marks are plainly visible only in good light or from a certain angle or when the bird is in flight.

Lesser Scaup, Greater Scaup

Apart from birds that come regularly to a back-yard feeder or congregate in public places, many species do not provide the observer a good, long look. It is therefore necessary to make the most of the time that the bird does allow. Take as long a look as possible, getting an impression of the bird from head to toe. Notice its shape and any prominent marks; take a few notes, if you can. But mostly look. When the bird flies away is the time to reach for your field guide, and begin the process of sorting out the information you have. In this guide, the most distinctive features for each species in each plumage are usually listed first in the text account, for quick reference. Keep in mind, though, that not every bird seen can be identified, even by experts.

Parts of a Bird

Although all birds share feathered bodies and other common features, the sizes, shapes, and configurations of their various parts are different from family to family and species to species. Each part of a bird's body can yield important clues to identification. It is therefore necessary to become acquainted with all the terms used in describing the parts of a bird and the location of those parts on the bird.

Shape

Most birds have a shape and stance that is characteristic of their species or family. Even at great range and in poor light, the short-tailed, pointed-billed, and rather chunky body shape of the perched European Starling (page 16) is unmistakable. Shape can change, though, depending on environmental conditions. In cold weather many species fluff their feathers and hunker down. This makes them look bigger, and often shorter, and alters their characteristic posture.

superciliuim
postocular stripe
ear patch (auricular)
moustachial stripe
submoustachial stripe

median crown stripe
lateral crown stripe
supraloral area
lores

malar stripe

Lark Sparrow

Head

Good birding should start at the top. A careful look at a bird's head can nearly always provide a correct identification of a species. Head shape should be the first aspect noted. For example, the blocky head of the Common Loon (page 22) stands out from afar across a misty lake.

eye line

Chipping Sparrow

The boldly marked head of an adult Lark Sparrow offers a nearly complete course in common head markings. Sparrows are a confusing group, and it is the often subtle differences in head markings that can help sort them out. At the top of the head there is often a pale or white *median crown stripe* bordered by dark *lateral crown stripes*. A line running from base of the bill up and over the eye is known as the *eyebrow*, or *supercilium*. Sometimes the area between bill and eye, the *lores*, has its own marking. The front part of the eyebrow, or *supraloral area*, may be of a different color—another useful marking. The eye color itself may be diagnostic in some species. Bird pupils are always black but the *iris* can be colored, as it is in many gulls. A ring of naked flesh, the *orbital ring*, may surround the eye as may a feathered one, usually called an *eye ring*. The Least Flycatcher has an unbroken, feathered, white eye ring. In some species the ring is interrupted, forming *eye crescents* instead. The dark stripe extending back from the Lark Sparrow's eye is known as a *postocular stripe*. If it extended through the eye itself, as in the Chipping Sparrow, it would be known as an *eye line*. A distinctive brown patch, bordered in black on the Lark Sparrow, marks the *ear patch* or *auricular*. Its lower border is a *moustachial stripe*. Below that is a white *submoustachial stripe*, bordered with yet another dark line, the *malar stripe*.

eye crescent

Northern Parula

gonys

Western Gull, California Gull

The shape of the bill must not be overlooked. Bills are specialized according to diet and method of feeding. The Lark Sparrow's short, stout bill indicates a seedeater. The Tennessee Warbler's is a fine-pointed insect probe, as is the case with many warblers, but it is also used for sipping nectar. Gulls have a special ridge on their lower mandible called the *gonys*, which forms a distinct angle. On the Western Gull it is very acute, giving the bill a bulbous tip, while on the California Gull the angle is much broader and the bill looks almost straight. The top of the bill is known as the *culmen*. In raptors, the patch of bare skin covering the upper mandible is called the *cere*, seen here in the Common Black-Hawk. Some species, such as pelicans or cormorants, have a fold of loose skin called a *gular pouch* hanging from the throat.

orbital ring

cere

Common Black-Hawk

Wings

Wings frequently give birders the ability to confirm an identification. They are most often observed in the folded position, providing useful diagnostic clues, but obscuring the wing's overall structure.

eye ring
scapulars
median coverts
greater coverts
wing bar
tertials
secondaries
primaries
tertials
Least
Flycatcher
scapulars
greater coverts
median coverts
lesser coverts
marginal coverts
secondaries
Great Black-backed Gull
upper wing
greater primary
coverts
primaries

mantle
primary tip
projection
scapulars
median
coverts
greater
coverts
tertials
tail
tibia
tarsus
Pacific
Golden-Plover

A bird's wing is composed basically of groups of strong *flight feathers,* covered on the upper and lower side by shorter, protective feathers called *coverts.* Each feather's shaft divides its *inner web* from its *outer web.* The outer nine or ten tapering flight feathers comprise the *primaries.* They are followed by the *secondaries.* The three innermost flight feathers are the *tertials.* Joining the wing and body are rows of short, protective feathers, the *scapulars.* A series of wing coverts cover the bases of the flight feathers and the leading edge of the wing. From *leading edge* to *trailing edge* of the wing they are the *marginal, lesser, median,* and *greater wing coverts.* The lesser coverts have several rows of feathers, while the others have a single row each. On long-winged species such as albatrosses, another set of feathers, the *humerals,* is well developed. The overall plumage of the back, extending to the scapulars and upperwing coverts, is called the *mantle,* a term used frequently in referring to gulls.

In some species the white tips of the greater and median coverts above the secondaries form *wing bars,* often an important diagnostic feature. In some ducks, such as the American Black Duck, the secondaries themselves are uniquely colored, forming a pronounced bar known as a *speculum.* If a bird, such as the immature Common Tern, shows a contrasting bar on the forward part of the upper wing, it is referred to as a *carpal bar.*

The spread underwing displays the undersides of the flight feathers and the underwing coverts, and offers features that prove useful in identifying birds in flight. The short, dense feathers of the *wing linings* often contrast with the rest of the underwing, as may the *axillaries,* the bird's "armpit."

A feature to notice in the folded bird wing is how far the primaries extend past the secondaries and longest tertials. Called

trailing
edge
scapulars
humerals
Short-tailed
Albatross
leading
edge

wing lining
speculum
American Black Duck

axillaries
Black-bellied Plover

the *primary tip projection*, its length can help distinguish between similar species such as the American and Pacific Golden-Plovers. We have labeled the visible feathers on the Pacific Golden-Plover (preceding page). On such shorebirds, note the prominence of the scapulars, and that the secondaries are completely hidden.

Tail

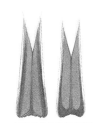

Last, tail shape and pattern are very important aids to identification. Most bird species have 12 tail feathers, called *rectrices*. A good part of the time we see only the folded tail. From above, usually only the one or two central tail feathers show, and from below only the outermost tail feather on each side. Similar-looking species, such as MacGillivray's and Connecticut Warblers (page 382), may be distinguished from each other from below by the length of tail projecting past the undertail coverts. In order to view the undertail properly, get in front of the bird and look at the tail from below. Subtle differences in undertail coloring, for instance, help distinguish the members of the perplexing fly-catcher group of the genus *Myiarchus*.

Flycatcher tails from below: Brown-crested, Ash-throated

But sometimes it takes more than the outer tail feathers to discern the pattern of a tail. Then it is best to see the bird in flight, as in the case of the four longspurs (pages 420, 422). In flight, too, tail shape shows well. Thus, we can distinguish the fan-shaped tail of the American Crow from the wedge-shaped tail of the Common Raven (page 318). The distinctive forked tail of the Barn Swallow (page 324) gets its shape from short central tail feathers and long outer ones.

Molt

Regular renewal of plumage, called *molt,* is essential to a bird's well-being and ability to fly. Yet molt produces variations of plumage within a species and between ages that create additional obstacles to identification. It is not enough for us to know what a bird's plumage looks like in only one season or sex or at one age. Most species undergo a complete molt in late summer or early fall, replacing all their feathers.

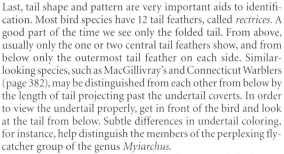

Adult male Scarlet Tanagers change their entire body plumage color from summer to fall. Adult Acadian Flycatchers (opposite, above) are brightest in spring, becoming worn and faded by late summer. Fresh fall plumage after molt can be brighter than the colors of August. This plumage is usually held through the fall and winter.

Scarlet Tanagers: breeding adult ♂, fall adult ♂

In some songbirds, such as the House Sparrow (opposite), the bright plumage of spring appears with the gradual wearing away of dull tips on the feathers of the winter plumage, with very little actual molting involved.

Often the molt occurs before the birds migrate, and thus we see the birds in this fresh plumage even if they spend the winter outside North America. In late winter or early spring, the birds undergo a partial molt—usually involving the head, body, and some wing coverts—to the plumage we see in spring and summer. To further complicate matters, some species suspend the molt during migration and complete it upon arrival at the wintering or breeding grounds. This applies to many shorebird species. On the whole, fall and winter plumage may vary considerably from spring and summer plumage, and a bird in the process of molting can confound even expert birders.

Some species molt over a considerably longer period than others. Birds of prey must rely on their wing feathers for successful hunting and thus molt very gradually so that only a few feathers are missing at any one time.

Acadian Flycatchers: spring adult, worn summer adult

Plumage Variation

In many species the male and female look quite different, and the young birds are unlike either parent. And some species, usually of the same genus, occasionally breed with other species, producing *hybrid* offspring that look partly like one parent, partly like the other. Different subspecies also interbreed, resulting in *intergrade* individuals or populations.

Some species have two or more *color morphs*—variations, in plumage color occurring regionally or within the same population. The Red-tailed Hawk (page 116) comes in two morphs, *dark* and *rufous* (rust-colored). Common terms, such as rufous and *buffy*, alternate with rarer usages, such as *hepatic* (reddish-brown), in describing the nuances of shading in a bird's plumage.

Where adult males and females of a species are similar, we show only one. When male (♂) and female (♀) look different, we usually show both. If spring and fall, or *breeding* and *non-breeding*, plumages differ only slightly or if only one of these plumages is usually seen in North America, we show only one figure. Juvenile and immature birds are illustrated when they hold a different-looking plumage after they are old enough to be seen away from their more easily recognizable parents.

Plumage Sequence

After hatching, not all birds go through the same sequences of plumage. Some young birds, such as the Painted Redstart (page 390), hold juvenile plumage for a few weeks, then move right into adult or adultlike plumage. Others, such as the Herring Gull (page 202) and the Bald Eagle (page 108) take years to acquire their adult look. Knowing these differences is essential to recognizing birds.

Some nestlings wear fluffy *down*, while others are hatched naked. The first coat of true feathers, acquired before the bird leaves the nest, is called the *juvenile*, or *juvenal*, plumage. True hawks and loons, and many other waterbirds, hold this plumage well into the winter. In many

House Sparrows: fall adult ♂, breeding adult ♂

species, juvenile plumage is replaced in later summer or early fall by a *first-fall* or *first-winter* plumage that more closely resembles the adult. First-fall and any subsequent plumages that do not resemble the adult are termed *immature* plumages. These may continue in a series that includes *first-spring* (when the bird is almost a year old), *first-summer*, and so on, until adult plumage is attained. When birds, such as the Bald Eagle, take several years to reach adult plumage, we have labeled the interim plumages as *subadult* or with the specific year or season shown. This terminology is often used with gulls.

Some species wear colorful plumage in the breeding season and molt to different colors for fall and winter. In other species, *breeding* plumage looks much like *winter* plumage. Some changes are evident only during the brief period of courtship. In herons, for example, the colors of bill, lores, legs, and feet may change or deepen. When these colors are at their height, the birds are said to be in *high breeding* plumage.

Most ducks, after mating, molt into an *eclipse* plumage in which males acquire a femalelike plumage and females show little change, although some become paler and duller. Eclipse plumage is usually held only for a few weeks, when another molt begins. In eclipse, all the flight feathers are lost simultaneously, and the ducks are unable to fly until new feathers grow in.

Measurements

Knowing the size of a bird is another key. If you are searching for a kinglet, for example, it helps to know that the bird in question is only about four inches long. Relative size is also important. In mixed flocks, Greater and Lesser Yellowlegs (page 160) are easily distinguished from each other by size alone.

The measurements in this book come from a large number of published works. Technical books give a variety of precise measurements, such as the *wing chord*—the measurement of a folded wing. Body length and wingspread measurements are by their nature more imprecise and may vary slightly from one source to another. For birders in the field, however, we felt that these were the most helpful aids. Thus, average length (L) from tip of bill to tip of tail for each species is given, with figures rounded off. Where size varies greatly within a species, either because of sex or geographical variation among subspecies, a range of smallest to largest is provided. And for large birds seen most often in flight, we give the wingspan (W), measured from wing tip to wing tip.

Voice

A bird's songs and calls not only reveal its presence but also, in many cases, its identity. Some species—particularly nocturnal or secretive birds such as owls, nightjars, and rails—are more often heard than seen. A few species are most reliably identified by voice even when they are seen well. Willow and Alder Fly-catchers, for example, are nearly identical in appearance, but their calls are different enough to distinguish them: Willow gives a liquid *wit* call, while Alder delivers a loud *pip.*

When birds assemble or travel in flocks, they often keep in touch with a *contact* or *flight call* that may be markedly different from their other calls. Flight calls are especially important for identifying flocks overhead. Flying Blackpoll Warblers and other warblers, for example, announce their identity with buzzy *zeet* notes.

Birds sensing danger let out an *alarm call,* which may be the same as or a variant of their basic call, but delivered in a more urgent tone. Dowitchers execute a series of call notes that increases in rapidity according to the birds' degree of alarm. Bushtits give an excited twittering when raptors are about.

While bird species have a number of vocalizations that are used for different purposes, some are multipurpose. The primary song is sung mainly by males on or near the breeding grounds, although some species sing year-round. Its purpose is to announce territorial claims or to woo females. Females themselves, such as the Northern Cardinal, sometimes sing also.

Learning songs and calls makes birding a more rewarding experience. Distinctive songs and calls are described in our text. Transcription into words, such as *cheerily cheer-up cheerio* for the American Robin's song, helps to express tone and pattern but is very subjective. You may find it best to transcribe sounds into your own words as you hear them; one birder's *chip* is another's *tsip* or *chik* or even *peek.*

Behavior

Body language and other kinds of behavioral traits also provide many clues to species identity. Look, for example, at a bird's flight. Is it direct or undulating? Does the bird beat its wings rapidly or slowly? Turkey Vultures soar with their wings held slightly raised in a shallow V, known as a *dihe-dral,* while Black Vultures soar on level wings.

Observe feeding. Does the bird forage on the ground or in the treetops? Among shore-birds, the two species of Yellowlegs and the Solitary Sandpiper peck at the water to get food, while the dowitchers drill the mud like a sewing machine.

Look for personality clues. Is the bird usu-ally visible and approachable, or shy and difficult to locate? How does the bird move? Mourning and MacGillivray's Warblers hop; Connecticut Warblers walk deliberately. Black-and-white War-blers climb up and down and around tree trunks; the superfi-cially similar Blackpoll Warbler does not. How does the bird use its tail? Among the hard to identify flycatchers of the genus *Empi-donax,* nearly all species flick their tails up except for the Gray Flycatcher, which drops its tail down. Such distinctive behavior is not only useful for identification but fascinating to watch.

Short-billed Dowitcher

Abundance and Habitat

Abundant:
European Starling

Abundance must be considered in relation to habitat. Habitat information included in the text will help you find a particular species within its range. Under the heading **Range:** in our species accounts, we include supplemental information about habitat, abundance (such as casual and accidental), and seasonal status that cannot be shown in a single map. Some species are highly local, found only in a very specialized habitat. Bank Swallows, for example, are common in summer only near the steep sandy or gravelly banks they require for nesting. Common Loons are fairly common to common on large bodies of water, but away from large lakes, as in parts of the southwest, they are very rare.

Seasons of the year, of course, also affect numbers. In spring, the Semipalmated Sandpiper is abundant on its northern breeding grounds; during migration it is common in the midwest and on the east coast but rare in the west; in the winter a few are still found in North America only in southernmost Florida.

Common:
Indigo Bunting

The following categories of abundance, or lack thereof, are used in this third edition of the Field Guide:

Abundant means a species is present in great numbers in an area. The European Starling is plainly abundant in varied habitats throughout most of North America.

Common means that a species is very likely to be seen in a given area, but in fewer numbers than an abundant one. The Indigo Bunting is common over much of eastern North America.

Fairly common is down a notch from common. Again it is a matter of probability and numbers.

Uncommon species can have an enormous range and still be seen infrequently. The Northern Goshawk, for example, is uncommon over much of its resident range.

Rare:
Black-headed Gull

Rare means that a species is present each year in very low density, or that very small numbers pass through in a given season. The Black-headed Gull is rare in New England.

Very rare species are annual in a region, but only one or a few will occur in a season.

Casual is used for species that do not occur annually, but over decades there is a pattern of their occurrence, as with the Redwing in Newfoundland.

Casual:
Redwing

Accidental refers to species that have been seen only once or a few times in an area that is far out of their normal range. In fact, it may be decades, or even centuries, before another one is seen there again. The Narcissus Flycatcher is an example, having been recorded twice on Attu Island in the westernmost Aleutians.

Vagrant is a bird that has strayed off its usual migration route.

Irruptive species, such as the Snowy Owl (opposite) are erratic or sporadic in their movements. One year they may be common in a given region, and the next year totally absent.

Range Maps

Accidental:
Narcissus Flycatcher

Maps are provided for all species with two general exceptions. One is those species with very limited ranges that instead are

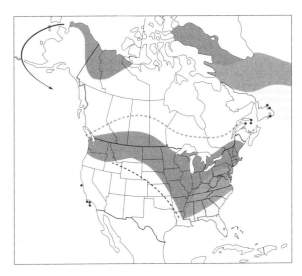

Range Map Symbols

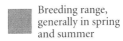 Breeding range, generally in spring and summer

 Extent of irregular breeding range, or of post-breeding dispersal in summer and fall

 Year-round range

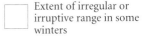 Extent of irregular or irruptive range in some winters

Winter range (*if no winter or year-round range is shown, winters outside North America*)

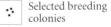 Species migrates chiefly east of this line

 Principal direction of migration

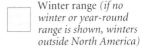 Selected breeding colonies

described in the text. The other is those species that do not ordinarily breed or winter in North America.

On each map, range boundaries are drawn where the species ceases to be regularly seen. Keep in mind that nearly every species will be rare at the edges of its range. The sample map shown here explains the colors and symbols used on our maps.

Remember that our maps are general guides for the entire continent. Specific, up-to-the-minute information for a particular area should be obtained from local checklists, books, and birders. A good place to start is with a local nature center or chapter of the National Audubon Society.

Birds, like any other animal, are not bound by maps. Ranges continually expand and contract, making any map a tool rather than a rule. The Shiny Cowbird, for instance, was

immature
Snowy Owl

not even included in the last edition of this field guide. Now it is found regularly in small numbers in south Florida and has been recorded as an accidental as far north as New Brunswick. Irruptive species, such as the Snowy Owl, move southward in some years in large or small numbers and for great or small distances. These irregular movements are generally but not specifically predictable; certainly they cannot be precisely mapped. In some species, birds leave the nesting grounds in late summer and move northward. These postbreeding wanderers, principally young birds, will migrate southward with the winter.

Range maps of pelagic species, birds that spend most of their time over the open sea, are somewhat conjectural, due to smaller numbers of seabird observations.

Range information is based on actual sightings and therefore depends upon the number of knowledgeable and active birders in each area. There is much to learn about bird distribution in every part of North America. Participation by amateur birders is necessary to the discovery of expanding ranges. Breeding-bird surveys and atlas projects undertaken by federal and state governments and by birding clubs make a vital contribution to the general fund of information about each species.

Extinct species:
Bachman's Warbler

How to Be a Better Birder

Time spent at home with your field guide will be repaid when you go out into meadows and woodlands, deserts and mountains, looking for birds. But much is also learned only from experience. When you have seen the Northern Harrier many times, for instance, its distinctive flight pattern signals its identity for you long before you can see its facial disk or white rump.

Experienced birders know how to move quietly and to stand patiently still. They know that a sudden riot of scolding songbirds may mean that an owl is roosting nearby; that a flock of familiar Bonaparte's Gulls should be studied closely to determine whether a Little or Black-headed Gull might also be present.

But there is more to responsible birding than maintaining a quiet demeanor. In fact, the American Birding Association (A.B.A.) publishes a comprehensive list of birding ethics in most of its publications. It can be obtained also by writing to the A.B.A. at P.O. Box 6599, Colorado Springs, CO 80934. The list stresses that special concern should be taken with threatened and endangered species and promotes the basic message that the welfare of any bird is more important than whether or not you see it.

The bird life of our continent has, on the whole, declined with the advance of human populations, with its resultant destruction of habitat, overhunting, and other hazards. In the last century and a half, we have lost such species as the Labrador Duck, the Great Auk, and the Passenger Pigeon. Since the publication of the last edition of this guide, it now appears virtually certain that the Ivory-billed Woodpecker has disappeared from North America, and that Bachman's Warbler

Endangered species:
Red-cockaded
Woodpecker

(opposite, above) has also become extinct. We have also lost various subspecies, such as the "Heath Hen" in the 1930s. More recently, the Dusky Seaside Sparrow has become extinct, the last one dying in captivity in 1987. In the species accounts describing birds presently on the federal list of threatened or endangered species—such as the Red-cockaded Woodpecker species (opposite, below) and *extimus* subspecies of Willow Flycatcher (endangered), or Florida Scrub-Jay (threatened)—we have placed the symbols **E** or **T**.

Many local and national organizations, such as the The Nature Conservancy, the National Audubon Society, and ABA, work tirelessly toward the preservation of habitat and protection of individual species. There are many opportunities for the amateur birder to get involved in this work through participation in lectures, bird walks, Christmas counts, and other activities. After learning the state distribution of a species, amateurs can also help by reporting rare sightings. If you believe you have seen a rare bird, watch it carefully while taking notes; photographs or tape recordings are particularly important if you can obtain them. Then report your findings promptly to the local birding authorities. Informed amateurs have made many significant contributions to our knowledge of North American birds.

Extinct subspecies: nigrescens Dusky Seaside Sparrow

Keeping Track

Most birders make lists of the birds they see. Some keep several lists, ranging from birds seen in a certain area to all birds ever seen—a life list. Such lists are a source of great pride and pleasure, enabling you to look back and remember the first time you saw an American Robin or a Downy Woodpecker.

The index in this guide includes a check-off box beside the common-name entry for each species; you can use this for your life list. Better still, keep a notebook in which to record not only the name of the bird you see but also the date and place and notes about field marks, behavior, and voice.

To make this easier, the National Geographic Society has published a companion *Birder's Journal*. This attractive volume includes a fully illustrated life list and ample space for recording bird sightings and taking notes. An introductory section presents a list of the Latin names of the orders and families of North American birds, along with the common and scientific names of the different species.

Endangered subspecies: extimus Willow Flycatcher

To become acquainted with the United States' top birding areas, you will want to consult the *National Geographic Guide to Birdwatching Sites*. These guides appear in two volumes: Eastern and Western United States. Written by travel writer and birding enthusiast Mel White, they list both popular and lesser known observation sites from forests to seashores, and provide all the information you need to locate them and enjoy their rewards. Precise travel and visitor information along with seasonal advice is combined with detailed maps and more than 250 color photographs of birds in their habitats.

Loons (Family Gaviidae)

All five members of this family occur in North America. In all species, juvenile-like plumage is held through the first summer.

Red-throated Loon *Gavia stellata* L 25" (64 cm)
Thin bill often appears slightly upturned; tends to hold head tilted up. **Breeding adult** has gray head with brick red throat patch that appears dark in flight; dark brown upperparts with no contrasting white patches as in all other loons in breeding plumage. **Winter adult** has sharply defined white on face and extensive white spotting on back. **Juvenile**'s head is grayish-brown; throat may have dull red markings. In all plumages, white on flanks extends upward a bit on sides of rump, which may cause confusion with Arctic Loon. In flight, shows smaller head and feet than Common and Yellow-billed Loon (next page); wingbeat is quicker; often flies with drooping neck, unlike other loons. Flight **call,** heard on breeding range, is a rapid, gooselike *kak-kak-kak.* **Range:** Migrates coastally; also overland in the east, where most numerous on northern and eastern Great Lakes. Casual inland in western North America and throughout the interior during winter.

Pacific Loon *Gavia pacifica* L 26" (66 cm)
In all plumages, has dark flanks, with no white extending upward on sides of rump. Bill is slim and straight; head smoothly rounded and held level. **Breeding adult**'s head and nape are pale gray; white stripes on sides of neck show only moderate contrast; throat's iridescent purple patch, sometimes washed with green, usually appears black unless seen clearly on swimming bird. **Juvenile**'s crown and nape are slightly paler than back, unlike Common Loon (next page); in juveniles and **winter** birds, dark cap extends to eye. Winter adults and most juveniles have a thin, brown "chin strap," though it may be faint in juveniles. In flight, resembles Common, but head and feet are smaller. **Range:** A coastal and offshore migrant; unlike other loons, often migrates in small to moderate-size flocks. Rare inland throughout the west; very rare in midwest; casual on east coast.

Arctic Loon *Gavia arctica* L 28" (73 cm)
Range: Old World species. To date, only the larger Siberian race, *G. a. viridigularis,* has been recorded in North America. Breeds in northwestern Alaska. Seen in migration in coastal western Alaska, especially at St. Lawrence Island. Casual elsewhere on west coast. Larger than Pacific Loon, with less rounded head; best distinguished in all plumages from Pacific by more extensive white on flanks, coming up over sides of rump. Visibility of white area depends on how buoyantly the bird is swimming. When diving, often only a small white rump patch is evident. At rest, Arctic Loon shows much more white; note Pacific can also show some white. Nape in **breeding adult** is darker, and black and white stripes are bolder, than in Pacific; white stripes on face connect more to sides of neck; greenish throat bar usually hard to see.

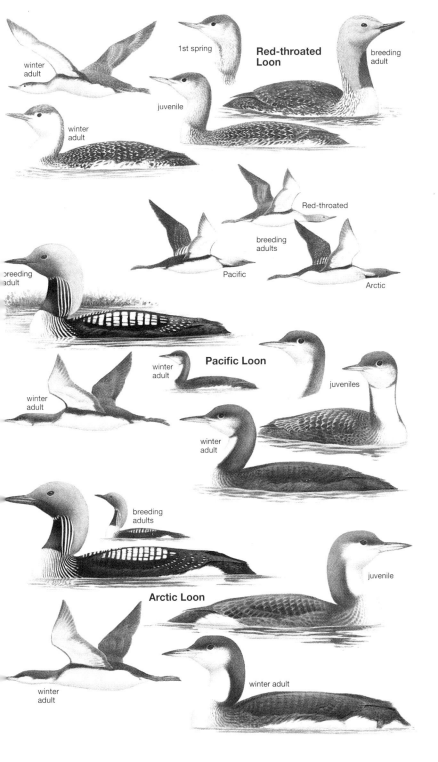

winter adult

1st spring

Red-throated Loon

breeding adult

juvenile

winter adult

Red-throated

breeding adults

Pacific

Arctic

breeding adult

Pacific Loon

winter adult

winter adult

juveniles

winter adult

breeding adults

Arctic Loon

juvenile

winter adult

winter adult

winter adult

Common Loon *Gavia immer L 32" (81 cm)*

Large, thick-billed loon with slightly curved culmen. Bill is black in **breeding** plumage, blue-gray in **winter adults** and **juveniles,** but the culmen remains dark. In winter plumage, crown and nape are darker than back; dark on nape extends around sides of neck, but note the white indentation above this. In winter adults the white extends up and around the eye; the face pattern is more blended in juveniles. Forehead is steep, crown is peaked at front. Holds head level. Juvenile Common and Yellow-billed Loons have whitish scalloping on their scapulars, distinguishing them from the plainer-backed winter adults. Full juvenile plumage is kept through most of the winter, with a partial molt in spring. Most winter adults retain at least a few spotted coverts, often visible on swimming birds. In flight, large head and feet help distinguish Common from Arctic, Pacific, and Red-throated Loons (preceding page). Loud yodeling **calls** are heard all year, but most often on breeding grounds. **Range:** Fairly common; nests on large lakes. Migrates overland as well as coastally. Under most conditions, Common and Yellow-billed fly quite high above the water when migrating, while the other loon species fly lower. Winters mainly in coastal waters or on large, ice-free inland bodies of water.

Yellow-billed Loon *Gavia adamsii L 34" (86 cm)*

Breeding adult has straw yellow bill, usually longer than in Common Loon; culmen is straight, giving bill a slightly uptilted look; head often tilted back, which enhances this effect. Crown is peaked at front and rear, giving a subtle double-bump effect. Bill is duskier at the base in **winter** and **juvenile** plumages, but always shows strong yellow cast toward the tip. Note also pale face and distinct dark mark behind eye; eye is smaller, back and crown are paler and browner than in Common. **Calls** are similar to Common. **Range:** Yellow-billed Loon breeds on tundra lakes and rivers. Migrates coastally; rare south of Canada on west coast, where it is recorded annually south to northern California, casually to southern California. Very rare inland in west; casual east to Great Lakes region.

winter adult

breeding adult

winter adult

Common Loon

juvenile

breeding adult

swimming juveniles

Common Yellow-billed Arctic Pacific Red-throated

winter adult

breeding adults

Yellow-billed Loon

winter adult

juvenile

Grebes (Family Podicipedidae)

A worldwide family; seven species occur in North America. Lobed toes make them strong swimmers. Grebes are infrequently seen on land or in flight.

Horned Grebe *Podiceps auritus* L 13½" (34 cm)

Breeding adult has chestnut foreneck, golden "horns." In **winter** plumage, white cheeks and throat contrast with dark crown and nape; some are dusky on lower foreneck. Black on nape narrows to a thin stripe. All birds show a pale spot in front of eye. In flight (next page), white secondaries show as patch on trailing edge of wing. Bill is short and straight, thicker than Eared Grebe's; neck is thicker too, crown flatter. Smaller size and shorter, dark bill most readily separate winter Horned from Red-necked Grebe (next page). **Range:** Breeds on lakes and ponds. Winters mostly on salt water but also on ice-free lakes of eastern North America; a few winter inland in west. Casual in Newfoundland.

Eared Grebe *Podiceps nigricollis* L 12½" (32 cm)

Breeding adult has blackish neck, golden "ears" fanning out behind eye. In **winter** plumage, throat is variably dusky; cheek dark; whitish on chin extends up as a crescent behind eye; compare with Horned Grebe. Note also Eared Grebe's longer, thinner bill; thinner neck; more peaked crown. Lacks pale spot in front of eye. Generally rides higher in the water than Horned Grebe, exposing fluffy white undertail coverts. In flight, white secondaries show as white patch on trailing edge of wing. **Range:** Usually nests in large colonies on freshwater lakes. Rare in eastern North America.

Pied-billed Grebe *Podilymbus podiceps* L 13½" (34 cm)

Breeding adult is brown overall, with black ring around stout, whitish bill; black chin and throat; pale belly. **Winter** birds lose bill ring; chin is white, throat tinged with pale rufous. Juveniles resemble winter adult but throat is much redder; eye ring absent, head and neck streaked with brown and white. First-winter birds lack streaking; throat is duller. A short-necked, big-headed, stocky grebe. In flight, shows almost no white on wing. **Range:** Nests around marshy ponds and sloughs; sometimes hides from intruders by sinking until only its head shows. Common but not gregarious. Winters on fresh or salt water. Casual to Alaska.

Least Grebe *Tachybaptus dominicus* L 9¾" (25 cm)

A small, short-necked grebe with golden yellow eyes, a slim, dark bill, and purplish-gray face and foreneck. **Breeding adult** has blackish crown, hindneck, throat, and back. **Winter** birds have white throat, paler bill, less black on crown. In flight, shows large white wing patch. **Range:** Rather uncommon and local; may hide in vegetation near shores of ponds, sloughs, ditches. May nest at any season on any quiet, inland water. Casual straggler to southern Arizona, southeast California, south Florida, and upper Texas coast.

Horned Grebe

breeding adult

winter

Eared Grebe

winter

breeding adult

Pied-billed Grebe

breeding

winter

Least Grebe

breeding

winter

Red-necked Grebe *Podiceps grisegena L 20" (51 cm)*
Large grebe with heavy, tapered, yellowish bill almost as long as the head. **Breeding adult**'s whitish throat and cheeks contrast with reddish foreneck. In **winter** plumage, throat is dusky, white of chin extends onto rear of face in a crescent. **First-winter** bird has rounder head, paler eye; lacks strong facial crescent. **Juvenile** has striped head. In flight, Red-necked Grebe shows a white leading and trailing edge on inner wing; thick neck is often held slouched down. **Calls,** usually heard only on breeding grounds, include a *crick-crick* note and drawn out braying calls. Generally solitary. **Range:** Breeds on shallow lakes; winters mostly along coasts. Rare in interior south of northern tier of states; casual south to southwest and Gulf coast states.

Clark's Grebe *Aechmophorus clarkii L 25" (64 cm)*
Resembles Western Grebe but bill is orange; back and flanks are paler; black cap does not extend to eye in **breeding** plumage; **downy young** are paler. In **winter adult,** lore region acquires more dark color, pattern looks more like Western; best distinction then is bill color. In flight, Clark Grebe's white wing stripe is more extensive than on Western. **Call** is a single, two-syllabled, upslurred *kree-eek* note. **Range:** Limits of range in both species are not well-known; Clark's occupies same general area and habitat as Western but is much less common in northern and eastern part of range. Formerly considered one species with Western.

Western Grebe *Aechmophorus occidentalis L 25" (64 cm)*
Large grebe, strikingly black-and-white, with a long, thin neck and long bill. Resembles Clark's Grebe but bill is yellow-green; black cap extends to include eyes; back and flanks are darker; **downy young** are darker. In **winter adult,** lore region acquires more whitish color, and pattern can closely resemble winter Clark's. In flight, Western Grebe's white wing stripe is less extensive than Clark's. **Call** is a loud, two-note *crick-kreek*. **Range:** Gregarious; nests in reeds along broad, freshwater lakes. Winters on seacoasts and sheltered bays and large inland bodies of water. Occupies same general range and habitat as Clark's but greatly predominates in northern and eastern part of range. Casual during migration and winter to eastern North America. Formerly considered one species with Clark's; hybrids occasionally seen.

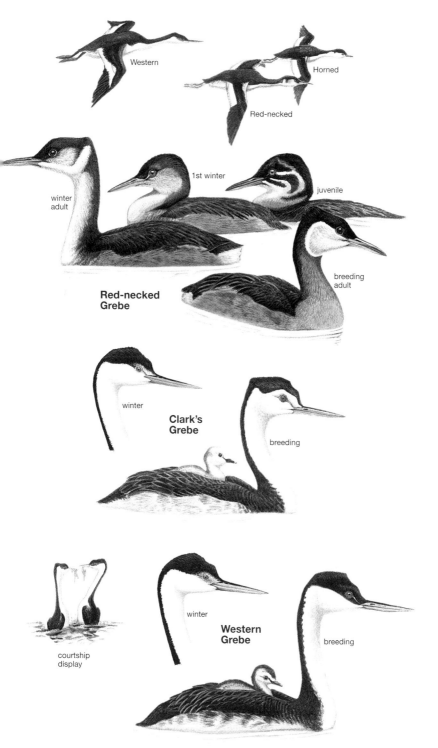

Western

Horned

Red-necked

winter adult

1st winter

juvenile

breeding adult

Red-necked Grebe

winter

Clark's Grebe

breeding

courtship display

winter

Western Grebe

breeding

Albatrosses (Family Diomedeidae)

Gliding on extremely long, narrow wings, these largest of seabirds spend most of their lives at sea, alighting on the water when becalmed or when feeding on squid, fish, and refuse. Rarely can they be seen from shore. Most species nest in large colonies on remote oceanic islands; pairs mate for life. In flight, feet and legs may not be visible.

Short-tailed Albatross *Phoebastria albatrus* E
L 36" (91 cm) W 87" (215-230 cm) **Range:** Common until end of 19th century; now extremely rare off west coast from Aleutians to California. Breeds on islands off southern Japan, where it is estimated that world population is now approaching 1,000. Large size, massive pink bill with pale bluish tip, dark humerals, and pale feet distinctive in all plumages. **Adult** is mostly white, with golden wash on head. **Juvenile** is blackish-brown except for traces of white below and behind eye and on chin. **Older juvenile** has more white around bill; compare with Black-footed Albatross. **Subadult** shows white forehead and face, dark cap; acquires white patches on scapulars and inner secondary coverts; with age becomes progressively whiter, but retains dark hindneck.

Shy Albatross *Thalassarche cauta*
L 37" (90-99 cm) W 87-101" (220-256 cm) **Range:** Accidental off northern Pacific coast. Southern Hemisphere bird; of the three races found there, only *T. c. cauta* has appeared in Northern Hemisphere. Superficially similar to Laysan Albatross but much larger, with a thicker bill that is yellowish-gray with yellow tip in **adults** and grayer with darker tip in younger birds. Paler back than Laysan, longer and grayer tail, more extensive white on rump; flight more languid, displaying in all ages extensively white underwings and characteristic dark "thumb mark" at beginning of leading edge. In immatures, gray shading on back and sides of neck sometimes forms collar.

Laysan Albatross *Phoebastria immutabilis*
L 32" (81 cm) W 79" (195-203 cm) Back and upperwing are blackish-brown except for white flash in primaries; underwing white, with black margins and variable internal markings. Occasionally hybridizes with Black-footed Albatross. **Range:** Most numerous spring to summer off Alaska; rare but regular off west coast late fall to spring; casual inland in spring, chiefly in southeastern California. Breeds mainly on Hawaiian Islands.

Black-footed Albatross *Phoebastria nigripes*
L 32" (81 cm) W 80" (203 cm) Mostly dark in all plumages. White area around bill is more extensive on **old** birds; reduced or absent on immatures. Most birds of all ages have dark undertail coverts. Some **adults** have white undertail coverts, and white may extend onto belly; these birds can be confused with subadult Short-tailed Albatross, but lack white upperwing patches and have smaller, darker bills. **Range:** Seen year-round off west coast; most common in spring, summer. Chiefly breeds on Hawaiian Islands.

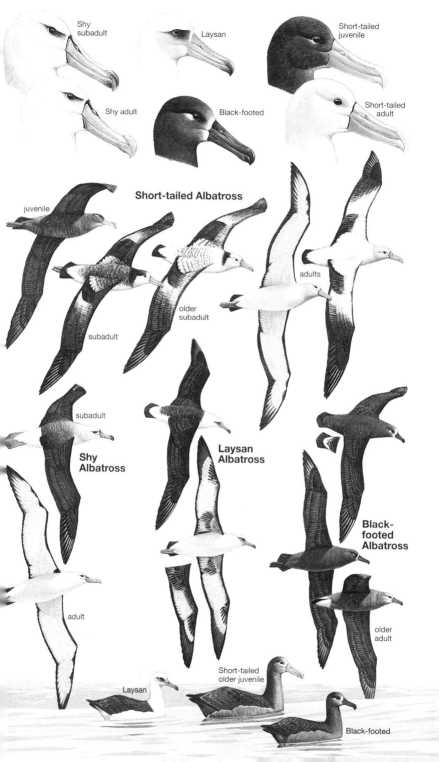

Shy subadult

Laysan

Short-tailed juvenile

Shy adult

Black-footed

Short-tailed adult

Short-tailed Albatross

juvenile

older subadult

subadult

adults

Shy Albatross

subadult

adult

Laysan Albatross

Black-footed Albatross

older adult

Laysan

Short-tailed older juvenile

Black-footed

Yellow-nosed Albatross *Thalassarche chlororhynchos*
L 32" (81 cm) W 80" (203 cm) **Range:** Casual off the Atlantic and Gulf coasts. Sometimes seen from shore or even inland. Widespread species in South Atlantic and Indian Oceans. Many pairs of the nominate subspecies breed on Tristan da Cunha and Gough islands, probable source of North American sightings in the western North Atlantic. Often confused with Black-browed, but Yellow-nosed is smaller and slimmer, with longer neck. **Adult**'s bill appears black; at close range, yellow ridge on top and reddish tip are visible. In fresh plumage, adult has a light gray wash on head. Underwing is extensively white with a narrow dark border; some juveniles show more dark on the leading edge, which can cause confusion with adult Black-browed. Otherwise **juvenile** resembles adult Yellow-nosed except for all-dark bill.

Black-browed Albatross *Thalassarche melanophris*
L 35" (89 cm) W 88" (224 cm) **Range:** A circumpolar Southern Hemisphere species. Casual in the North Atlantic, where most records are from the northeast part. Several sightings off east coast, one of which is well documented. Most easily confused with Yellow-nosed Albatross but larger, with proportionately shorter neck and chunkier body. **Adult** has a broad, dark leading edge to the underwing; compare with juvenile Yellow-nosed. Note the heavier bill, bright orange with redder tip, unlike mostly black bill of Yellow-nosed; also the black eyebrow, with Yellow-nosed has a more triangular black mark in front of the eye. **Juveniles** have darker bills and gray shading about the head and neck, forming a collar; underwing mainly dark. **Subadults** have more yellowish bill with dark tip; more white in center of underwings.

Shearwaters, Petrels (Family Procellariidae)

These gull-size seabirds have longer wings than gulls; bills are topped with large nostril tubes. Rapid wingbeats alternating with stiff-winged glides present a distinctive flight pattern as these birds skim the waves in search of food. Pelagic; most species are rarely seen from shore.

Northern Fulmar *Fulmarus glacialis*
L 19" (48 cm) W 42" (107 cm) In most morphs, color is rather uniform, with no strong contrasts. **Light morphs** predominate over much of the North Atlantic; darker birds are more numerous in the high Arctic. On breeding grounds in Pacific region, light morphs predominate in the Bering Sea area, **dark morphs** on the Aleutians and off south coastal Alaska. Both morphs disperse south in winter down the west coast. **Intermediates** of all shades are also seen. Distinguished from gulls by short, thick bill with nostril tubes and shearwater-like flight; from shearwaters by thick, yellow bill, stockier shape, and more rounded wings. **Range:** Common and increasing. Some summer south to California and Maine. Within winter range, numbers fluctuate annually. Winters north to limits of open water.

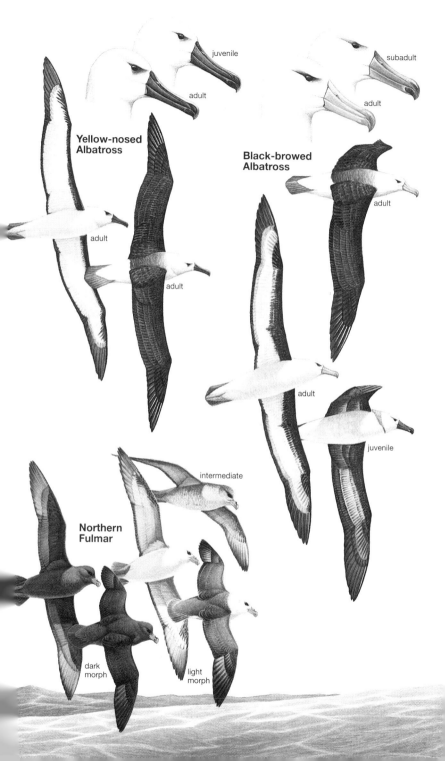

Yellow-nosed Albatross

juvenile

adult

adult

adult

Black-browed Albatross

subadult

adult

adult

adult

juvenile

intermediate

Northern Fulmar

dark morph

light morph

Gadfly Petrels

Fluttery wingbeats and high, erratic soaring named these fast-flying petrels. Unlike shearwaters, petrels typically hold their wings slightly forward from the shoulder and bent sharply back at the wrist.

Black-capped Petrel *Pterodroma hasitata*
L 16" (41 cm) W 37" (94 cm) Distinct dark cap; white collar; broad white band on uppertail coverts and base of tail. White wing lining, with variable dark diagonal bar on leading edge. Wing and bill shape, white forehead, broader band on tail, and languid, arching flight distinguish this species from Greater Shearwater (page 40). Some birds have less white at base of tail and duskier collar. **Range:** Breeds on Hispaniola and Cuba. Common in Gulf Stream off North Carolina from late May to mid-October; uncommon in winter; casual north to Nova Scotia and in Gulf of Mexico. Recorded inland in the east after hurricanes.

Fea's Petrel *Pterodroma feae*
L 14" (36 cm) W 37" (94 cm) **Range:** Breeds in the Madeira and Cape Verde islands off West Africa. Rare visitor off North Carolina in late May and early June, casual into the fall; accidental to Nova Scotia. Sightings here believed to be Fea's, not Zino's Petrel (*P. madeira,* an endangered species breeding only on Madeira), based on larger bill size and likelihood. Fea's is brownish-gray above with dark M pattern, pale uppertail coverts and tail. White below; partial breast band; mostly dark underwings.

Bermuda Petrel *Pterodroma cahow* **E**
L 15" (38 cm) W 35" (89 cm) Endangered species. Believed extinct, but rediscovered early in 20th century; population increasing, now estimated at about 200. **Range:** Nests only on islets off Bermuda; recent documented sightings off the Carolinas in late spring and summer. Note that larger Black-capped Petrel has heavier bill and proportionately shorter wings. Bermuda Petrel's whitish rump, sometimes lacking, is restricted to base of uppertail coverts. Without Black-capped's white collar, dark on head is more like cowl than cap; Bermuda more buoyant in flight, with darker underwings than Black-capped.

Herald Petrel *Pterodroma arminjoniana*
L 15½" (39 cm) W 37½" (95 cm) **Range:** Tropical Southern Hemisphere species. South Atlantic birds of the nominate race nest on islands off Brazil; mid-Atlantic region sightings likely from these populations. Rare visitor late May to late September in Gulf Stream off North Carolina. Long-winged, slender-bodied species with languid wingbeats. Occurs in three morphs: **dark morph,** predominant in U.S., has pale-based flight feathers and greater primary coverts on underwing. Compare with chunkier Sooty Shearwater with its shorter tail, thinner bill, paler underwings, and faster wingbeats. **Light morph** has brownish-gray head and chest, variably whitish throat, white belly, pale underwings. **Intermediate morphs** are variably mottled below.

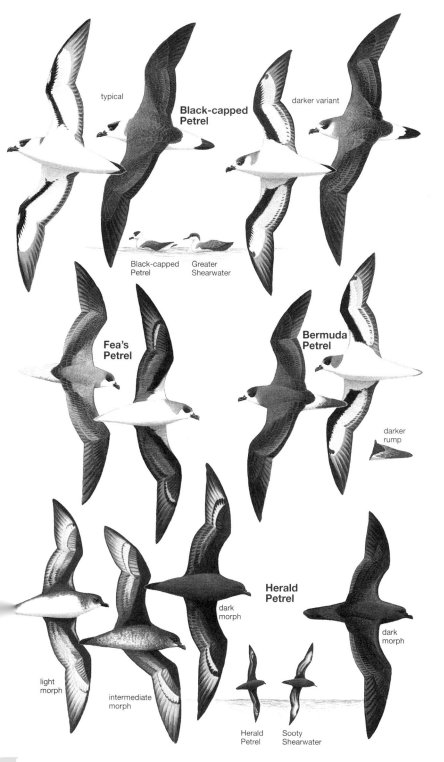

typical

Black-capped Petrel

darker variant

Black-capped Petrel

Greater Shearwater

Fea's Petrel

Bermuda Petrel

darker rump

Herald Petrel

dark morph

dark morph

light morph

intermediate morph

Herald Petrel

Sooty Shearwater

Dark-rumped Petrel *Pterodroma phaeopygia*
L 17" (43 cm) W 36" (91 cm) **Range:** Casual well off California coast. Populations of *P. p. sandwichensis* on Hawaiian islands and nominate race on Galápagos sometimes treated as separate species, though they are not separable in the field, based on present knowledge. Large and long-winged; mostly black crown extends down sides of neck. Uniformly dark above, lacking M pattern; often has some white on rump. Underwing shows blackish diagonal bar and sometimes small blackish patch on axillaries.

Murphy's Petrel *Pterodroma ultima*
L 16" (41 cm) W 38" (97 cm) **Range:** Fairly common visitor in spring well off California and Oregon coasts. Breeds on remote central South Pacific islands. Depending on light, color varies from brownish to gray. Note faint dark M pattern on back, wedge-shaped tail, and white underwing flash. Variable white around bill, most conspicuous on chin and throat. Two to three recent records of similar Great-winged Petrel (not shown) off central California coast, but note larger bill; more extensive white around bill, including forehead; overall color warmer brown, less grayish; lacks dark M on back. Other dark Pacific petrels, notably Kermadec (*P. neglecta*) and Solander's (*P. solandri*), not yet recorded off North America, but could occur. Compare Murphy's also to dark-morph Northern Fulmar (page 30).

Mottled Petrel *Pterodroma inexpectata*
L 14" (36 cm) W 32" (81 cm) White throat and center of breast contrast with rest of mostly gray underparts. Shows prominent black bar on otherwise white underwings; dark M across upperwings. **Range:** Breeds on islands off New Zealand. Probably regular well off southern Alaska and Aleutians in summer; rare and irregular well off the west coast, chiefly in late fall.

Cook's Petrel *Pterodroma cookii*
L 10" (25 cm) W 26" (66 cm) **Range:** Breeds on islands off New Zealand. Found well off California coast from spring through late fall, where it is the most numerous *Pterodroma* petrel. Casual off Aleutians and on Salton Sea in summer. Small, with long wings and a rather short tail. Crown and back uniformly gray. Note mainly white underwings and distinct dark M across upperwings. White on outer tail feathers and dark tip to central tail feathers can be hard to see.

Stejneger's Petrel *Pterodroma longirostris*
L 10" (25 cm) W 26" (66 cm) **Range:** Breeds on Juan Fernández Islands off Chile. Casual well off the California coast, chiefly in the fall. Resembles Cook's Petrel but distinct dark half hood contrasts with grayish back; tail is longer and more uniformly colored, with less white in outer tail feathers.

Dark-rumped
Petrel

Murphy's
Petrel

Mottled
Petrel

Cook's
Petrel

Stejneger's
Petrel

Buller's Shearwater *Puffinus bulleri*

L 16" (41 cm) W 40" (102 cm) Gleaming white below, including wing linings. Gray above, with a darker cap and a long, dark, wedge-shaped tail. Dark bar across leading edge of upperwing extends across back, forming a distinct M. Flight is graceful and buoyant, with long periods of soaring. **Range:** Breeds on islands off New Zealand. Irregular off west coast during southward migration. Most common from Washington to central California; rarer north and south along west coast.

Streaked Shearwater *Calonectris leucomelas*

L 19" (48 cm) W 48" (122 cm) **Range:** Asian species, casual off central California in the fall. Pale, finely streaked head looks white at a distance. Pale fringes give upperparts a scaly look. Bill is mostly pink. Note also the white axillaries and dark underwing primary coverts. Languid, soaring flight is typical of *Calonectris* shearwaters (see also Cory's, page 40).

Pink-footed Shearwater *Puffinus creatopus*

L 19" (48 cm) W 43" (109 cm) Uniformly blackish-brown above; white wing linings and underparts are variably mottled; pink bill and feet distinctive at close range. Flies with slower wingbeats and more soaring than Sooty Shearwater (next page). Spring birds of this and other Southern Hemisphere species may be in heavy **molt,** often resulting in whitish wing bars and odd wing shape. **Range:** Breeds on islands off Chile; winters (our summer) in the northern Pacific. Common from spring through fall; rare throughout the rest of the year.

Black-vented Shearwater *Puffinus opisthomelas*

L 14" (36 cm) W 34" (86 cm) Dark brown above, white below, with dark undertail coverts. Variable dusky mottling on sides of breast, often extending across entire breast. **Range:** Seen off California from August to May; often visible from shore. Nests chiefly on islands off the Baja peninsula. Strictly casual north of central California to southwestern British Columbia. Formerly considered a subspecies of the Atlantic species Manx Shearwater which is rare in fall off central California.

Buller's Shearwater

Streaked Shearwater

worn

variant with white upper-tail coverts

dark

light

Black-vented Shearwater

typical

typical

n molt

light

dark

Pink-footed Shearwater

dark

Manx Shearwater for comparison

dark

Wedge-tailed Shearwater *Puffinus pacificus*

L 18" (46 cm) W 40" (101 cm) **Range:** Polymorphic species from warm waters of Pacific and Indian Oceans. Casual in summer and fall to waters off central California; accidental on Salton Sea. Long tail held in a point; wedge shape visible only when fanned. Slender, grayish bill has darker tip. Head and upperparts of **light morph** grayish-brown; mostly white with mottled brown below. Most sightings are of wholly brown **dark morph,** which has paler base to flight feathers. Languid flight with prolonged soaring on bowed wings angled forward to wrist, then swept back.

Flesh-footed Shearwater *Puffinus carneipes*

L 17" (43 cm) W 41" (104 cm) Dark above and below except for pale flight feathers, distinctive pale pink base of bill. Compare especially with Sooty Shearwater, which has whitish wing linings, all-dark bill, less languid flight. **Range:** Breeds on islands off Australia and New Zealand. Winters (our summer) in North Pacific; rare off west coast.

Bulwer's Petrel *Bulweria bulwerii*

L 10" (26 cm) W 26" (66 cm) **Range:** Bird of tropical and subtropical oceans; accidental summer visitor off Monterey, California, and Outer Banks, North Carolina. Sooty brown overall with pale diagonal bar across secondary coverts. Long tail usually held in a point; wedge shape visible only when fanned. Flight is buoyant and erratic, long wings slightly bowed and held forward. Flies within a few feet of the water; flight, when it is windy, is more like gadfly petrels.

Short-tailed Shearwater *Puffinus tenuirostris*

L 17" (43 cm) W 39" (99 cm) Plumage variable. Usually dark overall, but often with pale wing linings like Sooty Shearwater; white is more evenly distributed, when present, forming a panel. Has shorter bill than Sooty, slightly steeper forehead, more rounded crown. Some birds, unlike Sooty, have pale throat and dark-capped appearance. **Range:** Breeds off Australia. Winters (our summer) in North Pacific to Alaska. Seen along west coast from British Columbia to California during southward migration in fall and winter.

Sooty Shearwater *Puffinus griseus*

L 18" (46 cm) W 40" (101 cm) Whitish underwing coverts contrast with overall dark plumage. Flies with fast wingbeats and, except when it is windy, short glides. Almost identical to Short-tailed Shearwater. White on underwings usually most prominent on primary coverts. **Range:** Breeds in Southern Hemisphere. Fairly common off east coast in spring, and in summer off New England and Canada. Abundant off west coast, often seen from shore. Very rare in Gulf of Mexico.

dark morph

dark morph

Wedge-tailed Shearwater

light morph

Flesh-footed Shearwater

Bulwer's Petrel

Short-tailed Shearwater

Sooty Shearwater

Short-tailed

Sooty

Cory's Shearwater *Calonectris diomedea*

L 18" (46 cm) W 46" (117 cm) Grayish-brown upperparts merge into white underparts without sharp contrast; bill is yellowish. Similar Greater Shearwater has dark cap, dark bill, all-white underwings. Flight of Cory's Shearwater is more languid than that of most other shearwaters, with slower, less frequent wing-beats. **Range:** Nominate race *C. d. diomedea* breeds in the Mediterranean, and *borealis* on the Azores and the Canary and Salvage Islands in the eastern Atlantic. Seen (mainly *borealis)* off the east coast, primarily from late spring through fall. Uncommon in the Gulf of Mexico.

Greater Shearwater *Puffinus gravis*

L 18" (46 cm) W 44" (112 cm) Dark brown cap contrasts with grayish-brown upperparts and white cheeks. Rump usually shows a narrow, white, U-shaped band. Bill is dark; underparts white with indistinct dusky patch on belly. Compare especially with Cory's Shearwater. Many Greater Shearwaters have a white nape; may be confused with Black-capped Petrel (page 32), but lack white forehead and wide black bar on underwing; also have shorter, less wedge-shaped tail with less extensive white at base. **Range:** Breeds in South Atlantic. Fairly common off the east coast during migration, chiefly in spring. Summers in large numbers from the Gulf of Maine north.

Manx Shearwater *Puffinus puffinus*

L 13½" (34 cm) W 33" (84 cm) Blackish above, white below, with white wing linings. Pure white undertail coverts extend to end of short tail. Note that white on throat wraps around dark ear coverts. **Range:** Most breed on islands around Scotland, southwest Wales, and Ireland; some from the Canaries and Azores to Iceland; one colony nests in Newfoundland. Winters off eastern South America. Fairly common off the northern Atlantic coast from June to October; less common farther south. Rare in winter from Maryland south. Rare in fall off central California.

Little Shearwater *Puffinus assimilis*

L 11" (28 cm) W 25" (64 cm) **Range:** Three records exist: Two fall specimens from Nova Scotia and North Carolina from the race *P. a. baroli,* which breeds on the Azores and nearby islands of the eastern Atlantic; and one early winter sighting in 1984 off North Carolina. Similar to larger Audubon's Shearwater but has shorter tail, more white on underwing, and grayer, two-toned upperwing; undertail coverts are white, and face more extensively white. Flies with rapid, stiff, shallow wingbeats and short glides. Often jerks head upward at end of glide.

Audubon's Shearwater *Puffinus lherminieri*

L 12" (31 cm) W 27" (69 cm) Dark brown above, white below, with long tail, dark undertail coverts (some individuals have pale ones); undersides of primaries dark. **Range:** Breeds on Caribbean islands. Common off the southern Atlantic coast, chiefly from May through October. Rare in winter.

Cory's

Greater

Black-capped Petrel

Cory's Shearwater
borealis

Greater Shearwater

Manx Shearwater

Little Shearwater
baroli

Audubon's Shearwater

Storm-Petrels (Family Hydrobatidae)

Sprightly fliers, these small seabirds hover close to the water, pattering or hopping across the waves to pluck up small fish and plankton. Some species follow ships. Identification is often difficult. Flight patterns may help to distinguish the various species, but flight can vary deceptively depending on weather.

Wilson's Storm-Petrel *Oceanites oceanicus*
L 7¼" (18 cm) W 16" (41 cm) Skims across the waves with shallow, fluttery wingbeats like a swallow. Wings short and rounded; has long legs; in flight, feet trail behind tip of squarish or rounded tail. Often hovers to feed, pattering its yellow-webbed feet on the water; a distinctive trait. Bold white U-shaped rump band extends onto undertail coverts; white on lower flanks is conspicuous even on sitting bird. Brownish-black overall with pale wing patch. Smaller than Leach's and Band-rumped Storm-Petrels. **Range:** Common to abundant off Atlantic coast from May to September; rare off Gulf coast; rare off central California coast in the fall. On the west coast, compare carefully to Wedge-rumped Storm-Petrel (next page).

Band-rumped Storm-Petrel *Oceanodroma castro*
L 9" (23 cm) W 17" (43 cm) **Range:** Breeds on tropical islands. Fairly common from late May to late August in Gulf Stream, especially off North Carolina; rare or casual farther north to waters off Massachusetts; uncommon well off Gulf coast. Rather shallow wing strokes are followed by stiff-winged glides, like the flight of a shearwater but unlike the erratic flight of Leach's Storm-Petrel or the fluttery flight of Wilson's. White rump patch narrower and less extensive on undertail coverts than on Wilson's. Tail squarish or very slightly notched; no foot projection in flight. Larger, longer-winged than Wilson's; darker than Leach's, with fainter carpal bar.

Leach's Storm-Petrel *Oceanodroma leucorhoa*
L 8" (20 cm) W 18" (46 cm) Distinctive erratic flight, with deep strokes of long, pointed wings. Wings are much longer and more sharply angled than Wilson's. In close view, note dusky line dividing white rump band on most birds. No white is visible on flanks of sitting bird. Brown overall, with pale wing stripes and forked tail. Amount of white on rump varies; a few birds seen off southern California have brown rumps. **Range:** Fairly common well off Pacific coast; uncommon south of breeding range along Atlantic coast. Very rare in Gulf of Mexico; casual on Salton Sea.

White-faced Storm-Petrel *Pelagodroma marina*
L 7½" (19 cm) W 17" (43 cm) **Range:** Very rare off the Atlantic coast from North Carolina to Massachusetts. Flies with stiff, shallow wingbeats and short glides. Habitually angles to water at 45 degrees, then bounces off the surface with long legs in a pogo-stick fashion. Distinctive white underparts, wing linings, and face. Dark eye stripe, crown, and upperparts; paler rump.

Band-rumped Storm-Petrel

Wilson's Storm-Petrel

Leach's Storm-Petrel

White-faced Storm-Petrel

Wilson's

Band-rumped

Leach's west coast

northern

intermediate

southern

Wedge-rumped

Black Storm-Petrel *Oceanodroma melania*

L 9" (23 cm) W 19" (48 cm) Deep, languid wing strokes, graceful flight. Largest of the all-dark storm-petrels. Blackish-brown overall with pale bar on upper surface of wing. Tail forked and fairly long. Slow, deep wingbeats and larger size distinguish Black Storm-Petrel from brown-rumped individuals of Leach's Storm-Petrel (preceding page). **Range:** Breeds from May to December off Baja California and in Gulf of California; small colony in vicinity of Santa Barbara Island. Common off southern California coast from late spring; by late summer north to Monterey Bay. Casual in interior of southern California and in southwest Arizona after tropical storms.

Ashy Storm-Petrel *Oceanodroma homochroa*

L 8" (20 cm) W 17" (43 cm) Fluttery wingbeats, but flight fairly direct; not as swallowlike as Wilson's Storm-Petrel (preceding page). Gray-brown overall; pale mottling on underwing coverts may be visible at close range. Viewed from the side, Ashy appears long-tailed. Distinguished from Black Storm-Petrel by rapid, shallow wingbeats and overall paler, grayer appearance. **Range:** Fairly common most of the year; rare in winter. Breeds on islands off central and southern California.

Least Storm-Petrel *Oceanodroma microsoma*

L 5¾" (15 cm) W 5½" (14 cm) Our smallest storm-petrel. Swift, indirect flight, low over the water, with deep wingbeats like the much larger Black Storm-Petrel. Blackish-brown overall. Short-tailed; appears almost tailless in flight. **Range:** Irregular: Rare to common off the coast of southern California in late summer and fall; in peak years, small numbers occur to central California; after tropical storms, may be seen in southeast California and southwest Arizona.

Fork-tailed Storm-Petrel *Oceanodroma furcata*

L 8½" (22 cm) W 18" (46 cm) Wingbeats shallow, rapid, often followed by glides. Looks fairly long-tailed in flight. Occasionally makes shallow dives for food. Distinctively bluish-gray above, pearl gray below. Note also dark gray forehead and eye patch, dark wing linings. **Range:** Found regularly south to central California; rare off southern California coast.

Wedge-rumped Storm-Petrel *Oceanodroma tethys*

L 6½" (17 cm) W 13¼" (34 cm) **Range:** Breeds on the Galápagos Islands and on islands off Peru. Casual off the California coast from August to January. Distinctive bold white triangular patch on tail gives the appearance of a white tail with dark corners. Compare with the rounded rump band and white flanks of Wilson's Storm-Petrel (preceding page). Wedge-rumped is almost as small as Least Storm-Petrel, with similar deep wingbeats.

Black
Storm-Petrel

Ashy
Storm-Petrel

Fork-tailed
Storm-Petrel

Least Storm-Petrel

Wedge-rumped
Storm-Petrel

Frigatebirds (Family Fregatidae)

These large, dark seabirds have the longest wingspan, in proportion to weight, of all birds.

Magnificent Frigatebird *Fregata magnificens*
L 40" (102 cm) W 90" (229 cm) Long, forked tail; long, narrow wings. **Male** is glossy black; orange throat pouch becomes bright red when inflated in courtship display. **Female** is blackish-brown, with white at center of underparts. **Juveniles** show varying amount of white on head and underparts; require four to six years to reach adult plumage. Frigatebirds skim the sea, snatching up food from surface; also harass other birds in flight, forcing them to disgorge food. **Range:** Generally seen along coast, but also casual inland, especially after storms. Rare but regular in summer on Salton Sea. Breed on Dry Tortugas islands off Florida. Rare north along California coast, casual farther north; rare on east coast north to North Carolina, casual farther north.

Tropicbirds (Family Phaethontidae)

Long central tail feathers identify adults. They are usually seen far out at sea, diving for fish or resting on the waves, streamers held high.

White-tailed Tropicbird *Phaethon lepturus*
L 30" (76 cm) W 37" (94 cm) **Range:** Tropical species, rare but regular in Gulf Stream off North Carolina; rare and irregular on Dry Tortugas islands, Florida; casual elsewhere off east coast. Smaller and slimmer than Red-billed Tropicbird; distinctive black stripe on upperwing coverts; primaries show less black than in Red-billed. Bill orange in Atlantic **adults. Juvenile** lacks tail streamers; upperparts are boldly barred, bill more yellowish.

Red-billed Tropicbird *Phaethon aethereus*
L 40" (102 cm) W 44" (112 cm) **Range:** Tropical species, rare well off southern California coast; very rare in Gulf of Mexico and off Atlantic coast to North Carolina; casual to Massachusetts. Flies with rapid, stiff, shallow wingbeats, unlike other tropicbirds, whose flight is more ternlike. **Adult** has red bill, black primaries, barring on back and wings, white tail streamers. **Juvenile** has black collar; lacks streamers; tail is tipped with black; barring on upperparts is finer than in other young tropicbirds. Also bill is yellowish, but soon becomes orange-red.

Red-tailed Tropicbird *Phaethon rubricauda*
L 37" (94 cm) W 44" (112 cm) **Range:** Species from tropical and subtropical Pacific and Indian Oceans. Very rare, usually well off California coast. Languid wingbeats. Flight feathers mostly white. **Adult** has red bill; red tail streamers, narrower than in other tropicbirds. **Juvenile** lacks streamers; tail is all-white; upperparts barred; bill black, gradually changing to yellow and then red. Note also lack of black collar on nape.

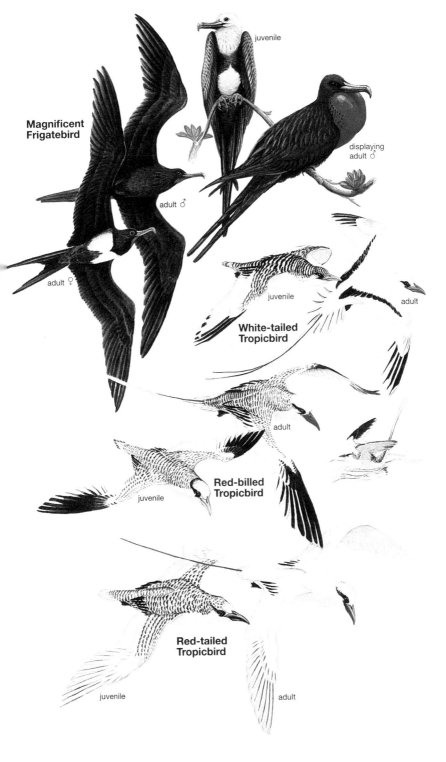

Magnificent Frigatebird

juvenile

displaying adult ♂

adult ♂

adult ♀

White-tailed Tropicbird

juvenile

adult

Red-billed Tropicbird

adult

juvenile

Red-tailed Tropicbird

juvenile

adult

Boobies, Gannets (Family Sulidae)

High-diving seabirds noted for their sudden, headlong plunges after prey. All are gregarious, nesting in colonies on small islands. The rest of the year, gannets roost at sea, boobies primarily on land.

Red-footed Booby Sula sula
L28" (71 cm) W 60" (152 cm) **Range:** Tropical species; casual on Florida's Dry Tortugas and California coast. All **adults** show bright coral red feet and blue and pink at base of bill. Four principal morphs occur: **brown, white-tailed brown, white,** and an additional **white morph** with a **black tail;** note that white morphs have black primaries, secondaries, and underwing median primary coverts. All **juveniles** and **subadults** are brownish overall, with mainly dark underwings and flesh pink legs and feet. Smallest of the boobies, with rounded head, the Red-footed Booby flies with grace and speed.

Brown Booby Sula leucogaster
L 30" (76 cm) W 57" (145 cm) **Adults** of nominate race and female S.l.brewsteri from western Mexico have dark brown heads and necks with sharply contrasting white bellies and underwing coverts; **adult male** brewsteri has white on head and neck. Adult female's bill, facial skin, legs, and feet are bright yellow; male's soft parts washed with grayish-green, throat bluish. **Juveniles** are dark brown, with little or no contrast between breast and belly; underwing muted. **Subadults** show white on belly and sharp line of contrast with darker neck. **Range:** A few found on Dry Tortugas and vicinity; rare north off both Florida coasts. Very rare through Gulf of Mexico; casual up Atlantic coast to Nova Scotia, and in California and the southwest (brewsteri).

Blue-footed Booby Sula nebouxii
L 32" (81 cm) W 62" (158 cm) Feet bright blue in adults, darker in young; long, attenuated bill is dark bluish-gray. **Adults** have streaked heads, whitish patches on upper back and rump. **Juvenile** has darker head and neck; compare with immature Masked Booby; note pale dorsal patches, all-dark underwing primary coverts. **Range:** Breeds on islands in Gulf of California. Rare and irregular to inland California and southwest Arizona in late summer and fall. Absent in U.S. most years. Occurs on Salton Sea; casual to California coast; accidental to Washington and Texas.

Masked Booby Sula dactylatra
L 32" (81 cm) W 62" (158 cm) Proportionately, the shortest tailed booby. **Adult** distinguished from Northern Gannet (next page) by yellow bill and extensive black facial skin; black tail; and solid black trailing edge to wing. On **juvenile,** note more white on underwing, with contrasting dark median primary coverts and pale collar. **Subadult** has paler head and broader collar; note yellow on bill. **Range:** Breeds on Dry Tortugas, Florida; uncommon in Gulf of Mexico in summer. Rare in Gulf Stream north to Outer Banks, North Carolina. Casual to coastal California.

Red-footed Booby

juvenile

adult white morphs

adult brown morph

adult white-tailed brown morph

subadult brown morph

adult white morph with black tail

juvenile

Brown Booby

adult ♂ *brewsteri*

adult ♀

adult ♂

subadult ♀

juvenile

juveniles

Blue-footed Booby

adult

adults

juveniles

Northern Gannet immature

Masked Booby

adult

adult

adult

juvenile

subadult

juvenile

subadult

Northern Gannet *Morus bassanus*

L 37" (94 cm) W 72" (183 cm) Large, white seabird with long, black-tipped wings, pointed white tail. **Juvenile** is dark gray above, with pale speckling; grayish below. **First-year** birds are whiter below; distinguished from juvenile and immature Masked Booby (preceding page) by more uniformly dark underwings and, at close range, by different feathering pattern around the bill. Full **adult** plumage is acquired in three to four years. **Range:** Common; breeds in large colonies on rocky cliffs; winters at sea. Often seen from shore during migration and winter. Casual in Great Lakes region in fall.

Pelicans (Family Pelecanidae)

These large, heavy waterbirds have massive bills and huge throat pouches used as dip nets to catch fish. In flight, pelicans hold their heads drawn back.

American White Pelican *Pelecanus erythrorhynchos*

L 62" (158 cm) W 108" (274 cm) White, with black primaries and outer secondaries. **Breeding adult** has pale yellow crest; bill is bright orange, usually with a fibrous plate on upper mandible. Plate is shed after eggs are laid; crown and nape become grayish. Juvenile is white with brownish wash on head, neck, and lesser coverts; soft parts more dully colored. White Pelicans do not dive for food but dip their bills into the water while swimming. **Range:** Usually found in flocks. **Nonbreeding** birds are seen in summer throughout area enclosed by dashed line on map. In fall, vagrants may appear almost anywhere, increasingly in northeast.

Brown Pelican *Pelecanus occidentalis* **E**

L 48" (122 cm) W 84" (213 cm) **Nonbreeding adult** has white head and neck, often washed with yellow; grayish-brown body; blackish belly. In **breeding** bird, hindneck is dark chestnut; yellow patch appears at base of foreneck. On eastern race, *P. o. carolinensis* (shown here), gular pouch is grayish; breeding *californicus* from the west coast has a bright red gular pouch. Molt during incubation and **chick-feeding** produces speckled head and foreneck. Adult eye color is light except during chick-feeding, when it darkens. Juvenile is grayish-brown above, tipped with pale buff; underparts whitish. **First-year** bird is browner; acquires adult plumage by third year. Dives from the air after prey, capturing fish in its pouch. **Range:** Very rare inland except at Salton Sea, where may be common. Wanderers are seen mainly in spring and summer, to limit of dashed line on map.

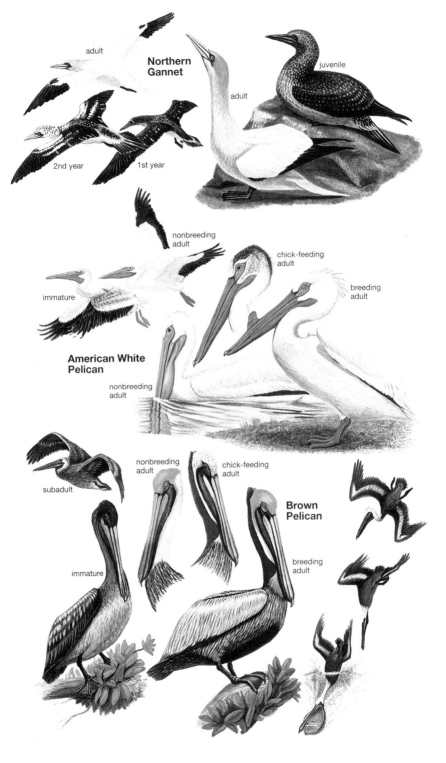

Northern Gannet

adult

adult

juvenile

2nd year

1st year

nonbreeding adult

immature

chick-feeding adult

breeding adult

American White Pelican

nonbreeding adult

subadult

nonbreeding adult

chick-feeding adult

Brown Pelican

immature

breeding adult

Darters (Family Anhingidae)

Long, slim neck helps to distinguish Anhingas from cormorants. Anhingas often swim submerged to the neck. Sharply pointed bill is used to spear fish.

Anhinga *Anhinga anhinga L 35" (89 cm) W 45" (114 cm)*

Black above, with green gloss; silvery-white spots and streaks on wings and upper back. During breeding season, **male** acquires pale, wispy plumes on upper neck; bill and bare facial skin become brightly colored. **Female** has buffy neck and breast. Immatures resemble adult female but are browner overall. Anhingas prefer freshwater habitats; often seen perched on branches or stumps with wings spread to dry. In flight, profile looks headless. Flies with slow, regular wingbeats and circles like raptor on thermals. **Range:** Casual wanderer north of breeding range.

Cormorants (Family Phalacrocoracidae)

Dark birds with set-back legs; long, hooked bill; and colorful bare facial skin and throat pouch. Dive from the surface for fish. May briefly soar, and may swim submerged to the neck.

Neotropic Cormorant *Phalacrocorax brasilianus*

L 26" (66 cm) W 40" (102 cm) Small, long-tailed cormorant with white-bordered yellow-brown or dull yellow throat pouch that tapers to a sharp point behind bill. In **breeding** plumage, **adult** acquires short white plumes on sides of neck. Distinguished from Double-crested Cormorant (next page) by smaller size, longer tail, and smaller, angled throat pouch that does not extend around eye. Neotropic **immatures** are browner than adults, particularly on underparts. **Range:** Fairly common; found at marshy ponds or shallow inlets near perching stumps and snags. Regular to Arizona; casual to southeast California, Colorado, and the western midwest. Formerly called Olivaceous Cormorant.

Great Cormorant *Phalacrocorax carbo*

L 36" (91 cm) W 63" (160 cm) Large, short-tailed cormorant with small, lemon yellow throat pouch broadly bordered with white feathering. **Breeding adult** shows white flank patches and wispy white plumes on head. Smaller Double-crested Cormorant (next page) has orange throat pouch; lacks flank patches; note also Great Cormorant's larger, blockier head and heavier bill. **First-year** birds are brown above; white belly contrasts with streaked brown neck, breast, and flanks. **Second-year** immatures resemble nonbreeding adults more closely but have a brown tinge above; compare with young Double-crested, which has a slimmer bill, deep orange facial skin, and, often, a darker belly. **Range:** Winters in small numbers regularly south to South Carolina, very rarely as far south as Florida.

Anhinga

breeding adult ♂

♀

♀

Double-crested adult

Great adult

Neotropic immature

breeding adult

immature

nonbreeding adult

eastern Double-crested breeding adult

Neotropic Cormorant

2nd year

Great Cormorant

breeding adult

1st year

Double-crested Cormorant *Phalacrocorax auritus*

L 32" (81 cm) W 52" (132 cm) Large, rounded throat pouch is yellow-orange year-round. **Breeding adult** has a tuft curving back on either side of its head from behind eyes. Tufts are largely white in western birds, black and less conspicuous in eastern birds (see figure preceding page). **First-year** birds are brown above, variably pale below, but usually palest on upper breast and neck. Immatures sometimes have pouch edged with white, which can cause confusion with Neotropic Cormorant (preceding page). Among west coast cormorants, Double-crested's kinked neck is distinctive in flight; its wings are also longer and more pointed than Brandt's and Pelagic. **Range:** Common and widespread; found along coasts, inland lakes, and rivers. Breeding populations in the interior have greatly increased in the last two decades.

Brandt's Cormorant *Phalacrocorax penicillatus*

L 35" (89 cm) W 48" (122 cm) A band of pale buffy feathers bordering the throat pouch identifies all ages. Throat pouch becomes bright blue in **breeding** plumage; head, neck, and scapulars acquire fine, white plumes. **First-year** birds are dark brown above, slightly paler below. In all ages, appears more uniformly dark above than Double-crested Cormorant; wings and tail are proportionately shorter. Head and bill are larger than in Pelagic Cormorant. **Range:** Common and gregarious; often fishes in large flocks; flies in long lines between feeding and roosting grounds. Much more likely to be seen over open ocean than Pelagic Cormorant. A tiny breeding colony exists on Seal Rocks near Prince William Sound, Alaska; casual in southeast Alaska.

Pelagic Cormorant *Phalacrocorax pelagicus*

L 26" (66 cm) W 39" (99 cm) **Adults** are dark and glossy overall; bill dark. Smaller and slenderer than other western cormorants. **Breeding adult** has tufts on crown and nape; fine white plumes on sides of neck; white patches on flanks. Distinguished from Red-faced Cormorant by darker and less extensive red facial skin and lack of yellow in bill. **First-year** bird is uniformly dark brown; closely resembles young Red-faced, but note dark bill, lack of pink facial skin, and smaller size. Pelagic Cormorant is distinguished in flight from Brandt's by smaller head, slimmer neck, smaller overall size, and proportionately longer tail. Less gregarious than other species; breeds in smaller colonies.

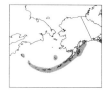

Red-faced Cormorant *Phalacrocorax urile*

L 31" (79 cm) W 46" (117 cm) Partly yellow bill distinguishes all ages from the very similar Pelagic Cormorant. In **adult,** dull brown wings contrast with glossy upperparts. Lower mandible is bluish. Throat patch is red; dull red facial skin becomes brighter in **breeding** season. **First-year** bird is uniformly dark brown, with pink facial skin. More gregarious than Pelagics, Red-faced Cormorants nest in colonies on the ledges of steep coastal cliffs and on rocky sea islands, alongside gulls, murres, and auklets.

1st year

western
breeding
adult

**Double-crested
Cormorant**

Double-crested
adult

Pelagic
adult

Brandt's
adult

**Brandt's
Cormorant**

nonbreeding
adult

nonbreeding
adult

**Pelagic
Cormorant**

1st year

breeding
adult

1st year

breeding
adult

1st year

**Red-faced
Cormorant**

breeding
adult

Herons, Bitterns (Family Ardeidae)

Wading birds; most have long legs, neck, and bill for stalking food in shallow water. Graceful crests and plumes adorn some species in breeding season.

Least Bittern *Ixobrychus exilis* L 13" (33 cm) W 17" (43 cm)
Buffy inner wing patches identify this small, rather secretive heron as it flushes briefly from dense marsh cover. When alarmed, it may freeze with bill pointing up. In **male** back and crown are black; in **female** they are browner. **Juvenile** resembles female but has more prominent streaking on back and breast. Dark morph (not shown), known as "Cory's Least Bittern" and seldom now reported, is chestnut where typical plumage is pale. Least Bittern's **calls** include a series of harsh *kek* notes; its song, a softer series of *ku* notes, is heard only on the breeding ground. Fairly common. May breed sporadically beyond mapped range in west.

American Bittern *Botaurus lentiginosus*
L 28" (71 cm) W 42" (107 cm) Rich brown upperparts are set off by black neck streaks. Contrasting dark flight feathers are conspicuous in flight; note also that wings are somewhat pointed, not rounded as in night-herons. **Juvenile** lacks neck patches. Distinctive spring and early summer **song,** *oonk-a-lunk,* is most often heard at dusk in dense marsh reeds. When alarmed, freezes with bill pointing up, or flushes with rapid wingbeats. **Range:** Fairly common; casual breeder south of range. Casual in winter into southern part of breeding range.

Black-crowned Night-Heron *Nycticorax nycticorax*
L 25" (64 cm) W 44" (112 cm) Stocky heron with short neck and legs. **Adult** has black crown and back; white hindneck plumes are longest in breeding season. **Juvenile** distinguished from young Yellow-crowned Night-Heron by browner upperparts with bolder white spotting; thicker neck; paler, less contrasting face with smaller eyes; and longer, thinner bill with mostly pale lower mandible. In flight, legs barely extend beyond tail. Full adult plumage is not acquired until third year. **Calls** include a low, harsh *woc*, more guttural than in Yellow-crowned. Mainly nocturnal feeder. Typically roosts in trees. Fairly common to common.

Yellow-crowned Night-Heron *Nyctanassa violacea*
L 24" (61 cm) W 42" (107 cm) **Adult** has buffy-white crown, black face with white cheeks; acquires head plumes in breeding season. **Juvenile** distinguished from young Black-crowned Night-Heron by grayer upperparts with less conspicuous white spotting; thinner neck; stouter, mostly dark bill; and larger eyes. In flight, its legs extend well beyond its tail and it shows darker flight feathers and trailing edge on wings. Full adult plumage is acquired in third year. **Calls** include a short *woc*, higher and less harsh than in Black-crowned. **Range:** Uncommon to fairly common; roosts in trees in wet woods and swamps. Casual in California and north to dashed line on map; casual also in Newfoundland.

adult ♂

Least Bittern

adult ♂   adult ♀

juvenile

adult

American Bittern

juvenile

adult

2nd spring

breeding adult

Black-crowned Night-Heron

1st spring

juvenile

juvenile

breeding adult

juvenile   breeding adult

breeding adult

Yellow-crowned Night-Heron

Green Heron *Butorides virescens*

L 18" (46 cm) W 26" (66 cm) Small, chunky heron with short legs. Back and sides of **adult**'s neck are deep chestnut; green on upperparts is mixed with blue-gray; center of throat and neck white. Greenish-black crown feathers, sometimes raised to form shaggy crest. Legs are usually dull yellow but in **male** turn bright orange in high breeding plumage. **Juvenile** is browner above; white throat and underparts heavily streaked with brown. Common **call** is a loud, sharp *kyowk*. When alarmed, raises crest and flicks tail. **Range:** Usually solitary; found in a variety of habitats, but prefers streams, ponds, and marshes with woodland cover; often perches in trees. Generally common; a few winter north of resident limit.

Tricolored Heron *Egretta tricolor*

L 26" (66 cm) W 36" (91 cm) White belly and foreneck contrast with mainly dark blue upperparts; bill long and slender. **Immature** has chestnut hindneck and wing coverts. **Range:** Common inhabitant of salt marshes and mangrove swamps of the east and Gulf coasts. Rare inland, but has bred in North Dakota and Kansas. Rare but regular on southern California coast, chiefly in winter; casual in the southwest.

Little Blue Heron *Egretta caerulea*

L 24" (61 cm) W 40" (102 cm) Slate blue overall. During most of year, plumage, head, and neck are dark purple; legs and feet dull green. In high **breeding** plumage, head and neck become reddish-purple, legs and feet black. **Immature** is easily confused with immature Snowy Egret (next page); note Little Blue Heron's dull yellow legs and feet; two-toned bill with thicker, gray base and dark tip; mostly grayish lores; and, usually, narrow, dusky primary tips. During first spring, immature's white plumage begins gradual **molt** to adult plumage. Little Blue Herons are slow, methodical feeders in freshwater ponds, lakes, and marshes and coastal saltwater wetlands. **Range:** Common; disperses north in spring and during post-breeding dispersal. Casual north on the west coast to southern British Columbia, and on the east coast to Newfoundland.

Reddish Egret *Egretta rufescens*

L 30" (76 cm) W 46" (117 cm) While feeding, this heron lurches, dashing about with wings spread in a canopy. **Breeding adult** has shaggy plumes on rufous head, neck. Bill is pink with black tip; legs cobalt blue. Nonbreeding plumage varies, but in general is duller, plumes shorter, bill dark. **Immature** is gray with some pale cinnamon on head, neck, inner wing; bill is dark. **White-morph** adult resembles immature Little Blue Heron or Snowy Egret (next page), but note larger size, longer bill, dark legs and feet. A few dark-morph birds have considerable white on wings and resemble molting immature Little Blue Heron. **Range:** Inhabits shallow, open salt pans. Wanders along Gulf coast in postbreeding dispersal; casual inland to midwest and up Atlantic coast to New England; rare in southern California.

juvenile

adult

Green Heron

adult

immature

Tricolored Heron

adult

molting immature

Little Blue Heron

breeding adult

immature

nonbreeding adult

white morph breeding adult

canopy feeding

immature

dark morph breeding adult

Reddish Egret

Cattle Egret *Bubulcus ibis L 20" (51 cm) W 36" (91 cm)*
Small, stocky white heron with large, rounded head; note throat feathering extends far out on bill. **Breeding adult** is adorned with orange-buff plumes on crown, back, and foreneck. At height of breeding season, bill is red-orange, lores purplish, legs dusky-red. **Nonbreeding adult** has short yellow bill, yellowish legs. Juvenile's bill is black; begins to turn yellow in late summer. **Immature** resembles nonbreeding adult. Often seen among livestock in fields, feeding on insects. In flight, resembles Snowy Egret but is smaller; bill and legs shorter; wingbeats faster. **Range:** An Old World species, Cattle Egret came to South America from Africa, spread to Florida in the early 1950s, reached California by the mid-1960s, and continues to expand. In spring, summer, and especially fall, wanders well north of breeding range.

Little Egret *Egretta garzetta L 24" (60 cm) W 36" (91 cm)*
Range: Old World species. Casual spring and summer visitor to east coast, from Newfoundland to mid-Atlantic states. Closely resembles Snowy Egret, but often appears larger, with longer neck; longer, thicker bill and legs, the latter always entirely black; mostly grayish lores; and more extensive throat feathering out on lower mandible. Little Egret's crown is rounder; feet are yellow, like Snowy, but average slightly duller. In **breeding** plumage, lore color is variable, but can be yellow. Note the two or three long, tapering plumes on back, rather than Snowy's many curved plumes. Often feeds less frenetically than Snowy, with long neck bent over in a posture like Little Blue Heron.

Snowy Egret *Egretta thula L 24" (61 cm) W 41" (104 cm)*
White heron with slender black bill, yellow eyes, black legs, and bright golden-yellow feet. Graceful plumes on head, neck, and back (where they curve upward) are striking in **breeding adult**. In **high breeding** plumage, lores turn red, feet orange. Nonbreeding plumage is similar but plumes shorter; also note yellow on backs of legs. Compare to Little Egret. **Immature** resembles nonbreeding adult, but lacks plumes and shows some bluish-gray at base of lower mandible. Can be confused with immature Little Blue Heron (preceding page); note young Snowy Egret's slimmer, mostly black bill; yellow lores; predominantly dark legs; and white wing tips. Snowy Egrets are active feeders. **Range:** Common in various wetland habitats. Disperses north of mapped range in spring and after breeding season.

Great Egret *Ardea alba L 39" (99 cm) W 51" (130 cm)*
Large white heron with heavy yellow bill, blackish legs and feet. In **breeding** plumage, long plumes trail from back, extending beyond tail. In immature and **nonbreeding adult,** bill and leg colors are duller, plumes absent. Distinguished from most other white herons by large size; from white morph of the larger Great Blue Heron by black legs and feet. **Range:** Common in wetlands. Partial to open habitats for feeding; stalks prey slowly, methodically. Occasionally breeds far north of usual range. Postbreeding wanderers reach far north of mapped breeding range.

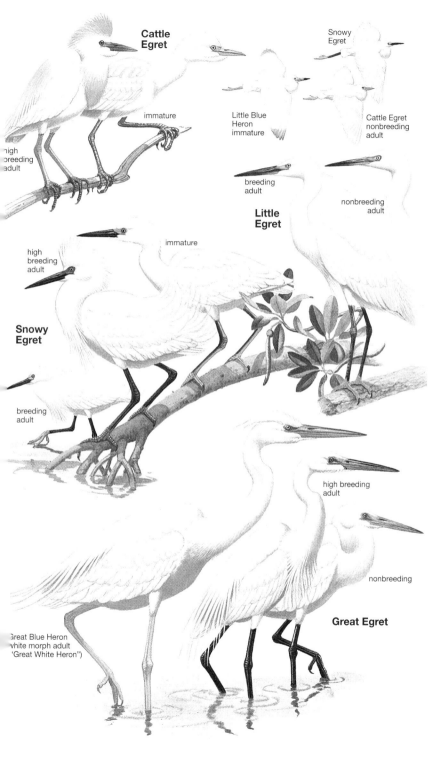

Cattle Egret

Snowy Egret

immature

Little Blue Heron immature

Cattle Egret nonbreeding adult

high breeding adult

breeding adult

nonbreeding adult

Little Egret

immature

high breeding adult

Snowy Egret

breeding adult

high breeding adult

nonbreeding

Great Egret

Great Blue Heron white morph adult ("Great White Heron")

Great Blue Heron *Ardea herodias*

L 46" (117 cm) W 72" (183 cm) Large, gray-blue heron; black stripe extends above eye; white foreneck is streaked with black. **Breeding adult** has yellowish bill and ornate plumes on head, neck, and back. Nonbreeding adult lacks plumes; bill is yellower. **Juvenile** has black crown, no plumes. All-white morph found in southern Florida formerly considered a separate species, **"Great White Heron"** (preceding page). **"Wurdemann's Heron"** morph found chiefly in Florida Keys, has all-white head. **Range:** Common. A few winter far north into breeding range.

Storks (Family Ciconiidae)

Large, long-legged birds that walk sedately and fly with slow, deliberate beats of their long, broad wings, soaring and circling like hawks.

Wood Stork *Mycteria americana* **E**

L 40" (102 cm) W 61" (155 cm) Black flight feathers and tail contrast with white body. **Adult** has bald, blackish-gray head; thick, dusky, downcurved bill. **Juvenile**'s head is feathered largely with grayish-brown; bill is yellow. **Range:** Wood Storks inhabit wet meadows, swamps, ponds, coastal shallows. A few wander north in late summer; accidental as far north as Maine and British Columbia.

Jabiru *Jabiru mycteria* *L 52" (132 cm) W 90" (229 cm)*

Range: Huge stork of Central and South America, casual straggler in south Texas; recorded once in Oklahoma. Distinguished from Wood Stork by larger size; large bill, slightly upturned; and all-white wings and tail. Red throat pouch brightens and inflates during breeding season. **Juvenile** is patchy brown-gray; head is blackish-brown. Usually seen with flocks of Wood Storks.

Flamingos (Family Phoenicopteridae)

Large waders with big, bent bills, used to strain food from the waters of shallow lakes and lagoons.

Greater Flamingo *Phoenicopterus ruber*

L 46" (117 cm) W 60" (152 cm) **Range:** Birds seen in Florida are of the nominate race, which breeds as close to Florida as southern Bahamas and Cuba. Note pink legs, black flight feathers, tricolored bill. **Immature** is grayer, with pink wash below; paler bill. Sightings in south Florida may or may not be wild birds; others (except possibly in south Texas) may include escaped zoo birds, which are sometimes duller pink. Similar escapes include a widespread Old World subspecies *(P. r. roseus)*, with pink-and-white plumage; the Chilean Flamingo *(P. chilensis)*, with grayish legs with pink joints; and the Lesser Flamingo *(Phoeniconaias minor)*, with dark red bill and blotchy red wing coverts and axillaries.

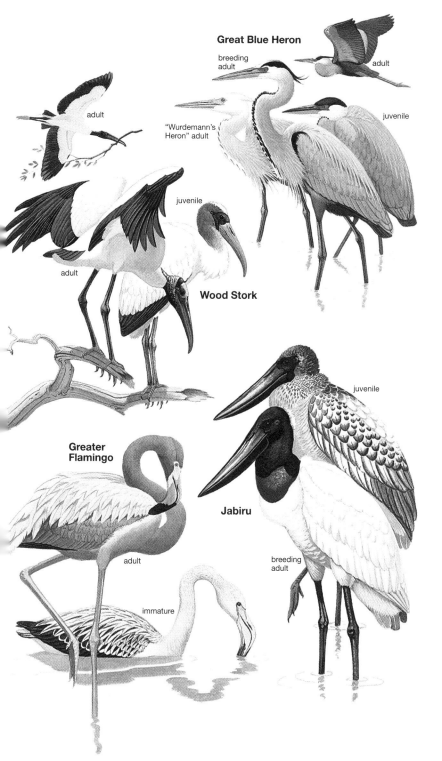

Great Blue Heron

breeding adult

adult

"Wurdemann's Heron" adult

juvenile

adult

Wood Stork

juvenile

adult

Greater Flamingo

adult

immature

Jabiru

juvenile

breeding adult

Ibises, Spoonbills (Family Threskiornithidae)

Gregarious, heronlike birds, these long-legged waders feed with long, specialized bills: slender and curved downward in ibises, wide and spatulate in spoonbills.

Glossy Ibis *Plegadis falcinellus L 23" (58 cm) W 36" (91 cm)*
Breeding adult's chestnut plumage is glossed with green or purple; looks all-dark at a distance. Distinguished from White-faced Ibis by brownish-olive bill, brown eye, gray-green legs with red joints, and lack of distinct white border to bare facial skin. Blue edge to gray facial skin does not extend behind eye or under chin. **Winter adult** closely resembles winter White-faced; look for gray facial skin partiallly bordered by blue line. **First-fall** bird closely resembles first-fall White-faced Ibis, but note gray facial skin and trace of blue line on most birds. Adult breeding plumage is acquired in second spring. **Range:** Glossy Ibises inhabit freshwater and saltwater marshes. Fairly common but local. Expanding north along the east coast. Rare but annual in Texas. Rare inland wanderer, chiefly in spring; casual west to Colorado.

White-faced Ibis *Plegadis chihi L 23" (58 cm) W 36" (91 cm)*
Breeding adult distinguished from Glossy Ibis by bronzer tones in chestnut plumage, reddish bill, red eye, all-red legs, and white feathered border around red facial skin; border extends behind eye and under chin. **Winter adult** plumage is like Glossy, but lacks pale blue line from eye to bill; facial skin is pale pink. **First-fall** bird closely resembles first-fall Glossy until winter when facial skin turns pinkish; look for lack of blue line (or a hint of white border) and reddish tinge to eye. **Range:** Breeds in freshwater marshes; may frequent brackish areas or feed in flooded fields. Very rare in midwest; casual on east coast north to New England.

White Ibis *Eudocimus albus L 25" (64 cm) W 38" (97 cm)*
Adult's white plumage and pink facial skin are distinctive. In **breeding adult,** facial skin, bill, and legs turn scarlet. Dark tips of primaries most easily seen in flight. Immatures have white underparts and wing linings, pinkish bill; gradually molt into adult plumage by second fall. **Range:** Locally common to abundant in coastal salt marshes, swamps, mangroves. Expanding north, now breeds to Virginia. Casual north to New Jersey, midwest, southwest. Closely related Scarlet Ibis *(E. ruber),* a South American species introduced or escaped in Florida, hybridizes with White Ibis; offspring are various shades of pink or scarlet.

Roseate Spoonbill *Ajaia ajaja L 32" (81 cm) W 50" (127 cm)*
Adult has pink body with red highlights; long, spatulate bill; unfeathered greenish head. The head may become buffy during courtship. **First-fall** bird has white feathering on head; body is mostly pale pink. Spoonbills feed in shallow waters, swinging their bills from side to side. **Range:** Fairly common locally along the Gulf coast; casual north to mid-Atlantic coast, southern midwest, and southwest.

breeding adult

1st fall

1st fall

winter adult

Glossy Ibis

breeding adult

winter adult

1st fall

White-faced Ibis

breeding adult

1st fall

White Ibis

breeding adult

breeding adult

1st fall

1st spring

Scarlet Ibis adult

Roseate Spoonbill

1st fall

breeding adult

breeding adult

1st fall

Ducks, Geese, Swans (Family Anatidae)

Worldwide family. Aquatic, web-footed, gregarious birds ranging from small ducks to large swans. Most feed on water; geese, swans, and some "puddle ducks" such as Wigeons also graze on land.

Tundra Swan *Cygnus columbianus L 52" (132 cm)*
In **adult,** black facial skin tapers to a point in front of eye and cuts straight across forehead; most birds have a yellow spot of variable size in front of eye. Head is rounded, bill slightly concave. In Eurasian race, **"Bewick's Swan,"** seen casually on the west coast, facial skin and base of bill are yellow, but usually only above the nostril; compare with Whooper Swan. **Immature** Tundras molt earlier than immature Trumpeter and Whooper Swans; appear much whiter by late winter. Immature "Bewick's" has whitish bill patch. Tundra's **call** is a noisy, high-pitched whooping or yodeling. **Range:** Nests on tundra or sheltered marshes; winters in flocks on shallow ponds, lakes, estuaries. Rare to uncommon in winter over parts of interior U.S.; casual south to the Gulf coast and north to the Maritimes.

Trumpeter Swan *Cygnus buccinator L 60" (152 cm)*
Adult's black facial skin tapers to broad point at the eye, dips down in a V on forehead. Forehead slopes evenly to straight bill. **Immatures** retain gray-brown plumage through first spring. Common **call** is a single or double honk like an old car horn. **Range:** Locally fairly common in its breeding areas. Reintroduced into parts of former range and introduced elsewhere. Rare in winter south to California and in western interior south of mapped range.

Whooper Swan *Cygnus cygnus L 60" (152 cm)*
Range: Eurasian species closely related to Trumpeter Swan. Regular winter visitor to outer and central Aleutians; has bred on Attu Island. Casual records in winter in Oregon and California are debatable; may be either wild or escaped birds. Large yellow patch on lores and bill usually extends in a point to the nostrils; compare with "Bewick's Swan." Forehead slopes evenly to the straight bill. Common **call** is a buglelike double note. **Immature** retains dusky plumage through first winter; by first fall, bill attains whitish patches in same shape as adult's bill patch.

Mute Swan *Cygnus olor L 60" (152 cm)*
Prominent black knob at base of orange bill. **Juvenile** plumage may be white or brownish; bill gray with black base. Darker juvenile begins to molt to white plumage by midwinter; bill becomes pinkish. Mute Swan often holds its long neck in an S-curve, with bill pointed down. Often swims with wings arched over back. Gives a variety of hisses and snorts, but generally silent. **Range:** An Old World species, introduced in the U.S. Seen in parks. East coast populations are increasing. Mute Swan is now established on the southeastern portion of Vancouver Island, British Columbia, and in parts of the Midwest. It is being systematically removed from the Great Lakes with other areas under consideration.

Tundra Swan

immature

adult

"Bewick's Swan" adult

Whooper Swan

Trumpeter Swan

adult

immature

immature

adult

Mute Swan

adult

juvenile

Greater White-fronted Goose *Anser albifrons*

L 28" (71 cm) Named for the distinctive white band at base of bill. Medium-size, grayish-brown goose, with irregular black barring on underparts; orange feet and legs. Bill pink or orangish with whitish tip. In flight, note grayish-blue wash on wing coverts and white U-shaped rump band. Most **immatures** acquire white front above bill and white bill tip during first winter; acquire black belly markings by second fall; distinguished from similar Bean Goose by bill color; from Pink-footed Goose by bill and leg color; compare also with immature blue-morph Snow Goose (next page). Color and size vary in **adults:** Small, pale, Arctic tundra birds have heavy barring; taiga-breeding race *A. a. elgasi* is larger, darker, with less barring; Greenland's intermediate-size tundra subspecies, *flavirostris,* rare in the northeast, is darkest, with the heaviest barring and an orange bill. **Range:** Breeds and feeds near fresh water; seen in wetlands, grassy fields, grainfields. Large populations are found on eastern Great Plains (with small to moderate numbers east to Mississippi Valley) and Pacific coast. Rare on western Great Plains and in eastern North America. Flocks may number in the thousands. **Call** is a high-pitched, laughing *kah-lah-aluck.* Rare winter visitor outside mapped range in all western states and north into southern Canada. Breeding distribution in Canada may be more extensive than shown.

Bean Goose *Anser fabalis L 31" (79 cm)*

Range: Eurasian species; rare spring migrant on western and central Aleutians, casual on islands in Bering Sea and on Seward Peninsula in western Alaska; a few scattered records elsewhere in North America. Grayish-brown goose with plain underparts, orange legs and feet. Similar to plain-bellied, immature Greater White-fronted Goose; best distinguished by different bill color: Black with orange-yellow band above the tip in eastern Siberian races; lacks white front, though some show a narrow white ring at base of bill. In flight, Bean Goose shows browner primary coverts and greater secondary coverts than Greater White-fronted. Of the two Siberian races shown here, *A. f. middendorffii* of the taiga, largest of all Bean Goose races, has only one definite record, on the Pribilofs; bill is long and of moderate depth; bill of tundra race *serrirostris* is shorter with an extremely thick base. **Call** is a low, reedy *ung-unk,* suggestive of barnyard geese.

Pink-footed Goose *Anser brachyrhynchus L 26" (66 cm)*

Range: East coast vagrant from breeding grounds in eastern Greenland. Several records between eastern Pennsylvania and Newfoundland; most sightings, especially in Newfoundland, are thought to be wild birds. Distinguished from plain-bellied immature Greater White-fronted Goose by pink legs and variable dark base and tip to pinkish bill; bill is also stubbier, neck shorter than Greater White-fronted. Juvenile is browner, looks more scaly than barred; legs duller. In flight, Pink-footed shows an extensive area of bluish-gray on mantle and all wing coverts; darker head and neck contrast with grayish body; tail base is grayer and paler than Greater White-fronted and Bean Goose.

Greater White-fronted Goose

immature

taiga adult
elgasi

tundra adult

Greenland adult
flavirostris

Bean Goose

adult
middendorffii

adult
serrirostris

Pink-footed Goose

adult

Snow Goose *Chen caerulescens*
L 26-33" (66-84 cm) W 52-65" (132-165 cm) Two color morphs. All adults distinguished from smaller Ross's Goose by larger, pinkish bill with black "grinning patch," longer neck, flatter head. Flies with slower wingbeat than Ross's; rusty stains often visible on face in summer. **White-morph immature** is grayish above, with dark bill. **Blue morph** was formerly considered a separate species, Blue Goose: **Adult** has mostly white head and neck, brown back, variable amount of white on underparts. Primaries and secondaries are black, wing coverts bluish-gray. **Immature** has dark head and neck, overall slaty body coloring; distinguished from Greater White-fronted Goose (preceding page) by dark legs and bill and lack of white on face. Intermediates between white and blue morphs have mainly white underparts and whitish wing coverts. Immatures of both morphs resemble adults by first spring. **Range:** Abundant. Breeds on high Arctic tundra; seen in winter in grasslands, grainfields, coastal wetlands. Occasionally hybridizes with Ross's Goose. A larger subspecies, the "Greater Snow Goose," (not shown) breeds around Baffin Bay, winters only along mid-Atlantic coast; blue morph almost unknown. Smaller form, the "Lesser Snow Goose" (morphs shown here), is rare in winter throughout interior U.S. and in southern Canada outside mapped range. Blue morph is abundant on the Gulf coast; rare west of the Great Plains; uncommon but increasing in the east.

Ross's Goose *Chen rossii L 23" (58 cm)*
Stubby, triangular bill, mostly deep pinkish-red, shows warty bluish protuberances at base that are visible at close range; more prominent in older birds. Neck shorter, head rounder than Snow Goose, white head generally lacks rusty stains; in flight, note smaller size and faster wingbeat; **calls** higher pitched. Ross's has two color morphs. **White-morph immature** may have very pale gray wash on head, back, and flanks, but far less than immature white-morph Snow Goose. Extremely rare **blue morph** is darker than blue-morph Snow Goose; face and belly are white. **Range:** Ross's Goose nests on lake islands on high Arctic tundra; occasionally hybridizes with Snow Goose. Seen during migration in grasslands and grainfields in eastern Great Plains and Mississippi Valley; rare but regular farther east to western Vermont. Rare winter visitor to mid-Atlantic states; rare visitor also to much of west outside mapped range. Usually seen with Snow Geese.

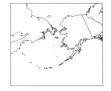

Emperor Goose *Chen canagica L 26" (66 cm)*
Fairly stocky, small goose with short, thick neck. Head and back of neck white; chin and throat black; face often stained rusty in summer. Bill pinkish; lower mandible is sometimes black. Black-and-white edging to silvery gray plumage creates a scaled effect below; upperparts appear barred. **Juvenile** has dark head and bill. During first fall, acquires white flecking on head; resembles adult by first winter. **Range:** Emperor Goose breeds in tidewater marsh and tundra; winters on seashores, reefs. Casual south on Pacific coast to central California and inland to Sacramento Valley.

Snow Goose

blue morph adults

white morph immature

white morph adult

blue morph immature

Ross's Goose

white morph immature

white morph adult

blue morph adult

Emperor Goose

juvenile

adult

Canada Goose *Branta canadensis*

L 25"-45" (64 cm-114 cm) Our most common and familiar goose. Black head and neck marked with distinctive white "chin strap" stretching from ear to ear. In flight, shows large, dark wings, white undertail coverts, white U-shaped rump band. Subspecies vary geographically in breast color, generally paler in eastern populations, darker in western; ranges from pale *B. c. canadensis* of the eastern seaboard to dark *occidentalis* of northern Gulf of Alaska coast. Size decreases northward, the smallest forms breeding on the high Arctic coastal tundra: pale-breasted *hutchinsii* in central and western Canada, and *minima*, smallest of all, in western Alaska. Threatened Aleutian subspecies, *leucopareia* (**T**), is distinguished from *minima* by slightly larger size, paler breast, and often a broad white neck ring; *minima* may show a very narrow ring. **Call** is a deep, musical *honk-a-lonk* in larger races, a rapid, high cackle in smaller ones. **Range:** Canada Geese breed in open or forested areas near water. Flocks usually migrate in V-formation, stopping to feed in wetlands, grasslands, or cultivated fields. Breeding programs have produced expanding populations south of mapped range and along Atlantic and Pacific coasts; explosive increase has prompted control measures in east.

Brant *Branta bernicla L 25" (64 cm)*

A small, dark, stocky sea goose with black head, neck, and breast and whitish patch on either side of neck. Extensive white upper-tail coverts almost conceal black tail. White undertail coverts conspicuous in flight. Wings comparatively long and pointed, wingbeat rather rapid. **Immature** birds show bold white edging to wing coverts and secondaries, and fainter neck patches than **adults.** Juveniles usually lack neck patches entirely. In more easterly subspecies *B.b. hrota,* "American Brant," pale belly contrasts with black chest, and neck patches do not meet in front. Western *nigricans,* "Black Brant," has dark belly, and neck patches meet in front. **Call** is a low, rolling. slightly upslurred *raunk-raunk.* **Range:** Primarily a sea goose; flocks fly low in ragged formation and feed on aquatic plants of shallow bays and estuaries. Locally common. Western *nigricans* is regular at Salton Sea in spring and summer. Brant is rare inland, but some *hrota* are sighted during migrations through the Great Lakes region, particularly in fall. Both races are casual during migration and winter on opposite coasts. Eastern *hrota* also casual south of mapped range.

Barnacle Goose *Branta leucopsis L 27" (69 cm)*

Part of world population breeds in northeastern Greenland; accidental vagrant in Maritime Provinces. Distinctive head pattern: white or creamy face with black streak extending from bill to eye; rest of head, neck, and breast black. Bluish-gray upperparts, barred with black, and white U-shaped rump band. Silver-gray wing linings show in flight. **Range:** More of a land goose than the Brant, feeding in fields near the ocean. Fairly common in captivity. Numerous east coast sightings south of the Maritime Provinces are probably mostly escaped birds; inland and western birds are almost certainly escapes.

Canada Goose

canadensis

occidentalis

leucopareia

minima

hutchinsii

adult
hrota

adult
nigricans

Brant

immature *hrota*

Barnacle Goose

Whistling-Ducks

Named for their whistling calls, these gooselike ducks have long legs, long necks. Wingbeats are slower than ducks, faster than geese.

Fulvous Whistling-Duck *Dendrocygna bicolor*
L 20" (51 cm) Rich tawny color overall; back darker, edged with tawny. Dark stripe along hindneck is continuous in female, usually broken in male. Bill and legs dark. Whitish rump band conspicuous in flight. **Call,** a squealing *pe-chee.* Forages in rice fields, marshes, shallow waters; often dives to feed. More active at night than day. **Range:** Irregular summer wanderer north to dashed line on map; casual farther north. Declining in the west.

Black-bellied Whistling-Duck
Dendrocygna autumnalis L 21" (53 cm) Gray face with white eye ring, red bill. Legs red or pink; belly, rump, and tail black. White wing patch shows as broad white stripe in flight. **Juvenile** is paler, with gray bill. **Call** is a high-pitched, four-note whistle. Inhabits wetlands; nests in trees, nest boxes. **Range:** Casual west to southeastern California; recent sightings in the east north to Canada may include wild birds.

Perching Ducks

These surface-feeding, woodland ducks are equipped with sharp claws for perching in trees. They nest in tree cavities or nest boxes.

Wood Duck *Aix sponsa L 18½" (47 cm)*
Male's glossy, colorful plumage and sleek crest are distinctive. Head pattern and bill colors are retained in drab eclipse plumage. **Female** identified by short crest and large, white, teardrop-shaped eye patch; compare with female Mandarin Duck (page 96). **Juvenile** resembles female but is spotted below. In all plumages, flight profile (page 98) is distinctive: large head with bill angled downward; long, squared-off tail. Male gives soft, upslurred whistle when swimming; female's squealing flight **call** is a rising *oo-eek.* **Range:** Fairly common in open woodlands near water. Rare during winter throughout most of breeding range.

Muscovy Duck *Cairina moschata L 26-33" (66-84 cm)*
Range: Tropical species; tame escaped birds occur in parks across North America. A nest box program in northeastern Mexico helped spread of wild Muscovies to Rio Grande area, where they are now present near Falcon Dam, Texas. Bulky, blackish duck with green and purple gloss above; white patches on upper- and underwing. **Male** has blackish to dark reddish knob at base of bill, bare facial skin; (usually brighter red in **domestic** male, whose color varies; can be all-white). Female is smaller, duller; lacks knob and bare facial skin. **Juvenile** even duller; slowly acquires wing patches in first winter. Wild Muscovies are shy, usually silent; seen mostly in slow, gooselike flight at dawn and dusk.

Fulvous Whistling-Duck

adult

Black-bellied Whistling-Duck

juvenile

Wood Duck

♀

juvenile ♂

♂

juvenile ♀

adult ♂

adult ♂

Muscovy Duck

domestic variety ♂

Dabbling Ducks

Surface-feeding members of the genus *Anas:* the familiar "puddle ducks" of freshwater shallows and, chiefly in winter, salt marshes. Dabblers feed by tipping tail-up to reach aquatic plants, seeds, and snails. They require no running start to take off but spring directly into flight. Most species show a distinguishing swatch of bright color, the speculum, on the secondaries. Many are known to hybridize.

Mallard *Anas platyrhynchos L 23" (58 cm)*
Male readily identified by metallic green head and neck, yellow bill, narrow white collar, chestnut breast. Black central tail feathers curl up. Both sexes have white tail, white underwings, bright blue speculum with both sides bordered in white (see also page 99). **Female**'s mottled plumage resembles other *Anas* species; look for orange bill marked with black. **Juvenile** and **eclipse male** resemble female but bill is dull olive. Abundant and widespread. Mallards in central Mexico, formerly considered a separate species, "Mexican Duck," are darker, lack distinctive male plumage; **intergrades** occur in southwestern U.S.

Mottled Duck *Anas fulvigula L 22" (56 cm)*
Both sexes closely resemble American Black Duck but body is slightly paler, throat and face unstreaked; speculum bluish. Differs from female Mallard by darker plumage and absence of white in tail or black on bill. Western Gulf coast race, *A. f. maculosa,* is darker than nominate Florida race. **Range:** Mottled Duck has been introduced to coastal South Carolina. Common year-round in coastal marshes. Very rare north to Arkansas and Kansas. Begins pairing in January or February, earlier than the migratory American Black Ducks and Mallards. Some authorities consider the Mottled Duck to be a subspecies of the Mallard.

American Black Duck *Anas rubripes L 23" (58 cm)*
Blackish-brown, paler on face and foreneck. In flight (page 98), white wing linings contrast more sharply with otherwise dark plumage than in similar female Mallard. Violet speculum is bordered in black, may show a thin white trailing edge. **Male**'s bill is yellow; **female**'s dull green, may be flecked with black. **Range:** Nesting pairs favor woodland lakes and streams, freshwater or tidal marshes. Small introduced populations are now established in British Columbia and Washington. In many parts of range, especially deforested areas, Mallards are replacing American Black Ducks; the two species **hybridize** frequently.

Spot-billed Duck *Anas poecilorhyncha L 22" (56 cm)*
Range: Asian species, casual vagrant on Aleutians and Kodiak Island. Pale tertials and sharply defined yellow tip of black bill, visible at a great distance, set this species apart from similar American Black Duck and female Mallard. The subspecies, *A. p. zonoahyncha,* that has reached North America lacks the red spots at base of bill for which this duck is named.

eclipse ♂

Mallard

juvenile

♀

♂

♂

Mottled Duck

♂

**"Mexican"-Mallard
intergrade**

♂

**American Black x
Mallard hybrid**

♀

**American
Black Duck**

♂

**Spot-billed
Duck**

Gadwall *Anas strepera L 20" (51 cm)*

Male is mostly gray, with white belly, black tail coverts, pale chestnut on wings. **Female**'s mottled brown plumage resembles female Mallard (preceding page), but belly is white, forehead steeper, upper mandible gray with orange sides. Both sexes have white inner secondaries that may show as small patch on swimming bird and identify the species in flight (page 99).

Falcated Duck *Anas falcata L 19" (48 cm)*

Range: Asian species, rare visitor to the western Aleutians; casual to Pribilofs. Named for **male**'s long, falcated (sickle-shaped) tertials that overhang tail. Both sexes are chunky, with large head. **Female**'s all-dark bill distinguishes her from female wigeons (next page) and Gadwall; note slight bump on back of head. In flight (page 99), both sexes show a broad, dark speculum bordered in white. Birds sighted on or near west coast may or may not be wild birds.

Green-winged Teal *Anas crecca L 14½" (37 cm)*

Our smallest dabbler. **Male**'s chestnut head has dark green ear patch outlined in white. **Female** distinguished from other female teals (see also page 83) by smaller bill and by largely white undertail coverts that contrast with mottled flanks. A fast-flying, agile duck. In flight (page 98), shows green speculum bordered in buff on leading edge, white on trailing edge. In the subspecies seen in most of North America, *A. c. carolinensis,* **male** has vertical white bar on side. Eurasian race, *crecca,* lacks vertical bar but has white stripe along scapulars. **Range:** Fairly common to Aleutians and Pribilofs; rare to very rare elsewhere on west and east coasts. Eurasian *crecca* was formerly considered a separate species, "Common Teal."

Baikal Teal *Anas formosa L 17" (43 cm)*

Range: Asian species; populations of northeast Asia have declined sharply in recent decades. A casual vagrant in Alaska and in west coast states; birds seen away from Alaska, and particularly away from the west coast, may well be escapes from captivity. **Adult male**'s intricately patterned head is distinctive. Long, drooping dark gray scapulars are edged in rufous and white. Gray sides are set off front and rear by vertical white bars. **Female** similar to smaller female Green-winged Teal, but coloration more tawny; note well defined white spot at base of bill, and whiter throat color that angles up to rear of eye. Narrow eyebrow is bordered by darker crown. On a few females, face has **bridle** marking. In flight (page 98), Baikal Teal's underwing is like Green-winged, but has blacker leading edge. Green speculum has a cinnamon-buff inner border.

Gadwall

♀

♂

Falcated Duck

♀

♂

crecca ♂

carolinensis ♀

carolinensis ♂

Green-winged Teal

Baikal Teal

bridled ♀

♀

♂

American Wigeon *Anas americana L 19" (48 cm)*

Male's white forehead and cap are conspicuous in mixed flocks foraging in fields, marshes, and shallow waters; in flight (page 98), identified by mainly white wing linings and, in **adult males,** by large white patches on upperwing. Wing patches are grayish on **adult female** and immatures. Female lacks white on head, closely resembles gray-morph female Eurasian Wigeon; distinguishing field marks in flight are female American's white wing linings and contrast between gray throat and brown breast; Eurasian female's throat and breast are of uniform color. **Range:** Common. A recently established breeder on the east coast. Fairly common during winter north to Lake Erie, rare on northern Great Lakes; rare to the Aleutians.

Eurasian Wigeon *Anas penelope L 20" (51 cm)*

Dark rufous head and gray back and sides make males conspicuous in flocks of American Wigeons; dusky wing linings are distinctive in all plumages. **Adult male** has reddish-brown head and neck with creamy forehead and cap; large white patches on upperwings. Many fall males retain some brown eclipse feathers but show distinctive reddish head. **Immature male** begins to acquire adult head and breast color but retains some brown juvenile plumage, particularly on forewing, similar to American Wigeon. **Gray-morph female** closely resembles female American, but note dusky wing linings and uniform color on throat and breast. **Rufous morph** has reddish head. **Range:** Eurasian Wigeon is a rare but regular winter visitor along both coasts, more common in the west; rare in interior of North America. Regular migrant and winter visitor on western and central Aleutians.

Northern Pintail *Anas acuta ♂ L 26" (66 cm) ♀ L 20" (51 cm)*

Male's chocolate brown head tops long, slender white neck, the white extending in a thin line onto head. Black central tail feathers extend far beyond rest of long, wedge-shaped tail. **Female** is mottled brown, paler on head and neck; bill uniformly grayish. In both sexes, flight profile (page 98) shows long neck; slender body; long, pointed wings; dark speculum bordered in white on trailing edge. In flight, female's mottled brown wing linings contrast with white belly; tail long and wedge-shaped but lacks male's extended feathers. **Range:** A common, widespread duck, found in marshes and open areas with ponds, lakes; in winter often feeds in grainfields. Much more common in west than in east. Rare in winter north to southern Alaska and Great Lakes region.

White-cheeked Pintail *Anas bahamensis L 17" (43 cm)*

Range: Casual vagrant from the West Indies to southern Florida. White cheeks and throat contrast with dark forehead and cap; blue bill has a red spot near base. Long, pointed tail is buffy; tawny or reddish underparts are heavily spotted. Female is paler than **male;** tail slightly shorter. In flight, both sexes show green speculum broadly bordered on each side with buff. Sightings even from Florida are of uncertain origin; those away from Florida are most likely birds escaped from captivity.

American Wigeon

♂

eclipse ♂

♀

rufous morph ♀

gray morph ♀

Eurasian Wigeon

♂

immature ♂

Northern Pintail

♂

♀

♂

White-cheeked Pintail

Northern Shoveler *Anas clypeata L 19" (48 cm)*

Large, spatulate bill, longer than head, identifies both sexes. **Male** distinguished by green head, white breast, brown sides; in early **fall** has a white crescent on each side of face, like Blue-winged Teal. **Female**'s grayish bill is tinged with orange on cutting edges and lower mandible. In flight (page 99), both sexes show blue forewing patch. **Range:** Common to abundant in the west; increasing in the east. Found in marshes, ponds, bays.

Blue-winged Teal *Anas discors L 15½" (39 cm)*

Violet-gray head with white crescent on each side identifies **male**. **Female** distinguished from female Green-winged Teal (page 78) by larger bill, more heavily spotted undertail coverts, yellowish legs. Compare also with female Cinnamon Teal; note Blue-winged's grayer plumage, smaller bill, and bolder facial markings, including whiter lore and more prominent, broken eye ring. Male in eclipse plumage resembles female. In flight (page 99), wing patterns of both sexes match those of Cinnamon. **Range:** Blue-winged Teal is fairly common in marshes and on ponds and lakes in open country. Uncommon on the west coast.

Garganey *Anas querquedula L 15½" (39 cm)*

Range: Old World species. Regular migrant on western Aleutians; very rare on Pribilofs and in Pacific states; casual elsewhere in North America. Prominent whitish edge to tertials is an important field mark in swimming birds; head shape is less rounded than in Blue-winged and Cinnamon Teal. **Male**'s bold white eyebrows separate dark crown, red-brown face; in flight (page 99), shows gray-blue forewing and green speculum bordered fore and aft with white. Wing pattern is retained when male acquires female-like eclipse plumage, held well into **fall**. **Female** has strong facial pattern: dark crown, pale eyebrow, dark eye line, white lore spot bordered by a second dark line; note also dark bill and legs, dark undertail coverts. Larger and paler overall than female Green-winged Teal (page 78). Female in flight shows gray-brown forewing, dark green speculum bordered in white. Note also pale gray inner webs of primaries, visible in flight from above.

Cinnamon Teal *Anas cyanoptera L 16" (41 cm)*

Cinnamon head, neck, and underparts identify **male. Female** closely resembles female Blue-winged Teal but plumage is a richer brown; lore spot, eye line, and broken eye ring less distinct; bill longer and more spatulate. Compare also with Green-winged Teal (page 78). Young birds and males in eclipse plumage resemble female. Males more than a couple of months old have red-orange eyes; Blue-winged's eyes are dark. Wing pattern (see page 99) is almost identical to Blue-winged. **Range:** Common in marshes, ponds, lakes. Regular from eastern Great Plains south to east Texas. Casual to eastern midwest and east. Some sightings may be escaped birds. Cinnamon Teal is known to interbreed with Blue-winged Teal.

Northern Shoveler

fall ♂

♀

♂

♀

Blue-winged Teal

♂

♀

Garganey

♂

fall ♂

Cinnamon Teal

♂

♀

Pochards

Diving ducks of the genus *Aythya* have legs set far back and far apart, which makes walking awkward. Heavy bodies require a running start on water for takeoff. Various species hybridize; seemingly rare birds sighted outside their normal range may in fact be hybrids.

Canvasback   *Aythya valisineria*   L 21" (53 cm)

Forehead slopes to long, black bill. **Male**'s head and neck are chestnut, back and sides whitish. **Female** and eclipse male have pale brown head and neck, pale brownish-gray back and sides. In flight (page 100), whitish belly contrasts with dark breast, dark undertail coverts. Wings lack contrasting pale stripe of Common Pochard and Redhead. **Range:** Locally common in marshes, lakes; feeds in large flocks; has decreased significantly but decline has stabilized. Migrating flocks fly in irregular V's or in lines.

Common Pochard   *Aythya ferina*   L 18" (46 cm)

Range: Eurasian species, rare migrant to Pribilofs and to western and central Aleutians; accidental to south coastal Alaska and southern California. Resembles Canvasback in plumage and head shape. Bill similar to Redhead's but dark at base and tip, gray in center. Gray on upperparts immediately distinguishes **female** from female Redhead and Ring-necked Duck (next page). In flight (page 100), wings show gray stripe along trailing edge.

Redhead   *Aythya americana*   L 19" (48 cm)

Rounded head and shorter, tricolored bill separate this species from Canvasback. Bill is mostly pale blue (male) or slate (female), with narrow white ring bordering black tip. **Male**'s back and sides are smoky gray. **Female** and eclipse male are brown, with darker crown, pale patch bordering black bill tip; compare female scaup (next page). Redheads in flight (page 100) show gray stripe on trailing edge of wings. **Range:** Locally common in marshes, ponds, lakes; is declining in the east.

Canvasback

♀

♂

Common Pochard

♂

♀

Redhead

♀

♂

Ring-necked Duck *Aythya collaris L 17" (43 cm)*

Peaked head; bold white ring near tip of bill. **Male** has second white ring at base of bill; white crescent separates black breast from gray sides. Cinnamon collar is very hard to see in the field. **Female** has dark crown, white eye ring; may have a pale line extending back from eye; face is mainly gray. In flight (page 100), all plumages show a gray stripe on secondaries. **Range:** Fairly common in freshwater marshes and on woodland ponds, small lakes; during winter, found also in southern coastal marshes. Range is variable; may breed south or winter north of mapped range; regular breeder in Alaska.

Tufted Duck *Aythya fuligula L 17" (43 cm)*

Range: Old World species; regular visitor to western Alaska. Rare winter visitor along east coast as far south as Maryland, and on west coast to southern California; casual elsewhere in west; very rare in Great Lakes region. Found on ponds, rivers, bays, often with Ring-necked Ducks and scaup. Head is rounded; crest distinct in **male,** smaller in **female** and immatures; may be absent in eclipse male. Gleaming white sides further distinguish male from male Ring-necked Duck. **First-winter male** has gray sides but lacks the white crescents conspicuous in male Ring-necked. Female is blackish-brown above; lacks white eye ring and white bill ring of female Ring-necked. Bills of both male and female Tufted have a wide black tip. Some females also have a small white area at base of bill. In flight (page 100), all plumages show a broad white stripe on secondaries and extending onto primaries.

Greater Scaup *Aythya marila L 18" (46 cm)*

Larger size and smoothly rounded head help distinguish this species from Lesser Scaup. In close view, note Greater Scaup's slightly larger bill with wider black tip. In good light, **male**'s head may show a green gloss. In both species, **female** has bold white patch at base of bill. Some female Greater Scaup, especially in spring and summer, have a paler head with a distinct whitish ear patch. In flight (page 100), Greater Scaup typically shows a bold white stripe on secondaries and well out onto primaries, unlike Lesser Scaup. **Range:** Locally common; found on large, open lakes and bays. Migrates and winters in small or large flocks, often with Lesser Scaup. Rare to uncommon winter visitor throughout the Gulf states.

Lesser Scaup *Aythya affinis L 16½" (42 cm)*

Smaller size and peaked crown help distinguish from Greater Scaup. In close view, note Lesser Scaup's slightly smaller bill with smaller black tip. In good light, **male**'s head may show a purple gloss, sometimes mixed with green. **Female** is brown overall, with bold white patch at base of bill. In some females, especially in spring and summer, head is paler, with whitish ear patch less distinct than in female Greater Scaup. In flight (page 100), Lesser Scaup shows bold white stripe on secondaries only. **Range:** Common; breeds in marshes, small lakes, and ponds. In winter, found in large flocks on sheltered bays, inlets, and lakes.

Ring-necked Duck

♂ ♀

Tufted Duck

♂ 1st winter ♂ ♀ ♀

Greater Scaup

1st winter ♂ ♀ ♂ ♀

Lesser Scaup

♂ ♀

Eiders

These large, bulky diving sea ducks have dense down feathers that help insulate them from the cold northern waters. Females pluck their own down to line nests.

Common Eider *Somateria mollissima* L 24" (61 cm)
Female distinguished from female King Eider by larger size, sloping forehead, and evenly barred sides and scapulars. Feathering extends along sides of bill to or beyond nostril, with minimal feathering on top of bill. Females range in overall color from rust to gray. Eastern *S. m. dresseri* is reddish-brown. Western *v-nigra* is duller brown; **eclipse** plumage paler. **Male**'s head pattern is distinctive. Most western and a few eastern males show a thin black V on throat; *v-nigra* male has orange-yellow bill. **Eclipse** and **first-winter** males are dark; first-winter has white on breast; full adult plumage is attained by fourth winter. In flight (page 100), adult male shows white back with black tail, black primaries and secondaries. **Range:** Locally abundant on shallow bays, rocky shores; casual on Great Lakes. Rare in winter to North Carolina; casual on east coast to Florida.

King Eider *Somateria spectabilis* L 22" (56 cm)
Female distinguished from female Common Eider by smaller size, more rounded head, and crescent or V-shaped markings on sides and scapulars. Feathering extends only slightly along sides of bill but extensively down the top, making bill look stubby. **Male**'s head pattern is distinctive. In flight (page 101), shows partly black back, black wings with white patches. **First-winter male** has brown head, pinkish or buffy bill, buffy eye line; lacks white wing patches; full adult plumage attained by third winter. **Range:** Common on tundra and coastal waters in northern part of range; generally very rare on Great Lakes except on Lake Ontario where rare and increasing. Rare in winter on east coast to Virginia; casual to Florida and on west coast.

Spectacled Eider *Somateria fischeri* **E** L 21" (53 cm)
Male has green head with white, black-bordered eye patches and orange bill. In flight (page 101), black breast separates adult male from other eiders, smaller size from Common Eider. Drab **female** has fainter spectacle pattern; bill is gray-blue; feathering extends far down upper mandible. **Range:** Uncommon and declining; found on coastal tundra near lakes and ponds. Flocks winter in openings in ice pack on Bering Sea. Casual on Aleutians.

Steller's Eider *Polysticta stelleri* **E** L 17" (43 cm)
Greenish head tufts, black eye patch, chin, and collar identify **male**. **Female** is dark cinnamon brown with distinct pale eye ring, unfeathered dark bill. In flight (page 101), adults, immature males, and some immature females show blue speculum bordered fore and aft in white. **Range:** Found along rocky coasts; nests on inland grassy areas or tundra. Winters casually south to northern California coast. Numbers reduced over last decade.

Common Eider

eclipse adult ♂ *v-nigra*

eclipse ♀ *v-nigra*

♀ *dresseri*

1st winter ♂ *dresseri*

adult ♂ *dresseri*

adult ♂ *v-nigra*

1st winter ♂

adult ♂

King Eider

♀

adult ♂

Spectacled Eider

♀

Common Eiders in flight

Steller's Eider

♀

1st winter ♂

adult ♂

Sea Ducks

Stocky, short-necked diving ducks, most species breed in the far north and migrate in large, compact flocks to and from their coastal wintering grounds.

Black Scoter *Melanitta nigra* L 19" (48 cm)

Male is black, with orange-yellow knob at base of dark bill. **Female**'s dark crown and nape contrast with pale face and throat; feathering does not extend onto bill. In both, forehead is strongly rounded; feet and legs are dark. In flight (page 101), adult male's blackish wing linings contrast with paler flight feathers. Juveniles resemble females but are whitish on belly; **first-winter male** has some yellow at base of bill by early winter. **Range:** Nests along tundra and woodland waterways. Small numbers seen in fall on Great Lakes (common on Lake Ontario, where some winter); rare elsewhere in eastern interior; casual in western interior.

White-winged Scoter *Melanitta fusca* L 21" (53 cm)

White secondaries, conspicuous in flight (page 100), may show as a small white patch on swimming bird. Forehead slightly rounded. Feathering extends almost to nostrils on top and sides of bill. **Female** and juveniles lack contrasting dark crown and paler face of other scoters; white facial patches are distinct on juveniles, often indistinct on adult female. Juveniles and immatures are whitish below. **Adult male** has black knob at base of colorful bill; crescent-shaped white patch below white eye, brownish flanks. **Range:** Fairly common on inland lakes and rivers in breeding season, coastal areas in winter. Uncommon inland migrant. Large numbers winter on Lake Ontario since introduction of zebra mussels. Rarest scoter in the south.

Surf Scoter *Melanitta perspicillata* L 20" (51 cm)

Male's black plumage sets off colorful bill, white eye, white patch on forehead and nape; forehead is sloping, not rounded. **Female** is brown, with dark crown; usually has two white patches on each side of face; feathering extends down top of bill only. Adult female and **first-winter male** may have whitish nape patch. All juveniles have whitish belly, usually white face patches. In flight (page 100), more uniform color of underwings helps distinguish Surf from Black Scoter; also orangish legs and feet. **Range:** Common; nests on tundra and in wooded areas near water. Rare inland migrant. A few winter on Great Lakes; most in coastal waters.

Harlequin Duck *Histrionicus histrionicus* L 16½" (42 cm)

Small duck, with steep forehead, rounded head, stubby bill. **Male**'s colorful plumage appears dark at a distance. **Female** has three white spots on each side of head; belly is pale. Juvenile resembles adult female. Flight is rapid, low. Compare female in flight (page 101) with female Bufflehead. Male's **call** is a high-pitched nasal squeaking. **Range:** Locally common on rocky coasts; moves inland along swift streams for nesting. Regular in winter south to Virginia; rare on Great Lakes in migration and winter.

Black Scoter

1st winter ♂

adult ♂

adult ♀

White-winged Scoter

adult ♂

1st winter ♂

1st winter ♀

adult ♀

Surf Scoter

adult ♂

adult ♀

1st winter ♀

1st winter ♂

Harlequin Duck

♀

1st winter ♂

adult ♂

Oldsquaw *Clangula hyemalis* ♂ *L 22" (56 cm)* ♀ *16" (41 cm)*

Male's long tail is conspicuous in flight, may be submerged in swimming bird. Male in winter and spring is largely white; breast and back dark brown, scapulars pearl gray; stubby bill shows pink band. By late spring, male becomes mostly dark, with pale facial patch, bicolored scapulars; in later, supplemental molt, acquires paler crown and shorter, buff-edged scapulars. Molt into full eclipse plumage continues until early fall. **Female** lacks long tail; bill is dark; plumage whiter overall in winter, darker in summer. First-fall birds (see page 101) are even darker. Oldsquaws are identifiable at some distance by their swift, careening flight and loud, yodeling, three-part **calls,** heard all year. Both sexes show uniformly dark underwings. **Range:** Away from Great Lakes, Oldsquaw is rare in the interior and south to the Gulf coast.

Barrow's Goldeneye *Bucephala islandica L 18" (46 cm)*

Male has white crescent on each side of face; white patches on scapulars show on swimming bird as a row of spots; dark color of back extends forward in a bar partially separating white breast from white sides. **Female** and male in eclipse plumage closely resemble the Common Goldeneye. Puffy, oval-shaped head, steep forehead, and stubby, triangular bill help identify Barrow's. Adult female's head is slightly darker than female Common; bill mostly yellow, except in young females, which may have only a yellow band near tip of bill. In all plumages, white wing patches visible in flight (page 101) differ subtly between the two species. **Range:** Both summer on open lakes and small ponds; winter in sheltered coastal areas, inland lakes, and rivers. Barrow's is much less common; rare to casual outside mapped winter range.

Common Goldeneye *Bucephala clangula L 18½" (47 cm)*

Male has round white spot on each side of face; scapulars are mostly white. **Female** and eclipse male closely resemble Barrow's Goldeneye. Head of Common is more triangular; forehead more sloped; bill longer. Female's head is slightly paler than female Barrow's; bill generally all-dark or with yellow near tip only; rarely all dull yellow. In all plumages, there are subtle differences between the two species in white wing patches visible in flight (page 101). **Range:** Both summer on open lakes, often near woodlands where nest holes are available and winter in coastal areas, inland lakes, and rivers.

Bufflehead *Bucephala albeola L 13½" (34 cm)*

A small duck with a large, puffy head, steep forehead, short bill. **Male** is glossy black above, white below, with large white patch on head. **Female** is duller, with small, elongated white patch on each side of head. **Young male** and male in eclipse resemble female. In flight (page 101), males show white patch across entire wing; female has white patch only on inner secondaries. **Range:** Generally common, Buffleheads nest in woodlands near small lakes, ponds. During migration and winter, found also on sheltered bays, rivers, and lakes.

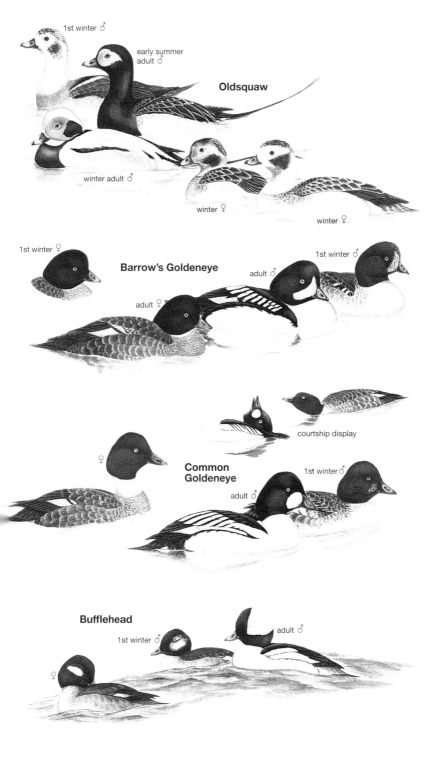

1st winter ♂

early summer
adult ♂

Oldsquaw

winter adult ♂

winter ♀

winter ♀

1st winter ♀

Barrow's Goldeneye

adult ♀

adult ♂

1st winter ♂

courtship display

**Common
Goldeneye**

♀

adult ♂

1st winter ♂

Bufflehead

adult ♂

1st winter ♂

♀

Mergansers

Long, thin, serrated bills help these divers catch fish, crustaceans, and aquatic insects. Mergansers in flight show pointed wings and a distinctive profile: Head looks like a bump between long neck and bill.

Common Merganser *Mergus merganser* L 25" (64 cm)
Large duck with long, slim neck and thin, hooked, red bill. White breast and sides, often tinged with pink, and lack of crest distinguish **male** from Red-breasted Merganser. **Female**'s bright chestnut, crested head and neck contrast sharply with white chin, white breast. Adult male in flight (page 100) shows white patch on upper surface of entire inner wing, partially crossed by a single black bar. Eclipse male resembles female but retains wing pattern. Female's white inner secondaries and greater coverts are partially crossed by a black bar. As in all species on this page, **young male** resembles adult female. **Range:** Common Mergansers nest in woodlands near lakes and rivers; in winter, sometimes also found on brackish water. In eastern North America, regular in winter south to Ohio River region, casual to Gulf coast.

Red-breasted Merganser *Mergus serrator* L 23" (58 cm)
Shaggy double crest, white collar, and streaked breast distinguish **male** from male Common Merganser. **Female**'s head and neck are paler than female Common; chin and foreneck white. Adult male in flight (page 100) shows white patch on upper surface of inner wing, partly crossed by two black bars. Eclipse male resembles female but retains male wing pattern. Female's white inner secondaries and greater coverts are crossed by a single black bar. Smaller size helps distinguish Red-breasted Merganser in mixed flocks. **Range:** Nests in woodlands near fresh water or in sheltered coastal areas; prefers brackish or salt water in winter. Abundant migrant on Great Lakes, where moderate numbers winter; elsewhere, fairly common to common migrant in interior.

Hooded Merganser *Lophodytes cucullatus* L 18" (46 cm)
Puffy, rounded crest; thin bill. **Male**'s bill is dark; white head patches are fan-shaped and conspicuous when crest is raised. Compare with male Bufflehead (preceding page). **Female** brownish overall; upper mandible dark, lower yellowish. Rapid wingbeats in flight (page 101); both sexes show black-and-white inner secondaries. Crest is flattened in flight, male's head patch shows only as a white line. **Range:** Uncommon in west; common over much of east. In breeding season, found on woodland ponds, rivers, backwaters. Winters chiefly on fresh water.

Smew *Mergellus albellus* L 16" (41 cm)
Range: Eurasian species, rare visitor to Aleutians; casual on Pribilofs; accidental on or near the west and east coasts and the Great Lakes. Bill is dark and relatively short. In **female,** white throat and lower face contrast sharply with reddish head and nape. **Adult male** is white with black markings; black-and-white wings are conspicuous in flight (page 101).

Common Merganser

♀

adult ♂

1st spring ♂

Red-breasted Merganser

adult ♂

1st winter ♂

♀

Hooded Merganser

1st spring ♂

adult ♂

♀

Smew

♀

adult ♂

1st spring ♂

Stiff-tailed Ducks

Long, stiff tail feathers serve as a rudder for these diving ducks. In both species, male's bill is blue in breeding season.

Ruddy Duck *Oxyura jamaicensis* L 15" (38 cm)
Chunky, with large head, broad bill, long tail, often cocked up. **Male**'s white cheeks are conspicuous both in **breeding** plumage and in dull **winter** plumage. In **female,** single dark line crosses cheek. Young resemble female through first winter. **Range:** Common; nests in dense vegetation of freshwater wetlands. During migration and winter, found on lakes, bays, salt marshes.

Masked Duck *Nomonyx dominicus* L 13½" (34 cm)
Range: Tropical species, rare visitor to southern and southeastern Texas; casual in Louisiana and Florida. Accidental in east, north to Wisconsin and New England. Shy; found on densely vegetated ponds. **Male**'s black face on reddish-brown head is distinctive. In **female, winter male,** and **juvenile,** two dark stripes cross face. White wing patches show in flight (page 99).

Exotic Waterfowl

Many waterfowl species are brought into North America from other continents for zoos, farms, parks, and private collections. They occasionally escape from captivity. The species shown here are among those now seen all over; some are becoming established in the wild.

Ruddy Shelduck *Tadorna ferruginea* L 26" (66 cm)
Afro-Eurasian species. Popular in zoos and private collections.

Northern Shelduck *Tadorna tadorna* L 25" (64 cm)
Eurasian species. Female smaller, lacks knobs on bill.

Egyptian Goose *Alopochen aegyptiacus* L 27" (68 cm)
African species. A recent addition to the list of exotics.

Chinese Goose *Anser cygnoides* L 45" (114 cm)
Asian species, more widely known as Swan Goose. Wild form is slim, has long, swanlike bill lacking knob at base.

Mandarin Duck *Aix galericulata* L 16" (41 cm)
Asian species. Compare female to female Wood Duck (page 74).

Domestic Goose *Anser "domesticus"*
L 22-45" (56-114 cm) Common on farms.

Greylag Goose *Anser anser* L 34" (86 cm)
Eurasian species, progenitor of most domestic geese. Compare carefully to White-fronted Goose (page 68).

Bar-headed Goose *Anser indicus* L 30" (76 cm)
Asian species. Fairly common in zoos and private collections.

Ruddy Duck

breeding ♀

breeding ♂

winter ♂

winter ♀

breeding ♂

winter ♀

winter ♂

breeding ♀

Masked Duck

juvenile

Ruddy Shelduck

Northern Shelduck ♂

Egyptian Goose

Chinese Goose

Mandarin Duck ♀ ♂

Domestic Goose

Greylag Goose

Bar-headed Goose

Ducks in Flight

Northern
Pintail

American
Black Duck

Eurasian
Wigeon

adult
♂

gray morph
♀

American
Wigeon

adult
♂

♀

Baikal
Teal

♂

♀

Wood
Duck

♂

♀

Green-winged
Teal

carolinensis
♂

Ruddy
Duck

breeding
♂

♀

carolinensis ♀

Mallard

Gadwall

Northern
Shoveler

Falcated
Duck

Cinnamon
Teal

Blue-winged
Teal

Garganey

immature ♂

Masked
Duck

breeding ♂

Ducks in Flight

Common Merganser adult ♂ ♀

Common Eider *dresseri* ♂ *dresseri* ♀

Red-breasted Merganser adult ♂ ♀

White-winged Scoter adult ♂ adult ♀

Surf Scoter adult ♂ immature ♀

Canvasback ♂ ♀

Common Pochard ♂ ♀

Redhead ♂ ♀

Greater Scaup ♂ ♀

Lesser Scaup ♂ ♀

Tufted Duck ♂ ♀

Ring-necked Duck ♂ ♀

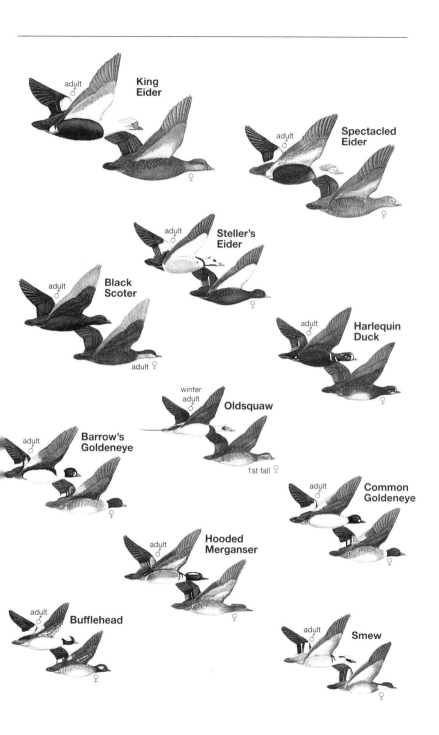

King
Eider

adult
♂

♀

Spectacled
Eider

adult
♂

♀

Steller's
Eider

adult
♂

♀

Black
Scoter

adult
♂

adult ♀

Harlequin
Duck

adult
♂

♀

Oldsquaw

winter
adult
♂

1st fall ♀

Barrow's
Goldeneye

adult
♂

♀

Common
Goldeneye

adult
♂

♀

Hooded
Merganser

adult
♂

♀

Bufflehead

adult
♂

♀

Smew

adult
♂

♀

New World Vultures (Family Cathartidae)

Small, unfeathered head and hooked bill aid in consuming carrion. Recent evidence indicates a relationship to storks.

Turkey Vulture *Cathartes aura* L 27" (69 cm) W 69" (175 cm)
Seen from below, contrastingly two-toned wings aid identification: flight feathers silver-gray; linings black. Wings are often held upward in a shallow V. Rocks side to side in flight, seldom flapping its wings; long tail extends beyond legs and feet. **Adult** has red head, white bill, brown legs; **juvenile**'s head and bill are dark, legs paler. Feeds chiefly on carrion and refuse. **Range:** Common in open country, woodlands, farms. Range is expanding in east.

Black Vulture *Coragyps atratus* L 25" (64 cm) W 57" (145 cm)
In flight, shows large white patches at base of primaries. Tail is shorter than Turkey Vulture; wings shorter and broader; legs white; feet usually extend to edge of tail or beyond. Flight includes rapid flapping and short glides, usually with wings flat. Gregarious and aggressive. Less efficient at spotting carrion, Black Vultures may claim Turkey Vultures' find. **Range:** Common in open country and near human settlements, where they scavenge in garbage dumps. Range expanding in the northeast; casual north to Ontario, Maritimes. Accidental in California, New Mexico.

California Condor *Gymnogyps californianus* **E**
L 47" (119 cm) W 108" (274 cm) **Range:** Last wild birds captured in April 1987. Before that, found in arid foothills and mountains of southern and central California. Decline to near extinction caused largely by lead poisoning and illegal shooting. Recently reintroduced in southern California and introduced in northern Arizona. Huge size distinctive. **Adult** has white wing linings, orange head; **juvenile**'s wing linings mottled, head dusky. Soars on flat wings, without flapping, in search of large carrion.

Hawks, Kites, Eagles (Family Accipitridae)

A large, worldwide family of diurnal birds of prey, equipped with hooked bills and strong talons. Males are usually smaller than females.

Osprey *Pandion haliaetus*
L 22-25" (56-64 cm) W 58-72" (147-183 cm) Dark brown above, white below, with white head, prominent dark eye stripe. Females average darker streaking on neck; **juvenile** plumage is fringed with pale buff above. In flight, long, narrow wings are bent back at wrist, dark carpal patches conspicuous; wings slightly arched in soaring. Nests near fresh or salt water; eats mostly fish. Hovering over water, dives down, then plunges feetfirst to snatch prey. Bulky nests are built in trees, on sheds, poles, docks, and special platforms. **Call** is a series of loud, whistled *kyews*. **Range:** Conservation programs have halted decline of species. Now fairly common in coastal range. Uncommon and local inland.

Turkey Vulture

adults

adult

juvenile

adult

Black Vulture

adult

juvenile

adult

California Condor

adult

adult

Osprey

adult

juvenile

adult

Mississippi Kite *Ictinia mississippiensis*

L 14½" (37 cm) W 35" (89 cm) Long, pointed wings with first primary distinctly shorter; long, flared tail. Dark gray above, paler below, with pale gray head, paler on **male.** White secondaries show in flight as white wing patch. Black tail readily distinguishes Mississippi from White-tailed Kite. Compare also with male Northern Harrier (next page); note Mississippi never hovers. **Juvenile** is heavily streaked and spotted, with pale bands on tail. **First-summer** bird (page 126) more like adult but retains juvenile flight feathers. At all ages, may be confused with Peregrine Falcon (page 124); compare wing and tail shapes. Mississippi Kites capture and eat their prey, mainly insects, on the wing. Gregarious; often hunt in groups, nest in loose colonies. **Range:** Found in woodlands, swamps, rangelands. Regular straggler (chiefly immatures in spring) to mid-Atlantic states. Casual north to Great Lakes region and California. Winters in South America.

Swallow-tailed Kite *Elanoides forficatus*

L 23" (58 cm) W 48" (122 cm) Seen in flight, deeply forked tail and sharply defined pattern of black and white are like no other large bird except the young Magnificent Frigatebird (page 46). Perched, Swallow-tailed Kite's coloring more closely resembles White-tailed and Mississippi Kites; again, note long, forked tail. Juveniles are similar to **adults,** but tail is shorter, flight feathers and tail narrowly tipped with white. Agile and graceful, Swallow-tailed snatches flying insects; also drops down upon snakes, lizards, young birds; does not hover. Often eats prey in flight; also drinks in flight, skimming the water like a swallow. Found in open woods, bottomlands, wetlands. Nests in the tops of tall trees. Somewhat social; several may hunt in the same territory. **Range:** Casual in spring and summer as far north as Ontario and Nova Scotia; accidental as far west as Arizona. Most winter in South America.

White-tailed Kite *Elanus leucurus*

L 16" (41 cm) W 42" (107 cm) Long, pointed wings; long tail. White underparts and mostly white tail distinguish **adults** from similar Mississippi Kite. Compare also with male Northern Harrier (next page). **Juvenile**'s underparts and head are lightly streaked with rufous, which rapidly fades. In all ages, black shoulders show in flight as black leading edge of inner wings from above, small black patches from below. Hovers while hunting, unlike any other North American kite. Eats mainly rodents, insects. **Range:** Populations fluctuate. Fairly common in grasslands, farmlands, even highway median strips. Casual well north of mapped range to British Columbia, Wyoming, and New York. Often forms winter roosts of more than a hundred birds.

Mississippi Kite

juvenile

adult ♂

adult ♂

adult ♀

Swallow-tailed Kite

adults

juvenile

adult

White-tailed Kite

Snail Kite *Rostrhamus sociabilis* **E**

L 17" (43 cm) W 46" (117 cm) This kite's wings are paddle-shaped, bill thin and deeply hooked. **Male** is gray-black above and below, with white uppertail and undertail coverts, square, white tail with broad, dark band and paler terminal band; legs orange-red; eyes and facial skin reddish. **Female** is dark brown, with distinctive head pattern. Juvenile has dark brown eyes, duller facial skin and legs, streaked crown and underparts. Hunting flight is slow, with considerable flapping of wings, and head held down as the kite searches for apple snails, its chief and perhaps only food. **Range:** A tropical species. Endangered; uncommon and local resident in southern Florida.

Hook-billed Kite *Chondrohierax uncinatus*

L 16" (41 cm) W 33" (84 cm) **Range:** Tropical species, uncommon over most of its range. Rare resident in lower Rio Grande Valley from Santa Ana to Falcon Dam. Found in dense woodlands, from which it thermals upward in late morning. Plumage varies considerably, but look for large, heavy bill with long hook, white eyes, banded tail, and heavily barred underparts, including underwings. **Males** are generally gray overall. **Females** are brown, with a rufous collar and rufous, barred underparts. **Juveniles** have brown eyes, white collar, and whitish underparts with variable dark brown barring. In the **black morph,** not yet seen in the U.S., **adult** is all-black except for a single white or grayish tail band and whitish tail tip; **immatures** are mostly brownish-black, with two or more grayish tail bands. Hook-billed Kite flies with deep, languid wingbeats, its wrists slightly cocked upward and hands angled down. Wings are paddle-shaped, slightly tapered in at the base. It eats insects and small amphibians, but prefers snails of various kinds. A pile of broken snail shells beneath a tree may indicate a favorite perch or a nest site above.

Northern Harrier *Circus cyaneus*

L 17-23" (43-58 cm) W 38-48" (97-122 cm) White uppertail coverts and owl-like facial disk distinctive in all ages and both sexes. Body slim; wings long and narrow with somewhat rounded tips; tail long. **Adult male** is grayish above; mostly white below with variable chestnut spotting; has black wing tips and black tips to secondaries. **Female** is brown above, whitish below with heavy brown streaking on breast and flanks, lighter streaking and spotting on belly. **Juveniles** resemble adult female but are cinnamon below, fading to creamy buff by spring; streaked only on the breast; wing linings are cinnamon, distinctly darker on inner half. Harriers generally perch low and fly close to the ground, wings upraised, as they search for birds, mice, frogs, and other prey. Seldom soar high except during migration and in exuberant, acrobatic courtship display. **Range:** Fairly common in wetlands and open fields. Adult males migrate later in fall and earlier in spring than females and immatures. In winter, Harriers form communal ground roosts, sometimes with Short-eared Owls.

Snail Kite

adult ♂

adult ♀

juvenile

adult ♂

black morph adult

black morph immature

molting immature

adult ♂

adult ♀

Hook-billed Kite

juvenile

juvenile

adult ♀

Northern Harrier

adult ♂

Golden Eagle *Aquila chrysaetos*

L 30-40" (76-102 cm) W 80-88" (203-224 cm) Brown, with variable yellow to tawny brown wash over back of head and neck; bill mostly horn-colored; tail faintly banded. Tawny greater upperwing coverts form a bar. **Juveniles,** seen in flight from below, show well-defined white patches at base of primaries, white tail with distinct dark terminal band. Compare with juvenile Bald Eagle's larger head, shorter tail, blotchier tail and underwing pattern. **Adult** plumage is acquired in four years. Golden Eagle often soars with wings slightly uplifted. **Range:** Inhabits mountainous or hilly terrain, hunting over open country for small mammals, snakes, birds, carrion. Also found in valleys and western plains, especially in migration and winter. Nests on cliffs or in trees. Uncommon to rare in the east; fairly common in the west.

White-tailed Eagle *Haliaeetus albicilla*

L 26-35" (66-89 cm) W 72-94" (183-239 cm) **Range:** Flies over northern Eurasia and Greenland in diminishing numbers. Very rare visitor to Attu in outer Aleutians, where it has nested. Note short, wedge-shaped white tail. Plumage mottled; head may be very pale and appear white at a distance; undertail coverts are dark, unlike Bald Eagle. **Juvenile**'s tail has variable dark mottling and tip and is less wedge-shaped, underwing darker, than Bald Eagle.

Steller's Sea-Eagle *Haliaeetus pelagicus*

L 33-41" (84-104 cm) W 87-96" (221-244 cm) **Range:** Nests in northeastern Asia; casual in Alaska; recorded on Aleutians, Pribilofs, Kodiak Island, near Juneau in southeastern Alaska. In flight, white shoulders show as white leading edge of wings; trailing edge of wing more curved than in White-tailed or Bald Eagles. Immense yellow-orange bill; long, white, wedge-shaped tail; white thighs. **Juvenile** lacks white shoulders; end of tail is dark.

Bald Eagle *Haliaeetus leucocephalus* **T**

L 31-37" (79-94 cm) W 70-90" (178-229 cm) **Adults** readily identified by white head and tail, large yellow bill. **Juveniles** are mostly dark, may be confused with juvenile Golden Eagle; compare blotchy white on underwing coverts, axillaries, and tail with Golden Eagle's more sharply defined pattern; note also Bald Eagle's proportionately larger head, shorter tail. Neck is shorter and tail longer than White-tailed Eagle; Steller's Sea-Eagle has longer, wedge-shaped tail. Flat-winged soar distinguishes young Bald Eagle from Turkey Vulture (page 102). Bald Eagles require four or five years to reach full adult plumage. Seen most often on seacoasts or near rivers and lakes. Feed mainly on fish in breeding season, regularly on carrion, and on roadkill in winter, particularly in the southwest. Nest in tall trees or on cliffs. **Range:** Most abundant in Alaska; common in winter along Mississippi and Missouri Rivers, fairly common in the northwest. Banning of pesticides and intense recovery programs have increased populations that had been seriously diminished in the east.

Golden Eagle

juvenile

adult

adult

White-tailed Eagle

juvenile

adult

Steller's Sea-Eagle

adult

juvenile

Bald Eagle

juvenile

2nd year

3rd year

juvenile

adults

Accipiters

Comparatively long tails and short, rounded wings give these woodland hawks greater agility. Flight is several quick wingbeats and a glide. The three species in North America are confusingly similar.

Sharp-shinned Hawk *Accipiter striatus*

L 10-14" (25-36 cm) W 20-28" (51-71 cm) Distinguished from Cooper's Hawk by shorter, squared tail, often appearing notched when folded, thinner legs, and by proportionately smaller head and neck. **Adult** lacks Cooper's strong contrast between crown and back. **Juveniles** are whitish below, some streaked with brown (like Cooper's), others spotted with reddish-brown. Note also the pale eyebrows, narrow white tip on tail, entirely white undertail coverts, less tawny head than other accipiters. In flight (see also page 127), again compare smaller head and proportionately shorter tail than Cooper's. **Range:** Sharp-shinned Hawk is fairly common over much of its range; found in mixed woodlands. Preys chiefly on small birds. Migrates singly or in loose groups.

Cooper's Hawk *Accipiter cooperii*

L 14-20" (36-51 cm) W 29-37" (74-94 cm) Distinguished from Sharp-shinned Hawk by longer, rounded tail, larger head, and, in **adult,** stronger contrast between back and crown. **Juvenile** has whitish or buffy underparts with fine streaks on breast, streaking reduced or absent on belly; tawny rufous color on head is much richer, white tip on tail is broader, than in Sharp-shinned; undertail coverts entirely white. Note that some juveniles may have a pale eyebrow like Sharp-shinned. In flight (see also page 127), again compare larger head and proportionately longer tail. Preys largely on songbirds, some small mammals. Often perches on telephone poles, unlike Sharp-shinned. **Range:** Inhabits broken woodlands or streamside groves, especially deciduous. Usually migrates singly. Rare, mainly in fall, in the Maritimes.

Northern Goshawk *Accipiter gentilis*

L 21-26" (53-66 cm) W 40-46" (102-117 cm) Conspicuous eyebrow, flaring behind eye, separates **adult**'s dark crown from blue-gray back. Underparts are white with dense gray barring; appear gray at a distance; has wedge-shaped tail with fluffy undertail coverts. Note proportionately shorter tail, longer wings, than Cooper's Hawk. **Juvenile** is brown above, buffy below, with thick, blackish-brown streaks, heaviest on flanks; tail has wavy dark bands bordered with white and a thin white tip; undertail coverts usually have dark streaks. In flight (see also page 127), note tawny bar on upperwing on greater secondary coverts. Juvenile also can be confused with Gyrfalcon (page 124) and Red-shouldered Hawk (page 114). **Range:** The Northern Goshawk inhabits deep, conifer-dominated, mixed woodlands; preys on birds and mammals as large as hares. Uncommon; winters irregularly south of mapped range in the east. Southward irruptions occur in some winters.

Sharp-shinned Hawk

adult ♂

juvenile ♀

juvenile

juvenile

Cooper's Hawk

juvenile ♀

adult ♂

juvenile

juvenile

juvenile ♀

Northern Goshawk

adult ♂

Buteos

High-soaring hawks, buteos are among the easiest daytime birds of prey to spot. Often soar with wings in a shallow V, called a dihedral.

Common Black-Hawk *Buteogallus anthracinus*
L 21" (53 cm) W 50" (127 cm) Wings broad and rounded; tail short, broad. **Adult** blackish overall; tail has broad white band and narrow white tip. Legs and cere (fleshy area at base of bill) orange-yellow. In flight, whitish patch at base of primaries smaller than on Black Vulture (page 102); wingbeats deep and slow. Distinguished from Zone-tailed Hawk by broader wings; broader, less banded tail; larger bill; more yellow-orange under eye. **Juvenile** has strong face pattern; heavily streaked underparts; many-banded tail; buffy wing panel visible from above and below. **Call** is a series of loud whistles. **Range:** Found along waterways. Rare, local, and declining; casual in spring west to southeastern California; very rare in southwestern Utah and southern Texas.

Harris's Hawk *Parabuteo unicinctus*
L 21" (53 cm) W 46" (117 cm) Chocolate brown overall, with conspicuous chestnut shoulder patches, leggings, and wing linings; white at base and tip of long tail; rounded wingtips. **Juvenile** is heavily streaked below; chestnut shoulder patches are less distinct. Inhabits semiarid woodland, brushland. Gregarious; sometimes hunts in small, cooperative groups. **Range:** May straggle north and west of mapped range, but birds sighted there and especially elsewhere in U.S. may not be wild birds.

Zone-tailed Hawk *Buteo albonotatus*
L 20" (51 cm) W 51" (130 cm) Grayish-black overall, with barred flight feathers. Legs and cere bright yellow. Has much slimmer wings than Common Black-Hawk; longer tail, variably banded according to sex and age. Soars teetering on uptilted wings like Turkey Vulture; compare Zone-tailed Hawk's banded tail; smaller bill; yellow cere; larger, feathered head. **Juvenile** has grayish tail, some white flecking on breast. **Call** is a squealing whistle. **Range:** Uncommon; found in mesa and mountain country, often near watercourses; drops from low glide on small birds, rodents, lizards, fish. Rare in southern California and southern Texas.

Short-tailed Hawk *Buteo brachyurus*
L 15½" (39 cm) W 35" (89 cm) Small hawk with two color morphs. Secondaries seen from below are paler than primaries. Scarcer **light morph** (in Florida) has dark helmet and underwing resembling Swainson's Hawk (page 116), but wings and tail are shorter, broader; lacks chest band. All **adults** have wide, dark, subterminal tail band; light morph's sides are lightly streaked; **dark morph**'s underparts and wing linings are spotted with white. In juveniles tail bands are of equal width. Nearly all observations of this species are in flight. **Range:** Found in mixed woodland-grassland. Casual to south Texas and mountains of southeast Arizona in spring and summer.

Common Black-Hawk

adult

juvenile

juvenile

adult

Turkey Vulture for comparison

juvenile

adult ♂

Harris's Hawk

adult

adult

juvenile

adult

Zone-tailed Hawk

adult

Short-tailed Hawk

light morph adult

light morph adult

dark morph adult

Broad-winged Hawk *Buteo platypterus*

L 16" (41 cm) W 34" (86 cm) White underwings have dark borders; tail has broad black and white bands, with last white band broader than the others. Wings broad but more pointed than in Red-shouldered Hawk; wing linings buffy or white; tail shorter, broader. Wingbeats are slower than in *B. l. elegans* race of Red-shouldered. **Juveniles** typically have black moustachial streak; dark-bordered underwings, indistinct bands on tail; very similar to juvenile eastern Red-shouldered but paler below; may have a pale area at base of primaries but lack the distinct pale crescent. Rare **dark morph** breeds in western and central Canada. Broad-winged is a woodland species. **Call,** heard on breeding and winter grounds, is a thin, shrill, slightly descending whistle: *pee-teee.* **Range:** Often migrates in very large flocks. Rare migrant in the west. Most winter in South America; a few winter in southern Florida and very rarely in coastal California.

Gray Hawk *Asturina nitida*

L 17" (43 cm) W 35" (89 cm) Gray upperparts, gray-barred underparts and wing linings, and rounded wing tips distinguish Gray from Broad-winged Hawk (see also page 127). Flight is accipiter-like: several rapid, shallow wingbeats and a glide. **Juvenile** resembles juvenile Broad-winged, but has much longer tail projection, stronger face pattern, and white, U-shaped rump band; dark trailing edge on wings is smaller or absent. Gray Hawk inhabits deciduous growth along streams with nearby open land. **Calls** include a loud, descending whistle. **Range:** Tropical species; local nester in southeastern Arizona. Casual in New Mexico; rare in Rio Grande Valley, where seen year-round, and very rare north along the river to Big Bend region.

Red-shouldered Hawk *Buteo lineatus*

L 15-19" (38-48 cm) W 37-42" (94-107 cm) Relatively long-tailed and long-legged. In flight, shows pale crescent at base of primaries. **Adult** has reddish shoulders and wing linings and extensive pale spotting above. Widespread eastern nominate race *B. l. lineatus* shows dark streaks on reddish chest. Southeastern *alleni* (not shown) is smaller, with grayish cast to head and back; usually lacks breast streaking. South Florida *extimus*, is the smallest and palest race. California *elegans* and central Texas *texanus* (not shown) are decidedly more rufous below; *elegans* is often solidly rufous across the chest and has broader white tail bands. **Juveniles** show extensive variations; *lineatus* shows more finely streaked breast and more closely resembles juvenile Broad-winged Hawk; other eastern races show more coarsely marked underparts; *elegans* is quite dark and has more adultlike features, including some rufous on shoulders and wing linings. Flight of all ages of *elegans* is accipiter-like, with several quick wingbeats and a glide, while *lineatus* flies with slower wingbeats, more like Broad-winged. **Call** is an evenly spaced series of clear, high *kee-ah* or *kah* notes. **Range:** Found in moist, mixed woodlands; often seen near water.

Broad-winged Hawk

juveniles

juveniles

dark morph adult

adult

juvenile

adult

Gray Hawk

juveniles

adult

juvenile

adult

Red-shouldered Hawk

adult *lineatus*

juvenile *lineatus*

juvenile *lineatus*

adult *elegans*

juvenile *elegans*

adult *extimus*

adult *lineatus*

juvenile *lineatus*

juvenile *elegans*

Red-tailed Hawk *Buteo jamaicensis*

L 22" (56 cm) W 50" (127 cm) Our most common buteo; wings broad and fairly rounded; plumage extremely variable. Looks heavy-billed, unlike Rough-legged (next page) and Swainson's Hawks. Variable pale mottling on scapulars, contrasts with dark mantle, often forming a broad-sided V on perched birds. Most **adults,** especially in the east, show a belly band of dark streaks on whitish underparts; dark bar on leading edge of underwing, contrasting with paler wing linings (see also page 128). Note reddish uppertail; paler red undertail. Great Plains race *B. j. krideri,* known as "Krider's Red-tailed," has paler upperparts, whitish tail with pale reddish wash, and in flight shows pale rectangular patches at base of primaries on upperwing. Many southwestern birds of the *fuertesi* race (not shown) lack belly band and have entirely light underparts. Widespread dark and **rufous morphs** of western race, *calurus,* have dark wing linings and underparts, obscuring the bar on leading edge and belly band; tail is dark reddish above. In *harlani,*"Harlan's Hawk," formerly considered a separate species, dark morph has dusky-white tail, diffuse blackish terminal band; shows some white streaking on its dark breast; may lack scapular mottling. Very rare *harlani* light morph has typical tail pattern, but plumage resembles *krideri.* Red-tailed *harlani* breeds in Alaska and east to northwestern Canada; winters primarily in central U.S. **Juveniles** of all morphs except *harlani* have gray-brown tails with many blackish bands; otherwise heavily brown-streaked and spotted below. Distinctive **call,** a harsh, descending *keeeeer.* Habitat variable: woods with nearby open land; also plains, prairie groves, desert. Preys on rodents.

Swainson's Hawk *Buteo swainsoni*

L 21" (53 cm) W 52" (132 cm) Distinguished from most other buteos by long, narrow, pointed wings; plumage is extremely variable. Lacks Red-tailed Hawk's pale mottling on scapulars; bill is smaller. White below, with pale uppertail coverts; shows contrast between dark flight feathers and paler wing linings from below. In **light morph,** whitish or buffy-white wing linings contrast with darkly barred brown flight feathers (see also page 128); dark bib; underparts otherwise whitish to pale buff. **Dark-morph** bird is dark brown with white undertail coverts; shows less sharp contrast between wing linings and flight feathers; darkest birds show none. Compare with first-year White-tailed Hawk (next page). **Intermediate** colorations between light and dark morphs include a rufous morph. Intermediate and **light-morph juveniles** have dark moustachial stripe and conspicuous whitish eyebrows that meet on the forehead; variable streaking below, very heavy on dark morphs. Show less contrast between wing linings and flight feathers than adult birds (page 128). Swainson's soars over open plains and prairie with uptilted wings in teetering, vulturelike flight. **Range:** Very rare spring and fall migrant in eastern North America. Gregarious; usually migrates in large flocks, often with Broad-winged Hawks (preceding page). Winters chiefly in South America; rarely in southern Florida and Central Valley of California.

Red-tailed Hawk

eastern adult *borealis*

eastern juvenile *borealis*

adult *harlani*

adult *krideri*

rufous morph adult *calurus*

eastern adult *borealis*

light morph juvenile

Swainson's Hawk

dark morph adult

light morph adult

light morph adult

intermediate morph adult

Rough-legged Hawk *Buteo lagopus*
L 22" (56 cm) W 56" (142 cm) Long, white tail with dark band or bands helps to identify this hawk in all plumages; bill small. Thin legs are feathered to the toes, the feathering barred in adults, unbarred in juveniles. **Adult male** has multibanded tail with a broad blackish subterminal band. **Adult female**'s tail is brown toward tip with a thin, black subterminal band. **Juveniles** have a single broad, brown tail band. Wings are long, fairly narrow. Seen in flight from above, white at base of tail is conspicuous; note also the small white patches at base of primaries on upperwings. In the common light morph, pale head contrasts with darker back and dark belly band, especially in females and immatures. Adult male has darker breast markings that may create a bib effect; belly is paler. Observe the square, black carpal patches at the "wrists" of the wings. **Dark morph** is less common. A bird of the open country also seen in marshes in winter, Rough-legged often hovers while hunting. During breeding season gives a soft, plaintive courting whistle. Alarm **call** is a loud screech or squeal.

Ferruginous Hawk *Buteo regalis*
L 23" (58 cm) W 53" (135 cm) This hawk has a pale head; extended "gape line" going back under eye; tail is a mixture of pale rust, white, or gray. Wings are long, broad, and pointed; note large, white, crescent-shaped patches on upperwing surface. Seen from below, flight feathers lack barring. **Adults** show rusty color on back and shoulders; rusty leggings form a conspicuous V against whitish underparts spotted with rufous. **Dark morph** is rare; varies from dark rufous to dark brown, with dark undertail coverts. Absence of dark tail bands separates it from similar dark-morph Rough-legged Hawk. **Juvenile** Ferruginous Hawk almost or entirely lacks rusty leggings and is less rufous above; resembles "Krider's" type of Red-tailed Hawk (preceding page), but wings are longer and more pointed. Ferruginous gives harsh alarm **calls,** *kree-a* or *kaah,* chiefly in breeding season. Inhabits dry, open country. Often hovers when hunting or soars in a dihedral. Perches in trees, on poles, on the ground. **Range:** Casual east to Wisconsin, Illinois, Arkansas, Louisiana, Florida in migration, winter. Very rare migrant to Minnesota; casual in summer.

White-tailed Hawk *Buteo albicaudatus*
L 23" (58 cm) W 50" (127 cm) Legs longest of any North American buteo. Wings fairly long and pointed; at rest, **adult**'s wing tips project well beyond end of short tail; tail is white with single black band and other finer bands. Rusty shoulders are highly visible against dark gray upperparts. Underparts and wing linings vary from white on most to lightly barred. Females are darker above, more barred below. **Juveniles** brown above, variable below from mostly blackish to paler; most show a white patch on breast; tail is pale gray; undertail and uppertail coverts whitish, the latter forming a pale U at tail base. Compare with dark morphs of Swainson's (preceding page) and Ferruginous Hawks. **Range:** Rare to fairly common in open coastal grasslands and semiarid inland brush country. Casual to southwest Louisiana.

Rough-legged Hawk

adult ♀

adult ♂

dark morph adult ♂

juvenile

Ferruginous Hawk

juvenile

adult

dark morph adult

adults

White-tailed Hawk

juvenile

adult

adult

juvenile

dark juvenile

Caracaras, Falcons (Family Falconidae)

These powerful hunters are distinguished from hawks by their long wings, which are bent back at the wrist and, except in the Crested Caracara, narrow and pointed. Females are larger than the males. Birds of the genus *Falco* use their notched beaks to kill prey by severing its spinal column at the neck.

Eurasian Hobby *Falco subbuteo*
L 12¼" (31 cm) W 30¼" (77 cm) **Range:** Old World species. Casual in late spring and summer in Bering Sea region and on western Aleutians. Record of a bird on a ship off Newfoundland. Small, short-tailed falcon with long, slender wings; in folded wing, wingtips extend well past tip of tail. Graceful and powerful flier. White cheeks; thin, pale eyebrow; thin, dark moustachial stripe; heavily streaked below. **Adult** has rufous-red undertail coverts; is dark gray above. **Juveniles** are blackish-brown above with buffy feather fringes; lack rufous below. By following spring some look like adults, others intermediate in appearance. Compare all ages carefully to Merlin and Peregrine Falcon (next two pages).

Aplomado Falcon *Falco femoralis* **E**
L 15-16½" (38-42 cm) W 40-48" (102-122 cm) **Range:** Once found in open grasslands and deserts from southern Texas to southern Arizona. Disappeared by early 20th century; vagrants seen in New Mexico and west Texas probably from a small extant population in northern Chihuahua, Mexico. A reintroduction project is now under way in south Texas. In flight, often hovers; long, pointed wings and long, banded tail resemble young Mississippi Kite (page 104); underwings are dark, with pale trailing edge. Note slate gray crown, boldly marked head. Pale eyebrows join at back of head. Dark patches on sides sometimes extend across breast. **Juvenile** is cinnamon below with a streaked breast, and browner above.

Crested Caracara *Caracara plancus*
L 23" (58 cm) W 50" (127 cm) Large head, long neck, long legs. Blackish-brown overall, with white throat and neck and red-orange to yellow bare facial skin; underparts barred with black. **Juvenile** is browner; upperparts are edged and spotted with buff; underparts streaked with buff, unlike **adult** barring. In flight, shows whitish patches near ends of rounded wings. Flapping, ravenlike flight; soars with flat wings. **Calls** include a low rattle and a single *wuck* note. Inhabits open brushlands; often seen on the ground in company with vultures. Feeds chiefly on carrion; also hunts insects and small animals. **Range:** Fairly common in Texas part of range. Rare in Louisiana and southern Arizona. Casual to southern New Mexico. Records from well outside known range are probably of captive or escaped birds.

Eurasian Hobby

adult

juvenile

adult

juvenile

adult

juvenile

Aplomado Falcon

juvenile ♀

adult ♂

adult

Crested Caracara

juvenile

adults

American Kestrel *Falco sparverius*

L 10½" (27 cm) W 23" (58 cm) Smallest and most common of our falcons. Identified by russet back and tail, double black stripes on white face. Seen in flight from below, **adults** show pale underwings, and **males** a distinctive row of white, circular spots on trailing edge of wings. Male also has blue-gray wing coverts; compare with Merlin and much larger Peregrine Falcon (next page). **Juvenile male** is like adult male, but breast heavily streaked, back completely barred; by first fall looks more like adult, but some dark markings remain. **Call** is a shrill *killy killy killy.* Found in open country and in cities, American Kestrel feeds on insects, reptiles, and small mammals, hovering over prey before plunging. Also eats small birds, chiefly in winter. Often perches on telephone wires; frequently bobs its tail.

Eurasian Kestrel *Falco tinnunculus*

L 13½" (34 cm) W 29" (74 cm) **Range:** Casual on western Aleutians and in Bering Sea region; accidental in fall and winter on the east coast from New Brunswick to New Jersey, and on the west coast to British Columbia. Resembles American Kestrel, but note larger size and single, not double, dark facial stripe. In flight, distinguished by wedge-shaped tail and two-toned upperwing, with back and inner wing paler. Hovers as it hunts. **Adult male** has russet wings, gray tail; **female** duller, often with gray rump. **Juvenile** similar to adult female, but dark barring heavier on upperparts and tail.

Merlin *Falco columbarius* L 12" (31 cm) W 25" (64 cm)

Adult male is gray-blue above; **female** and juveniles usually dark brown. Merlins lack the strong facial markings and russet upperparts of kestrels, and have broader wings than American Kestrel. Plumage varies geographically from the very dark race, *F. c. suckleyi,* of the Pacific northwest to the pale *richardsonii* that breeds on northern Great Plains from southern Canada to northern U.S. A few *suckleyi* winter to southern California; this race has dark cheeks and narrow, incomplete tail bands. All *richardsonii* have pale cheeks; male is pale blue-gray above; female and juvenile are brown, the latter with wide, pale tail bands. Winter to southern Great Plains, a few to the Great Basin and Pacific states. The widespread nominate race, *columbarius,* which breeds in the taiga region, is intermediate in plumage; western *columbarius* average slightly paler than eastern. In flight, strongly barred tail distinguishes Merlin from the much larger Peregrine and Prairie Falcons (next page). Underparts and underwings darker than in kestrels, particularly in *suckleyi* and *columbarius,* and head larger. Nests in open woods or wooded prairies; otherwise found in a variety of habitats. Powerful flyer; does not hover. Catches birds in flight by a sudden burst of speed rather than by diving. Also eats large insects, small rodents. **Range:** Fairly common to common on east coast during fall migration. Many individuals in the Prairie Provinces do not migrate but winter in or near cities. Generally uncommon throughout U.S. in winter.

American Kestrel

adult ♀

adult ♂

adult ♂

juvenile ♂

adult ♂

Eurasian Kestrel

adult ♂

juvenile

♀

adult ♂

Merlin
columbarius

♀

♀

adult ♂

♀ *suckleyi*

adult ♂
suckleyi

adult ♀
richardsonii

adult ♂

adult ♂ *richardsonii*

Prairie Falcon *Falco mexicanus*

L 15½-19½" (39-50 cm) W 35-43" (89-109 cm) Pale brown above; creamy white and heavily spotted below. Crown is streaked; also note pale stripe between dark moustachial and ear coverts; facial markings narrower and plumage paler overall than Peregrine Falcon. Compare also with female and juvenile male Merlin (preceding page), especially subspecies *F. c. richardsonii.* In flight (see also next page), all ages show distinctive dark axillaries and dark bar on wing lining, broader on **females.** Juvenile is streaked below, rather than spotted, and darker overall above. Preys chiefly on birds and small mammals. **Range:** Inhabits dry, open country, prairies. Uncommon to fairly common. Rare migrant and winter visitor in western midwest. Casual elsewhere in midwest and southeast. Small numbers winter throughout breeding range.

Peregrine Falcon *Falco peregrinus* **E**

L 16-20" (41-51 cm) W 36-44" (91-112 cm) Crown and nape black; black wedge extends below eye, forming a distinctive helmet, absent in Prairie Falcon and smaller Merlin (preceding page). Tail is shorter than in Prairie; wing tips almost reach the end; also lacks dark bar and axillaries on underwings. Plumage varies from pale in subspecies *F. p. tundrius* of the north to very dark in *pealei,* found from Queen Charlotte Islands to the Aleutians. In *pealei,* the largest race, adult has heavy spotting on whitish breast, underparts very dark. Intermediate *anatum* race has thickest moustachial stripe; **adult** shows rufous wash below; **juvenile** is dark brownish above, and underparts are heavily streaked. Juvenile *tundrius* has a pale eyebrow and larger pale area on side of face; underparts more finely streaked. **Range:** Peregrines inhabit open wetlands near cliffs; prey chiefly on birds. Now established also in cities; nest on bridges, tall buildings. Use of pesticides helped eliminate eastern *anatum* breeding populations; now reintroduced in parts of their former range, Peregrines are seen year-round. Most east coast sightings in the fall are of *tundrius* birds. Uncommon to rare in winter in U.S.

Gyrfalcon *Falco rusticolus*

L 20-25" (51-64 cm) W 50-64" (127-163 cm) Heavily built; wings broader based than in other falcons. **Adult** has yellow-orange eye ring, cere, and legs (bluish-gray in juveniles). Tail broad and tapered; may be barred or unbarred; in perched bird, tail extends far beyond wingtips, unlike other falcons. Compare also with Northern Goshawk (page 110). Plumages vary from **white morph** to **gray morph,** to very **dark,** with paler gray morphs intermediate between typical gray and white. Facial markings range from none on white morph to all-dark cheeks on dark morph. **juveniles** of white and gray morphs are much browner above; **juveniles** of gray and dark morphs show darker wing linings and paler flight feathers. Gyrfalcon inhabits open tundra near rocky outcrops and cliffs. Flies with slow, powerful wingbeats. Preys chiefly on birds. **Range:** Uncommon; winters irregularly south to dashed line on map. Casual to central California, southern Great Plains, and southern Great Lakes and mid-Atlantic regions.

Prairie Falcon

adult ♂

♀

juvenile *pealei*

adult *pealei*

adult *pealei*

Peregrine Falcon

adult *anatum*

juvenile *anatum*

juvenile *tundrius*

adult *tundrius*

Gyrfalcon

gray morph juvenile

gray morph adult

dark morph juvenile

white morph adult

Female Hawks in Flight

White-tailed Kite
adult

Mississippi Kite
1st summer

Hook-billed Kite
adult

Snail Kite
adult

American Kestrel

Peregrine Falcon
adult

Merlin
columbarius

Gyrfalcon
gray morph juvenile

Prairie Falcon
adult

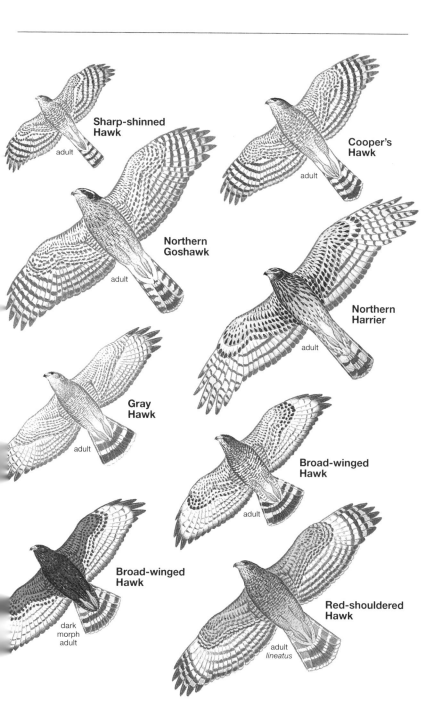

Sharp-shinned Hawk
adult

Cooper's Hawk
adult

Northern Goshawk
adult

Northern Harrier
adult

Gray Hawk
adult

Broad-winged Hawk
adult

Broad-winged Hawk
dark morph adult

Red-shouldered Hawk
adult *lineatus*

Female Hawks in Flight

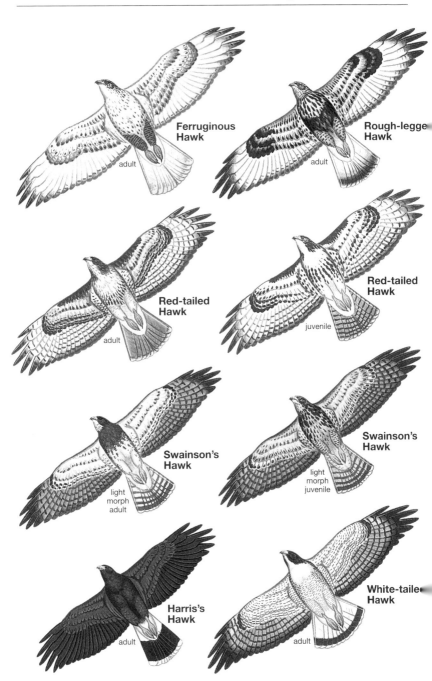

Ferruginous Hawk
adult

Rough-legge Hawk
adult

Red-tailed Hawk
adult

Red-tailed Hawk
juvenile

Swainson's Hawk
light morph adult

Swainson's Hawk
light morph juvenile

Harris's Hawk
adult

White-taile Hawk
adult

Crested Caracara — adult

Osprey — adult

Zone-tailed Hawk — juvenile

Bald Eagle — 2nd year

Common Black-Hawk — adult

Golden Eagle — adult

Black Vulture — adult

Turkey Vulture — adult

Chachalaca (Family Cracidae)

These tropical-forest birds have short, rounded wings and long tails. Generally secretive but highly vocal. One species of this family is found in the United States.

Plain Chachalaca *Ortalis vetula* L 22" (56 cm)
Gray to brownish-olive above, with small head, slight crest; long, lustrous, dark green tail tipped with white. Patch of bare skin on throat, usually grayish, is pinkish-red in **breeding male.** Male's **call** is a deep, ringing *cha-cha-lac;* female's voice higher pitched. **Range:** Inhabits tall chaparral thickets along the Rio Grande; feeds in trees, chiefly on leaves and buds. Introduced to Georgia's Sapelo Island.

Partridges, Grouse, Turkeys
(Family Phasianidae)

Ground-dwellers with feathered nostrils, short, strong bills, and short, rounded wings. Flight is brief but strong. Males perform elaborate courting displays. In some species, birds gather at the same strutting grounds, known as leks, every year.

Chukar *Alectoris chukar* L 14" (36 cm)
Old World species, introduced in North America as a game bird. Gray-brown above; flanks boldly barred black and white; buffy face and throat outlined in black; breast gray; belly buff; outer tail feathers chestnut. Bill and legs are red. Sexes are similar, but males are slightly larger and have small leg spurs. **Juvenile** is smaller and mottled; lacks bold black markings of **adults. Calls** include a series of loud, rapid *chuck chuck chuck* notes and a shrill *whitoo* alarm note. **Range:** Chukars have become established in rocky, arid, mountainous areas of the west; game farm birds are released for hunting in the east. In fall and winter, Chukars feed in coveys of 5 to 40 birds.

Gray Partridge *Perdix perdix* L 12½" (32 cm)
Grayish-brown bird with rusty face and throat, paler in **female. Male** has dark chestnut patch on belly; patch is smaller or absent in females. Flanks are barred with reddish-brown; outer tail feathers rusty. **Calls** include a hoarse *kee-ah.* **Range:** Widely introduced from Europe. Has declined over parts of North American range. Inhabits open farmlands, grassy fields. In fall, forms coveys of 12 to 15 birds.

Plain Chachalaca

breeding ♂

Gray Partridge

♀

♂

Chukar

♀

juvenile

Ring-necked Pheasant *Phasianus colchicus*

♂ *L 33" (84 cm)* ♀ *L 21" (53 cm)* Introduced from Asia, this large, flashy bird has a long, pointed tail and short, rounded wings. **Male** is iridescent bronze overall, mottled with brown, black, and green; head varies from dark, glossy green to purplish, with fleshy red eye patches and iridescent ear tufts. Often shows a broad white neck ring. **Female** is buffy overall, much smaller and duller than male. Distinguished from female Sharp-tailed Grouse (page 138) by larger size, longer tail, lack of barring below, and white in tail. Male's territorial **call** is a loud, penetrating *kok-cack*. Both sexes give hoarse, croaking alarm notes. When flushed, rise almost vertically with a loud whirring of wings. **Range:** Locally common; declining in parts of the east. Found in open country, farmlands, brushy areas, woodland edges. A group of subspecies with white wing coverts (not shown) has become established in parts of the west. The Japanese **Green Pheasant,** *P. versicolor,* now considered a separate species, has been introduced in tidewater Virginia and southern Delaware.

Wild Turkey *Meleagris gallopavo*

♂ *L 46" (117 cm)* ♀ *L 37" (94 cm)* Largest game bird in North America; slightly smaller, more slender than the domesticated bird. **Male** has dark, iridescent body, flight feathers barred with white, red wattles, blackish breast tuft, spurred legs; bare-skinned head is blue and pink. Tail, uppertail coverts, and lower rump feathers are tipped with chestnut on eastern birds, buffy-white on western birds. **Female** and immature are smaller and duller than male, often lack breast tuft. Of the two races seen in North America, *M. g. silvestris* predominates in the east, *merriami* in the west. Birds of the open forest, Wild Turkeys forage mostly on the ground for seeds, nuts, acorns, insects. At night they roost in trees. In spring a male's gobbling **call** may be heard a mile away. **Range:** Restocked in much of its former range and introduced in other areas.

Himalayan Snowcock *Tetraogallus himalayensis*

L 28" (71 cm) **Range:** Large Asian bird, successfully established only in the Ruby Mountains of northeastern Nevada. Gray-brown overall, with tan streaking above. Whitish face and throat, outlined with chestnut stripes; undertail coverts white. Inhabits mountainous terrain; flies downhill in the morning, then walks back up, feeding. Clucks and cackles constantly as it feeds.

Ring-necked Pheasant

♂

♀

♀

Green
Pheasant

♂

♀

eastern
silvestris

**Wild
Turkey**

♀

♂

**Himalayan
Snowcock**

western
merriami

♂

Ruffed Grouse *Bonasa umbellus* L 17" (43 cm)

Small crest; black ruffs on sides of neck, usually inconspicuous; multibanded tail with a wide, dark band near tip; dark band is incomplete in **female.** The two color **morphs, red** and **gray,** are most apparent by tail color. Red morphs predominate in the humid Pacific northwest and Appalachian region; gray morphs predominate in the north and west outside the Pacific northwest area. Ten different subspecies have also been recognized. In spring, the **male** attracts females to his territory by raising ruffs and crest, fanning his tail, and beating his wings to make a hollow, accelerating, drumming noise. **Range:** Fairly common in deciduous and mixed woodlands. Flushed birds burst into flight with a roar of wings.

Spruce Grouse *Falcipennis canadensis* L 16" (41 cm)

Male has dark throat and breast, edged with white; red eye combs. Over most of range, both sexes have black tail with chestnut tip. Birds of the northern Rockies and Cascades, **"Franklin's Grouse,"** *F. c. franklinii,* have white spots on uppertail coverts; **male**'s tail is all-dark. In all subspecies of Spruce Grouse, **females** have two color **morphs, red** and **gray;** generally resemble female Blue Grouse but are smaller and have black barring and white spots below. Juveniles resemble red-morph female. Spruce Grouse inhabit open coniferous forests with dense undergrowth. Often seen along roadsides, especially in fall, or perched in trees. Female's high-pitched **call** is thought to be territorial. In courtship strutting display, male spreads his tail, erects the red combs above his eyes, and rapidly beats his wings; some males also give a series of low-pitched hoots. In territorial flight display, the male flutters upward on shallow wing strokes; "Franklin's Grouse" ends this performance by beating his wings together, making a clapping sound.

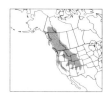

Blue Grouse *Dendragapus obscurus* L 20" (51 cm)

Male's sooty-gray plumage sets off yellow-orange comb above eye. On each side of neck, white-based feathers cover an inflatable bare patch, the yellow or reddish-purple neck sac. **Females** are mottled brown above, with plain gray belly. Both sexes have dark tail with gray band, except populations in the northern Rockies, which show no band. Coastal subspecies, *D. o. fuliginosus,* also known as Sooty Grouse, is darker overall than interior races. **Call** is a series of hoots, higher pitched than those of Spruce Grouse. Courting males stand on high spots (often perch in trees) and inflate their neck sacs to amplify their hooting. Display also involves fluttering above the ground or making short circular flights, then strutting with tail fanned, body tipped forward, head drawn in, wings dragging. **Range:** Blue Grouse inhabit open coniferous or mixed woodlands, brushy lowlands, and mountain slopes, moving to higher altitudes in winter.

gray morph ♂

red morph ♂

red morph ♀

Ruffed Grouse

red morph ♀

Spruce Grouse

gray morph ♀

♂

"Franklin's Grouse" *franklinii* ♂

coastal ♂ *fuliginosus*

northern Rockies ♂ *obscurus*

Blue Grouse

southern Rockies ♀ *richardsonii*

White-tailed Ptarmigan *Lagopus leucurus*
L 12½" (32 cm) As with all ptarmigans legs and feet are feathered and plumage is molted three times a year, matching seasonal changes in habitat. Distinguished from other ptarmigans in all seasons by white tail. **Winter** bird is white except for dark bill and eyes and red eye combs. In **summer,** body is mottled blackish or brown with white belly, wings, and tail. Spring and **fall molts** give a patchy appearance. **Calls** include a henlike clucking and soft, low hoots. **Range:** Locally common on rocky alpine slopes, high meadows. Small numbers have been successfully introduced in the central High Sierra and Uinta Mountains, Utah.

Rock Ptarmigan *Lagopus mutus L 14" (36 cm)*
Mottled **summer** plumage is black, dark brown, or grayish-brown; **male** generally lacks the reddish tones of male Willow Ptarmigan. There are many recognized subspecies, with color variations according to geography. In **winter** plumage, **male** has a black line from bill through eye, lacking in male Willow. Acquires breeding plumage later in spring than does Willow. In both sexes, bill and overall size are slightly smaller than in Willow. **Females** are otherwise difficult to distinguish from Willows. Plumage is patchy white during spring and fall molts. Both species retain white wings and black tail year-round. **Calls** include low growls and croaks and noisy cackles. **Range:** The Rock Ptarmigan is common on high, rocky slopes and tundra. In breeding season, generally prefers higher and more barren habitat than does Willow Ptarmigan. Accidental in northern Minnesota and Queen Charlotte Islands, British Columbia, in spring.

Willow Ptarmigan *Lagopus lagopus L 15" (38 cm)*
Mottled **summer** plumage of **male** is generally redder than in Rock Ptarmigan. White **winter** plumage lacks the black eye line of male Rock Ptarmigan; bill and overall size are slightly larger in Willow Ptarmigan. **Female** is otherwise difficult to distinguish from Rock Ptarmigan. Both species retain white wings and black tail year-round. Plumage is patchy white during spring and fall **molts. Calls** include low growls and croaks, noisy cackles. In courtship and territorial displays, male utters a raucous *go-back go-back go-backa go-backa go-backa*. Ptarmigans' red eye combs can be concealed, or inflated during courtship and aggression. **Range:** Willow Ptarmigan is common on tundra, especially in thickets of willow and alder. In breeding season, generally prefers wetter, brushier habitat than Rock Ptarmigan. Casual in spring and winter to northern tier of U.S. states.

White-tailed Ptarmigan

winter

summer ♀

molting fall ♂

summer ♂

Rock Ptarmigan

winter ♀

winter ♂

fall ♂

summer ♀

summer ♂

Willow Ptarmigan

summer ♀

molting spring ♂

winter

summer ♂

summer ♂

Greater Prairie-Chicken *Tympanuchus cupido*

L 17" (43 cm) Heavily barred with dark brown, cinnamon, and pale buff above and below. Short, rounded tail is all-dark in **male,** barred in **female.** Male has fleshy yellow-orange eye combs. Both sexes have elongated dark neck feathers, longer in males and erected during courtship to display inflated golden neck sacs. Courting males make a *deep oo-loo-woo* sound known as "booming," as if one blew across the top of an empty bottle. **Range:** Uncommon, local, and declining. Found in areas of natural tall-grass prairie interspersed with cropland. A smaller, darker race, endangered "Attwater's Prairie-Chicken," *T. c. attwateri* (**E**) of southeastern Texas, is nearly extinct. The "Heath Hen," formerly resident along the Atlantic seaboard from Massachusetts to Virginia, is now extinct—last record on Martha's Vineyard in 1932.

Lesser Prairie-Chicken *Tympanuchus pallidicinctus*

L 16" (41 cm) Resembles Greater Prairie-Chicken, but slightly smaller, paler, less heavily barred below. Male's courtship notes are higher pitched than Greater. Courting male displays dull orange-red neck sacs and erects dark neck tufts. **Range:** Uncommon, local, and declining; found in sagebrush and shortgrass prairie country, especially where shinnery oak grows.

Sharp-tailed Grouse *Tympanuchus phasianellus*

L 17" (43 cm) Similar to prairie-chickens, but underparts are scaled and spotted; tail is mostly white and pointed; yellowish eye combs are less prominent. Compare with female Ring-necked Pheasant (page 132). Birds are darkest in Alaska and northern Canada (standing figure), palest in the Plains (flying figure). **Male**'s purplish neck sacs are inflated during courtship display. His courting notes include cackling and a single, low *coo-oo* **call** accompanied by the rattling of wing quills. **Range:** Inhabits grasslands, sagebrush, woodland edges, and river canyons. Fairly common over range; rare in western U.S. Where ranges overlap, can hybridize with Greater Prairie-Chicken and Blue Grouse.

Gunnison Sage-Grouse *Centrocercus minimus* ♂ *L 22"*

(56 cm) ♀ *L 18" (46 cm)* Distinguished from Greater Sage Grouse by smaller size and more strongly white-banded tail. Longer, denser filoplumes are erected to form a distinct, recurved crest on **courting male. Range:** Small, declining population in south-central Colorado and southeastern Utah is geographically isolated from Greater Sage-Grouse.

Greater Sage-Grouse *Centrocercus urophasianus* ♂ *L 28"*

(71 cm) ♀ *L 22" (56 cm)* Blackish belly, long pointed tail feathers, and large size are distinctive. **Male** is larger than **female** and has yellow eye combs, black throat and bib, and large white ruff on breast. In flight, dark belly, absence of white outer tail feathers and larger size distinguish it from Sharp-tailed Grouse. Courting male fans tail and rapidly inflates and deflates air sacs, emitting a loud, bubbling popping. **Range:** Fairly common but local; found in sagebrush areas of foothills and plains.

Greater Prairie-Chicken

displaying ♂

displaying ♂

♀

Lesser Prairie-Chicken

♀

Sharp-tailed Grouse

displaying ♂

♀

Gunnison Sage-Grouse

displaying ♂

Greater Sage-Grouse

displaying ♂

♀

♀

♂

displaying males on lek

New World Quail (Family Odontophoridae)

Scientific evidence has recently placed the New World Quails in their own family. All have chunky, rounded bodies and crests or head plumes; most live in western North America.

Gambel's Quail *Callipepla gambelii* L 11" (28 cm)

Grayish above, with prominent teardrop-shaped plume or double plume. Chestnut sides and crown, and lack of scaling on underparts, distinguish Gambel's from California Quail. **Male** has dark forehead, black throat, black patch on belly. Smaller **juvenile** is tan and gray with pale mottling and streaking. Shows less scaling and streaking than darker California juvenile; nape and throat are grayer. **Calls** include varied grunts and cackles and a plaintive *qua-el;* loud, querulous *chi-ca-go-go* call is similar to California Quail but higher pitched and usually has four notes. **Range:** Common in desert scrublands and thickets, usually near permanent water source. Gregarious; in fall and winter, forms large coveys. Sometimes hybridizes with Scaled Quail (next page) and California Quail where ranges overlap. Introduced populations exist in Idaho and on California's San Clemente Island.

California Quail *Callipepla californica* L 10" (25 cm)

Gray and brown above, with prominent teardrop-shaped plume or double plume. Scaled underparts and brown sides and crown separate California from Gambel's Quail. Body color varies from grayish, seen over most of range, to brown in coastal mountains of California; extremes are shown here in **females. Male** has pale forehead, black throat, and chestnut patch on belly. **Juvenile** is smaller; resembles Gambel's juvenile, but is darker, with traces of scaling on underparts. **Calls** include varied grunts and cackles; loud, emphatic *chi-ca-go* call is similar to Gambel's Quail but lower pitched and usually has three notes rather than four. **Range:** Common in open woodlands, brushy foothills, stream valleys, suburbs, usually near permanent water source. Gregarious; in fall and winter, assembles in large coveys. Populations in northeastern portion of range and Utah are probably introduced.

Mountain Quail *Oreortyx pictus* L 11" (28 cm)

Gray and brown above, with two long, thin head plumes that often appear to be one plume. Gray breast; chestnut sides boldly barred with white; chestnut throat outlined in white. **Male** and **female** are alike, but female has shorter head plumes. Amount of brown and gray in upperparts varies in different races of this species; birds of humid coastal northwest are browner than three gray interior subspecies. Smaller **juvenile** has grayer underparts and longer head plumes than Gambel's or California Quail juveniles. Male's mating **call,** a clear, descending *quee-ark,* can be heard up to a mile away. **Range:** Locally common in chaparral, brushy ravines, mountain slopes, at altitudes up to 10,000 feet. Nonmigratory but descends to lower altitudes in winter. Gregarious, forming small coveys in fall and winter. Secretive; best seen in late summer in family groups along roadsides.

Gambel's Quail

♂   ♀   juvenile

Scaled x Gambel's hybrid

♂

♀ *californica*

coastal ♀ *brunescens*

California Quail

coastal juvenile *brunescens*

♂ *californica*

Mountain Quail

coastal ♂ *palmeri*   interior ♀

juvenile

Northern Bobwhite *Colinus virginianus L 9¾" (25 cm)*
Mottled reddish-brown quail with short gray tail. Flanks are
striped with reddish-brown. Throat and eye stripe are white in
male, buffy in **female. Juvenile** is smaller and duller. Male's **call**
is a rising, whistled *bob-white,* heard chiefly in late spring and
summer; whistled *hoy* call is heard year-round. **Range:** Uncommon to common in brushlands and open woodlands, the Bobwhite feeds and roosts in coveys except during nesting season.
The population in the northwest is introduced. At northern edge
of range, numbers have greatly declined over the last couple of
decades. **"Masked Bobwhite,"** *C. v. ridgwayi* (**E**), which was formerly found from southeastern Arizona to central Sonora, Mexico, was eliminated from the U.S. part of its range by the early
1900s. Reintroduced in 1970 from Mexico to Altar Valley in southeastern Arizona, it remains endangered. Male has black throat
and cinnamon underparts.

Montezuma Quail *Cyrtonyx montezumae L 8¾" (22 cm)*
Plump, short-tailed, round-winged quail. **Male** has distinctive
facial pattern and rounded pale brown crest on back of head.
Back and wings mottled black, brown, and tan; breast dark chestnut; sides and flanks dark gray with white spots. **Female** is mottled pinkish-brown below with less distinct head markings.
Juvenile is smaller, paler, with dark spotting on underparts.
Call heard in breeding season is a loud, quavering, descending
whistle. **Range:** Uncommon, secretive, and local in grassy undergrowth of open juniper-oak or pine-oak woodlands on semiarid
mountain slopes.

Scaled Quail *Callipepla squamata L 10" (25 cm)*
Grayish quail with conspicuous white-tipped crest. Bluish-gray
breast and mantle feathers have dark edges, creating a shingled
or scaly effect. **Female**'s crest is buffy and smaller. **Males** in
southernmost Texas tend to show a dark chestnut patch on belly,
unlike the common subspecies, *C. s. pallida,* found over much of
the U.S. range. **Juvenile** resembles adult but is more mottled
above, with less conspicuous scaling. During breeding season,
both sexes give a location **call** when separated, a low, nasal *chip-
churr,* accented on the second syllable. **Range:** Fairly common;
found on barren mesas and plateaus, semidesert scrublands, and
grasslands with mixed scrub. In fall, forms large coveys.

Northern Bobwhite

♂

♀

juvenile

"Masked Bobwhite"
♂ *ridgwayi*

Montezuma Quail

♂

♀

juvenile

Scaled Quail

pallida ♂

juvenile

South Texas ♂
castanogastris

Limpkins (Family Aramidae)

Large, long-necked wading bird, named for its unusual limping gait.

Limpkin *Aramus guarauna* L 26" (66 cm)

Chocolate brown overall, densely streaked with white above. Long bill, slightly downcurved. Long legs and large, webless feet are dull grayish-green. Juvenile is paler than **adult. Call,** heard chiefly at night, is a wailing *krr-oww*. **Range:** Locally common in swamps and wetlands, where it wades or swims in search of snails, frogs, insects. Rare to fairly common in Florida; casual in southern Georgia; accidental north to Maryland.

Rails, Gallinules, Coots (Family Rallidae)

These marsh birds have short tails and short, rounded wings. Most species are local and secretive. Some, especially the rails, are identified chiefly by call and habitat.

King Rail *Rallus elegans* L 15" (38 cm)

Large freshwater rail with long, slightly downcurved bill. Much larger than similar Virginia Rail (next page). **Adult** distinguished from Clapper Rail by tawny edges on black-centered back feathers, tawny wing coverts. Head slate, with brown or grayish cheeks, buffy eyebrow; underparts cinnamon; flanks strongly barred black-and-white. **Juvenile** is darker above, paler below. King Rail favors freshwater and brackish swamps and marshes but hard to see. Most often heard at dusk and dawn. Usually distinctive **call** is a series of fewer than ten *kek kek kek* notes, fairly evenly spaced. **Range:** Fairly common to common in freshwater habitat near Gulf coast; generally rather rare and local well inland in east. Rare in west Texas, where it may breed. Casual west to Colorado. Some birds winter in coastal marshes with Clapper Rails. Hybridizes with Clapper Rail in narrow zone of overlap; some calls of the two are identical.

Clapper Rail *Rallus longirostris* L 14½" (37 cm)

Much larger than Virginia Rail (next page). Plumage variable but always has grayish edges on brown-centered back feathers, olive wing coverts. East coast subspecies such as *R.l.crepitans* are much duller than King Rail: buffy below; cheeks gray; flanks less strongly barred than in King. Gulf coast races such as *scottii* are brighter cinnamon below. West coast races such as *levipes* (**E**) and inland *yumanensis* are brighter below than east coast birds; cheeks brownish-gray. Clappers **call** chiefly at dusk and dawn. Distinctive call is a series of ten or more dry *kek kek kek* notes, accelerating and then slowing. **Range:** Common in coastal salt marshes except on west coast, where populations have declined since introduction of the red fox; also found along lower Colorado River and at Salton Sea. In east, casual north to Maritimes.

Limpkin

King Rail

juvenile

crepitans

yumanensis

Clapper Rail

levipes

scottii

Virginia Rail *Rallus limicola* L 9½" (24 cm)
Similar to King Rail (preceding page) but smaller; cheeks grayer; wings richer chestnut; legs and bill often redder. **Juvenile** is blackish-brown above, mottled black or gray below. **Song** a series of *kid kid kidick kidick* phrases, heard chiefly in breeding season; common **call,** heard year-round, is a descending series of *oink* notes. **Range:** Common but a bit secretive; found in freshwater and brackish marshes and wetlands; also in coastal salt marshes.

Sora *Porzana carolina* L 8¾" (22 cm)
Short, thick bill, yellow or greenish-yellow. **Breeding adult** is coarsely streaked above. Face and center of throat and breast are black. In **winter** plumage, black throat is somewhat obscured by gray edgings. **Juvenile** lacks black on face and throat; underparts are paler. Compare with Yellow Rail; juvenile Sora is not as black above; upperparts streaked, not barred, with white. **Calls** heard year-round are a descending whinny and a sharp, high-pitched *keek;* a whistled *ker-wheer* is heard on breeding grounds. **Range:** Common in freshwater and brackish marshes, rice fields, grain-fields; found in saltwater marshes during migration and winter.

Yellow Rail *Coturnicops noveboracensis* L 7¼" (18 cm)
A small, dark rail, deep tawny-yellow above with wide dark stripes crossed by white bars. In flight, shows a large white patch on trailing edges of wings. Bill is short and thick; color varies from yellowish to greenish-gray. **Juvenile** is darker than **adult.** Distinctive **call,** heard chiefly in breeding season, a four- or five-note *tick-tick, tick-tick-tick* in alternate twos or twos and threes, sounds like tapping two pebbles together. **Range:** Uncommon and local; secretive. Breeds in grassy marshes, boggy swales, damp fields; not found in deepwater marshes or swamps. Rare in the west. Winters in fresh, brackish, or salt marshes, rice fields, dry fields.

Black Rail *Laterallus jamaicensis* L 6" (15 cm)
Very small, extremely secretive. Blackish above, with white speckling; chestnut nape. Bill short and black. Underparts grayish-black, with narrow white barring on flanks. Newly hatched juveniles of other rails resemble Black Rail. Unlike other rails, most vocal in the middle of the night. Distinctive **call,** heard chiefly in breeding season, is a repeated *kik-kee-do* or *kik-kee-derr;* sometimes four notes: *kik-kik-kee-do.* **Range:** Uncommon and local; inhabits marshes, swamps, wet meadows. Very irregular inland; range speculative; declining in some coastal areas.

Corn Crake *Crex crex* L 10½" (27 cm)
Range: European species, formerly a very rare vagrant in fall along the east coast; recently only two fall records, one from Saint-Pierre off Newfoundland and one from Nova Scotia. Western European populations have seriously declined over last decades. Found in damp, grassy fields, croplands, not in marshes. Dull buffy-yellow overall, with short, thick, brownish bill; distinctive large chestnut wing patch.

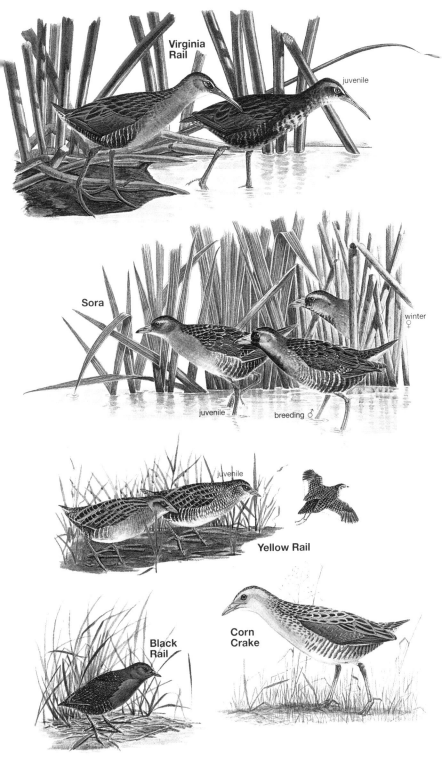

Virginia Rail

juvenile

Sora

juvenile

breeding ♂

winter ♀

juvenile

Yellow Rail

Black Rail

Corn Crake

Purple Gallinule *Porphyrula martinica* L 13" (33 cm)

Bright purplish-blue head, neck, and underparts, with pale blue forehead shield, red-and-yellow bill. Back is brownish-green, legs and feet yellow. **Juvenile** is buffy-brown overall, with brownish-olive back, greenish wings; forehead dark brown, bill mostly dark olive, legs and feet dull olive. Molts into winter plumage after fall migration but may retain traces of juvenile plumage into first spring. In all ages, all-white undertail coverts are conspicuous. **Range:** Fairly common in overgrown swamps, lagoons, marshes. Highly migratory; winters from southern Florida to Argentina. Wanderers are seen in all seasons far north of mapped range; frequently breeds north of area shown, occasionally far north.

Common Moorhen *Gallinula chloropus* L 14" (36 cm)

Black head and neck, with red forehead shield, red bill with yellow tip. Back brownish-olive; underparts slate; white streaking on flanks shows as a thin white line. Outer undertail coverts white, inner ones black. Legs and feet yellow. **Juvenile** is paler, browner; throat whitish; bill and legs dusky. Distinguished at all ages from Purple Gallinule and coots by white line along side. **Winter adult** has brownish facial shield and usually a brownish bill with dusky-yellow tip. **Range:** Common in freshwater marshes, ponds, placid rivers; uncommon in brackish marshes.

American Coot *Fulica americana* L 15½" (39 cm)

Blackish head and neck, with small, reddish-brown forehead shield, whitish bill with dark band near tip. Body slate; outer feathers of undertail coverts are white, inner ones black. Leg color ranges from greenish-gray in **immature** birds to yellow or orangish in **adults.** Toes are lobed, unlike gallinules. Juvenile is quite pale; by first winter more like adult, but still paler, with whitish feather tips, especially below. In flight, white trailing edge on most of wing is distinctive. A few American Coots have extensively white facial shields like Caribbean Coot, *F. caribaea*, of the West Indies. Regarded by some as a subspecies of American, Caribbean has not yet been verified in Florida. **Range:** American Coot is common to abundant. Nests in freshwater marshes, wetlands, or near lakes or ponds; winters in both fresh and salt water, usually in large flocks. Often dives to feed.

Eurasian Coot *Fulica atra* L 15¾" (40 cm)

Range: Accidental straggler to Newfoundland, Labrador, and the Pribilofs. Slightly larger and darker than American Coot; undertail coverts all-black. Forehead shield and bill entirely white.

juvenile

Purple Gallinule

Common Moorhen

winter

juvenile

breeding

immature

variant

American Coot

Eurasian Coot

150

Cranes (Family Gruidae)

Tall, stately birds with long necks and legs and fairly long, heavy bills. Tertials droop over the rump in a "bustle" that distinguishes cranes from herons. Cranes fly with their necks fully extended and circle in thermals like raptors. Courtship includes a frenzied, leaping dance.

Sandhill Crane *Grus canadensis*

L 34-48" (86-122 cm) W 73-90" (185-229 cm) Races vary in size: northern nominate race smallest and southern *G. c. tabida* largest. Resident Florida race, *pratensis,* and endangered Gulf coast race, *pulla,* are intermediate. **Adult** is gray, with dull red skin on crown and lores; whitish chin, cheek, and upper throat; and black primaries. **Juvenile** lacks red patch; head and neck vary from pale to tawny; gray body is irregularly mottled with brownish-red; full adult plumage reached after two and a half years. Great Blue Heron (page 62), sometimes confused with Sandhill Crane, lacks bustle. Preening with muddy bills, cranes may stain feathers of upper back, lower neck, and breast with ferrous solution in mud. Common **call** is a trumpeting, rattling *gar-oo-oo,* audible for more than a mile. **Range:** Locally common; breeds on tundra and in marshes and grasslands. In winter, regularly feeds in dry fields, returning to water at night. Resident near parts of the Gulf coast, in Florida, and in Cuba; other North American subspecies migratory. Very rare during fall and winter on east coast from Massachusetts south. Migrating flocks fly at great heights, sometimes too high to be seen from the ground.

Common Crane *Grus grus*

L 44-51" (112-130 cm) W 79-91" (202-231 cm) **Range:** Eurasian species, casual vagrant on the Great Plains, accidental further east; almost always with migrating flocks of Sandhill Cranes. **Adult** distinguished from Sandhill Crane by blackish head and neck marked by broad white stripe. **Juvenile** bird resembles juvenile Sandhill; may show trace of white head stripe in spring. In flight, in all ages, black primaries and secondaries show as a broad black trailing edge on gray wings.

Whooping Crane *Grus americana* **E**

L 52" (132 cm) W 87" (221 cm) **Range:** Sparse wild population breeds in freshwater marshes of Wood Buffalo National Park, Alberta, and winters in Aransas National Wildlife Refuge on Gulf coast of Texas. A small population has been introduced in Florida. **Adult** is white overall, with red facial skin; black primaries show in flight. **Juvenile** bird is whitish, with pale reddish-brown head and neck and scattered reddish-brown feathers over the rest of its body; begins to acquire adult plumage after first summer. A few abnormally colored Sandhill Cranes of *G. c. tabida* race ("Greater Sandhill Crane") have been taken for Whooping Cranes; check wingtip pattern. **Call** is a shrill, trumpeting *ker-loo ker-lee-loo.* Endangered: Breeding birds currently number about 150, including introductions. Intensive management and protection programs seem to be slowly succeeding.

juvenile

adult

Sandhill Crane

stained adult

adult

juvenile

adult

Common Crane

adult

adult

juvenile

Whooping Crane

Lapwings, Plovers (Family Charadriidae)

These compact birds dart across the ground, stop, then run off again. Shape and behavior identify plovers in general; species are harder.

Black-bellied Plover *Pluvialis squatarola* L 11½" (29 cm) Black-and-white **breeding male** has frosty crown and nape, white belly region; **female** averages less black. **Winter** and **juvenile** birds distinguished from Pacific and American Golden-Plovers by larger size, larger bill, grayer plumage, underparts streaked rather than softly barred, but note that juvenile can be gold-speckled above. In flight shows black axillaries and white uppertail coverts, barred white tail, bold white wing stripe. **Call** is a drawn-out, three-note whistle, the second note lower pitched. **Range:** Nests on Arctic tundra. Common migrant in Great Lakes region. Uncommon to rare elsewhere in interior.

American Golden-Plover *Pluvialis dominica* L 10¼" (26 cm) Smaller, with a smaller bill than Black-bellied Plover; wing stripe indistinct and underwings are smoky gray with no black in axillaries; no contrasting white rump. Note the four evenly spaced primary tips. **Breeding male** shows broad white patches on sides of neck; underparts otherwise black. **Female** has less black. Flight **call** is a shrill *ku-wheep*. **Range:** March arrivals are in winter plumage; breeding plumage slowly acquired on migration north. Rare fall migrant in west (nearly all **juveniles**). Winters in South America.

Pacific Golden-Plover *Pluvialis fulva* L 9¾" (25 cm) Similar to American, but shorter primary tip projection with three, not four, staggered primary tips, the outer two close together; bill appears thicker, legs longer. **Breeding male** has less extensive white on sides of neck than American; white continues down sides and flanks; undertail coverts whiter; slightly larger gold markings above. Female has less black below. **Juveniles** and **winter** birds typically appear brighter than American. **Call,** a loud, rich *chu-wheet*. In Alaska, Americans favor less vegetated slopes; Pacifics, the coast and river valleys. **Range:** Breeds from northern Siberia to western Alaska. Winters from southern Asia to Pacific islands; a few on west coast and in central California. Some adults migrate earlier in fall than other golden-plovers.

European Golden-Plover *Pluvialis apricaria* L 11" (28 cm) **Range:** Breeds from Greenland and Iceland to western Siberia. Winters from Europe to North Africa. Irregular spring migrant to Newfoundland. Similar to Pacific Golden-Plover; note larger size, plumper body shape, white underwings; also small bill, bolder wing bar and longer primary tip projection. On **breeding males,** white nearly meets on front of breast; sides, flanks, and undertail coverts are more purely white than on Pacific; note dense pattern of smaller gold spots on upperparts, unlike coarser pattern of larger spots on other golden-plovers. **Call** is a mournful, drawn-out whistle.

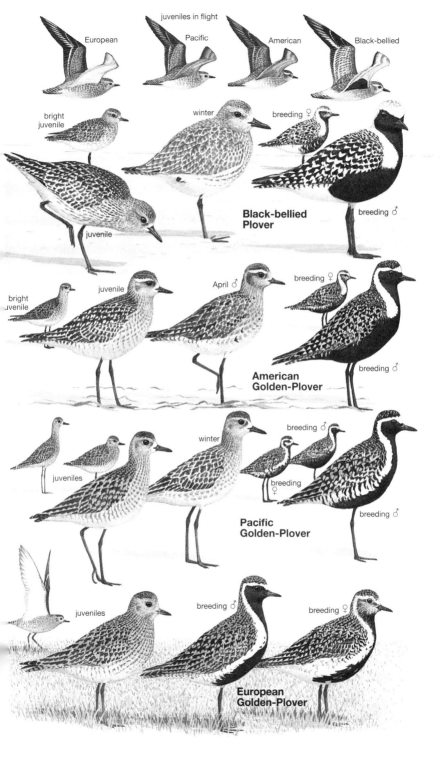

juveniles in flight

European

Pacific

American

Black-bellied

bright juvenile

winter

breeding ♀

Black-bellied Plover

breeding ♂

juvenile

bright juvenile

juvenile

April ♂

breeding ♀

American Golden-Plover

breeding ♂

juveniles

winter

breeding ♂

breeding ♀

Pacific Golden-Plover

breeding ♂

juveniles

breeding ♂

breeding ♀

European Golden-Plover

Snowy Plover *Charadrius alexandrinus* L 6¼" (16 cm)
Pale above, very pale in Gulf coast birds; thin dark bill; dark or grayish legs; partial breast band; dark ear patch. **Females** and **juveniles** resemble Piping Plover; note Snowy Plover's thinner bill, darker legs. **Calls** include a low *krut* and a soft, whistled *ku-wheet.* **Range:** Inhabits barren sandy beaches and flats. Uncommon and declining on Gulf coast.

Piping Plover *Charadrius melodus* **E** L 7¼" (18 cm)
Very pale above; orange legs; white rump conspicuous in flight (page 188). In **breeding** plumage, shows dark narrow breast band, sometimes incomplete, especially in **females** and east coast birds. In **winter,** bill is all-dark. Distinguished from Snowy Plover by thicker bill, paler back; legs are brighter than in Semipalmated Plover. Distinctive **call,** a clear *peep-lo.* **Range:** Found on sandy beaches, lakeshores, dunes. Endangered: Generally uncommon; rare and declining breeder in the midwest; casual winter visitor to coastal California.

Wilson's Plover *Charadrius wilsonia* L 7¾" (20 cm)
Long, very heavy, black bill; broad neck band is black in **breeding male,** brown in **female** and winter male; legs grayish-pink. **Juvenile** resembles adult female but note scaly-looking upperparts. Breeding male may have cinnamon-buff ear patch. **Call** is a sharp, whistled *whit.* **Range:** Fairly common but declining on barrier islands, sandy beaches, mud flats. Recorded casually to California and the Maritimes, and inland to Great Lakes region.

Semipalmated Plover *Charadrius semipalmatus*
L 7¼" (18 cm) Dark back distinguishes this species from Piping and Snowy Plovers; bill much smaller than in Wilson's Plover (flight figures page 188). At very close range, Semipalmated shows partial webbing between toes. **Breeding adult male** often lacks white above eye; shows orangish eye ring. **Juvenile** has darker legs than adults. Distinctive **call** is a whistled, upslurred *chu-weet;* **song** a series of same. **Range:** Common on beaches, lakeshores, tidal flats; seen throughout the continent in migration.

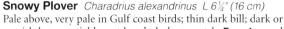

Common Ringed Plover *Charadrius hiaticula*
L 7½" (19 cm) Almost identical to Semipalmated Plover; best distinguished by **call,** a soft, fluted *pooee;* **song,** delivered in display flight, is a series of these notes. Breast band averages slightly broader in center than in Semipalmated. White eyebrow is more distinct; eye ring is partial or lacking altogether; webbing between toes less extensive. Bill is slightly longer, of more even thickness, and shows more orange at base; black on face meets bill where mandibles join. **Range:** Regular but rare spring migrant on western Alaska islands; occasionally breeds on St. Lawrence Island.

Snowy Plover

Gulf Coast ♂ *tenuirostris*

♀

western *nivosus*

juvenile

♂

Piping Plover

winter

breeding ♂

breeding ♂

breeding ♀

Wilson's Plover

juvenile

breeding ♂

♀

winter

breeding ♂

Semipalmated Plover

juvenile

breeding ♀

Common Ringed Plover

breeding ♂

breeding ♀

Mongolian Plover *Charadrius mongolus L 7½" (19 cm)*

Range: Asian species, rare migrant on Aleutians and on islands off western Alaska; casual along west coast. Casual in summer in western and northwestern Alaska, where it has bred. Accidental in eastern North America. Bright rusty red breast; black-and-white facial pattern. **Females** are duller. **Juvenile** has broad buffy wash across breast; edged with buff above. In **winter** birds, underparts are white except for broad grayish patches on sides of breast.

Little Ringed Plover *Charadrius dubius L 6" (15 cm)*

Range: Old World species. Casual spring vagrant to western Aleutians. A small, slim plover with conspicuous yellow eye ring; legs rather dull color. In flight (page 188) note lack of wing bar. In **breeding adult,** white line separates brown forecrown from rear of head. In winter and **juvenile** plumages, brown replaces black on head and breast, and eye ring is slightly duller; juvenile often shows yellow-buff tint to pale areas on head and throat. Rather solitary. **Call** is a descending *pee-oo* that carries a long way.

Killdeer *Charadrius vociferus L 10½" (27 cm)*

Double breast bands distinctive, as is Killdeer's loud, piercing **call:** *kill-dee or dee-dee-dee.* Bright reddish-orange rump is visible in flight (page 188). Downy young have only one breast band. **Range:** Common in grassy fields and on shores. Nests on open ground, usually on gravel. May form loose flocks and linger into early winter in summer range. Vagrant north of breeding range.

Mountain Plover *Charadrius montanus L 9" (23 cm)*

In **breeding** plumage, unbanded white underparts separate this plover from all other brown-backed plovers. Buffy tinge on breast is more extensive in **winter** plumage; compare with winter American Golden-Plover (page 152); in flight, Mountain Plover shows white underwings, American Golden-Plover's are grayish. **Calls** heard on breeding grounds include low, drawn-out whistles and harsh notes. In migration and winter, gives a harsh *krrr* note. **Range:** Inhabits plains; local and declining in many areas. Gregarious in winter; usually found on grassy or bare dirt fields.

Northern Lapwing *Vanellus vanellus L 12½" (32 cm)*

Range: Eurasian species, casual primarily in late fall in northeast states and provinces; accidental elsewhere in east; recorded south to Florida. Most sightings of birds in **winter** plumage: dark and green-glossed above, white below, with black breast; wispy but prominent crest. Wings broad and rounded, with white tips, white wing linings. Flight **call** is a whistled *pee-wit.*

Eurasian Dotterel *Charadrius morinellus L 8¼" (21 cm)*

Range: Eurasian species, very approachable; uncommon, sporadic breeder in northwestern Alaska; casual along west coast in fall. Whitish band on lower breast is somewhat obscured in young and **winter** birds. Bold white eyebrow extends around entire head. Unlike other plovers, **females** are brighter than males. **Juvenile** is darker above, buffy below.

breeding ♀

Mongolian Plover
stegmanni

breeding ♂

winter

juvenile

winter

Little Ringed Plover

juvenile

breeding ♂

Killdeer

Mountain Plover

breeding

winter

juvenile

breeding ♂

Eurasian Dotterel

Northern Lapwing

winter

breeding ♀

winter

winter

winter

winter

juvenile

Jacanas (Family Jacanidae)

Extremely long toes and claws allow these tropical birds to walk on lily pads and other floating plants.

Northern Jacana *Jacana spinosa* *L 9½" (24 cm)*
Range: Mexican and Central American species, rare and irregular visitor to ponds and marshes in southern Texas, where it has probably bred; casual in southern Arizona. Often raises its wings, revealing yellow flight feathers.

Oystercatchers (Family Haematopodidae)

These chunky shorebirds have laterally flattened, heavy bills that can reach into mollusks and pry the shells open; they also probe sand for worms and crabs.

Black Oystercatcher *Haematopus bachmani*
L 17½" (45 cm) Large red-orange bill, all-dark body, pinkish legs. On immatures, outer half of bill is dusky during first year. **Range:** Resident on rocky shores and islands along the Pacific coast from the Aleutians to Baja California.

American Oystercatcher *Haematopus palliatus*
L 18½" (47 cm) Large red-orange bill. Black head and dark brown back; white wing and tail patches, white underparts. **Juvenile** is scaly-looking above; dark tip on bill is kept through first year. Birds feed in small, noisy flocks on coastal beaches and mud flats. **Range:** Expanding northward in the east. Casual in southern California, where has hybridized with Black Oystercatcher.

Stilts, Avocets (Family Recurvirostridae)

Sleek and graceful waders with long, slender bills and spindly legs. Two species inhabit North America.

American Avocet *Recurvirostra americana* *L 18" (46 cm)*
Black-and-white above, white below; head and neck rusty in breeding plumage, gray in winter. **Juveniles** have cinnamon wash on head and neck. Avocets feed by sweeping their bills from side to side through the water. **Male**'s bill is longer, straighter, than **female**'s. Common **call** is a loud *wheet*. **Range:** Fairly common on shallow ponds, marshes, lakeshores.

Black-necked Stilt *Himantopus mexicanus* *L 14" (36 cm)*
Male's glossy black back and bill contrast sharply with white underparts, long red or pink legs. Female is browner on back. **Juvenile** is brown above, with buffy edgings. Common **call** is a loud *kek kek kek*. **Range:** Black-necked Stilt breeds and winters in a wide variety of wet habitats. Breeding range is spreading north. Casual north to Great Lakes.

adult

**Black
Oystercatcher**

**Northern
Jacana**

immature

adult

adults

juvenile

**American
Oystercatcher**

breeding ♀

juvenile ♂

breeding ♀

winter ♂

**American
Avocet**

juvenile

Black-necked Stilt

♂

Sandpipers, Phalaropes
(Family Scolopacidae)

The majority of these shorebirds have at least three plumages. Most begin molting to winter plumage as they near or reach winter grounds.

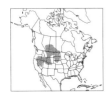

Willet *Catoptrophorus semipalmatus* L 15" (38 cm)
Large, plump bird. **Breeding adult** is heavily mottled; belly white; legs gray. Eastern *C. s. semipalmatus* is smaller, shorter-billed, more heavily barred below than western *inornatus*. **Winter** birds are pale gray above; in flight (page 187), show black-and-white wing pattern. **Call** is *pill-will-willet.* **Range:** Fairly common. Nests in wetlands. Early fall migrants are *semipalmatus,* interior ones *inornatus.* Winters on coastal beaches and at Salton Sea.

Greater Yellowlegs *Tringa melanoleuca* L 14" (36 cm)
Legs yellow to orange. Larger than Lesser Yellowlegs; bill longer, stouter, often slightly upturned, and in **winter** faintly two-toned. In **breeding** plumage, throat and breast are heavily streaked; sides and belly are spotted and barred; bill is all-black. **Call** is a loud, slightly descending series of three or more *tew* notes. **Range:** Fairly common; nests on muskeg, winters in wetland habitats.

Lesser Yellowlegs *Tringa flavipes* L 10½" (27 cm)
Legs yellow to rarely orange. Smaller than Greater Yellowlegs; all-dark bill is shorter, thinner, straight. In **breeding** plumage, breast is finely streaked; sides and flanks show fine, short bars. **Call** is higher, shorter than in Greater: one to three *tew* notes. **Range:** Common in east and midwest; uncommon in far west. Nests on tundra or woodland. Most winter in South America, a few in U.S.

Common Redshank *Tringa totanus* L 11" (28 cm)
Range: Old World species; breeds in Iceland. Probably casual to Newfoundland; numerous records for Greenland. Bright orange legs, stout bill, brownish plumage, streaking below. In flight (page 187) shows white dorsal wedge and distinctive broad white trailing edge to secondaries and inner primaries. **Calls** are a loud *twek-twek* and a mournful, liquid whistle.

Common Greenshank *Tringa nebularia* L 13½" (34 cm)
Range: Eurasian species; rare to Aleutians and Pribilofs; casual to northeast Canada and St. Lawrence Island. Looks similar to Greater Yellowlegs but less heavily streaked; legs are greenish. In flight (page 187), white wedge extends up to middle of back. Typical flight **call** is a loud *tew-tew-tew,* all on one pitch.

Spotted Redshank *Tringa erythropus* L 12½" (32 cm)
Range: Eurasian species, rare spring and fall visitor to Aleutians and Pribilofs; casual on both coasts in migration and winter; accidental elsewhere. Long bill droops at tip. **Breeding adult** is black overall with white spots above; legs dark red. **Juvenile** and **winter adult** paler, with orange legs. In flight (page 187), shows white wedge on back, white wing linings. **Call,** a loud rising *chu-weet.*

Willet
western
inornatus

breeding

winter

juvenile

breeding

winter

juvenile

Greater Yellowlegs

breeding

winter

juvenile

Lesser Yellowlegs

juvenile

breeding

Common Redshank

Common Greenshank

juvenile

breeding

juvenile

breeding

winter

Spotted Redshank

Wandering Tattler *Heteroscelus incanus L 11" (28 cm)*
Uniformly dark gray above; white eyebrow flecked with gray; bill dark, legs dull yellow. In **breeding** plumage, underparts are heavily barred. **Juvenile** and **winter** birds have only a dark gray wash over breast and sides; juvenile has pale spots above. Closely resembles Gray-tailed Tattler; best distinguished by voice. Wandering Tattler's **call** is a rapid series of clear, hollow whistles, all on one pitch. Often teeters and bobs as it feeds. **Range:** Breeds chiefly on gravelly stream banks. Winters on rocky coasts. Generally seen singly or in small groups. Casual inland during migration. Accidental to eastern North America.

Gray-tailed Tattler *Heteroscelus brevipes L 10" (25 cm)*
Range: Asian species, regular spring and fall migrant on outer Aleutians, Pribilofs, and St. Lawrence Island; casual visitor to northern Alaska. Accidental in fall to Washington and California. Closely resembles Wandering Tattler; upperparts are slightly paler; barring on underparts finer and less extensive; whitish eyebrows are more distinct and meet on forehead. **Juvenile** has less extensive gray on underparts; white sides and belly. Best distinction is voice. Gray-tailed Tattler's common **call** is a loud, ascending *too-weet*, similar to call of Common Ringed Plover.

Green Sandpiper *Tringa ochropus L 8¾" (22 cm)*
Range: Eurasian species, casual in spring on outer Aleutians, Pribilofs, and St. Lawrence Island. Resembles Solitary Sandpiper (see also next page) in plumage, behavior, and calls. Note white rump and uppertail coverts, with less extensively barred tail; lacks solidly dark central tail feathers of Solitary; wing linings are darker. Similar Wood Sandpiper has more spotting above, more barring on tail, and paler wing linings.

Wood Sandpiper *Tringa glareola L 8" (20 cm)*
Range: Eurasian species, fairly common spring migrant and occasional breeder on the outer Aleutians; uncommon on the Pribilofs; rare on St. Lawrence Island. Casual to British Columbia and northeast North America. Dark upperparts are heavily spotted with buff; prominent whitish eyebrow. In flight (page 187), distinguished from Green Sandpiper by paler wing linings, smaller white rump patch, and more densely barred tail. Note also the shorter bill. Common **call** is a loud, sharp whistling of three or more notes, similar to the call of Long-billed Dowitcher.

Wandering Tattler

breeding

winter

juvenile

Gray-tailed Tattler

breeding

juvenile

Solitary Sandpiper breeding

juvenile

breeding

Green Sandpiper

Green Sandpiper breeding

juvenile

breeding

Wood Sandpiper

breeding

Solitary Sandpiper *Tringa solitaria L 8½" (22 cm)*

Dark brown above, heavily spotted with buffy-white. White below; lower throat, breast, and sides streaked with blackish-brown. Bolder white eye ring and shorter, olive legs distinguish Solitary Sandpiper from Lesser Yellowlegs (page 160). In flight (page 187), shows dark central tail feathers, white outer feathers barred with black. Underwing is dark. **Calls** include a shrill *peet-weet,* higher pitched than calls of Spotted Sandpiper. Often keeps wings raised briefly after alighting; on the ground, often bobs its tail. Generally seen singly or in small flocks. Fairly common at shallow backwaters, pools, small estuaries, even rain puddles.

Spotted Sandpiper *Actitis macularia L 7½" (19 cm)*

Striking in **breeding** plumage, with barred upperparts, spotted underparts. **Juvenile** and **winter** birds lack spotting below, resemble Common Sandpiper. Note Spotted Sandpiper's shorter tail; in flight, shows shorter white wing stripe, shorter white trailing edge. In juvenile and first-winter birds, barred wing coverts contrast with back; tertials have a black bar on tip; and barring, if any, on edge of tertials extends no farther than halfway along each feather. **Calls** include a shrill *peet-weet* and, in flight, a series of *weet* notes, lower pitched than the calls of Solitary Sandpiper. Both Spotted and Common Sandpipers fly with stiff, rapid, fluttering wingbeats. On the ground, both nod and teeter constantly. **Range:** Spotted is common and widespread, found at sheltered streams, ponds, lakes, or marshes. Generally seen singly; may form small flocks in migration. Most winter in Central and South America. Rare in winter to southern edge of breeding range.

Common Sandpiper *Actitis hypoleucos L 8" (20 cm)*

Range: Eurasian species, rare but regular migrant, usually in spring, on the outer Aleutians, Pribilofs, St. Lawrence Island; casual to Seward Peninsula. **Breeding adult** is brown above with dark barring and streaking; white below; upper breast finely streaked. **Juvenile** and winter birds resemble Spotted Sandpiper. Note Common Sandpiper's longer tail; in juvenile, barring on edge of tertials extends along the entire feather. In flight, shows longer white wing stripe and longer white trailing edge. **Call** in flight is a shrill, piping *twee-wee-wee.*

Terek Sandpiper *Xenus cinereus L 9" (23 cm)*

Range: Eurasian species, rare migrant on outer Aleutians; casual on Pribilofs, St. Lawrence, and in Anchorage area. Accidental in fall to coastal British Columbia, California, and Massachusetts. Note long, upturned bill, short orange-yellow legs. In **breeding adult,** dark-centered scapulars form two dark lines on back. In flight, shows distinctive wing pattern: dark leading edge, grayer median coverts, dark greater coverts, white-tipped secondaries. Flight **call** is a series of shrill whistled notes on one pitch, usually in threes.

breeding

Solitary Sandpiper

juvenile

1st winter

juvenile

juvenile

breeding

Spotted Sandpiper

breeding

juvenile

juvenile

Common Sandpiper

breeding

breeding

juvenile

Terek Sandpiper

Eskimo Curlew *Numenius borealis* **E** *L 14" (36 cm)*
Range: Nested on Arctic tundra; wintered in South America. Most sightings in this century on Texas coast in spring. Probably extinct; last certain record was from Barbados in 1963. Resembles Whimbrel but smaller; upperparts darker; bill less curved; wing linings pale cinnamon. **Calls** are soft, twittering whistles.

Whimbrel *Numenius phaeopus* *L 17½" (45 cm)*
Boldly striped crown; dark eye line; long, downcurved bill. Call is a series of hollow whistles on one pitch. Fairly common; nests on open tundra; winters in wetlands. In flight (page 186), North American race, *N. p. hudsonicus,* shows dark rump and underwings; European *phaeopus,* casual vagrant to east coast, white rump and underwings; Asian *variegatus,* regular migrant off western Alaska, whitish, variably streaked rump and underwings.

Little Curlew *Numenius minutus* *L 12" (30 cm)*
Range: Breeds in central and northeast Siberia; winters mainly in northern Australia. Casual fall vagrant to coastal California and one spring record for St. Lawrence Island, Alaska. Like a diminutive Whimbrel with shorter and only slightly curved bill; note mostly pale lores. **Calls** include a musical *quee-dlee* and a loud *tchew-tchew-tchew.* Vagrants here are mostly silent.

Bristle-thighed Curlew *Numenius tahitiensis*
L 18" (46 cm) Bright buff rump and tail distinguish this species from the Whimbrel. Stiff feathers on thighs and flanks are very hard to see in the field. **Call** is a loud, whistled *chu-a-whit.* **Range:** Breeds in Alaska. Casual in spring to west coast. Most migrate across Pacific to and from winter grounds on Pacific islands.

Long-billed Curlew *Numenius americanus* *L 23" (58 cm)*
Cinnamon-brown above, buff below, with very long, strongly downcurved bill. Lacks dark head stripes of Whimbrel. Juveniles have shorter bill. Cinnamon-buff wing linings, visible in flight (page 186) are distinctive in all plumages. **Call** is a loud, musical, ascending *cur-lee.* **Range:** Fairly common; nests in wet and dry uplands; in migration and winter, found on wetlands, grainfields. Rare on east coast from Virginia south in fall and winter.

Far Eastern Curlew *Numenius madagascariensis*
L 25" (64 cm) **Range:** Asian species, casual in spring and early summer on the Aleutians and Pribilofs; accidental in coastal British Columbia. Brown overall, with heavy streaking below; bill long and strongly downcurved. Wing linings (page 186) are white with dark barring; rump is same color as back.

Eurasian Curlew *Numenius arquata* *L 22" (56 cm)*
Range: Eurasian species, casual on east coast in fall and winter. Brown overall, heavily streaked below; bill long, strongly downcurved. Distinguished from Long-billed Curlew by white rump, white wing linings; from *phaeopus* race of Whimbrel by larger size, longer bill, lack of dark stripes on head.

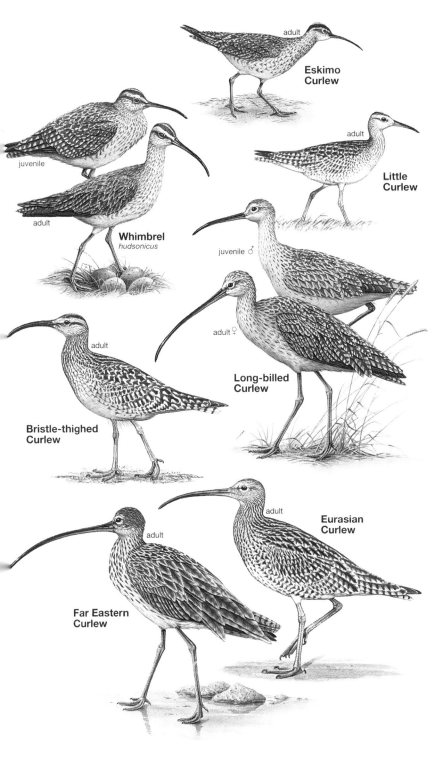

Eskimo Curlew
adult

Little Curlew
adult

juvenile

adult

Whimbrel
hudsonicus

juvenile ♂

adult ♀

Long-billed Curlew

Bristle-thighed Curlew
adult

Eurasian Curlew
adult

Far Eastern Curlew
adult

Black-tailed Godwit *Limosa limosa* L 16½" (42 cm)

Range: Eurasian species, rare but regular spring migrant on western Aleutians; casual to Pribilofs; casual along Atlantic coast. Long, bicolored bill is straight or only slightly upcurved. Tail is mostly black, uppertail coverts white. In **breeding** plumage, shows chestnut head and neck and heavily barred sides and flanks. East coast records are of *islandica,* which in the breeding male is of a deeper and more extensive reddish color below. **Winter** birds are gray above, whitish below. In all plumages, white wing linings and broad wing stripe are conspicuous in flight (page 186).

Hudsonian Godwit *Limosa haemastica* L 15½" (39 cm)

Long, bicolored bill, slightly upcurved. Tail is black, uppertail coverts white. **Breeding male** is dark chestnut below, finely barred. Female is larger and much duller. **Juvenile**'s buff feather edges give upperparts a scaly look. **Winter adult** resembles Black-tailed Godwit; dark wing linings and narrower white wing stripe are distinctive in flight (page 186). **Range:** Breeding range not fully known. Migrates through central and eastern Great Plains in spring, much farther east in fall. Casual to Pacific states.

Bar-tailed Godwit *Limosa lapponica* L 16" (41 cm)

Long, bicolored bill, slightly upcurved. **Breeding male** is reddish-brown below; lacks heavy barring of Black-tailed Godwit. **Female** is larger and much paler than male. In **winter** plumage, Bar-tailed resembles Marbled Godwit but lacks cinnamon tones. Note also shorter bill, shorter legs. Black-and-white barred tail distinctive but hard to see. **Juvenile** resembles winter adult but is buffier overall. Two subspecies of this Eurasian godwit occur in North America. *L. l. baueri* (shown opposite) breeds in Alaska, appears casually in migration along Pacific coast; rump is heavily mottled, wing linings brown with white barring. European *lapponica,* very rare migrant along Atlantic coast, has a whiter rump, white wing linings, and brown-barred axillaries. (Both races are shown in flight on page 186.)

Marbled Godwit *Limosa fedoa* L 18" (46 cm)

Long, bicolored bill, slightly upcurved. Tawny-brown; mottled with black above, barred below. Barring is much less extensive on **winter** birds and **juveniles.** In all birds, bill and legs are longer than in Bar-tailed Godwit. In flight (page 186), cinnamon wing linings and cinnamon on primaries and secondaries are distinctive. Nests in grassy meadows, near lakes and ponds. **Range:** Common on west coast in winter, fairly common on Texas Gulf coast and in Florida; rare but regular in the east.

Black-tailed Godwit
melanuroides

juvenile

juvenile

winter

islandica ♂
breeding

breeding ♂

breeding ♀

juvenile

juvenile

molting fall
adult ♂

Hudsonian Godwit

breeding ♂

breeding ♀

juvenile

winter

Bar-tailed Godwit
baueri

breeding ♂

breeding ♀

juvenile Hudsonian,
Bar-tailed, and Marbled
(L to R)

breeding ♂

Marbled Godwit

winter ♀

Ruddy Turnstone *Arenaria interpres* L 9½" (24 cm)
Striking black-and-white head and bib, black-and-chestnut back, and orange legs mark this stout bird in **breeding** plumage. Female is duller than **male.** Bib pattern and orange leg color are retained in **winter** plumage. **Juvenile** resembles winter adult but back has a scaly appearance. Distinctive **call,** a low-pitched, guttural rattle. Turnstones use their slender bills to flip aside shells and pebbles in search of food. In flight, complex pattern on back and wings identifies both Ruddy and Black Turnstones. **Range:** Nests on coastal tundra. Rare inland migrant except in Great Lakes region, where much more numerous.

Black Turnstone *Arenaria melanocephala* L 9¼" (24 cm)
Black upperparts. In **breeding** plumage head is marked by white eyebrow and lore spot; white spotting visible on sides of neck and breast. Legs dark reddish-brown in all plumages. Juvenile and **winter adult** are slate gray, lack lore spot and mottling. **Calls** include a guttural rattle, higher than call of Ruddy Turnstone. **Range:** Breeds in coastal Alaska. Winters on rocky coasts.

Surfbird *Aphriza virgata* L 10" (25 cm)
Base of short, stout bill is yellow; legs yellowish-green. **Breeding adult**'s head and underparts are heavily streaked and spotted with dusky-black; upperparts edged with white and chestnut; scapulars mostly rufous. **Winter adult** has a solid dark gray head and breast. **Juvenile**'s head and breast are flecked with white; back appears scaly. In flight, all plumages show a conspicuous black band at end of white tail and rump. **Range:** Nests on mountain tundra; winters along rocky beaches and reefs. Casual in spring on Texas coast, also at Salton Sea.

Rock Sandpiper *Calidris ptilocnemis* L 9" (23 cm)
Black patch on lower breast in **breeding** plumage; compare with belly patch of Dunlin (next page). Crown and back are black, edged with chestnut. In flight (page 189), shows white wing stripe and all-dark tail. *C. p. ptilocnemis* birds breeding on Pribilofs are larger, have paler chestnut above, less black below, bolder white wing stripe. Long, slender bill is slightly downcurved, base greenish-yellow. Legs greenish-yellow. **Winter** bird separated from Purple Sandpiper by range, duller bill base and legs; from Surfbird by longer bill, smaller size, more patterned upperparts and breast. **Range:** Nests on tundra; winters on rocky shores, often with Black Turnstones and Surfbirds. Migrates late in fall.

Purple Sandpiper *Calidris maritima* L 9" (23 cm)
Breeding adult has tawny-buff crown, streaked with black; back is edged with white and tawny-buff; breast and flanks spotted with blackish-brown. Long, slender bill is slightly downcurved, base orange-yellow. Legs orange-yellow. In flight (page 189) and in **winter,** adult resembles Rock Sandpiper. **Range:** Migrates late in fall. Rare fall migrant on Great Lakes. Casual elsewhere inland in the east and in winter on the Gulf coast. Winters on rocky shores, jetties, often with Ruddy Turnstones and Sanderlings.

juvenile

winter

Ruddy Turnstone

breeding ♂

breeding ♂

Black Turnstone

winter

winter

winter

juvenile

breeding

winter

Surfbird

Rock Sandpiper
tschuktschorum

breeding Pribilofs
ptilocnemis

winter

juvenile

breeding

Purple Sandpiper

juvenile

breeding

winter

Great Knot *Calidris tenuirostris L 11" (28 cm)*
Range: Asian species, casual spring migrant in western Alaska. Larger than Red Knot, with longer bill; less rufous on back, none on head and breast. Compare also with Surfbird and Rock Sandpiper (preceding page). In **breeding** plumage, shows black breast and black flank pattern. **Juvenile** has buffy wash and distinct spotting below; dark back feathers edged with rust. Resembles Red Knot in flight but primary coverts darker, wing bar fainter.

Red Knot *Calidris canutus L 10½" (27 cm)*
Chunky and short-legged. **Breeding adult** is dappled brown, black, and chestnut above, with buffy chestnut face and breast. In **winter**, back is pale gray; underparts white. Distinguished from dowitchers (page 180) by shorter bill, paler crown, and, in flight (page 187), by whitish rump finely barred with gray. **Juveniles** similar to winter adults but have distinct spotting below, scaly-looking upperparts. **Range:** Feeds along sandy beaches and mud flats, often with dowitchers. Rare migrant in the interior.

Sanderling *Calidris alba L 8" (20 cm)*
Palest sandpiper of **winter;** pale gray above, white below. Bill and legs black. Prominent white wing stripe shows in flight (page 189). In **breeding** plumage (not acquired until late April), head, mantle, and breast are rusty. Feeds on sandy beaches, running out of surf's reach to snatch up mollusks and crustaceans exposed by retreating waves. **Juveniles** are blackish above, with pale edges near tips of feathers. **Call** is a sharp *kip,* often given in a series.

Dunlin *Calidris alpina L 8½" (22 cm)*
Distinctive **breeding** plumage: reddish back; whitish, finely streaked underparts with conspicuous black belly patch. Rock Sandpiper (preceding page) has similar patch, but on chest. Note Dunlin's sturdy bill, curved at tip. Short-necked; appears hunchbacked. In flight (page 189), shows dark center on rump. In **winter** plumage, the upperparts are grayish-brown; breast is washed with gray-brown; belly is white. **Juveniles** are rusty above, spotted below. Distinctive **call,** a harsh, reedy *kree.* **Range:** Rare on Great Plains. Most stay well north in summer, where all ages, including juveniles, molt into winter plumage; mostly in winter plumage when seen in south Canada and U.S.

Curlew Sandpiper *Calidris ferruginea L 8½" (22 cm)*
Range: Eurasian species, rare on east coast, casual elsewhere. Long, downcurved bill has whitish area at base. In **breeding** plumage, rich chestnut underparts and mottled chestnut back are distinctive. Female is slightly paler than male. Many sightings are of birds in patchy spring plumage or molting to winter plumage, showing grayer upperparts and partly white underparts. **Juvenile** appears scaly above; shows rich buff wash across breast; young birds seen in south Canada and U.S. are in full juvenile plumage; compare with young Dunlins, which are mostly in winter plumage. White rump is conspicuous in flight (page 187). **Call** is a soft, rippling *chirrup.* Has bred in northern Alaska.

Great Knot

juvenile

breeding

Red Knot

juvenile

winter

breeding

Sanderling

juvenile

winter

breeding

Dunlin

molting juvenile

winter

breeding

Curlew Sandpiper

juvenile

breeding ♂

Semipalmated Sandpiper *Calidris pusilla L 6¼" (16 cm)*
Black legs; tubular-looking, straight bill, of variable length. Easily confused with Western Sandpiper. In **breeding** birds, note that Semipalmated usually lacks spotting on flanks and shows only a tinge of rufous on crown, ear patch, and scapulars. **Juveniles** are distinguished by stronger eyebrow, darker crown, and more uniform upperparts. **Winter** plumage of these two species is very similar (see also page 189), but Semipalmated is plumper; bill shape is different; face shows slightly more contrast; center of breast never shows the faint streaks visible on some winter Westerns. **Call** is a short *churk*. **Range:** Abundant. A common migrant in eastern half of continent. Rare migrant in the west south of British Columbia; very rare in winter in south Florida.

Western Sandpiper *Calidris mauri L 6½" (17 cm)*
Black legs; tapered bill, of variable length; tip is usually slightly drooped. Easily confused with Semipalmated Sandpiper. In **breeding** plumage, Western has arrow-shaped spots along sides, rufous at base of scapulars, and a bright rufous wash on crown and ear patch. **Juvenile** is distinguished from juvenile Semipalmated by less prominent eyebrow, paler crown and face, and brighter rufous edges on back and inner scapulars. **Winter** plumage is very similar to Semipalmated (see also page 189). **Call** is a high, raspy *jeet*. **Range:** Common in wet habitats.

Least Sandpiper *Calidris minutilla L 6" (15 cm)*
Note small size and short, thin bill, slightly downcurved. Always darker above than Western and Semipalmated Sandpipers. In **winter** plumage (see also page 189) has a prominent brown breast band. **Juvenile** has a strong buffy wash across breast. Legs are yellowish, but appear dark in poor light or when smeared with mud. **Call** is a high *kreee*. **Range:** Common in wet habitats.

White-rumped Sandpiper *Calidris fuscicollis*
L 7½" (19 cm) Long primary tip projection beyond tertials in standing bird. Similar to Baird's Sandpiper but grayer overall and usually has an entirely white rump. In **breeding** plumage, streaking extends to flanks. **Juvenile** (see also page 189) shows rusty edges on crown and back. In winter birds, head and neck are dark gray, giving a hooded look. **Call** note, a high-pitched, insectlike *jeet*. **Range:** Fairly common; feeds in marshes and on mud flats. Casual in the west.

Baird's Sandpiper *Calidris bairdii L 7½" (19 cm)*
Long primary tip projection beyond tertials in standing bird. Buff-brown above and across breast. Pale edgings on **juvenile**'s back give a scaly appearance (see also page 189). Distinguished from Least Sandpiper by larger size, longer and straighter bill. **Call** is a low, raspy *kreeep*. **Range:** Fairly common; found on upper beaches and inland on lakeshores, wet fields. Migration is through center of continent. Uncommon migrants, usually juveniles, to both coasts in fall.

Semipalmated Sandpiper

breeding

juvenile

winter

Western Sandpiper

breeding

winter

juvenile

Least Sandpiper

winter

breeding

juvenile

White-rumped Sandpiper

fall molting adult

juvenile

breeding

Baird's Sandpiper

juvenile

breeding

Long-toed Stint   *Calidris subminuta*   *L 6" (15 cm)*

Range: Asian species, casual in spring on St. Lawrence Island and the Pribilofs; can be fairly common on the outer Aleutians. Accidental elsewhere on the west coast. Distinguished in all plumages from Least Sandpiper (preceding page) by dark forehead and region above lores; bolder, split eyebrow, broadening behind eye; and white-edged median coverts; note also greenish base of lower mandible. Gives a lower-pitched **call** than Least Sandpiper.

Little Stint   *Calidris minuta*   *L 6" (15 cm)*

Range: Eurasian species, casual on east and west coasts; very rare off western Alaska islands in spring and fall. **Breeding** birds are brightly fringed with rufous above; throat and underparts white, with bright buff wash and bold spotting on sides of breast. Redder above than Western and Semipalmated Sandpipers (preceding page); compare also with Red-necked Stint. **Juvenile** best distinguished from juvenile Red-necked by extensively black-centered wing coverts and tertials usually edged with rufous.

Temminck's Stint   *Calidris temminckii*   *L 6¼" (16 cm)*

Range: Eurasian species, rare spring and fall migrant on Pribilofs, Aleutians, and St. Lawrence Island. White outer tail feathers distinctive in all plumages. **Breeding adult** resembles in plumage and shape the larger Baird's Sandpiper (preceding page), but legs are yellow or greenish-yellow; note dark legs in Baird's and primary tip projection. In Temminck's Stint **juvenile,** feathers of upperparts have dark subterminal edges, buffy fringe. **Call** is a repeated, rapid dry rattle.

Red-necked Stint   *Calidris ruficollis*   *L 6¼" (16 cm)*

Rufous on throat and upper breast may be pale and indistinct; look for necklace of dark streaks on white lower breast. **Juvenile** distinguished from juvenile Little Stint by plainer gray wing coverts and tertials. **Range:** Asian species, casual migrant on both coasts; regular migrant on western Alaska coast and islands. Breeding range in Alaska is conjectural.

Spoonbill Sandpiper   *Eurynorhynchus pygmeus*

L 6" (15 cm) **Range:** Asian species, casual migrant in Alaska, accidental in coastal British Columbia. In **breeding** plumage, is easily mistaken for Red-necked Stint. Bill is longer; bill shape is distinctive but requires a close view. **Juvenile** has darker cheek patch than juvenile Red-necked.

Broad-billed Sandpiper   *Limicola falcinellus*

L 7" (18 cm) **Range:** Eurasian species, casual fall migrant on the Aleutians. Accidental in fall in coastal New York. All sightings so far have been of **juveniles.** Plump body, short legs, and long bill form a distinctive profile. Upper mandible droops at tip. Note also the unusual forked eyebrow.

Long-toed Stint

juvenile

Little Stint

juvenile

breeding

Temminck's Stint

juvenile

breeding

breeding

Red-necked Stint

juvenile

breeding

breeding

Spoonbill Sandpiper

breeding

juvenile

breeding

Broad-billed Sandpiper

juvenile

Pectoral Sandpiper *Calidris melanotos* L 8¾" (22 cm)
Prominent streaking on breast, darker in **male**, contrasts sharply with clear white belly. Male is larger than **female. Juvenile** has buffy wash on streaked breast. Compare especially with juvenile Sharp-tailed Sandpiper (see also page 189). **Call** is a rich, low *churk*. **Range:** Often feeds in wet meadows, marshes, pond edges. Common in midwest; fairly common on east coast; scarcer from Great Plains to west coast, where mainly juveniles are seen in fall.

Sharp-tailed Sandpiper *Calidris acuminata*
L 8½" (22 cm) **Range:** Siberian breeder; casual spring and fairly common fall migrant in western Alaska; rare fall migrant along entire Pacific coast. Casual in fall across rest of continent. Most sightings are **juveniles,** distinguished from juvenile Pectoral Sandpiper by white eyebrow that broadens behind the eye; bright buffy breast lightly streaked on upper breast and sides; streaked undertail coverts; and brighter rufous cap and edging on upperparts (see also page 189). **Adult** in **breeding** plumage is similar to juvenile, but more spotted below with dark chevons on flanks; also distinct white eye ring. **Call** is a mellow, two-note whistle.

Upland Sandpiper *Bartramia longicauda* L 12" (31 cm)
Small head, with large, dark, prominent eyes; long, thin neck, long tail, long wings. Legs yellow. Prefers fields, where often only its head and neck are visible above the grass. Also perches on posts on breeding grounds. In flight (page 187), blackish primaries contrast with mottled brown upperparts. **Call,** a rolling *pulip pulip*, and a call like a wolf whistle, heard in flight on breeding grounds. **Range:** Fairly common except in eastern range, where declining. Casual on west coast and in the southwest in migration.

Buff-breasted Sandpiper *Tryngites subruficollis*
L 8¼" (21 cm) Dark eye stands out prominently on buffy face; underparts paler buff; legs orange-yellow. In flight, shows flashy white wing linings. **Juveniles** are paler below, with scaly white fringing to feathers above. **Range:** Prefers plowed fields, turf farms, wet rice fields. Migrates through the interior of the continent. In fall, rare on the west coast, uncommon to the east; most sightings west or east of eastern Great Plains are of juveniles (see also page 187).

Ruff *Philomachus pugnax* ♂ L 12" (31 cm) ♀ L 10" (25 cm)
Range: Old World species. Rare migrant in western Alaska and along west and east coasts and in Great Lakes region. Casual elsewhere. Very rare in winter in California; has bred in Alaska. **Breeding males** acquire dramatic ruffs in colors that range from black to rufous to white. **Female** lacks ruff, is smaller, and has a variable amount of black below. Both sexes have a plump body, small head, and white underwings. Leg color may be yellow, orange, or red. **Juvenile** is buffy below, has prominently fringed feathers above. In flight (page 189), the U-shaped white band on rump is distinctive in all plumages. Ruff and Buff-breasted Sandpiper are both silent away from breeding grounds.

Pectoral Sandpiper

breeding ♂

breeding ♀

juvenile

juvenile Sharp-tailed (center) with juvenile Pectorals

Sharp-tailed Sandpiper

breeding adult

juvenile

Upland Sandpiper

adult

juvenile

displaying adult

juvenile

Buff-breasted Sandpiper

breeding adult

Ruff

summer molting ♂

breeding males

♀

juvenile ♀

summer molting ♀

winter ♂

Dowitchers

Medium-size, chunky, dark shorebirds, dowitchers have long, straight bills and distinct pale eyebrows. Feeding in mud or shallow water, they probe with a rapid jabbing motion. Dowitchers in flight show a white wedge from barred tail to middle of back. Separating the two species is easiest with juveniles, more difficult with breeding adults, and very difficult in winter except by distinctive calls. Both species give the same song, a rapid *di di da doo,* year-round.

Short-billed Dowitcher *Limnodromus griseus*

L 11" (28 cm) In flight, tail usually looks paler than in Long-billed Dowitcher. **Breeding** plumage varies among the three subspecies: *L. g. griseus* (which breeds in northeast Canada), *hendersoni* (central and western Canada), and *caurinus* (Alaska). Unlike Long-billed, most Short-billed show some white on the belly, especially *griseus,* which also has a heavily spotted breast and may have densely barred flanks; *caurinus* is variable but similar to *griseus.* In *hendersoni,* which may be mostly reddish below, foreneck is much less heavily spotted than in Long-billed; sides have less or no barring; upperparts are brighter. In all forms, **juvenile** is brighter above, buffier and more spotted below than juvenile Long-billed; tertials and visible greater wing coverts have broad reddish-buff edges and internal bars, loops, or stripes. **Winter** birds are brownish-gray above, white below, with gray breast; at close range note fine dark speckling on and below the breast on many birds. **Call** is a mellow *tu tu tu,* repeated in a rapid series as an alarm call. **Range:** Common in migration along the Atlantic coast (*griseus*); from the eastern plains to Atlantic coast from New Jersey south (*hendersoni*); and along the Pacific coast (*caurinus*); a few *griseus* are seen on eastern Great Lakes in late spring. Fall migration begins earlier than Long-billed, usually in late June or early July for adults; end of July or early August for juveniles. Migrant juveniles are seen through early October.

Long-billed Dowitcher *Limnodromus scolopaceus*

L 11½" (29 cm) **Male**'s bill is no longer than on Short-billed Dowitcher, **female**'s is. In flight, tail usually looks darker than in Short-billed. **Breeding adult** is entirely reddish below; foreneck heavily spotted; sides usually barred. Bold white scapular tips in spring help separate this species from Short-billed. **Juvenile** is darker above, grayer below than Short-billed; tertials and greater wing coverts are plain, with thin gray edges and rufous tips; some birds show two pale spots near the tips. In **winter** birds, breast is unspotted and more extensively dark than on most Short-billed. **Call** is a sharp, high-pitched *keek,* given singly or in a rapid series. Adult Long-billed go to favored locations in late summer to molt; Short-billed molt when they reach winter grounds. **Range:** Common in migration in western half of continent; less common in the east in fall, rare in spring. Fall migration begins later than Short-billed, in mid-July (west) or late July (east). Juveniles migrate later than adults; rare before September. Dowitchers seen inland after mid-October are almost certainly Long-billed.

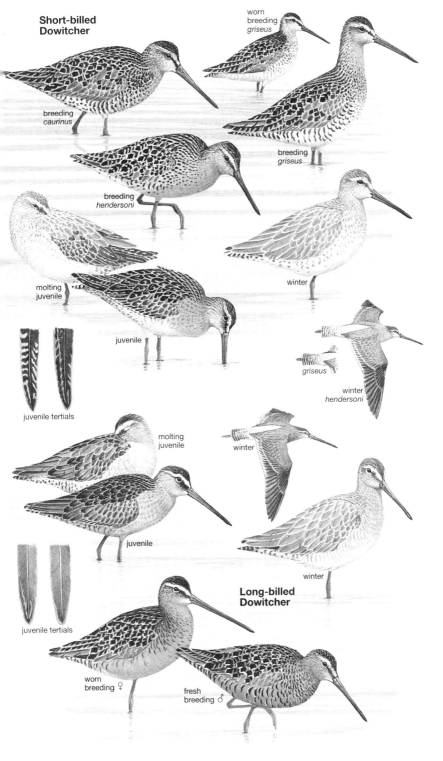

Short-billed Dowitcher

worn breeding *griseus*

breeding *caurinus*

breeding *griseus*

breeding *hendersoni*

molting juvenile

winter

juvenile

juvenile tertials

griseus

winter *hendersoni*

molting juvenile

winter

juvenile

Long-billed Dowitcher

juvenile tertials

winter

worn breeding ♀

fresh breeding ♂

Stilt Sandpiper *Calidris himantopus L 8½" (22 cm)*

Breeding adult has pale eyebrow, chestnut patches on sides of head, slender, slightly downcurved bill, and heavily barred underparts. **Winter adult** is grayer above, whiter below. **Juvenile** is like winter adult but has more sharply patterned upperparts; the two resemble Curlew Sandpiper (page 172), but note straighter bill, yellow-green legs, and, in flight (page 187), lack of prominent wing stripe; early juvenile has a buffy wash on breast. Feeds like dowitchers, with which it often associates. **Call** is a low, hoarse *querp,* but often silent. **Range:** Rare in spring on east coast; common in fall. Rare migrant on west coast; most occur in fall.

Common Snipe *Gallinago gallinago L 10½" (27 cm)*

Stocky, with very long bill; boldly striped head; barred flanks. Often not seen until flushed, when it gives a harsh two-syllable *ski-ape* **call** in rapid, zigzagging flight. On nesting grounds, males deliver loud *wheet* notes from perches. In swooping display flight, vibrating outer tail feathers make quavering hoots. Widespread nominate Eurasian race regular on Bering Sea islands makes different flight display sound; probably not the same species. Note paler, buffier color overall; white trailing edge to secondaries; fainter flank markings; paler, white-striped underwings. North American race, *G. g. delicata,* is widely known as Wilson's Snipe.

Pin-tailed Snipe *Gallinago stenura L 10" (26 cm).*

Range: Breeds in Siberia; winters chiefly in southeast Asia. Two certain records from Attu in western Aleutians. Chunkier, shorter billed, and shorter tailed than Common Snipe. On ground, note barred secondary coverts and even-width pale edges on inner and outer webs of scapulars, giving a scalloped look. In flight, note buffy secondary covert panel, uniformly dark underwings, no pale edge to secondaries, and distinct foot projection past tail. In the hand, razor-thin outer tail feathers are diagnostic. **Call** is a high-pitched, ducklike *squak.*

American Woodcock *Scolopax minor L 11" (28 cm)*

Very chunky, with long bill, barred crown, large eyes set high in head. Wings are rounded. Nocturnal and secretive; seldom seen until flushed. Flies up abruptly, wings making a twittering sound. Best seen when males give an elaborate flight display. Common **call** is a nasal *peent,* heard mostly in spring. **Range:** Fairly common but local; nests in moist woodlands. During mild winters, a few birds are found farther north. Casual west to east Colorado and east New Mexico. Accidental in southeast California.

Jack Snipe *Lymnocryptes minimus 7" (18 cm)*

Range: Small, chunky Eurasian species. Recorded on four occasions: Three late fall records for California and Labrador and one early spring for Pribilofs reflect its migration timing. Secretive, reluctant to flush, usually silent. Flight is low, short, fluttery, on rounded wings. Bobs body while feeding. Note extensive pale base to short bill, pale split eyebrow stripes with no median crown stripe, broad buffy back stripes, streaked flanks, pale underparts.

Stilt Sandpiper

juvenile

molting juvenile

breeding

winter

delicata underwing

displaying

delicata

gallinago underwing

Common Snipe

gallinago

Pin-tailed Snipe

underwing

American Woodcock

tail

Jack Snipe

Phalaropes

These elegant shorebirds have partially lobed feet and dense, soft plumage. Feeding on the water, phalaropes often spin like tops, stirring up larvae, crustaceans, and insects. Females, larger and more brightly colored than the males, do the courting; males incubate the eggs and care for the chicks. In fall, adults and juveniles (particularly Wilson's and Red Phalaropes) rapidly molt to winter plumage; many are seen in transitional plumage farther south.

Wilson's Phalarope *Phalaropus tricolor* L 9¼" (24 cm)
Long, thin bill; bold blackish stripe on face and neck. In **winter** plumage, upperparts are gray, underparts white; note also lack of distinct dark ear patch. Briefly held **juvenile** plumage resembles winter adult but back is browner with buffy edge to feathers, breast buffy. In flight, white uppertail coverts, whitish tail, and absence of white wing stripe distinguish juvenile and winter birds from other phalaropes. **Calls** include a hoarse *wurk* and other low, croaking notes. **Range:** Wilson's is chiefly an inland phalarope, nesting on grassy borders of shallow lakes, marshes, reservoirs. Feeds as often on land as on water. Common to abundant in western North America; uncommon to rare in the east; rare in southern California in winter.

Red-necked Phalarope *Phalaropus lobatus*
L 7¾" (20 cm) Chestnut on front and sides of neck distinctive in **breeding female,** less prominent in **male.** Both have dark back with bright buff stripes along sides; bill shorter than in Wilson's Phalarope, thinner than in Red Phalarope. **Winter** birds are blue-gray above with whitish stripes; underparts and front of crown white; dark patch extends back from eye. In flight, show white wing stripe, whitish stripes on back, dark central tail coverts. Fresh **juvenile** resembles winter adult but is blacker above, with bright buff stripes. **Call:** a high, sharp *kit*, often given in a series. **Range:** Breeds on Arctic and subarctic tundra; winters chiefly at sea in Southern Hemisphere. Common inland in west and off west coast during migration; rare in midwest and east; uncommon off east coast; more numerous off Maine and Maritimes.

Red Phalarope *Phalaropus fulicaria* L 8½" (22 cm)
Bill shorter and much thicker than in other phalaropes; yellow with black tip in breeding adult, usually all-dark in juvenile and winter adult. **Female** in breeding plumage has black crown, white face, chestnut red underparts. **Male** is duller. **Juvenile** resembles male but is much paler below; juveniles seen in south Canada and the U.S. are **molting** to winter plumage; more closely resemble Red-necked Phalaropes. **Winter** bird is pale gray above. In flight, shows a bolder white wing stripe than Red-necked and dark central tail coverts. **Call,** a sharp *keip,* is higher-pitched than Red-necked's. **Range:** Breeds on Arctic shores; winters at sea. Irregularly common off west coast during fall migration; rare to very rare inland, chiefly seen in fall. Generally uncommon off east coast in spring and fall.

juvenile

winter

Wilson's Phalarope

molting juvenile

breeding ♀

winter

breeding ♂

juvenile

breeding adults with juvenile

Red-necked Phalarope

winter

breeding ♀

molting juvenile

breeding ♂

winter

juvenile

molting fall adults

winter

Red Phalarope

molting juvenile

breeding ♀

winter

breeding ♂

Shorebirds in Flight

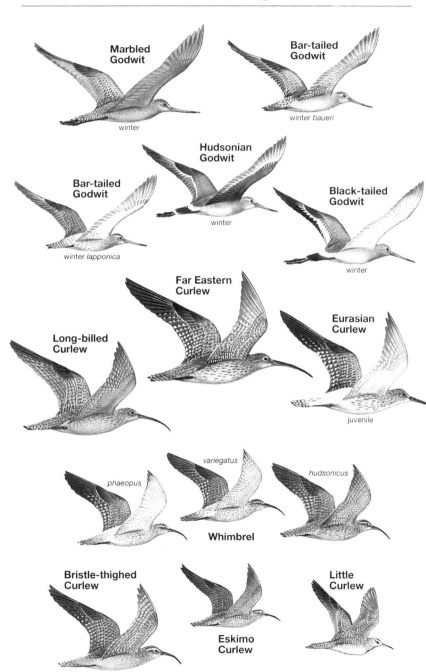

Marbled Godwit
winter

Bar-tailed Godwit
winter *baueri*

Bar-tailed Godwit
winter *lapponica*

Hudsonian Godwit
winter

Black-tailed Godwit
winter

Far Eastern Curlew

Long-billed Curlew

Eurasian Curlew
juvenile

phaeopus

variegatus

hudsonicus

Whimbrel

Bristle-thighed Curlew

Eskimo Curlew

Little Curlew

Willet winter

Greater Yellowlegs winter

Lesser Yellowlegs winter

een ndpiper juvenile

Wood Sandpiper juvenile

Solitary Sandpiper juvenile

Short-billed Dowitcher winter

Spotted Redshank winter

Common Greenshank winter

Common Redshank juvenile

Red Knot winter

Curlew Sandpiper juvenile

Stilt Sandpiper juvenile

Upland Sandpiper juvenile

Wilson's Phalarope juvenile

Buff-breasted Sandpiper juvenile

Shorebirds in Flight

Snowy
Plover ♀

Piping
Plover winter

Little
Ringed
Plover breed

Semipalmated
Plover juvenile

Common
Ringed
Plover juvenile

Mongolian
Plover winter

Wilson's
Plover ♀

Killdeer

Mountain
Plover winter

Eurasian
Dotterel juvenile

Pacific
Golden-Plover juvenile

American
Golden-Plover juvenile

European
Golden-Plover juvenile

Black-bellied
Plover juvenile

Rock Sandpiper — winter

Purple Sandpiper — winter

Dunlin — winter

Sanderling — winter

Red Phalarope — winter

Red-necked Phalarope — winter

Western Sandpiper — winter

Semipalmated Sandpiper — winter

Least Sandpiper — winter

Temminck's Stint — juvenile

Baird's Sandpiper — juvenile

White-rumped Sandpiper — juvenile

Pectoral Sandpiper — juvenile

Sharp-tailed Sandpiper — juvenile

Ruff — juvenile ♀

Skuas, Gulls, Terns, Skimmers
(Family Laridae)

Large seabirds with strong wings, powerful flight. Some species are highly pelagic, spending most of their time over the open sea. Others are seen in coastal waters, and some frequent inland waters.

Great Skua *Catharacta skua* L 22" (56 cm) W 54" (137 cm) Large, heavy, and barrel-chested; wings broader and more rounded than jaegers (next page); tail shorter, broader. Shows a distinctly hunchbacked appearance in flight and a conspicuous white bar at base of primaries; bill is heavier than in jaegers. Great Skua is distinguished from South Polar Skua by overall reddish or ginger brown color and heavy streaking on back, wing coverts, and much of underparts; sometimes shows dark brown cap. **Juvenile** and immature show less streaking, especially on underparts. A small number of juvenile dark morphs have much less rufous streaking; resemble juvenile South Polar Skuas. Strong, powerful fliers, skuas pursue gulls and other seabirds and rob them of their prey. **Range:** Uncommon; breeds in Iceland and northern Europe; winters in North Atlantic. Seen well offshore from November to April; rare in summer off Canadian coast.

South Polar Skua *Catharacta maccormicki*
L 21" (53 cm) W 52" (132 cm) Large, heavy, and barrel-chested; wings broader and more rounded than jaegers (next page); tail shorter, broader. Like Great Skua, shows a distinctly hunchbacked appearance in flight, a bold white bar at base of primaries, and a heavier bill than in jaegers. In all ages, South Polar Skua shows a uniform mantle coloring and lacks the reddish tones and streaking seen on upperparts of Great Skua. In **light-morph** birds, contrastingly pale gray nape is distinctive; also shows grayish head and underparts. **Dark morph** is uniformly blackish-brown across mantle, with golden hackles on nape; distinguished from subadult Pomarine Jaeger by larger size, broader and more rounded wings, more distinct white wing bar. **Juveniles** and immatures of both color morphs are darker than light-morph adults, ranging from dark brown to dark gray. In the field, birds under two years of age are generally indistinguishable from juveniles; birds over two years old are generally indistinguishable from full adults. **Range:** South Polar Skua winters (our summer) in the North Atlantic and North Pacific, usually from May to early November. Most numerous in spring and fall off the west coast, in spring off the east coast; casual off the south coast of Alaska; accidental in North Dakota. Very rarely seen from shore. Difficulty of identification makes range information somewhat speculative for both skua species.

Great Skua

typical adult

dark adult

pale adult

juvenile

South Polar Skua

dark morph adult

intermediate morph adult

juvenile

juvenile

light morph adults

Jaegers

Predatory seabirds with long, pointed, angled wings. Adult plumage and long central tail feathers take three or four years to develop. Complex and variable plumages make identification extremely difficult. Most molts occur after the fall migration.

Pomarine Jaeger *Stercorarius pomarinus*
L 21" (53 cm) W 48" (122 cm) Body bulkier, bicolored bill longer and thicker, wingbeats slower than Parasitic Jaeger. Most birds show a distinctive second pale underwing patch at base of primaries (fainter or lacking in Parasitic). **Adult**'s tail streamers, twisted at ends, form dark blobs when seen from side; length is variable, averages longer in male. Note extensive helmet on sides of head. Compare **dark-morph** adults and subadults with South Polar Skuas (preceding page). Some grayish-brown **juveniles** are dark, some pale, but none shows the foxy red tones of most juvenile Parasitics; underwing is paler than body; pale, barred uppertail covert forms a contrasting patch above. **Range:** Seen less often from shore than Parasitic. Common off west coast in spring migration and especially late in fall; often migrates in flocks. Uncommon in winter; casual inland away from Great Lakes.

Parasitic Jaeger *Stercorarius parasiticus*
L 19" (48 cm) W 42" (107 cm) Smaller size, more slender body, faster wingbeats than Pomarine Jaeger; also smaller head, thinner bill, pointed tail streamers. **Adult** lacks helmeted effect of Pomarine; is paler near bill, as juveniles sometimes are also. **Juvenile** is highly variable; shows rufous tips on primaries; distinctive rusty tones particularly evident on **light morphs;** tail coverts have fainter, wavier bars than Pomarine. **Range:** Fairly common; the jaeger species most often seen from shore in migration. Casual fall migrant inland; more regular on Great Lakes and Salton Sea.

Long-tailed Jaeger *Stercorarius longicaudus*
L 22" (56 cm) W 40" (102 cm) Most lightly built jaeger, with round chest, flat belly, narrow wings, and proportionately long tail in all ages; bill rather short and thick. Flight is more graceful, ternlike. Note distinctive contrast between grayish mantle and darker flight feathers; usually has only two to three white primary shafts; and no pale underwing patch except on **juvenile. Adult** has well-defined black cap, no breastband as in most jaegers, and usually very long, pointed central tail streamers. Juvenile's central tail feathers have round, often white-edged tips; bill is half dark, half gray; is grayer overall than Parasitic except for dark morph; fringing above whitish, never rusty. **Light-morph juveniles** show distinctive white belly and strong, even, black barring on upper- and undertail coverts; palest birds may have very pale gray heads. **Dark-morph juveniles** often lack barring on uppertail coverts. **Range:** Common in dry, upland-tundra breeding area; migrating birds uncommon to fairly common well off west coast; rare closer to shore and off east coast (mainly in fall); casual inland (mainly in fall), and off Gulf coast.

Pomarine Jaeger

dark morph breeding adult

light morph breeding adult

light morph subadult

juvenile

Parasitic Jaeger

light morph breeding adult

dark morph breeding adult

light morph juveniles

light morph subadult

Long-tailed Jaeger

breeding adult

subadult

light morph juvenile

dark morph juvenile

Gulls

A large, widespread group; often called seagulls, but many species nest inland. Gulls take from about two to four years to reach their first full breeding plumage. Many are highly variable and hard to identify in immature plumage. Most species have a complete molt in late summer and a partial molt in spring.

Heermann's Gull *Larus heermanni*

L 19" (48 cm) W 51" (130 cm) Four-year gull. **Adult** distinctive with white head, streaked gray-brown in winter; red bill; dark gray body; black tail with white terminal band; white trailing edge on wings. **Second-winter** bird is browner, bill two-toned, tail band buff. **First-winter** bird has dark brown body, lacks contrasting tail tip and trailing edge on wing. Wings are fairly long, flight bouyant. **Range:** Common postbreeding visitor along the west coast; very rare at Salton Sea. Casual elsewhere inland in California and the southwest; accidental to west Texas, Great Lakes, and southeast Alaska.

Franklin's Gull *Larus pipixcan* L 14½" (37 cm) W 36" (91 cm)

Three-year gull. **Breeding adult** has black hood, white underparts variably tinged with pink, slate gray wings with white bar and black-and-white tips on primaries. Distinguished from Laughing Gull by white bar and large white tips on primaries, pale gray central tail feathers, and broader white eye crescents. All **winter** birds have a dark half-hood, more extensive than in any winter Laughing Gull. Second-summer Franklin's has partial or no bar on primaries. **First-summer** bird like winter adult but lacks white primary bar; bill and legs black. **First-winter** bird resembles first-winter Laughing; note white outer tail feathers, half-hood, broader eye crescents, white underparts, and, in flight (page 212), pale inner primaries. Juvenile is like first-winter bird but back is brown. At all ages, distinguished from Laughing Gull by smaller size, smaller bill with less prominent hook, rounder forehead, less extensive dark on underside of primaries; shorter legs and wings give a stocky look when standing. **Range:** Rare migrant along both coasts; very rare in winter along Gulf coast and in southern California.

Laughing Gull *Larus atricilla* L 16½" (42 cm) W 40" (102 cm)

Three-year gull. **Breeding adult** has black hood, white underparts, slate gray wings with black outer primaries. In **winter**, shows gray wash on nape; compare with the half-hood of Franklin's Gull. Second-summer bird has partial hood, some spotting on tip of tail. **Second-winter** bird (see also page 212) is similar to second-summer but has gray wash on sides of breast, lacks hood. **First-winter** bird has extensively gray sides, complete tail band, gray wash on nape, slate gray back, dark brown wings; compare with first-winter Franklin's Gull. **Juvenile** is like first-winter bird but brown on head and body. **Range:** Common along Atlantic and Gulf coasts; rare inland except at Salton Sea where it is fairly common, chiefly as a postbreeding visitor.

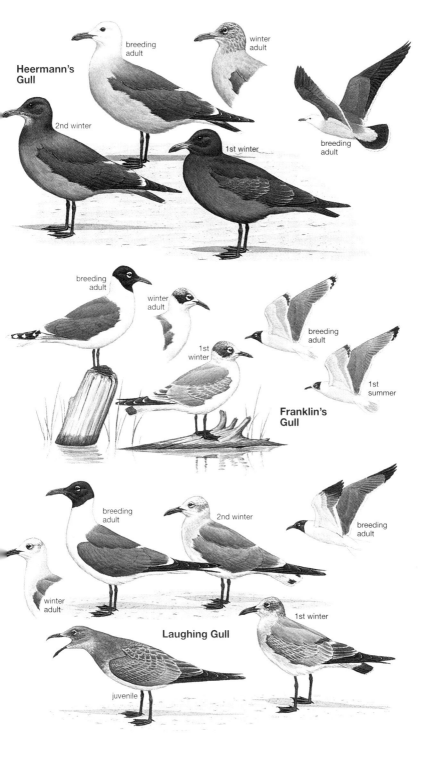

Heermann's Gull

breeding adult

winter adult

2nd winter

1st winter

breeding adult

breeding adult

winter adult

1st winter

breeding adult

1st summer

Franklin's Gull

breeding adult

2nd winter

breeding adult

winter adult

Laughing Gull

1st winter

juvenile

Bonaparte's Gull *Larus philadelphia*
L 13½" (34 cm) W 33" (84 cm) Two-year gull. **Breeding adult**
has slate black hood, black bill, gray mantle with black wing tips
that are pale on underside; white underparts, orange-red legs. In
flight, shows white wedge on wing. **Winter** bird lacks hood. **First-
winter** bird has a dark brown carpal bar on leading edge of wing,
dark band on secondaries, black tail band; compare with juvenile Black-legged Kittiwake (pages 210, 212). First-summer bird
may show partial hood; wings and tail are like first-winter. Flight
is buoyant, wingbeats rapid. **Range:** Uncommon inland migrant
in west; common on Great Lakes.

Black-headed Gull *Larus ridibundus*
L 16" (41 cm) W 40" (102 cm) Two-year gull. **Breeding adult** has
dark brown hood; maroon-red bill and legs; mantle slightly paler
gray than Bonaparte's Gull; black wing tips; white underparts.
Winter adult lacks hood; bill brighter red. **First-winter** birds have
orange-red bill, pale legs, dark tail band, dark brown carpal bar
(page 212). Distinguished from Bonaparte's by larger size and bill
color. **First-summer** bird's hood varies from minimal like first-
winter's to nearly complete; wings and tail like first-winter. In all
plumages, shows dark underside of primaries in flight, darker
on adults; compare with Bonaparte's. **Range:** Colonizer from
Europe. Fairly common in winter in Newfoundland, where a few
breed; rare off western Alaska, Maritimes, and coastal New England; casual elsewhere in North America.

Little Gull *Larus minutus L 11" (28 cm) W 24" (61 cm)*
Two- to three-year gull. **Breeding adult** has black hood, black
bill, pale gray mantle, white wing tips, white underparts, red legs.
Winter adult has dusky cap, dark spot behind eye. Wings uniformly pale gray above, dark gray to black below, with white
trailing edge. Some second-winter birds are like adult but underwing pattern is incomplete; show some dusky slate in primaries
(page 212). **First-winter** is like Bonaparte's but primaries blackish above, lack white wedge; wings show strong blackish W; crown
shows more black. In all plumages, note short, rounded wings,
fluttery wingbeat. **Range:** Western Palearctic species, has bred
irregularly from Great Lakes to Hudson Bay. Generally rare on
Great Lakes in migration and in winter on east coast; very rare
to casual elsewhere in North America.

Ross's Gull *Rhodostethia rosea*
L 13½" (34 cm) W 33" (84 cm) **Range:** East Siberian arctic
species, has bred in northern Canada and Greenland in last two
decades. Common fall migrant along northern coast of Alaska;
presumably winters at sea. Casual south to northern U.S. Two-
year gull. Variably pink below; upperwing pale gray; underwing
pale to dark gray. Black collar in summer, partial or absent in
winter. **First-winter** bird has black at tip of tail, dark spot behind
eye; acquires black collar by first summer; in flight, shows W pattern like Little Gull. In all plumages, note long, pointed wings;
long, wedge-shaped tail; and broad, white trailing edge to wings.

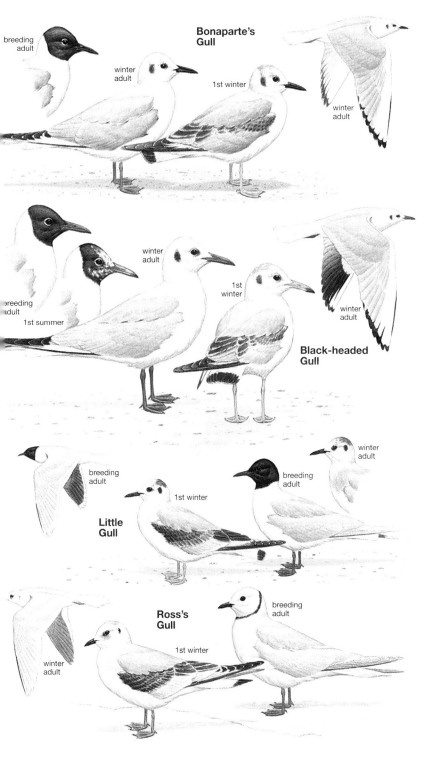

Bonaparte's Gull

breeding adult

winter adult

1st winter

winter adult

breeding adult

1st summer

winter adult

1st winter

winter adult

Black-headed Gull

breeding adult

Little Gull

1st winter

breeding adult

winter adult

winter adult

Ross's Gull

1st winter

breeding adult

Ring-billed Gull *Larus delawarensis*

L 17½" (45 cm) W 48" (122 cm) Three-year gull. **Adult** has pale gray mantle; yellow bill with black subterminal ring; pale eyes; yellowish legs; head streaked with brown in **winter. Second-winter** birds are like winter adult but bill has broader band, black on primaries is more extensive, tail usually has some blackish terminal spots. **First-winter** bird has gray back, brown wings with dark blackish-brown primaries, brown-streaked head and nape; underparts white with brown spots and scalloping on breast and throat; tail has medium-wide but variable brown band, and extensive mottling above band; uppertail and undertail coverts are lightly barred; secondary coverts medium gray; wing linings mostly white, with some barring (page 212). Distinguished from first-winter Mew Gull (*L.c.brachyrhynchus*) by white underparts spotted on breast and throat, tail pattern, darker primaries, heavier bill, and paler back. **Juvenile** plumage may be largely kept into early winter; resembles first-winter but back is brown, spotting below more extensive, bill more black. **Range:** Abundant and widespread; winters uncommonly outside mapped range.

Mew Gull *Larus canus* L 16" (41 cm) W 43" (109 cm)

Three-year gull. North American race *L.c.brachyrhynchus* is the smallest of three subspecies found here; has least black on wing tips; in flight, shows much more white on primaries than Ring-billed Gull. European nominate race, *canus* ("Common Gull"), and east Siberian *kamtschatschensis* (the largest race) have more extensive black on wing tips. All **adults** have white head, washed with brown in **winter;** dark gray mantle; thin yellow bill; most have large, dark eyes. **Second-winter** bird is like adult but bill is two-toned; has less white on primaries; variably spotty tail band. **First-winter** *brachyrhynchus* is heavily washed with brown below, almost solid brown on belly; spotted with white on breast. The head and nape are washed with soft brown; mantle dark gray; primaries light brown with pale edges. Tail is almost entirely brown, with heavily barred tail coverts; wing linings evenly pale brown (page 212). **Juvenile** is like first-winter, but brown on the back and head, darker below. Second-winter and adult *kamtschatschensis* have pale eyes; first winter birds are more like *brachyrhynchus,* but note dark tail band rather than all-dark tail, and paler tail coverts. In flight, first-winter's underwing coverts show intermediate coloration between *brachyrhynchus* (dark) and *canus* (pale). European *canus* resembles Ring-billed Gull in first winter; but note *canus's* mostly white tail with dark subterminal band, unbarred white tail coverts, darker gray back, white wing linings mottled with brown. Mew Gulls average smaller than Ring-billed Gulls, especially *brachyrhynchus,* with rounder heads, larger eyes, thinner bills. **Range:** Siberian race, rare on the Aleutians and islands in the Bering Sea. American race, rare inland in winter in Pacific states, casual east to Great Lakes region. European race, casual on east coast in winter, annual in Newfoundland.

Ring-billed Gull

breeding adult

winter adult

2nd winter

breeding adult

breeding adult

1st winter tail

1st winter

1st winter tail

juvenile

winter adult

2nd winter

breeding adults

juvenile

Mew Gull
brachyrhynchus

1st winter

kamtschatchensis

winter adult

1st winter

adult
kamtschatchensis

winter adult

canus

1st winter

adult
canus

California Gull *Larus californicus*

L 21" (53 cm) W 54" (137 cm) Four-year gull. **Adult** has darker gray mantle than Herring Gull (next page), paler than Lesser Black-backed Gull (page 208); white head, heavily streaked with brown in winter; dark eyes; yellow bill with black and red spots; black spot often smaller in breeding season; gray-green or greenish-yellow legs. In flight, shows dusky trailing edge on underwing. Third-winter plumage is like adult but bill is more extensively smudged with black; wings show some brown; tail has some brown spotting. **Second-winter** bird has gray back, brown wings, grayish legs, two-toned bill; compare with first-winter Ring-billed Gull (preceding page). **First-winter** bird is brown overall with veiled gray on scapulars; usually palest on throat, breast, and upper belly; legs pinkish; bill two-toned, the colors sharply defined. In flight (page 213), first-winter birds show double dark bar on inner half of wing, caused by darker secondaries and greater secondary covert bases. Distinctly smaller than Western Gull (page 206), with thinner bill. Compare first-winter birds with first- and second-winter Herring and Lesser Black-backed. **Juveniles** are variably pale below and lack pale bill base. **Range:** Casual on east coast and Gulf coast in winter.

Black-tailed Gull *Larus crassirostris*

L 18½" (47 cm) W 47¼" (120 cm) **Range:** East Asian species, casual in coastal Alaska and northeastern North America; accidental in California. Three-year gull, about size of Ring-billed Gull (page 198); bill and wings long; legs short. Distinctive white eye crescents except on **breeding adult** and third winter bird. Adult has black ring near red tip of bill; yellow iris, red orbital ring. Mantle dark slate gray; tail has broad subterminal band. Head of **winter** adult heavily streaked. **First-winter** bird has white on face, otherwise heavily washed with brown.

Band-tailed Gull *Larus belcheri*

L 20" (51 cm) W 49" (124 cm) **Range:** Resident on west coast of South America; accidental to California and Florida. Medium-size, three-year gull. Plumages and bill color similar to Black-tailed Gull, but Band-tailed has dark eyes, longer legs, and thicker bill. **Winter adults** and **second-winter** birds have dark hood, red only on tip of bill. Adult has yellow orbital ring. **First-winter**'s head and breast are smoky brown; belly white; mottled above.

Kelp Gull *Larus dominicanus*

L 23" (58 cm), W 53" (135 cm) **Range:** Widespread Southern Hemisphere species; casual to Gulf coast. A few Kelps have nested in recent years on Chandeleur Islands off southeast Louisiana. This results in pure Kelp pairings, and mixed pairings with Herring Gull that produce hybrids. Three-year gull, Kelp's size, structure, and bill shape suggest Western Gull (page 208). **Adult** Kelp has black back and dull greenish legs; head streaking in winter indistinct. Eye color variable. Note restricted white in outer primaries, unlike Great Black-backed (page 206). Change to adult plumage rapid; mantle blackish by **second summer.**

California Gull

winter adult

2nd winter

breeding adult

eeding adult

1st winter

pale juvenile

dark juvenile

Black-tailed Gull

breeding adult

winter adult

1st winter

2nd winter

breeding adult

Band-tailed Gull

breeding adult

2nd winter

1st winter

winter adult

breeding adult

Kelp Gull

moilting juvenile

2nd summer

winter adult

breeding adult

Herring Gull *Larus argentatus* L 25" (64 cm) W 58" (147 cm)
Highly variable four-year gull. **Adult** has pale gray mantle; white head streaked with brown in winter; legs and feet pink; bill yellow with red spot. **Third-winter** plumage is like winter adult but with black smudge on bill, some brown on body and wing coverts. **Second-winter** bird has pale gray back; brown wings; pale eye; two-toned bill. **First-winter** birds are brown overall, with dark brownish-black primaries and tail band, dark eye, dark bill, with variable pink at base; some may have bill like first-winter California Gull (preceding page); but usually distinguished by darker bill, paler face and throat, and, in flight (page 213), by pale panel at base of primaries and single dark bar on secondaries. Distinguished from first-winter Western Gull (page 206) by smaller bill, paler and more mottled body plumage, and in flight by paler wings with pale panel, and lack of contrast between back and rump. Distinguished from first-winter Lesser Black-backed Gull (page 208) by browner, less contrasting body plumage, usually darker belly, and in flight by pale primary and outer secondary coverts and less contrasting rump pattern. Widespread North American race is *L. a. smithsonianus;* Bering Sea region *vegae* has darker mantle in adult plumage and similar wing-tip pattern to Slaty-backed Gull (page 208); usually dark-eyed; head heavily streaked in winter. First-year birds are paler and more checkered; tail base is white. West European race, *argenteus,* noted casually from Newfoundland, is similar in adult plumage to *smithsonianus,* but first-winter bird is paler. **Range:** Herring Gull is generally local in the west; common in some regions, uncommon to rare in most. Common in eastern North America.

Yellow-legged Gull *Larus cachinnans*
L 24" (61 cm) W 57" (144 cm) **Range:** Palearctic species. Casual winter visitor to northeast coast from Newfoundland to mid-Atlantic. Size similar to Herring Gull, but Yellow-legged has squarer head, peaked at rear of crown; bill stouter and shorter. Adult mantle darker gray than Herring *L. a. smithonianus.* From above, wing tip darker than Herring; from below more gray, less black, on outermost primaries. Red gonys spot often extends onto upper mandible; orbital ring is redder than on Herring. Yellow legs distinctive, but some *smithsonianus* Herrings may show some yellow during winter. In Yellow-legged, winter head streaking is restricted to nape and crown, making white head stand out; by midwinter most **adults** are white-headed. **First-winter** birds are much paler on head and underparts than first-winter Herring; blocky head and extensive white on uppertail coverts and base of tail suggest same-age Great Black-backed Gull (page 208). Compare also to first-winter Lesser Black-backed. Molt to first-winter occurs earlier than in Herring; by fall, young Yellow-legged often appear worn. Recent evidence indicates that nominate *L. c. cachinnans* from Black Sea eastward is probably a distinct species from *michahellis* of Black and Mediterranean Seas and slightly darker-mantled *atlantis* of eastern Atlantic islands. Current North American records believed to be either *michahellis* or *atlantis.*

Herring Gull

juvenile

breeding adult

winter adult

3rd winter

1st winter

2nd winter

1st winter

1st winter *argenteus*

breeding adult *vegae*

1st winter *smithsonianus*

1st winter *vegae*

winter adult *vegae*

Yellow-legged Gull
michahellis

1st winter

winter adult

breeding adult

Glaucous Gull *Larus hyperboreus*

L 27" (69 cm) W 60" (152 cm) Heavy-bodied, four-year gull. In all ages, note translucent tips of white primaries. **Adult** has pale gray mantle, yellow eye, yellow bill with red spot. Head is streaked with brown in winter. Third-winter plumage like adult but has dark smudge on bill and some buff on body. Late **second-winter** bird has pale gray back and pale eye. **First-winter** birds may be buffy or almost all-white; bill is bicolored. Distinguished from Iceland Gull by size; heavier, longer bill; flatter crown; slightly paler mantle of adults; proportionately shorter wings, barely extending beyond tail. At all ages, distinguished from Glaucous-winged Gull (pages 206, 213) by more buffy white color, contrasting pale primaries; in first-winter birds by sharply two-toned bill. **Range:** Rare in winter south to Gulf states and southern California. Northern Alaskan birds are slightly smaller, adults slightly darker mantled, than birds from eastern Canada and Bering Sea. Occasionally hybridizes with Herring Gull.

Iceland Gull *Larus glaucoides L22" (56 cm) W 54" (137 cm)*

Highly variable four-year gull. **Adults** have translucent white tips on primaries, which are mostly marked with gray above; gray mantle; yellow bill with red spot; white head suffused with brown in winter; most have yellow eyes, a few brown. At rest, long wings extend well beyond tail. Late **second-winter** birds have pale eyes, gray back, two-toned bill. **First-winter** birds are buffy to mostly white; chiefly dark bill is short and thin; eyes dark; wing tips white or irregularly washed with brown; distinguished from first-winter Thayer's Gull by translucent primaries, checkered tertials, usually paler body plumage, and speckled or banded tail (see also page 213); from Glaucous Gull by smaller size, rounder head, dark bill, longer wings. **Range:** Casual south to Gulf states; uncommon to rare on Great Lakes; casual to Pacific States.

Thayer's Gull *Larus thayeri L 23" (58 cm) W 55" (140 cm)*

Variable four-year gull. In most **adults,** eye is dark brown, mantle slightly darker than Iceland Gull or Herring Gull (preceding page); bill yellow with dark red spot; legs darker pink than Herring. Primaries pale gray below, with thin, dark trailing edge; show some black or slaty gray from above. A few adults have yellow eye flecked with brown. **Second-winter** bird has gray mantle, contrasting gray-brown tail band, dark eye. **First-winter** birds variable but primaries always entirely pale below, darker than mantle above. Distinguished from Herring Gull by smaller size, paler checkered markings in plumage (see also page 213), and paler primaries with whitish edges. Distinguished from Iceland Gull by generally darker plumage, primaries darker than mantle, and usually by unspeckled tail. Compare with Glaucous-winged Gull (next page), which is larger, with larger bill, less noticeable speckling in immature plumage, and wing tips the same color as mantle. **Range:** Rare winter visitor to Great Lakes region, Ohio River, and through the interior, but identification difficult. Casual on east coast. Formerly treated as a subspecies of Herring Gull; considered by some a race of Iceland Gull.

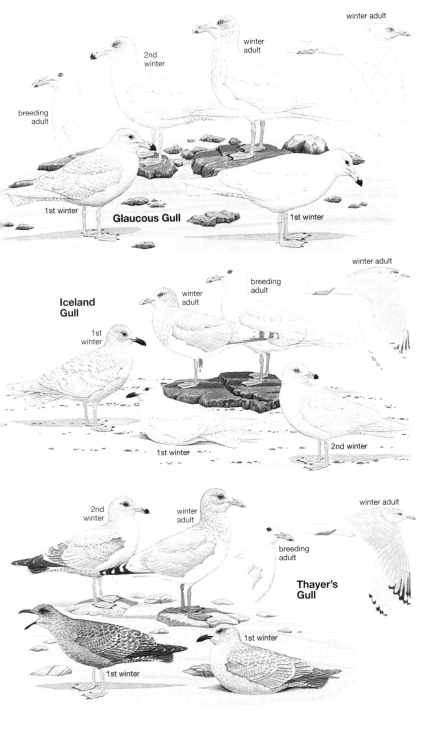

winter adult

2nd
winter

winter
adult

winter adult

breeding
adult

1st winter

Glaucous Gull

1st winter

**Iceland
Gull**

winter adult

winter
adult

breeding
adult

1st
winter

1st winter

2nd winter

2nd
winter

winter
adult

winter adult

breeding
adult

**Thayer's
Gull**

1st winter

1st winter

Yellow-footed Gull *Larus livens*

L 27" (69 cm) W 60" (152 cm) **Range:** Breeds in the Gulf of California. Fairly common postbreeding visitor in summer to Salton Sea; a few usually linger into winter; rarest in spring. Casual to coastal southern California. Three-year gull. **Adult** is like Western Gull but has yellow legs and feet; note also thicker yellow bill with red spot; dark slate gray wings; yellow eyes. **Second-winter** bird is like adult but tail looks entirely black, bill two-toned. In first-winter plumage (seen in flight page 213), head and body are mostly white, back and wings brown, eyes dark, bill mostly dark, legs pinkish. **Juvenile** resembles first-winter Western but white belly contrasts sharply with streaked breast; upperparts are more boldly patterned; rump whiter. Yellow-footed Gull's **calls** are lower pitched than Western.

Western Gull *Larus occidentalis*

L 25" (64 cm) W 58" (147 cm) Four-year gull. **Adults** north of Monterey have paler backs and darker eyes than southern birds. All adults have white head, dark gray back, pink legs, very large bill. In **winter,** head is moderately streaked with brown in northern birds, faintly streaked in southern. **Third-winter** plumage resembles second-winter Yellow-footed Gull but tail is mostly white. **Second-winter** bird has a dark gray back, yellow eyes, two-toned bill, dark brown wings. **First-winter** bird is one of the darkest young gulls; bill is black; in flight (page 213), distinguished from young Herring Gull by contrast of dark back with paler rump. Note also the often sootier underparts and head, heavier bill. **Juvenile** is like first-winter but darker. Western Gulls hybridize extensively with Glaucous-winged Gulls in the northwest; hybrids are seen all along the west coast in winter; two ages are shown here. These are easily confused with Thayer's Gull (page 204); note large bill, pattern of wing tips. **Range:** Western Gulls are very rare to casual well inland; definite records as far east as Illinois and Texas. Casual to southern Alaska.

Glaucous-winged Gull *Larus glaucescens*

L 26" (66 cm) W 58" (147 cm) Four-year gull. **Adult** has white head, moderately streaked with brown in winter. Body is white, mantle pale gray; primaries are the same color as rest of wing above, paler below. Eyes dark; large bill is yellow with red spot; legs pink. Third-winter bird is like adult but has some buff on body, bill is smudged black; some have a partial tail band. **Second-winter**'s back is gray, rest of body and wings are pale buff to white with little mottling; tail evenly gray; bill mostly dark. **First-winter** bird (shown in flight on page 213) is uniformly pale gray-brown to whitish with subtle mottling; primaries are the same color as the mantle; note young Glaucous Gull (pages 204, 213) has sharply two-toned bill, pale primaries; and young Thayer's Gull (page 204) is smaller, with smaller bill, more speckled body plumage, and darker primaries. Glaucous-winged Gull hybridizes with Western Gull; and with Herring Gull (page 202) in south-central Alaska. Hybrids are extremely variable. **Range:** Rare well inland in Pacific states; casual east to Great Lakes region.

2nd winter

adult

juvenile

adult

1st summer

Yellow-footed Gull

Western Gull

southern breeding adult *wymani*

southern 2nd winter *wymani*

1st winter

northern breeding adult *occidentalis*

juvenile

southern 3rd winter *wymani*

southern winter adult *wymani*

1st winter

breeding adult

Glaucous-winged x Western hybrid

breeding adult

2nd winter

Glaucous-winged Gull

breeding adult

1st winter

Slaty-backed Gull *Larus schistisagus*

L 25" (64 cm) W 58" (147 cm) **Range:** Coastal species of northeast Asia. Rare in coastal Alaska, most frequent in the Bering Sea. Casual in winter south to Pacific states. A four-year gull. **Adult** has dark slate gray back and wings, blackish outer primaries separated from mantle by a staggered row of whitish spots. Underside of primaries gray. Note broad white trailing edge to wings. Legs bright pink; eyes yellow. **Second-summer** bird has dark back, very pale wings. First-year birds show almost entirely dark tail and wing pattern like Thayer's Gull (page 204); also compare with *L. a. vegae* race of Herring Gull (page 202); *vegae* adult has slightly paler upperparts, lacks broad white trailing edge; underside of primaries darker than Slaty-backed.

Lesser Black-backed Gull *Larus fuscus*

L 21" (53 cm) W 54" (137 cm) **Range:** Western Palearctic species; generally rare to locally uncommon in eastern North America. Casual to west coast and Alaska. A four-year gull. **Adult** has white head, heavily streaked with brown in winter; white underparts; yellow legs. Third-winter bird has dark smudge on bill; some brown in wings. **Second-winter** bird resembles second-winter Herring Gull (page 202) but note dark gray back, much darker underwings. **First-winter** bird similar to first-winter Herring Gull but head and belly are paler, upperparts more contrastingly dark and light; bill is always entirely black. Identified in flight (page 213) by darker primary and secondary coverts, more extensively dark primaries and white outer tail feathers; paler rump contrasts with back. Much smaller than Great Black-backed Gull. Smaller on average than Herring Gull, with smaller bill, but there is substantial range of overlap; also note longer wings, usually extending well beyond tail at rest. Most birds seen here are of northern European race *L.f. graellsii.* A few darker mantled adults in eastern North America may be of Baltic race *intermedius.*

Great Black-backed Gull *Larus marinus*

L 30" (76 cm) W 65" (165 cm) Four-year gull. Huge size and large bill are distinctive. **Adult**'s white head is virtually unstreaked in winter; black upperparts; white underparts; variably pale eyed; pink legs. In flight, note extensive white on outer primary that merges with white spot on second primary to form solid white area. **Third-winter** bird is like adult but shows some dark on bill, some brown in wings, sometimes dark in tail. **Second-summer** bird has pale eye, black back; wings and tail are like first-winter. Second-winter is like first-winter, but base of bill is paler, secondary coverts more evenly brown. **First-winter** bird resembles Herring Gull (page 202) but head and body are much paler, back and wings have the checkered look of young Lesser Black-backed Gull; in flight (page 213), shows almost white rump, checkered tail band. **Range:** Breeding range is expanding southward on the Atlantic coast. Fairly common on eastern Great Lakes, more rare on western; casual inland throughout the east. Very rare on Gulf coast to Texas; casual west to Colorado and Montana; accidental in Alaska.

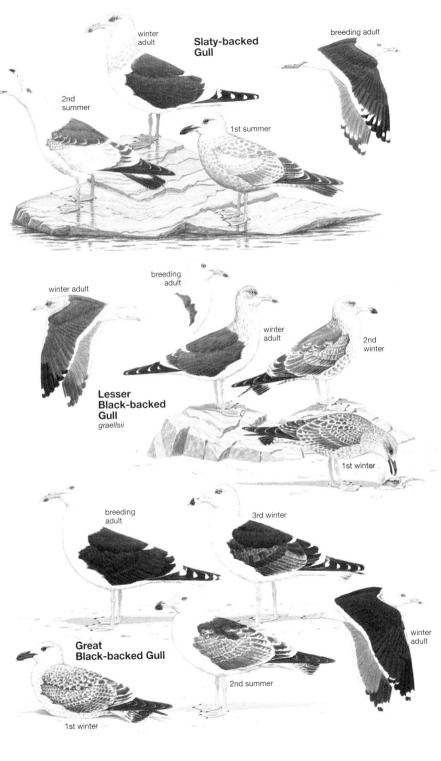

winter adult

Slaty-backed Gull

breeding adult

2nd summer

1st summer

winter adult

breeding adult

winter adult

2nd winter

Lesser Black-backed Gull
graellsii

1st winter

breeding adult

3rd winter

Great Black-backed Gull

winter adult

2nd summer

1st winter

Black-legged Kittiwake *Rissa tridactyla*

L 17" (43 cm) W 36" (91 cm) Pelagic three-year gull. **Adult** has white head, nape smudged with gray in winter; dark eye; yellow bill; white body with gray mantle. Inner primaries are pale, wing tips inky black; legs black. Second-year bird is like adult but with more black on outermost primary. **Juvenile** has dark half collar, retained into early winter; black bill; black spot behind eye; dark tail band; and in flight (page 212), dark W across the wings. Distinguished from young Sabine's Gull by half-collar, dark carpal bar. A very few young birds have pinkish legs. **Call** is a series of *kittiwake's*. **Range:** Nests in large cliff colonies; winters at sea. Seen uncommonly from shore on the west coast, commonly in some years when a few may summer; rarely on the east coast.

Red-legged Kittiwake *Rissa brevirostris*

L 15" (38 cm) W 33" (84 cm) Pelagic two-year gull. **Adult** distinguished from Black-legged Kittiwake by coral red legs; shorter, thicker bill; darker mantle; wings are not paler on flight feathers as in Black-legged; broader white trailing edge on wings; dusky underside of primaries. In first year, wing pattern resembles Sabine's Gull (page 212), but Red-legged Kittiwake is the only gull to have an all-white tail in first winter. Similar to young Black-legged but lacks W pattern on wings. **Call** is higher pitched and squeakier than Black-legged. **Range:** Breeds in cliff colonies, usually close to Black-legged Kittiwake. Very rare away from breeding grounds, even in winter. Casual on and off west coast.

Sabine's Gull *Xema sabini* *L 13½" (34 cm) W 33" (84 cm)*

Two-year gull with striking black-gray-and-white wing pattern in all ages. **Breeding adult** has dark gray hood with thin black ring at bottom; black bill with yellow tip; forked tail. First-summer bird is like adult but lacks hood; has dusky nape. In **juvenile** plumage (see also page 212), wing pattern is like adult but muted; crown and nape are soft gray-brown; bill black; tail has dark band. **Range:** Sabine's Gull winters at sea mainly in the Southern Hemisphere. Most adults migrate out of North America before acquiring white head and dark nape of winter plumage. Juveniles depart before acquiring first-winter plumage. Common migrant off west coast, rarely seen from shore. Rare in fall, casual in spring, in western interior. Very rare in fall east to Great Lakes region. Casual on and off east coast and in the south.

Ivory Gull *Pagophila eburnea* *L 17" (43 cm) W 37" (94 cm)*

Two-year arctic gull, ghostly pale. **Adults** in all plumages are strikingly white with a yellow-tipped bill, black eyes, black legs. Immature birds show a variable amount of speckling on the body, heaviest and often patchy on the face; have tail band, and spots on tips of primaries. A short-necked, stocky gull with long wings. **Range:** Winters primarily in Arctic seas. Uncommon in northern and western Alaska. Casual along the Atlantic coast to New York, and inland to the northern tier of states. Accidental to southern California and southern Tennessee.

Black-legged Kittiwake

breeding adult

winter adult

juvenile

Red-legged Kittiwake

breeding adult

breeding adult

juvenile

1st summer

Sabine's Gull

breeding adult

molting adult

breeding adult

juvenile

Ivory Gull

adult

1st winter

adult

Immature Gulls in Flight

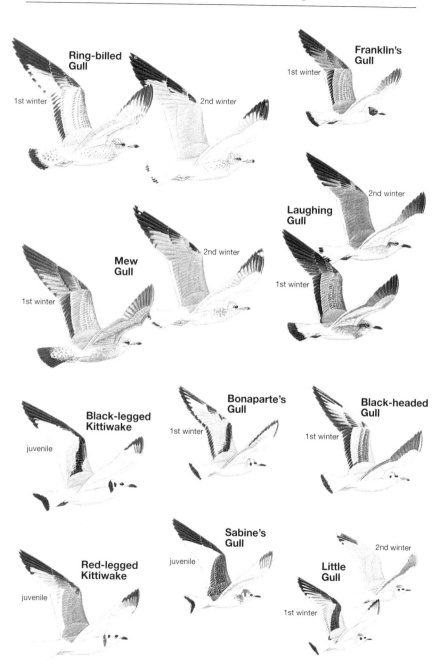

Ring-billed Gull
1st winter
2nd winter

Franklin's Gull
1st winter

Mew Gull
1st winter
2nd winter

Laughing Gull
2nd winter
1st winter

Black-legged Kittiwake
juvenile

Bonaparte's Gull
1st winter

Black-headed Gull
1st winter

Red-legged Kittiwake
juvenile

Sabine's Gull
juvenile

Little Gull
2nd winter
1st winter

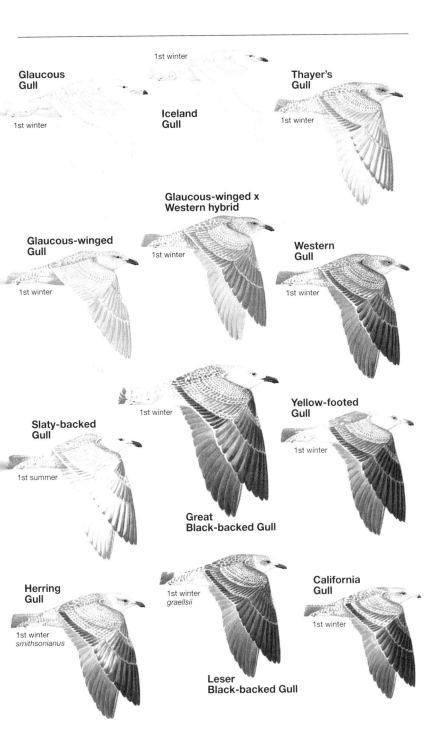

Glaucous Gull

1st winter

Iceland Gull

1st winter

Thayer's Gull

1st winter

Glaucous-winged x Western hybrid

1st winter

Glaucous-winged Gull

1st winter

Western Gull

1st winter

Slaty-backed Gull

1st summer

1st winter

Yellow-footed Gull

1st winter

Great Black-backed Gull

Herring Gull

1st winter
smithsonianus

1st winter
graellsii

California Gull

1st winter

Leser Black-backed Gull

Terns

Distinguished from gulls by long, pointed wings and bill and by feeding technique. Most terns plunge-dive into the water after prey. Most species have a forked tail.

Sandwich Tern *Sterna sandvicensis*
L 15" (38 cm) W 34" (86 cm) Slender, black bill, tipped with yellow. **Breeding adult** is pale gray above with black crown, short black crest. In flight, shows some dark in outer primaries. White tail is deeply forked, comparatively short. Adult in **winter** plumage, seen as early as July, has a white forehead, streaked crown, grayer tail. **Juvenile**'s tail less deeply forked; bill often lacks yellow tip, in a few it is entirely yellow. By late summer, juvenile loses dark V-shaped markings and spots on back and scapulars. **Calls** include abrupt *gwit gwit* and *skee-rick* notes, like calls of Elegant Tern. **Range:** Nests on coastal beaches and islands. Casual spring and summer visitor to coastal southern California.

Elegant Tern *Sterna elegans* *L 17" (43 cm) W 34" (86 cm)*
Bill longer, thinner than in Royal Tern; reddish-orange in adults, yellow in some juveniles. Body smaller, slimmer than Royal. In flight, shows mostly pale underside of primaries; compare with Caspian Tern. **Breeding adult** is pale gray above with black crown and nape, black crest; white below, often with pinkish tinge. **Winter adult** and **juvenile** have white forehead; black over top of crown extends forward around eye; compare with Royal. Juveniles have variably mottled upperparts, may have orange legs; some have less black on crown, like juvenile Royal. Sharp *kee-rick* **call** very similar to Sandwich Tern. **Range:** Postbreeding dispersal to northern Washington; casual to British Columbia; very rare spring and summer at Salton Sea; accidental in southwest.

Royal Tern *Sterna maxima* *L 20" (51 cm) W 41" (104 cm)*
Orange-red bill, thinner than in Caspian Tern. In flight, shows mostly pale underside of primaries; tail more deeply forked than Caspian. **Adult** shows white crown most of year; black cap is acquired briefly early in **breeding** season. In **winter adult** and **juvenile,** black on nape does not usually extend to encompass eye; compare Elegant Tern. **Calls** include a bleating *kee-rer* and ploverlike whistled *tourreee*. **Range:** Nests in dense colonies. Fairly common in winter on southern California coast, where a few breed; uncommon to rare north of breeding range along Atlantic coast in late summer; casual in interior of North America.

Caspian Tern *Sterna caspia* *L 21" (53 cm) W 50" (127 cm)*
Large, stocky; bill orange to coral red, much thicker than in Royal Tern. In flight, shows dark underside of primaries; tail less deeply forked than in Royal. **Adult** acquires black cap in **breeding** season; in **winter adult** and **juvenile,** crown is dusky or streaked; never shows fully white forehead of Royal. Adult's **calls** include a harsh *kowk* and *ca-arr;* immature's a distinctive, whistled *whee-you*. **Range:** Small colonies nest on coasts, in wetlands.

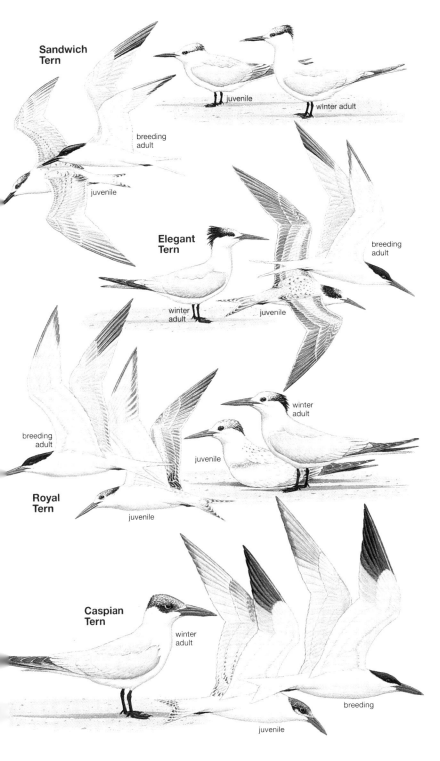

Sandwich Tern

juvenile

breeding adult

winter adult

juvenile

Elegant Tern

breeding adult

winter adult

juvenile

Royal Tern

breeding adult

winter adult

juvenile

juvenile

Caspian Tern

winter adult

breeding

juvenile

Roseate Tern *Sterna dougallii* **E**

L 15½" (39 cm) W 29" (74 cm) **Breeding adult** is white below with slight, variable pinkish cast visible in good light; pale gray above with black cap and nape. Much paler overall than Common and Arctic Terns (next page). Lacks dark trailing edge on underside of outer wing. Bill mostly black; during summer more red appears at base. Wings shorter than in Common and Arctic; flies with rapid wingbeats suggestive of Least Tern (page 220). Deeply forked all-white tail extends well beyond wings in standing bird. Legs and feet bright red-orange. **Juvenile**'s brownish cap extends over forehead; mantle looks coarsely scaled, lower back barred with black; bill and legs black. **First-summer** bird has white forehead; lacks dark secondaries of immature Common. Full adult plumage is attained by second spring. **Call** is a soft *chi-weep;* alarm signal a drawn-out *zra-ap,* like ripping cloth. **Range:** Uncommon and highly maritime, Roseate Terns usually come ashore only to nest. Rare on mid-Atlantic coast in late spring.

Forster's Tern *Sterna forsteri L 14½" (37 cm) W 31" (79 cm)*

Breeding adult is snow white below, pale gray above, with black cap and nape; mostly orange bill, orange legs and feet. Wingbeat much slower than in Roseate Tern. Legs and bill longer than in Common and Arctic Terns (next page). Long, deeply forked gray tail has white outer edges. In flight, shows pale upperwing area formed by silvery primaries; white rump contrasts with gray back, gray tail. **Winter** plumage resembles Common and Arctic but is acquired by mid- to late August, much earlier than those species, which molt chiefly after migration out of U.S. Note also lack of dark shoulder bars; most have dark eye patches not joined at nape as in Common, but many have dark streaks on nape. **Juvenile** and **first-winter** bird have shorter tails than adults and more dark color in wings. Juvenile has ginger brown cap, dark eye patch; shoulder bar is faint or absent. **Calls** include a hoarse *kyarr,* lower and shorter than in Common. **Range:** Forster's Terns nest in widely scattered colonies in marshes.

Gull-billed Tern *Sterna nilotica L 14" (36 cm) W 34" (86 cm)*

Breeding adult is white below, pale gray above, with black crown and nape, stout black bill, black legs and feet. Stockier and paler than Common Tern (next page); wings broader; tail shorter and only moderately forked. **Winter** birds have white crown with fine, dark streaks. **Juvenile** has pale edgings on upperparts, bill is brownish. Adult **call** is a raspy, sharp *kay-wack;* call of juvenile is a faint, high-pitched *peep peep.* **Range:** Fairly common but local; nests in salt marshes and on beaches; often seen hunting for insects over fields and marshes. Casual in interior of North America except at Salton Sea, where it nests. Breeds also in California in coastal San Diego County.

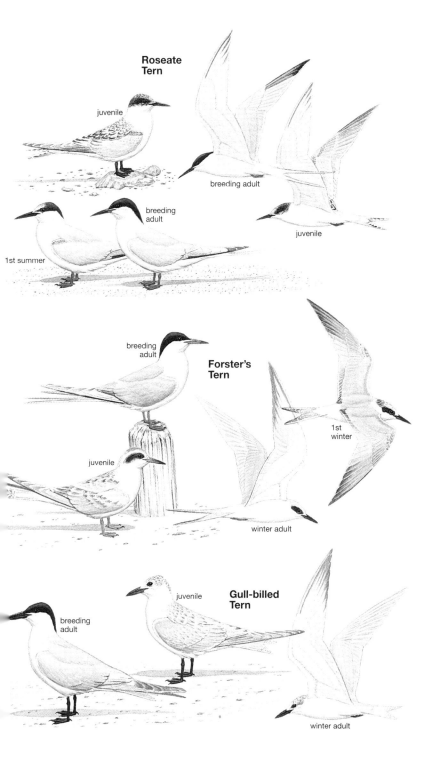

Roseate Tern

juvenile

breeding adult

juvenile

1st summer

breeding adult

Forster's Tern

breeding adult

juvenile

1st winter

winter adult

breeding adult

juvenile

Gull-billed Tern

winter adult

Common Tern *Sterna hirundo L 14½" (37 cm) W 30" (76 cm)*
Medium gray above, with black cap and nape; paler below. Bill red, usually black-tipped. Slightly stockier than the Arctic Tern, with flatter crown, longer neck and bill. In flight, usually displays a dark wedge, variably shaped, near tip of upperwing; in late summer all outer primaries can appear dark. Note also that head projects farther than in Arctic. Common Tern's shorter tail gives it a chunkier look. Early **juvenile** shows some brown above, white below, with mostly dark bill. Juvenile's forehead is white, crown and nape blackish, secondaries dark gray; compare with juvenile Forster's Tern (preceding page). All immature and winter plumages have a dark shoulder bar. Full **adult breeding** plumage is acquired by third spring. Some **calls** are similar to Arctic Tern; distinctive in Common, a low, piercing, drawn-out *kee-ar-r-r-r.* **Range:** Common Terns nest in large colonies. Common throughout breeding range; fairly common to common migrant on Pacific coast from Washington south; very rare in winter along the Gulf coast and in southern California. A Siberian subspecies, *S. h. longipennis,* seen regularly on the islands of western Alaska, is darker overall; bill and legs black.

Arctic Tern *Sterna paradisaea L 15½" (39 cm) W 31" (79 cm)*
Medium gray above, with black cap and nape; paler below. Bill deep red. Slightly slimmer than Common Tern, with rounder head, shorter neck and bill. In flight, upperwing appears uniformly gray, lacking dark wedge of Common; underwing shows very narrow black line on trailing edge of primaries; all flight feathers appear translucent. Note also that tail is longer and head does not project as far as in Common. **Juvenile** largely lacks brownish wash of early juvenile Common; shoulder bar less distinct; secondaries whitish and a portion of coverts whitish too, creating an effect like Sabine's Gull (page 210). Forehead is white, crown and nape blackish; compare juvenile Forster's Tern (preceding page). Full adult breeding plumage is acquired by third spring. **Calls** include a raspy *tr-tee-ar,* higher than Common Tern's call. **Range:** Arctic Terns migrate well offshore; casual inland during migration, especially in late spring.

Aleutian Tern *Sterna aleutica L 13½" (34 cm) W 29" (74 cm)*
Dark gray above and below, with white forehead, black cap, black bill, black legs. In flight, distinguished from Common and Arctic Terns by shorter tail and by white forehead and dark, white-edged bar on secondaries, most visible from below. **Juvenile** is buff and brown above; legs and lower mandible reddish. **Call** is a squeaky *twee-ee-ee,* unlike any other tern. **Range:** Aleutian Terns nest in loose colonies, sometimes with Arctic Terns. Casual in spring off British Columbia. Migration routes uncertain; has been seen in fall off Hong Kong and in the Philippines. Winter grounds still unknown, but probably in the South Pacific.

Common Tern

breeding adult

1st summer

juvenile

2nd summer

breeding adult *longipennis*

1st fall

breeding adult

Arctic Tern

juvenile

1st summer

breeding adult

breeding adult

juvenile

Aleutian Tern

breeding adult

juvenile

Least Tern *Sterna antillarum* **E**

L 9" (23 cm) W 20" (51 cm) Smallest North American tern. **Breeding adult** is gray above, with black cap and nape, white forehead, orange-yellow bill with dark tip; underparts are white; legs orange-yellow. By late summer, bill base is more greenish. In flight, black wedge on outer primaries is conspicuous; note also the short, deeply forked tail. **Juvenile** shows brownish, U-shaped markings; crown is dusky; wings show dark shoulder bar. By first fall, upperparts are gray, crown whiter, but dark shoulder bar is retained. **First-summer** birds are more like adults but have dark bill and legs, shoulder bar, black line through eye, dusky primaries. Flight is rapid and buoyant. **Calls** include high-pitched kip notes and a harsh *chir-ee-eep*. **Range:** Nests in colonies on beaches and sandbars; also on rooftops. Fairly common but local on east and Gulf coasts; declining inland and on the California coast. Winters from Central America south.

Black Tern *Chlidonias niger* L 9¾" (25 cm) W 24" (61 cm)

Breeding adult is mostly black, with dark gray back, wings, and tail; white undertail coverts. In flight, shows uniformly pale gray underwing and fairly short tail, slightly forked. Bill is black in all plumages. **Juvenile** and **winter** birds are white below, with dark gray mantle and tail; dark ear patch extends from dark crown; flying birds show dark bar on side of breast. Some juveniles show a contrastingly paler rump. Shoulder bar on upper wing is much darker than in juvenile White-winged Tern. **First-summer** birds can be like winter adults or may have some dark feathers on head and underparts; second-summer birds are like breeding adults, but show some whitish on head; full breeding plumage is acquired by third spring. Adults also appear patchy black-and-white as they molt into winter plumage in late summer; these birds are easily confused with the White-winged Tern. **Calls** include a metallic *kik* and a slurred *k-seek*. **Range:** Black Terns nest on lakeshores and in marshes; declining over part of range inland and on east coast; uncommon to rare on west coast.

White-winged Tern *Chlidonias leucopterus*

L 9½" (24 cm) W 23" (58 cm) **Range:** Eurasian species, very rare vagrant to east coast; casual to Great Lakes region; accidental in west, where recorded in western Aleutians, south coastal Alaska, coastal California. Bill and tail shorter than in Black Tern; tail less deeply notched. In **breeding** plumage, bill usually black, but sometimes red; white tail, whitish upperwing coverts, and black wing linings are distinctive; upperwing shows black outer primaries. **Molting** birds are patchy black-and-white, but whitish tail and rump are distinctive; black wing linings often last until late summer. **Winter adult** has white wing linings; lacks dark breast bar of Black Tern; crown, speckled rather than solid black, not usually connected to dark ear patch. First-summer bird resembles winter adult; second-summer usually like breeding adult; adult plumage reached by third spring. **Juvenile**'s head pattern resembles Black, but browner back shows greater contrast with grayish wing coverts and whitish rump than juvenile Black.

Least Tern

breeding adult

breeding adult

juvenile

1st summer

Black Tern

breeding adult

winter adult

breeding adult

1st summer

juvenile

White-winged Tern

breeding adult

molting adult

winter adult

juvenile

Bridled Tern *Sterna anaethetus L 15" (38 cm) W 30" (76 cm)*
Range: Nests in the West Indies and locally off Florida Keys. Regular in summer well offshore in the Gulf of Mexico, and in the Gulf Stream to North Carolina; rarely to off New Jersey. Tropical storms may drive Bridled Terns north to New England. Note white collar between brownish-gray upperparts and black cap on **breeding adult.** Similar to Sooty Tern, but slimmer; wings more pointed; underwings and tail edges more extensively white; tail grayer. Bridled's white forehead patch extends behind the eye, while Sooty's stops at the eye. **Juvenile** has pale mottling above.

Sooty Tern *Sterna fuscata L 16" (41 cm) W 32" (81 cm)*
Range: Large breeding colony on Dry Tortugas, Florida; also nests on islands off Texas and Louisiana. Regular in summer to North Carolina. Casual in southern coastal California. Tropical storms can carry birds inland to Great Lakes and north to Maritime Provinces. Blackish above, white below; white forehead. Lacks white collar of Bridled Tern. Tail is deeply forked, edged with white. **Juvenile** is sooty-brown overall, with whitish stippling on back; pale lower belly and undertail coverts; pale wing linings. Typical **call** is a high, nasal *wacky-wack.*

Black Noddy *Anous minutus L 13½" (34 cm) W 30" (76 cm)*
Range: Tropical species, rare in North America; casual to coastal Texas. A few, mostly immatures, seen among Brown Noddies on the Dry Tortugas. Black Noddy is smaller, with shorter legs; bill is thinner and proportionately longer; overall color is slightly blacker. In **immatures,** white area on head is very sharply defined.

Brown Noddy *Anous stolidus L 15½" (39 cm) W 32" (81 cm)*
Range: Nests in a colony on Dry Tortugas, Florida. Casual to Texas coast and off Outer Banks, North Carolina. Overall dark gray-brown with whitish-gray cap, blending at back; **immature** shows only a whitish line on forehead. Unlike other terns, noddies have long, wedge-shaped tail with only a small notch at tip. Usually silent; a crowlike *karrk* **call** is heard mostly around the breeding colonies.

Large-billed Tern *Phaetusa simplex*
L 14½" (37 cm) W 36" (92 cm) **Range:** A South American freshwater species. Accidental; recorded in late spring and summer from Illinois, Ohio, and New Jersey; additionally from Cuba and Bermuda. Mantle and short tail dark gray; white below with white forehead and black cap; legs and stout bill yellow. In flight shows striking Sabine's Gull-like pattern (page 210).

Black Skimmer *Rynchops niger L 18" (46 cm) W 44" (112 cm)*
No other bird has a lower mandible longer than the upper. A long-winged coastal bird, it furrows the shallows with its red, black-tipped bill. At rest, black back and crown, white face and underparts, red legs, and bill shape are distinctive. Female is distinctly smaller than the **male. Juvenile** is mottled dingy brown above. **Winter adults** show a white collar. **Range:** Casual inland.

Bridled Tern

breeding adult

juvenile

Sooty Tern

juvenile

breeding adult

Black Noddy

adult

immature

Brown Noddy

adults

immature

Large-billed Tern

breeding adult

juvenile

winter adults

breeding adult

Black Skimmer

Auks, Murres, Puffins (Family Alcidae)

These black-and-white "penguins of the north" have set-back legs that give them an upright stance on land. In flight, wingbeats are rapid and shallow.

Dovekie *Alle alle L 8¼" (21 cm)*
Small and plump with short neck, stubby bill. **Breeding adult** is black above, white below; black upper breast contrasts sharply with white underparts; dark wing linings. Usually swims tilted forward in the water. In **winter** plumage, throat, chin, and lower face are white, with white curving around behind eye. **Range:** Abundant on breeding grounds. Winters irregularly in North Atlantic south to off coast of North Carolina; rarely to Florida, but occasionally in large numbers; casual inland.

Common Murre *Uria aalge L 17½" (45 cm)*
Large, with a long, slender, pointed bill. Upperparts dark sooty-gray, head brownish; underparts white. Some Atlantic birds have a **"bridle,"** a white eye ring and spur. In **winter** plumage, a dark stripe extends from eye across white cheek. **Juvenile** has shorter bill; distinguished from Thick-billed Murre by white facial stripe, paler upperparts, thinner bill. Molting birds (early fall) are more difficult to identify. **Range:** Numerous off east and west coasts. Nests in dense colonies on rocky cliffs. Chick accompanies adult at sea and can be mistaken for Xantus's Murrelets (page 228).

Thick-billed Murre *Uria lomvia L 18" (46 cm)*
Stocky, with a thick, fairly short bill, arched at tip to form a blunt hook. Upperparts and throat of **adult** are darker than Common Murre; white of underparts usually rises to a sharp point on the foreneck. Most birds show a distinct white line on cutting edge of upper mandible; in Pacific birds, bill is slightly longer and thinner than in Atlantic birds. In immature and **winter adult,** face and neck are more extensively dark than in Common. First-summer bird is browner above than adult; otherwise similar to winter bird. **Range:** Nests in colonies on rocky cliffs. Common on breeding grounds. On east coast, much more regular in winter south of Canada than Common; casual to mid-Atlantic states; recorded to Florida. Casual on west coast south of breeding range, where most records are from the Monterey area in California.

Razorbill *Alca torda L 17" (43 cm)*
A chunky bird, big-headed and thick-necked; black above, white below. Rather long, pointed tail; heavy head; and massive, arching bill distinguish Razorbill from murres. Swimming birds often hold tail cocked up. A white band crosses the bill; in **breeding** plumage, a white line runs from bill to eye. **Immature** lacks white band; bill is smaller but still distinctively shaped. **Range:** Nests on rocky cliffs and among boulders. Winters in large numbers on the Grand Banks off Newfoundland. A few winter well offshore as far south as North Carolina, casually to Florida; irregular along the coast south of Long Island.

Dovekie

breeding adult

winter

breeding adult

winter

bridled breeding adult

breeding adult

Common Murre

breeding adult

winter

juvenile

Thick-billed Murre

Pacific winter *arra*

Atlantic breeding adults *lomvia*

immature

Razorbill

breeding adult

winter adult

breeding adult

Black Guillemot *Cepphus grylle L 13" (33 cm)*

Breeding adult black overall, with large white patch on upper-wing. **Winter adult** white; upperparts heavily mottled with black except on nape; wing patch less distinct. **Juvenile** is sooty above; sides and wing patches mottled. First-summer birds are patchily black-and-white; wing patches mottled. In all plumages, white axillaries and wing linings distinguish Black from Pigeon Guille-mot. In east coast race *C. g. arcticus,* juveniles and winter birds are darker than in high Arctic race, *mandtii.* **Range:** Fairly common in the east; usually seen close to shore in breeding season.

Pigeon Guillemot *Cepphus columba L 13½" (34 cm)*

Breeding and **winter adults'** plumage similar to smaller Black Guillemot, but note black bar on white upperwing patch; bar may be obscured in swimming bird. **Juvenile** is dusky above; crown and nape darker; wing patch marked with black edgings; breast and sides gray-mottled. Compare with juvenile Marbled Mur-relet. First-winter Pigeon Guillemot resembles winter adult but is darker. In all plumages, dusky axillaries and wing linings dis-tinguish Pigeon from Black Guillemot. **Range:** Fairly common; seen near shore in breeding season. Winter range not well-known.

Long-billed Murrelet *Brachyramphus perdix*

L 11½" (29 cm) **Range:** Found in coastal northeast Asia. Casual throughout North America; most records are in fall of winter-plumaged birds. In **winter,** lacks conspicuous white collar of sim-ilar Marbled Murrelet; shows small pale oval patches on sides of nape; in **breeding** plumage upperparts are less rufous, throat paler. In flight all plumages show whitish median underwing pri-mary coverts. Formerly considered a race of Marbled.

Marbled Murrelet *Brachyramphus marmoratus* **T**

L 10" (25 cm) Bill longer than in Kittlitz's Murrelet. Tail all-dark, but white on overlapping uppertail coverts. **Breeding adult** dark above, heavily mottled below. In **winter** plumage, white on scapu-lars distinguishes Marbled from other murrelets except Long-billed and Kittlitz's with shorter bill and breast band; white on face of Marbled is variable but less than Kittlitz's. **Juvenile** is like winter adult but mottled below; by first winter, underparts are mostly white. Highly vocal; **call** is a series of loud, high *kree* notes. **Range:** Nests inland, usually in trees. Fairly common in breeding range; rare in southern California. All murrelets have more pointed wings and faster flight than auklets.

Kittlitz's Murrelet *Brachyramphus brevirostris*

L 9½" (24 cm) Bill shorter than in Marbled Murrelet. Outer tail feathers white. **Breeding adult**'s buffy grayish-brown upperparts are heavily patterned; throat, breast, and flanks mottled; belly white. In **winter,** note extensive white on face, making eye con-spicuous; nearly complete breast band; and white edges on sec-ondaries. **Juvenile** distinguished from Marbled by shorter bill, paler face, white outer tail feathers. **Range:** Fairly common but local. Accidental to British Columbia and southern California.

Black Guillemot
arcticus

juvenile

winter adult

winter adult

breeding adult

winter adult

juvenile

Pigeon Guillemot

winter adult

breeding adult

Long-billed Murrelet

breeding adult

winter

juvenile

Marbled Murrelet

winter

breeding adult

winter

breeding adult

Kittlitz's Murrelet

breeding adult

winter

juvenile

winter

breeding adult

Xantus's Murrelet *Synthliboramphus hypoleucus*

L 9¾" (25 cm) Slate black above, white below. Southern California subspecies, *S. h. scrippsi,* has white eye crescents. The race that breeds on islands off Baja California, *hypoleucus,* has more white on face; seen rarely off southern and central California coast in fall. Both races distinguished from Craveri's Murrelet by lack of partial collar; slightly shorter, stouter bill; lack of black under the bill; and white wing linings, visible when birds rise to flap wings before taking off. Usually seen a few miles offshore; nests in colonies on rocky islands, ledges, and sometimes in dense vegetation. **Call,** a piping whistle or series of whistles, is heard year-round. **Range:** Uncommon to fairly common; rare late-summer and fall postbreeding wanderer as far north as Oregon; casual to south British Columbia. Rarely seen from shore.

Craveri's Murrelet *Synthliboramphus craveri*

L 8½" (22 cm) Slate black above, white below. Distinguished from Xantus's Murrelet by variably dusky-gray wing linings; dark partial collar extending onto breast; slightly slimmer, longer bill; and black color of face extending under the bill. In good light, upperparts have a brownish tinge. Usually seen a few or many miles offshore. **Call,** very different from Xantus's, is a cicadalike rattle, rising to a reedy trilling when agitated. **Range:** Breeds on rocky islands off Baja California. Regular late-summer and fall postbreeding visitor to coast of southern and central California. Rarely seen from shore.

Ancient Murrelet *Synthliboramphus antiquus*

L 10" (25 cm) Black crown and nape contrast with gray back. White streaks on head and nape of **breeding adult** give it an "ancient" look. Note also black chin and throat, yellowish bill. **Winter adult**'s bib is smaller and white-flecked, streaks on head less distinct. **Immature** lacks head streaks; throat is mostly white; distinguished from winter Marbled Murrelet (preceding page) by heavier, paler bill and by sharp contrast between head and back. In flight, the Ancient Murrelet holds its head higher than other murrelets; dark stripe on body at base of wing contrasts with white underparts, white wing linings. Call is a short, emphatic *chirrup.* **Range:** Uncommon to common; breeds primarily on the Aleutians and other Alaska islands; winters to central California, rarely to southern California. Casual inland throughout North America.

Cassin's Auklet *Ptychoramphus aleuticus* *L 9" (23 cm)*

Small, plump, dark gray bird; wings more rounded than in murrelets; bill short and stout, with pale spot at base of lower mandible; pale eyes. Upperparts are dark gray, shading to paler gray below, with whitish belly. Prominent white crescents above and below eye. Juvenile is paler overall; throat whitish; has darker eye and black bill. **Call,** heard only on the breeding grounds, is a weak croaking. **Range:** Common; nests in colonies on islands and on isolated coastal cliffs and headlands. Highly pelagic; usually seen farther from shore than murrelets.

Xantus's Murrelet

scrippsi

hypoleucus

scrippsi

Craveri's Murrelet

breeding adult

immature

Ancient Murrelet

breeding adult

winter adult

adults

Cassin's Auklet

Parakeet Auklet *Aethia psittacula L 10" (25 cm)*
In **breeding** plumage, acquired by late January, broad upturned bill is orange-red; white plume extends back from behind the eye; dark slate upperparts and throat contrast sharply with white underparts; sides are mottled gray. In **winter** plumage, bill becomes duskier; underparts, including throat, are entirely white. Compare especially with larger Rhinoceros Auklet (next page). Immature resembles winter adult. Silent except on breeding grounds, when **call** is a musical trill, rising in pitch. **Range:** Fairly common on breeding grounds; nests in scattered pairs on rocky shores, sea cliffs. Found in pairs or small flocks in winter, well out to sea. Winters irregularly as far south as California. Like other auklets, wings are rounded and wingbeats are fluttery in comparison to those of murrelets.

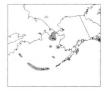

Crested Auklet *Aethia cristatella L 9" (23 cm)*
Sooty-black overall; prominent quail-like crest curves forward from forehead; narrow white plume trails from behind yellow eye. **Breeding adult**'s bill is enlarged by bright orange plates. In **winter,** bill is smaller and browner; crest and plume reduced. **Juvenile** may have short crest, lacks plume; bill much smaller. Compare with smaller Whiskered Auklet. First-summer bird has a single plume back from eye, but bill is still small. Common and gregarious; often seen in large flocks that may include Parakeet and Least Auklets. **Range:** Nests in crevices of sea cliffs, rocky shores. Accidental south to Baja California.

Whiskered Auklet *Aethia pygmaea L 7¾" (20 cm)*
Overall color like Crested Auklet, but note Whiskered is paler on belly and undertail coverts. Three white plumes splay from each side of face; thin crest curls forward. In **breeding** plumage, bill is orange-red with white tip. In **winter,** bill is dusky, plumes and crest less conspicuous. **Juvenile** is paler below; bill smaller; lacks crest and plumes. First-summer bird may lack crest and show only traces of plumes. Often seen feeding in riptides. **Range:** Fairly common but local; nests in Aleutians from Baby Island off Unalaska Island west to Buldir; and on islands off Siberia.

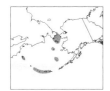

Least Auklet *Aethia pusilla L 6¼" (16 cm)*
Small, chubby, and short-necked; dark above, with white-tipped scapulars and primaries; forehead and lores streaked with white bristly feathers. Stubby, knobbed bill is dark red, with pale tip. In **breeding** plumage, acquired by January, a streak of white plumes extends back from behind eye; underparts are variable: heavily mottled with gray or nearly all-white. In **winter** plumage, underparts are entirely white. **Juvenile** resembles winter adult. **Range:** Abundant and gregarious, Least Auklets are found in immense flocks. Nest on boulder-strewn beaches and islands. Often seen far from shore. Accidental in Northwest Territories, Canada, and coastal California. Winter throughout Aleutians.

Parakeet Auklet

breeding adult

breeding adult

winter adult

Crested Auklet

breeding adult

juvenile

winter adult

breeding adult

Whiskered Auklet

breeding adult

breeding adult

juvenile

winter adult

Least Auklet

breeding adults

winter adults

juvenile

Rhinoceros Auklet *Cerorhinca monocerata L 15" (38 cm)*
Large, heavy-billed auklet with large head and short, thick neck. Blackish-brown above; paler on sides, neck, and throat. In flight, whitish on belly blends into dark breast; compare with extensively white underparts of similar Parakeet Auklet (preceding page). In **breeding** plumage, acquired by February, Rhinoceros Auklet has distinct white plumes and a pale yellow "horn" at base of orange bill. **Winter adult** lacks horn; plumes are less distinct, bill paler. Juvenile and **immature** lack horn and plumes; bill is dusky, eyes darker. Compare with much smaller Cassin's Auklet (page 228). **Range:** Rhinoceros Auklets are common along most of the west coast in fall and winter; often seen in large numbers close inshore.

Atlantic Puffin *Fratercula arctica L 12½" (32 cm)*
The only east coast puffin. **Breeding adult** identified by massive, brightly colored bill; pale face and underparts contrast with dark upperparts. **Winter adult** has smaller, duller bill, dusky face. In **juvenile** and first-winter birds, face is even duskier, bill much paler and smaller. Full adult bill takes about five years to develop. In flight, distinguished from murres and Razorbill (page 224) by red-orange legs, rounded wings, grayish wing linings, absence of white trailing edge on wing. **Range:** Locally common in breeding season; winters at sea, rarely south to Virginia.

Horned Puffin *Fratercula corniculata L 15" (38 cm)*
A stocky North Pacific species with thick neck, large head, massive bill; underparts are white in all plumages. **Breeding adult's** face is white, bill brightly colored. Dark, fleshy "horn" extending up from eye is visible only at close range. **Winter adult's** bill is smaller, duller; face is dusky. Bill of **juvenile** and first-winter birds smaller and duskier than adult; full adult bill takes several years to develop. In flight, bright orange legs are conspicuous; wings are rounded; wing linings grayish; wings lack white trailing edge. **Range:** Locally common; winters well out to sea. Irregular straggler off the west coast to southern California, mainly in late spring.

Tufted Puffin *Fratercula cirrhata L 15" (38 cm)*
Stocky, with thick neck, large head, massive bill. Underparts are dark in adults. **Breeding adult's** face is white, bill brightly colored; pale yellow head tufts droop over back of neck. **Winter adult** has smaller, duller bill; face is gray, tufts shorter or absent. **Juvenile** has smaller, dusky bill; dark eye; white or dark underparts. First-winter bird looks like juvenile until spring molt. As in other puffins, full adult bill and plumage take several years to develop. Red-orange feet are conspicuous in flight; wings are rounded; wing linings grayish; wings lack white trailing edge. **Range:** Common to abundant in northern breeding range; uncommon to rare off California. Winters far out at sea.

Rhinoceros Auklet

winter adult

immature

winter adult

breeding adult

Atlantic Puffin

breeding adult

breeding adult

winter adult

juvenile

Horned Puffin

juvenile

winter adult

breeding adult

Tufted Puffin

juvenile

juvenile

winter adult

breeding adult

Pigeons, Doves (Family Columbidae)

The larger species of these birds usually are called pigeons, the smaller ones doves. All are strong, fast fliers. Juveniles have pale-tipped feathers, lack the neck markings of adults. Pigeons and doves feed chiefly on grain, other seeds, and fruit.

Band-tailed Pigeon *Columba fasciata L 14½" (37 cm)*
Purplish head and breast; dark-tipped yellow bill, yellow legs; broad gray tail band; narrow white band on nape, absent on juvenile. Flocks in flight resemble Rock Doves but are uniform, not varied, in plumage and lack contrasting white rump and black band at end of tail. **Call** is a low *whoo-whoo.* **Range:** Locally common in low-altitude coniferous forests in the northwest, and oak or oak-conifer woodlands in the southwest; also increasingly common in suburban gardens, parks. Rare in Alaska; casual in eastern North America.

Red-billed Pigeon *Columba flavirostris L 14½" (37 cm)*
Dark overall, with a mainly red bill. Distinctive **call** heard in early spring and summer, a long, high-pitched *cooooo* followed by three loud *up-cup-a-coo's.* Perches in tall trees above a brushy understory; forages for seeds, nuts, figs. Seldom comes to the ground except to drink. **Range:** Uncommon, local, and declining in Texas; rare in winter.

White-crowned Pigeon *Columba leucocephala*
L 13½" (34 cm) **Range:** Flocks commute from nest colonies in coastal mangroves to feed inland on fruit. Most winter on Caribbean islands. A large, square-tailed pigeon of the Florida Everglades and Keys. Crown patch varies from shining white in **adult males** to grayish-white in most **females** and grayish-brown in juveniles Otherwise this species looks all-black; the iridescent collar is visible only in good light. **Calls** include a loud, deep *coo-cura-cooo* or *coo-croo.*

Rock Dove *Columba livia L 12½" (32 cm)*
The highly variable city pigeon; multicolored birds were developed over centuries of near domestication. The birds most closely resembling their wild ancestors have head and neck darker than back, black bars on inner wing, white rump, black band at end of tail. Flocks in flight show a variety of plumage patterns, unlike Band-tailed Pigeon. **Call** is a soft *coo-cuk-cuk-cuk-coooo.* **Range:** Rock Dove was introduced from Europe by early settlers, now widespread and common, particularly in urban settings. Nests and roosts chiefly on high window ledges, bridges, barns. Feeds during the day in parks and fields.

Band-tailed Pigeon

Red-billed Pigeon

White-crowned Pigeon

♂

♀

Rock Dove

color variations

Zenaida Dove *Zenaida aurita L 10" (25 cm)*
Range: Primarily West Indian species; now accidental on the Florida Keys (where it was reported as breeding by Audubon in 1832), and on southernmost Florida mainland. Distinguished from Mourning Dove by white on trailing edge of secondaries that shows as a square white spot on inner secondaries of folded wing; and by shorter, rounded, gray-tipped tail. Lacks white wing bars and tail tips of White-winged Dove. Feeds close to water. **Call,** similar to Mourning Dove's but faster. Generally shy.

Mourning Dove *Zenaida macroura L 12" (31 cm)*
Trim-bodied; long tail tapers to a point. Black spots on upperwing; pinkish wash below. In flight, shows white tips on outer tail feathers. **Juvenile** has heavy spotting; scaled effect on wings. **Call** is a mournful *oowoo-woo-woo-woo*. Wings produce a fluttering whistle as the bird takes flight. **Range:** Our most abundant and widespread dove, found in a wide variety of habitats.

Spotted Dove *Streptopelia chinensis L 12" (31 cm)*
Range: An Asian species introduced in Los Angeles in the early 1900s; now well established in southwestern California in suburban parks and gardens. Named for spotted collar, distinct in **adults,** obscured in **juveniles.** Wings and long, white-tipped tail are more rounded than in Mourning Dove; wings unmarked. **Calls** include a rather harsh c*oo-coo-croooo* and *coo-crrooo-coo,* with emphasis respectively on the last and middle notes.

Eurasian Collared-Dove *Streptopelia decaocto*
L 12½" (32 cm) Very pale gray-buff; black collar. Escapes of domesticated **Ringed Turtle-Dove,** "*S. risoria,*" an Old World species, may form small populations, but do not do well in the wild. Ringed Turtle-Dove is smaller, paler; has whitish undertail coverts, gray primaries; tail shorter, less black from below. Believed to derive from African Collared Dove, *S. roseogrisea.* **Range:** Eurasian species; introduced to Bahamas, spread to Florida. Common; spreading outside mapped range.

White-winged Dove *Zenaida asiatica L 11½" (29 cm)*
Large white wing patches and shorter, rounded tail distinguish this species from Mourning Dove. On sitting bird, wing patch shows only as a thin white line. Drawn-out, cooing **call,** *who-cooks-for-you,* has many variations. **Range:** Nests singly or in large colonies in dense mesquite, mature citrus groves, riparian woodlands, and saguaro-paloverde deserts; also found in desert towns. Casual mainly on east coast to the Maritime Provinces.

Oriental Turtle-Dove *Streptopelia orientalis*
L 13½" (24 cm) **Range:** Asian species; casual to western Aleutians and Bering Sea in spring and summer; accidental on Vancouver Island. Large and stocky; scaly pattern above due to buffy, gray, or reddish fringes on black feathers; black-and-white streaked patch on neck. North American records are nominate race *S. t. orientalis,* which is dark with gray rump and tail fringe.

Zenaida Dove

Eurasian-Collared

Ringed Turtle

Spotted

Mourning

Mourning Dove

♂ ♀

juvenile

Spotted Dove

Ringed Turtle-Dove

Eurasian Collared-Dove

juvenile

White-winged Dove

Oriental Turtle-Dove
orientalis

Common Ground-Dove *Columbina passerina*
L 6½" (17 cm) Very small, with pink at base of bill; scaled effect on head and breast; short tail, often raised. Plain scapulars; bright chestnut primaries and wing linings visible in flight. **Male** has a slate gray crown, pinkish-gray underparts. **Female** is grayer, more uniformly colored. **Call,** a repeated soft, ascending *wah-up*. **Range:** Forages on open ground in the east and brushy range-land in the west. Declining in Gulf coast region; casual as far north as New York and Oregon in fall and winter.

Ruddy Ground-Dove *Columbina talpacoti* L 6¾" (17 cm)
Range: Widespread in Latin America; casual from southern Texas to southern California. Dark bill; lacks scaling of Common Ground-Dove. **Male** of the subspecies *C.t.eluta* has a gray crown, rufous color on upperparts. **Female** is mainly gray-brown over-all. Both sexes show black on underwing coverts, black linear markings on scapulars. Most records in the U.S. are of west Mexican race *eluta;* some Texas records, however, are of east Mexican *rufipennis,* which is a richer cinnamon color overall.

Inca Dove *Columbina inca* L 8¼" (21 cm)
Plumage conspicuously scalloped. In flight, shows chestnut on wings like Common Ground-Dove, but note the Inca Dove's longer, white-edged tail. **Call,** a double *cooo-coo.* **Range:** Found usually near human habitations, often in parks and gardens. Casual wanderer north to North Dakota and Ontario.

White-tipped Dove *Leptotila verreauxi* L 11½" (29 cm)
This large, plump dove has a whitish forehead and throat and dark back. In flight, white tips show plainly on fanned tail. Low-pitched **call** is like the sound produced by blowing across the top of a bottle. Feeds on or near the ground, keeping close to wood-lands with dense understory.

Key West Quail-Dove *Geotrygon chrysia* L 12" (31 cm)
Range: West Indian species. Reported as breeding on Key West by Audubon in 1832. Population eliminated by about mid-19th century. Casual on the Florida Keys and south Florida. Larger and proportionately longer tailed than Ruddy Quail-Dove, with a white line under the eye. Upperparts, primaries, and tail are chestnut, glossed with purple and green. **Male** is highly irides-cent above; female is duller. Both sexes are whitish below.

Ruddy Quail-Dove *Geotrygon montana* L 9¾" (25 cm)
Range: A chunky tropical dove; five records for Florida and one for South Texas. **Male**'s primarily rich rufous upperparts and prominent buffy line under the eye are distinctive. **Females** are brown above; have a plainer facial pattern. In both sexes, under-parts are cinnamon-buff. Quail-doves are so named because they resemble quails and have a similar terrestrial lifestyle.

Common Ground-Dove ♂ ♀ ♂

Ruddy Ground-Dove
eluta ♀ ♂ ♂

Inca Dove

White-tipped Dove

Ruddy Quail-Dove ♂ ♀

Key West Quail-Dove ♂

Parakeets, Parrots (Family Psittacidae)

Most parrots in the wild in North America are descendants of escaped cage birds. We show species that have established populations, but others are seen, mostly in the south of California, Texas, and Florida.

White-winged Parakeet *Brotogeris versicolurus*
L 8¾" (22 cm) **Range:** From northern Amazon area. Small numbers established in south of Florida and California by 1960s, but have declined in recent years. Green body plumage; yellow greater secondary coverts; white inner primaries and outer secondaries.

Yellow-chevroned Parakeet *Brotogeris chiriri*
L 8¾" (22 cm) **Range:** From southern Amazon to northern Argentina. Now outnumbers White-winged in south of California and Florida. Once considered the same species, but note yellow-green body color; no white in primaries and secondaries.

Monk Parakeet *Myiopsitta monachus L 11½" (29 cm)*
Range: Species of temperate South America. The most widespread parrot in south Florida. Some also found in cities of northeast, midwest, Texas. Note extensive gray on face and underparts.

Dusky-headed Parakeet *Aratinga weddelli L 11" (28 cm)*
Range: From western Amazon basin. Small numbers established in Miami area. Gray head contrasts with white around eye and shiny black bill. Green below, shading to yellow on belly. In flight, dark flight feathers contrast with yellow-green wing linings.

Black-hooded Parakeet *Nandayus nenday*
L 13¾" (35 cm) **Range:** Southwest Brazil to north Argentina. Found Los Angeles area; established Pinellas County, Florida. Black on face, black bill, pale blue wash on breast, red thighs.

Green Parakeet *Aratinga holochlora L 13" (33 cm)*
Range: Mexican species; populations in towns in extreme southern Texas may include Mexican strays. Large, nearly all-green.

Blue-crowned Parakeet *Aratinga acuticaudata*
L 10" (25 cm) **Range:** South American species. Small numbers established on Key Biscayne and Key Largo, Florida, and in Los Angeles area. Blue face; bicolored bill; base of tail reddish below.

Mitred Parakeet *Aratinga mitrata L 13¾" (35 cm)*
Range: South American species. Numerous in Los Angeles area, a few in south Florida. Large, green, with white eye ring; red face, forehead, variable elsewhere on head; underwings yellow-olive.

Red-masked Parakeet *Aratinga erythrogenys*
L 13" (33 cm) **Range:** From southwest Ecuador and northwest Peru. In Los Angeles area, often associates with Mitred. Some also in Dade County, Florida. Similar to Mitred, but note red on leading edge of wing and underwing coverts, more red on head.

White-winged Parakeet

Yellow-chevroned Parakeet

Monk Parakeet

Black-hooded Parakeet

Dusky-headed Parakeet

Green Parakeet

Blue-crowned Parakeet

Mitred Parakeet

Red-masked Parakeet

Thick-billed Parrot *Rhynchopsitta pachyrhyncha*
L 16¼" (41 cm) **Range:** Declining species in northwest Mexico. Former sporadic visitor primarily to Chiricahua Mountains, Arizona; also neighboring ranges, including Animas Mountains, New Mexico. Last record in 1938. Releases into Chiricahuas in 1980s were unsuccessful. **Adult** green overall with red forehead, eyebrow, thighs, marginal coverts; tail long and pointed. Yellow underwing bar; slow, shallow wingbeats. Immature's bill paler, no red on eyebrow and wing. Loud, laughing **calls** carry far.

Rose-ringed Parakeet *Psittacula krameri*
L 15¾" (40 cm) **Range:** Small numbers of this Asian and African species are established in Miami and Los Angeles areas. Appear to be of Indian race, *P. k. manillensis.* Slender tail with very long central feathers; bright red upper mandible. **Adult males** show black, rose-edged collar. **Call** is a loud, flickerlike *kew.*

Red-crowned Parrot *Amazona viridigenalis*
L 13" (33 cm) **Range:** Native of northeast Mexico. Established in towns of southernmost Texas; some may be visitors from Mexico, but most or all are probably descendants of escaped cage birds. Also found in Los Angeles and Fort Lauderdale areas. Pale blue on sides of head, yellow eyes, yellowish band across tip of tail. **Adult male** has red crown; **female** and juvenile show less red. **Calls** generally raucous but include a mellow, rolling *rreeoo.*

Orange-winged Parrot *Amazona amazonica*
L 12¼" (31 cm) **Range:** South American species. Small numbers established in Miami area. Note blue stripe and nape on yellow head; orange at base of outer tail feathers.

Lilac-crowned Parrot *Amazona finschi* *L 13" (33 cm)*
Range: West Mexican species. Small numbers established in Los Angeles area; a few seen in south Texas and Florida. Like Red-crowned, but has lilac wash on crown and nape; maroon band across forehead; orange eye; longer tail has entirely green central tail feathers. **Calls** include a distinctive upslurred whistle.

Yellow-headed Parrot *Amazona oratrix L 14½" (37 cm)*
Range: Drastically declining species from Mexico and Belize. Small but declining numbers established in Los Angeles area; a few also in south Texas and Florida. Large, with yellow head; immature shows less yellow. Some escapes are of closely related Yellow-naped *(A. auropalliata)* and Yellow-crowned *(A. ochrocephala)* Parrots, formerly treated as subspecies of Yellow-headed.

Budgerigar *Melopsittacus undulatus L 7" (18 cm)*
Range: Australian species. Native birds green, as were populations established in southwest Florida in early 1960s; reached tens of thousands before 1980s. Only a few now present in Hernando and Pasco Counties, maybe due to competition for nest cavities with European Starling. Note barred upperparts and white wing stripe visible in flight. Escapes may be blue, white, or yellow.

Thick-billed Parrot

adult

adult

Rose-ringed Parakeet

♂

♀

♂

Red-crowned Parrot

♀

adult ♂

Orange-winged Parrot

Lilac-crowned Parrot

Budgerigar variants

Budgerigar

adults

Yellow-headed Parrot

Cuckoos, Roadrunners, Anis
(Family Cuculidae)

Of this large family, widespread in the Old World, only a few species are seen in North America. Most are slender and long-tailed; two toes point forward, two back.

Mangrove Cuckoo *Coccyzus minor L 12" (31 cm)*
Black mask and buffy underparts distinguish this species from other cuckoos. Upperparts grayish-brown; lacks rufous primaries of Yellow-billed Cuckoo. Black tail feathers are broadly tipped with white. In Florida subspecies, *C. m. maynardi*, paler throat and breast contrast with buffy flanks and belly. Underparts are entirely buffy in *continentalis*, an accidental vagrant along our Gulf coast from Mexico to northwest Florida. In all juveniles, mask is paler, tail pattern muted. Found chiefly in mangrove swamps. Like other cuckoos, perches quietly near center of tree. **Call** is a slow, guttural *gaw gaw gaw.*

Yellow-billed Cuckoo *Coccyzus americanus*
L 12" (31 cm) Grayish-brown above, white below; rufous primaries; lower mandible yellow. Undertail patterned in bold black and white. In **juvenile** plumage, held well into fall, tail has a much paler pattern and bill may show little or no yellow; may be confused with Black-billed Cuckoo. One **song** sounds hollow and wooden, a rapid staccato *kuk-kuk-kuk* that usually slows and descends to a *kakakowlp-kowlp* ending. **Range:** Common in open woods, orchards, and streamside willow and alder groves. Once numerous but now a rare breeder in California. Rare vagrant to the Maritimes during fall migration.

Black-billed Cuckoo *Coccyzus erythropthalmus*
L 12" (31 cm) Grayish-brown above, pale grayish below. Bill is usually all-dark. Lacks the rufous primaries of Yellow-billed Cuckoo. Note also reddish eye ring. Undertail patterned in gray with white tipping; compare juvenile Yellow-billed. **Juvenile** Black-billed has a buffy eye ring; undertail is paler; underparts may have buffy tinge, especially on undertail coverts; primaries may show a little rusty-brown. **Song** usually consists of monotonous *cu-cu-cu* or *cu-cu-cu-cu* phrases. **Range:** Uncommon to fairly common; found in woodlands and along streams. Very rare breeder in north Texas, west Tennessee, west Idaho.

Greater Roadrunner *Geococcyx californianus*
L 23" (58 cm) A large, ground-dwelling cuckoo streaked with brown and white. Note the long, heavy bill, conspicuous bushy crest, and long, white-edged tail. Short, rounded wings show a white crescent on the primaries. Eats insects, lizards, snakes, rodents, and small birds. **Song** is a dovelike cooing, descending in pitch. **Range:** Common in scrub desert and mesquite groves; less common in chaparral and open woodland.

continentalis

maynardi

**Mangrove
Cuckoo**

**Yellow-billed
Cuckoo**

juvenile

**Black-billed
Cuckoo**

juvenile

**Greater
Roadrunner**

Common Cuckoo *Cuculus canorus L 13" (33 cm)*

Range: Old World species, very rare spring and summer visitor to central and western Aleutians and Pribilofs. Closely resembles Oriental Cuckoo. **Adult male** and adult gray-morph female are gray above, paler below, with whitish belly narrowly barred with gray. In northeast Asian race *C. c. telephonus,* seen in Alaska, barring is often slightly narrower and underparts paler than in Oriental. Nominate European race is closer to Oriental. **Hepatic morph** (restricted to females in Common and Oriental Cuckoos) is pale rusty-brown above, heavily barred with black on back and tail; rump is paler than hepatic-morph Oriental and either unmarked or only lightly spotted. In flight, both species resemble small falcons. Male's **song** is the familiar *cuc-coo* for which the family is named but **call** is rarely heard in North America.

Oriental Cuckoo *Cuculus saturatus L 12½" (32 cm)*

Range: Eurasian species, casual in summer in western Aleutians and Pribilofs. **Adult male** and adult gray-morph female are darker gray above than Common Cuckoo, paler below, with pale belly barred in dark gray. Barring is often slightly broader, and lower belly and undertail covert region buffier than in Common Cuckoo. In the hand, underwing shows largely unmarked white feathering below the primary coverts that is barred in Common Cuckoo. **Hepatic-morph female** is rusty-brown above, heavily barred on back, rump, and tail. Oriental Cuckoo's **song,** a variable, hollow note often delivered four times, has not been heard here.

Smooth-billed Ani *Crotophaga ani L 14½" (37 cm)*

Bill size variable, but shape distinguishes both ani species from grackles (page 438). Black overall with iridescent bronze overtones. Long tail is often dipped and wagged. Found in brushy fields, scrublands; often feeds on insects stirred up by cattle. Both ani species are gregarious; several pairs usually share a nest and take turns incubating the eggs. **Call,** a whining, rising *quee-lick.* **Range:** Accidental north on east coast to North Carolina; also to Ohio. Has declined greatly in Florida.

Groove-billed Ani *Crotophaga sulcirostris L 13½" (34 cm)*

Bill is smaller than in Smooth-billed Ani; does not extend above crown. Plumage is black overall with iridescent purple and green overtones; long tail is often dipped and wagged. Grooves in bill are visible only at close range; these and call are distinctive. **Call** is a liquid *tee-ho,* accented on the first syllable. **Range:** Common in summer in woodlands. Casual north to Minnesota, west to California, and east to Virginia.

Common Cuckoo

hepatic morph ♀

hepatic morph ♀

♂

Oriental Cuckoo

hepatic morph ♀

hepatic ♀ morph

sunning

Smooth-billed Ani

Groove-billed Ani

Owls (Families Tytonidae and Strigidae)

These distinctive birds of prey are divided by structural differences into two families, the Barn Owls (Tytonidae) and the Typical Owls (Strigidae). All have immobile eyes in large heads. Fluffy plumage makes their flight nearly soundless. Many species hunt at night and roost during the day. To find an owl, search the ground for regurgitated pellets of fur and bone below a nest or roost. Listen for flocks of small songbirds noisily mobbing a roosting owl.

Barn Owl *Tyto alba L 16" (41 cm)*
A pale owl with dark eyes in a heart-shaped face. Rusty-brown above; underparts vary from white to cinnamon. Darkest birds are always **females,** palest birds **males.** Compare with Snowy Owl (next page). The Barn Owl roosts and nests in dark cavities in city and farm buildings, cliffs, trees. Typical **call** is a raspy, hissing screech. **Range:** Rare to uncommon in parts of western range, uncommon and declining in the east.

Short-eared Owl *Asio flammeus L 15" (38 cm)*
Tawny; boldly streaked on breast; belly paler, more lightly streaked. Ear tufts are barely visible. In flight, long wings show buffy patch above, black wrist mark below; these markings are usually more prominent than in Long-eared Owl. A bird of open country, marshes, tundra, weedy fields; nests on the ground. Flight is wavering, wingbeats erratic. During the day it roosts on the ground or on open, low perches: short poles, muskrat houses, duck blinds. Typical **call,** heard in breeding season and sometimes in winter, is a raspy, high barking. **Range:** Fairly common. Somewhat gregarious in winter; groups may gather where prey is abundant. Florida Short-eared Owls sighted on Florida Keys and Dry Tortugas are thought to have originated from West Indian populations.

Long-eared Owl *Asio otus L 15" (38 cm)*
A slender owl with long, close-set ear tufts. Boldly streaked and barred on breast and belly. Wings generally have a less prominent buffy patch and smaller black wrist mark than Short-eared Owl; facial disk is rusty. Lives in thick woods; hunts at night over open fields, marshes. By day it roosts in a tree, close to the trunk. Generally silent except in breeding season. Common **call** is one or more long *hooo's.* **Range:** Uncommon. More gregarious in winter; flocks may roost together.

Great Horned Owl *Bubo virginianus L 22" (56 cm)*
Size, bulky shape, and white throat separate this owl from the Long-eared Owl; ear tufts distinguish it from other large species. Nests in trees, caves, or on the ground. Chiefly nocturnal. Takes prey as large as skunks, grouse. **Call** is a series of three to eight loud, deep hoots, the second and third hoots often short and rapid. **Range:** Common; habitats vary from forest to city to open desert. Widespread interior race, *B. v. subarcticus,* is paler.

Barn Owl

Long-eared Owl

Short-eared Owl

Great Horned Owl

subarcticus

Barred Owl *Strix varia L 21" (53 cm)*
A chunky owl with dark eyes, dark barring on upper breast, dark streaking below. Chiefly nocturnal; daytime roost well hidden. Easily flushed; does not generally tolerate close approach. Distinctive **call** is a rhythmic series of loud hoots: *who-cooks-for-you, who-cooks-for-you-all;* also a drawn-out *hoo-ah,* sometimes preceded by an ascending agitated barking. Much more likely than other owls to be heard in daytime. **Range:** Common in dense coniferous or mixed woods of river bottoms and swamps; also in upland woods. Northwestern portion of range is expanding rapidly; now overlaps and has hybridized with similar Spotted Owl. May be very rare breeder in southeastern Alaska.

Great Gray Owl *Strix nebulosa L 27" (69 cm)*
Our largest owl. Heavily ringed facial disks make the yellow eyes look small. Lacks ear tufts. Hunts over forest clearings and nearby open country, chiefly by night but also at dawn and dusk; hunts by day during summer in northern part of range. **Call** is a series of deep, resonant *whoo's.* **Range:** Inhabits boreal forests and wooded bogs in the far north, dense coniferous forests with meadows in the mountains farther south. Generally uncommon; rare and irregular winter visitor to limit of dashed line on map.

Spotted Owl *Strix occidentalis L 17½" (45 cm)*
Large and dark-eyed, with white spotting on head, back, and underparts, rather than the barring and streaking of the similar Barred Owl. Tamer than Barred, with which it hybridizes. Strictly nocturnal. Main **call** is three doglike barks and cries; contact call, given mainly by females, is a hollow, upslurred whistle, *coooo-weep.* **Range:** Inhabits thickly wooded canyons, humid forests. Uncommon; decreasing in number and range due to habitat destruction, especially in the northwest. The threatened northern race, *S. o. caurina* (**T**), is the largest and darkest race, with smaller white spots.

Snowy Owl *Nyctea scandiaca L 23" (58 cm)*
Large white owl, with rounded head, yellow eyes. Dark bars and spots are heavier on females, heaviest on **immatures;** old males may be pure white. An owl of open tundra; nests on the ground; preys chiefly on lemmings, hunting by day as well as at night. **Range:** Retreats from northernmost part of range in winter; at least a few are seen annually to limit indicated by dashed line on map. In years when the lemming population plummets, Snowy Owls may wander in winter as far south as northern Alabama, Oklahoma, and central California. These irruptives, usually heavily barred younger birds, often perch conspicuously on the ground or on low stumps, fence posts, and buildings.

Barred
Owl

Great Gray
Owl

Spotted
Owl

Snowy
Owl

immature

Eastern Screech-Owl *Otus asio L 8½" (22 cm)*
All three owl species shown on this page are small, with yellow eyes and pale bill tip; bill base is yellow-green on Eastern and Whiskered Screech-Owls, and blackish or dark gray on Western. Ear tufts prominent if raised; when flattened, bird has a round-headed look. Underparts on all three are marked by vertical streaks crossed by dark bars: On Eastern, cross bars are spaced well apart and are nearly as wide as vertical streaks; on Western cross bars are closer together and much narrower; Whiskered is like Eastern, but markings have a bolder look. These markings are less distinct on the Eastern **red morph;** the latter predominates in the south, the **gray morph** on the Great Plains and in southernmost Texas. Lightest and whitest, the *O. a. maxwelliae* race is found in the northwestern part of the range. Eastern Screech-Owls are common in a wide variety of habitats: wood-lots, forests, swamps, orchards, parks, suburban gardens. Nocturnal; best located and identified by voice. Two typical **calls:** a series of quavering whistles, descending in pitch; and a long single trill, all on one pitch. **Range:** Formerly classified with Western Screech-Owl as one species; range separation is not yet fully known. Both species are found at Big Bend National Park in Texas: Western is uncommon, Eastern rare.

Western Screech-Owl *Otus kennicottii L 8½" (22 cm)*
Generally gray overall; some birds in the humid coastal northwest are brownish. Nocturnal; best located and identified by voice. Two common **calls:** a series of short whistles accelerating in tempo; and a short trill followed immediately by a longer trill. **Range:** Common in open woodlands, streamside groves, deserts, suburban areas, and parks. Where range overlaps that of Whiskered Screech-Owl, the Western Screech-Owl is generally found at lower elevations.

Whiskered Screech-Owl *Otus trichopsis L 7¼" (18 cm)*
Closely resembles gray Western Screech-Owl but slightly smaller with smaller feet and usually bolder cross barring, similar to Eastern. Identification best done by voice. Two common **calls:** a series of short whistles on one pitch and at a fairly even tempo; and a series of very irregular hoots, like Morse code. Nocturnal. **Range:** Inhabits dense oak and oak-conifer woodlands, at elevations from 4,000 to 6,000 feet, but mostly found around 5,000 feet. Generally at higher elevations than Western.

**Eastern
Screech-Owl**

red
morph

gray
morph

gray morph
juvenile

maxwelliae

northwest
coast
kennicottii

**Western
Screech-Owl**

**Whiskered
Screech-Owl**

Flammulated Owl *Otus flammeolus L 6¾" (17 cm)*

Dark eyes; small ear tufts, often indistinct; variegated red and gray plumage. Birds in the northwestern part of the range are the most finely marked; those in the Great Basin mountains are **grayish** and have the coarsest markings; and those in the southeast are **reddish.** Strictly nocturnal; nests and roosts in tree cavities, usually old woodpecker holes. Best located at night by its **call,** a series of single or paired low, hoarse, hollow hoots. **Range:** Common in oak and pine woodlands, especially ponderosa. Sometimes nests in loose colonies. Highly migratory. Accidental east to Louisiana and Florida. Rare in interior lowlands during migration.

Ferruginous Pygmy-Owl *Glaucidium brasilianum*

L 6¾" (17 cm) Long tail, reddish with dark or dusky bars. Upperparts gray-brown; crown faintly streaked. Eyes yellow; black nape spots look like eyes on the back of the head. White underparts streaked with reddish-brown. Unlike other North American owls, pygmy-owls fly with quick, unmuffled wingbeat. Chiefly diurnal; active any time of day. Roosts in crevices and cavities. Most common **call** is a rapid, repeated *took.* **Range:** Found at lower elevations than Northern Pygmy-Owl. Inhabits saguaro deserts, and woodlands north to near Kingsville, Texas. Rare in Arizona.

Elf Owl *Micrathene whitneyi L 5¾" (15 cm)*

Our smallest owl. Yellow eyes; very short tail. Lacks ear tufts. Strictly nocturnal; roosts and nests in cavities in saguaros and trees. **Call** is an irregular series of high *churp's* and chattering notes. **Range:** Common in desert lowlands and in canyons, especially among oaks and sycamores; fairly common in foothills. Now almost eliminated in California. Casual in winter in southernmost Texas.

Northern Pygmy-Owl *Glaucidium gnoma L 6¾" (17 cm)*

Long tail, dark brown with pale bars. Upperparts are either rusty-brown or gray-brown; crown spotted; underparts white with dark streaks. Eyes yellow; black nape spots look like eyes on the back of the head. The grayest birds are to be found in the **Rockies;** those on the **Pacific coast** as far north as British Columbia are browner. Inhabits dense woodlands in foothills and mountains. Chiefly diurnal; most active at dawn and dusk. Nests in cavities. **Call** is a mellow, whistled, *hoo* or *hoo hoo,* repeated in a well-spaced series; also gives a rapid series of *hoo* or *took* notes followed by a single *took.* An aggressive predator, sometimes catching birds larger than itself, this owl is a favorite target for songbirds. Birders may locate the owl by watching for mobbing songbirds. Nominate race, *G. g. gnoma,* seen from southeastern Arizona south through the mountains of Mexico, gives a series of double *took-took* notes with occasional single notes interspersed. Thought by some to be a separate species "Mountain Pygmy-Owl."

reddish type

Flammulated Owl

grayish type

Ferruginous Pygmy-Owl

Elf Owl

Northern Pygmy-Owl

Rockies type

Pacific coast type

256 OWLS

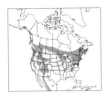

Northern Saw-whet Owl *Aegolius acadicus L 8" (20 cm)*
Reddish-brown above; white below with reddish streaks; bill dark; facial disks reddish, without dark border. **Juvenile** strongly reddish above, tawny-rust below. **Call,** heard primarily in breeding season from late winter to late spring, is a monotonously repeated single-note whistle; another, raspy call sounds like a saw being sharpened. Strictly nocturnal; roosts during day in or near nest hole in breeding season. In winter, preferred roost is in dense evergreens, usually close to end of branch. Large concentrations of regurgitated pellets and white "wash" build up below favored winter roosts. Once found, this species can be closely approached. **Range:** Northern Saw-whet Owls inhabit dense coniferous or mixed forests, wooded swamps, tamarack bogs. Very rare over most of winter range. A distinctive subspecies, *A. a. brooksi,* endemic to Queen Charlotte Islands, Canada, is much darker and buffier on facial disks and belly.

Northern Hawk Owl *Surnia ulula L 16" (41 cm)*
Long tail, falcon-like profile, and black-bordered facial disks identify this owl of the northern forests. Underparts are barred with brown. Flight is low and swift; sometimes hunts during daylight as well as at night. Is most often seen, however, perched high in a spruce tree. Usually can be closely approached. **Range:** Basically nonmigratory, but retreats slightly in winter from northernmost part of range. Vagrants are seen, but very rare, south of mapped range.

Boreal Owl *Aegolius funereus L 10" (25 cm)*
White underparts streaked with chocolate brown. Whitish facial disk has a distinct black border; bill is pale. Darker above than Northern Saw-whet Owl. **Juvenile** is chocolate brown below. Boreal Owls are strictly nocturnal; roost during daylight in dense cover, usually close to tree trunk. **Call,** heard primarily in breeding season from late winter to mid-spring, is a short, rapid series of hollow *hoo* notes. **Range:** Inhabit dense northern forests and muskeg. Irruptive, usually in small numbers; otherwise seldom seen south of mapped range, but this may be due to difficulty of locating them. Breed at isolated locations high in the Rockies.

Burrowing Owl *Athene cunicularia L 9½" (24 cm)*
Long legs distinguish this ground dweller from all other small owls. **Adult** is boldly spotted and barred. **Juvenile** is buffy below. An owl of open country, golf courses, airports. Nests in single pairs or small colonies. Nocturnal; flight low and undulating; often hovers like a kestrel. Perches conspicuously during daylight at entrance to burrow nest or on low post. **Calls** include a soft *coo-coooo* and a chattering series of *chack* notes. Disturbed in its nest, the Burrowing Owl often gives an alarm call that imitates the sound of a rattlesnake. **Range:** Casual vagrant in spring and fall to east coast, north to Maine. Declining in much of northern Great Plains; may be partly due to destruction of prairie dog towns, which it frequents, by agricultural growth. Florida birds are darker above with more whitish spotting; less buffy below.

Northern Saw-whet Owl

juvenile

Northern Hawk Owl

Boreal Owl

juvenile

Burrowing Owl
western *hypugaea*

juvenile

Nighthawks, Nightjars
(Family Caprimulgidae)

Wide mouths help these night-hunters snare flying insects. Most species are best located and identified by their distinctive calls.

Lesser Nighthawk *Chordeiles acutipennis* *L 8½" (22 cm)*
Resembles Common Nighthawk but wings are shorter and usually more rounded; whitish bar across primaries slightly closer to tip. Upperparts paler and more uniformly mottled. Throat is white in **males**, usually buffy in **females** and juveniles. Underparts buffy, with faint barring. Male has white tail band. Female lacks tail band; note buffy wing bar and markings at base of primaries, often indistinct in juvenile female. Juvenile male's wing bar much smaller. Distinctive **call**, a rapid, tremulous trill, heard only on breeding grounds. Seen chiefly around dusk. Flies with a fluttery wingbeat. **Range:** Fairly common; found in dry, open country, scrubland, desert. Very rare spring and fall migrant on Gulf coast. Casual in winter in southern California, Texas, Florida.

Common Nighthawk *Chordeiles minor* *L 9½" (24 cm)*
Wings long and pointed; tail slightly forked. Bold white bar across primaries slightly farther from wing tip than in Lesser Nighthawk. Subspecies range from dark brown in eastern birds to gray in the northern Great Plains race, *C. m. sennetti;* color variations are subtle in adults, distinct in juveniles. Pale spotting on wing coverts contrasts with darker back. Throat white in **male,** buffy in **female;** underparts whitish, with bold dusky bars. Female lacks white tail band. **Juvenile** shows less white on throat. In courtship display, male's wings make a hollow booming sound. Nasal *peent* **call** distinguishes Common from Lesser and Antillean Nighthawks. **Range:** Seen in woodlands, suburbs, towns; more active in daylight than nightjars. Roosts on the ground, on branches, posts, roofs. Fairly common over parts of range, but declining in east where generally uncommon and local.

Antillean Nighthawk *Chordeiles gundlachii*
L 8" (20 cm) **Range:** Rare but regular in summer on Florida Keys; also seen on Dry Tortugas and southeast Florida mainland. Accidental to Louisiana; Outer Banks, North Carolina. Wings are long, pointed; tail slightly forked. Females, juveniles lack white tail band. Very difficult to distinguish from variable Common Nighthawk. **Call,** a varying *pity-pit-pit,* best identifies Antillean.

Common Pauraque *Nyctidromus albicollis* *L 11" (28 cm)*
In flight, long, rounded tail separates it from nighthawks; also shorter, rounder wings. Broad white bands on wings distinguish it from other nightjars (next page). White tail patches conspicuous on **male,** smaller and often buffy on **female.** In close view, note chestnut ear patch. Common in woodland clearings and scrub. Seen just before dawn and after dusk. Flies close to the ground; often lands on roads or roadsides. Distinctive **song,** one or more low *pur* notes followed by a higher, descending *wheeer.*

Lesser
Nighthawk

Common
Nighthawk

Juvenile
annetti

Antillean
Nighthawk

Common
Pauraque

Chuck-will's-widow *Caprimulgus carolinensis*

L 12" (31 cm) Our largest nightjar. Mottled buff-brown overall; wings rounded; tail long and rounded. Loud, whistling **song** sounds like *chuck-will's-widow*, the first note often inaudible. Much larger and redder than Whip-poor-will; buff-brown throat and whitish necklace contrast with dark breast. **Male**'s tail has less white than in male Whip-poor-will; tips of outer feathers are buff. **Female**'s tail lacks white. This species is shy; not usually approachable even when roosting during the day. Unlike eastern Whip-poor-will, birds will flush when disturbed. **Range:** Fairly common but local in oak-pine woodlands, live oak groves.

Whip-poor-will *Caprimulgus vociferus L 9¾" (25 cm)*

Mottled gray-brown overall; wings rounded; tail long, rounded. **Song** is a loud *whip-poor-will*, clear and mellow in eastern birds, with accent on first and last syllables; rough and burry in southwestern race *C. v. arizonae* (probably a separate species), with strongest accent on last syllable. Whip-poor-will is much smaller and grayer than Chuck-will's-widow; dark throat contrasts with white or buffy necklace and pale underparts. **Male**'s tail shows much more white than in male Chuck-will's-widow, especially with eastern nominate race. **Female**'s tail has contrasting pale tip on dark outer feathers. Unlike Chuck-will's-widow, members of the eastern race are tame; sitting birds will habitually stay put during daylight hours. **Range:** Fairly common but local in open coniferous and mixed woodlands in the east, wooded canyons in the southwest. Breeds very locally in southern California.

Buff-collared Nightjar *Caprimulgus ridgwayi*

L 8¾" (22 cm) **Range:** Rare, irregular, and local in desert canyons of extreme southwestern New Mexico and southeastern Arizona. Accidental in southern California. Usually roosts on the ground by day. Gray-brown plumage resembles Whip-poor-will, but is lighter and more finely marked; shows distinct buff collar across nape. **Song** is an accelerating series of *cuk* notes ending with *cukacheea*.

Common Poorwill *Phalaenoptilus nuttallii L 7¾" (20 cm)*

Our smallest nightjar, distinguished by short, rounded tail and short, rounded wings. Outer tail feathers are tipped with white, more boldly in **males** than in females. **Song** is a whistled *poorwill*, with a final *ip* note audible at close range. Plumage is variable; upperparts range from brownish-gray to pale gray. Broad white band crosses dark throat and breast. **Range:** Fairly common in sagebrush and on chaparral slopes; often seen on roads or roadsides after dusk or before dawn. Roosts on the ground; flies up a short distance to catch an insect, then returns to the same or a nearby location. Known to hibernate in cold weather; may winter north into normal breeding range.

Chuck-will's-widow

♂

♀

Whip-poor-will
eastern *vociferus*

♂

vociferus ♀

vociferus ♂

♀

southwestern
arizonae ♂

**Buff-collared
Nightjar**

♂

**Common
Poorwill**

♂

Swifts (Family Apodidae)

These fast-flying birds spend most of the day aloft, feeding on insects. Long wings bend closer to the body than those of similar swallows.

Black Swift *Cypseloides niger* L 7¼" (18 cm)
Blackish overall; long, slightly forked tail, often fanned in flight. Nests in colonies on cliffs, beneath waterfalls; also on wet sea cliffs. Wingbeats rather more leisurely than in other swifts; often soars. **Range:** Uncommon. Thought to winter in South America.

Vaux's Swift *Chaetura vauxi* L 4¾" (12 cm)
Smaller than Chimney Swift; usually paler below and on rump; soars less. **Call** softer, higher, more insectlike. Nests in hollow trees. **Range:** Fairly common in woodlands near water. Rare in winter in southern California; casual on Gulf coast.

Chimney Swift *Chaetura pelagica* L 5¼" (13 cm)
Cigar-shaped body; short, stubby tail. Chimney Swift is larger than similar Vaux's Swift; usually darker below; wings longer; has louder, chattering **call** and greater tendency to soar. Both species give a rocking display: Wings upraised, bird rocks from side to side. Nests in chimneys, barns, hollow trees. **Range:** Rare in southern California. No winter records in the U.S.

Common Swift *Apus apus* L 6½" (17 cm)
Range: Breeds in Palearctic; winters in Africa. Accidental in summer on Pribilofs and Miquelon Island off Newfoundland; records from Bermuda and probably the northeast. Long, thin-winged, dark, with paler throat, long forked tail. Pribilofs specimen of eastern race *A. a. pekinensis* (illustrated) is paler than nominate.

White-collared Swift *Streptoprocne zonaris*
L 8½" (22 cm) **Range:** Tropical species, accidental at scattered coastal locations in the United States. A very large, black swift; note white collar, more indistinct in **immatures,** and slightly forked tail. Soars with wings bent down.

White-throated Swift *Aeronautes saxatalis*
L 6½" (17 cm) Black above, black-and-white below, with long, forked tail. Distinguished from Violet-green Swallow (page 322) by longer, narrower wings, bicolored underparts. In poor light, may be mistaken for Black Swift but is smaller, with faster wingbeats. Common in mountains, canyons, cliffs. Nests in crevices.

White-throated Needletail *Hirundapus caudacutus*
L 8" (21 cm) **Range:** Large Asian swift, casual in spring on outer Aleutians. Dark overall, with pale patch on back; white throat and undertail coverts. Tail short, stubby.

Fork-tailed Swift *Apus pacificus* L 7¾" (20 cm)
Range: Asian species, casual on western Aleutians and Pribilofs. Note white rump; long tail's deep fork not always apparent.

Black
Swift

juvenile

Vaux's
Swift

Chimney
Swift

White-collared
Swift

White-throated
Swift

soaring

Common
Swift

immature

soaring

Fork-tailed
Swift

White-throated
Needletail

264

Hummingbirds (Family Trochilidae)

These birds hover at flowers to sip nectar with needlelike bills. Often identified by twittery calls or chattering "chase notes" when driving off intruders. Males' throat feathers (gorget) look black in poor light.

Green Violet-ear *Colibri thalassinus* L 4¾" (12 cm)
Range: Tropical species. Most records in summer in the Hill Country in Texas; casual in eastern North America. Green overall; bill slightly downcurved. **Male** has blue-violet patches on face and breast. Female and **immature** slightly duller, immature grayer on belly. **Song** is a repeated *tsip-tsup*.

Green-breasted Mango *Anthracothorax prevostii*
L 4¾" (12 cm) **Range:** Found from eastern Mexico to northern South America. Casual in fall and winter to south Texas. Has curved bill and purplish color in outer tail feathers. **Male** is deep green overall. **Female** shows broad blackish-green stripe on underparts bordered in white. **Immature** is similar to female but shows cinnamon border to sides of underparts.

Buff-bellied Hummingbird *Amazilia yucatanensis*
L 4¼" (11 cm) Green overall with buff belly and chestnut tail; bill pinkish-red with black tip. **Calls** are shrill and squeaky. **Range:** Mexican species, fairly common in lower Rio Grande Valley. Very rare in winter along Gulf coast; casual to Florida.

Berylline Hummingbird *Amazilia beryllina* L 4¼" (11 cm)
Range: Very rare summer visitor from Mexico to mountains of southeastern Arizona; has bred there. Green above and below, with chestnut wings, rump, and tail. Base of lower mandible red. **Male**'s lower belly is chestnut, **female**'s grayish.

Bahama Woodstar *Calliphlox evelynae* L 3¾" (10 cm)
Range: Four records of five birds from southeast Florida. **Adult male** has broad white collar, light purple throat, and long, forked tail; mixed olive and rich buff below. In **female** note tail projection past primary tips, cinnamon tips to outer tail feathers, and slightly curved bill. **Immature male** gradually acquires purple throat. **Calls** are suggestive of Anna's Hummingbird.

Violet-crowned Hummingbird *Amazilia violiceps*
L 4½" (11 cm) Crown violet; underparts entirely white; upperparts bronze green; tail greenish. Long bill is mostly red. **Call** is a loud chattering; male's **song** is a series of sibilant *ts* notes. **Range:** Uncommon. Casual in California and west Texas.

Lucifer Hummingbird *Calothorax lucifer* L 3½" (9 cm)
Bill downcurved. **Male** has green crown, purple throat, long tail. **Female** is rich buff below, belly often whitish, tail rounded; outer tail feathers reddish at base, tipped with white. **Immature male** shows purple spotting on throat by late summer. **Range:** Uncommon; rare in southeast Arizona and southwest New Mexico.

Green Violet-ear

immature

♂

Green-breasted Mango

immature

♂

♀

Buff-bellied Hummingbird

Berylline Hummingbird

♂

♀

♂

Bahama Woodstar

♂

immature ♂

♀

♀

Lucifer Hummingbird

♂

♀

♂

Violet-crowned Hummingbird

♀

immature ♂

Broad-billed Hummingbird *Cynanthus latirostris*

L 4" (10 cm) **Adult male** is dark green above and below, with white undertail coverts, blue gorget, and mostly red bill. Broad, forked tail is blackish-blue. **Adult female** is duller above, gray below; often shows a narrow white eye stripe; tail is square-tipped. Juveniles resemble female; by late summer, male begins to show blue and green flecks on throat, green on sides; dark, forked tail helps distinguish it from White-eared Hummingbird. Chattering *je-dit* **call** is similar to Ruby-crowned Kinglet. Male's display call is a whining *zing*. **Range:** Common in desert canyons, low mountain woodlands. Very rare in southern California during fall and winter; casual in Texas and Louisiana.

White-eared Hummingbird *Hylocharis leucotis*

L 3¾" (10 cm) **Range:** Summer visitor to mountains of southwest: rare in southeastern Arizona; very rare in southwest New Mexico, west Texas. Bill shorter than in Broad-billed Hummingbird; broad white stripe extends back from eye; has black ear patch; square tail. **Adult male** has dark purple crown and chin, emerald green gorget; display **call** is a repeated, silvery *tink tink tink*. Chattering calls are loud and metallic.

Blue-throated Hummingbird *Lampornis clemenciae*

L 5" (13 cm) **Adult male**'s throat is blue, **female**'s gray. Broad white eye stripe and faint white malar stripe border dark ear patch. Tail has broad white tips on outer feathers; compare female Magnificent Hummingbird. Male's **call** is a loud, high, repeated *seep*. **Range:** Fairly common; found in mountain canyons, especially near streams. Casual north of mapped range.

Xantus's Hummingbird *Hylocharis xantusii*

L 3½" (9 cm) **Range:** Endemic to southern Baja California, Mexico. Accidental vagrant to southern California and southwest British Columbia. Plumages and **calls** similar to White-eared Hummingbird, but note buff on underparts and rufous in tail; male has black forehead and ear patches.

Magnificent Hummingbird *Eugenes fulgens*

L 5¼" (13 cm) **Adult male** is green above, with purple crown; metallic green throat; breast and upper belly black and green; lower belly dull brown. Tail is dark green and deeply notched. **Female** is duller, lacks purple crown; squarish tail has small, grayish-white tips on outer feathers; compare with female Blue-throated Hummingbird, which has stronger eyebrow. Main **call** is a sharp *chip*. **Range:** Fairly common in high mountain meadows and canyons. Casual north of mapped range.

Plain-capped Starthroat *Heliomaster constantii*

L 5" (13 cm) **Range:** Casual stray in summer and fall from Mexico to arid foothills and deserts of southeastern Arizona. Broad white malar stripe, white eye stripe, and white patches on sides of rump are conspicuous. Throat shows variable amount of red; note also very long bill. **Call** is a sharp *chip*.

Broad-billed Hummingbird ♀

immature ♂

♂

White-eared Hummingbird ♀

♂

♂

Blue-throated Hummingbird ♀

♂

♀ **Xantus's Hummingbird** ♂

♀

Magnificent Hummingbird ♂

Plain-capped Starthroat

Ruby-throated Hummingbird *Archilochus colubris*
L 3¾" *(10 cm)* The only hummingbird regularly seen over most of the east. Metallic green above. **Adult male** has a brilliant red throat and black chin; underparts are whitish; sides and flanks dusky green; tail forked. **Female**'s throat is whitish; underparts grayish-white, with buffy wash on sides; tail is similar to female Black-chinned Hummingbird. Immatures resemble adult female. Unlike Black-chinned, some **immature males** have a golden cast on upperparts; others begin to show red spotting on throat by early fall. As with all hummingbirds, adult males migrate much earlier than females and immatures. Ruby-throated Hummingbirds are fairly common in parts of range; found in gardens and woodland edges. *Archilochus* hummingbirds seen in the southeast in winter are more likely to be Black-chinned, but females and immatures of these two species are almost indistinguishable. Ruby-throated generally has a greener crown, shorter bill; note more pointed shape of darker primaries, especially outermost. **Calls** very similar. **Range:** Casual west to California.

Black-chinned Hummingbird *Archilochus alexandri*
L 3¾" *(10 cm)* Metallic green above. In good light, **male** shows violet band at lower border of black throat. Underparts whitish; sides and flanks dusky-green. **Female**'s throat can be all-white or show faint dusky or greenish streaks. Immatures resemble adult female; **immature male** may begin to show violet on lower throat in the fall. **Call** is a soft *tchew;* chase note combines high squeals and *tchew* notes. Twitches tail more than Ruby-throated while feeding. **Range:** Common in lowlands and low mountains. A few Black-chinned Hummingbirds winter in southeast.

Costa's Hummingbird *Calypte costae* L 3½" *(9 cm)*
Male has deep violet crown and gorget extending far down sides of neck. **Female** is generally grayer above, whiter below, than female Black-chinned Hummingbird; note also tail differences. Best distinguished by voice. **Call** is a high, metallic *tink,* often given in a series. Male's call is a loud *zing.* **Range:** Fairly common in desert washes, dry chaparral. Casual north to south coastal Alaska and east to west Texas.

Anna's Hummingbird *Calypte anna* L 4" *(10 cm)*
Male's head and throat are deep rose red, the color extending a short distance onto sides of neck. **Female**'s throat usually shows red flecks, often forming a patch of color. In both sexes, underparts are grayish, washed with a varying amount of green. Bill is proportionately short. Immatures resemble female; **immature male** usually shows some red on crown. **Juveniles** lack red on throat; compare with smaller female Black-chinned and Costa's Hummingbirds. Common **call** note, a sharp *chick;* chase call is a rapid dry rattling. Male's **song** is a jumble of high squeaks and raspy notes. **Range:** Abundant in coastal lowlands, mountains; also in deserts, especially in winter. Casual north to south coastal Alaska and in eastern North America.

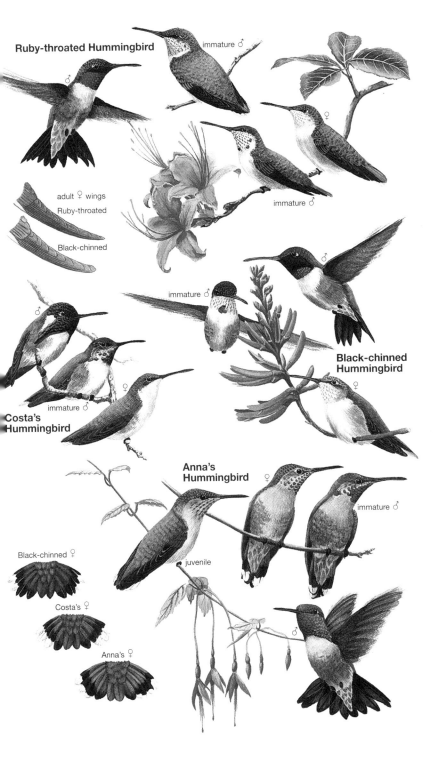

Ruby-throated Hummingbird

immature ♂

♂

♀

adult ♀ wings
Ruby-throated

Black-chinned

immature ♂

**Black-chinned
Hummingbird**

immature ♂

♂

♀

**Costa's
Hummingbird**

♂

immature ♂

♀

**Anna's
Hummingbird**

♀

immature ♂

Black-chinned ♀

Costa's ♀

Anna's ♀

juvenile

♂

Broad-tailed Hummingbird *Selasphorus platycercus*

L 4" (10 cm) Except during winter molt, all *Selasphorus* **adult males'** wingbeats produce a loud whistle, harsh and trilling in Broad-tailed. Male has rose red throat; white underparts with green sides. **Female** has blended buff on underparts; similar to female Calliope, but note tail tip extends well past primaries. **Calls** include a metallic *chip*, often given in a short series. Summers in mountains. **Range:** Casual fall and winter to Gulf coast.

Calliope Hummingbird *Stellula calliope* L 3¼" (8 cm)

Smallest North American bird; very short bill and tail; primary tips extend well past end of tail. Carmine streaks on **male**'s throat form a V-shaped gorget. **Female**'s underparts similar to female Broad-tailed. Immature male like female but shows some red on throat by late summer. Relatively silent. **Range:** Common; summers in mountains. Very rare in southeast in fall and winter.

Rufous Hummingbird *Selasphorus rufus* L 3¾" (10 cm)

Tail mainly rufous. **Adult male** has rufous back, sometimes marked with green, very rarely entirely green; orange-red gorget. **Immatures** resemble **adult female**; immature male may show reddish-brown back by winter before acquiring full gorget. Buzzy wing whistle and all **calls** identical to Allen's: Calls include a sibilant *chip*, often given in a series; chase note, *zeee-chuppity-chup*. **Range:** Rare in fall over much of the east.

Allen's Hummingbird *Selasphorus sasin* L 3¾" (10 cm)

Wing whistle and **calls** are identical to Rufous. **Adult male** has full, orange-red gorget; usually distinguishable from Rufous by solid green back. Adult female and immatures inseparable in the field from female Rufous, though tail feathers are comparatively narrower for each sex and age class. **Range:** Allen's migrates earlier in fall and spring than Rufous. Casual vagrant to eastern U.S.

Trogons (Family Trogonidae)

These highly colored tropical birds have short, broad bills.

Elegant Trogon *Trogon elegans* L 12½" (32 cm)

Yellow bill, white breast band; undertail delicately barred. **Male** is bright green above and has bright red belly. **Female** and juvenile are browner and duller. **Song** is a series of croaking *co-ah* notes. **Range:** Found in streamside woodlands, mostly at altitudes from 4,000 to 6,000 feet. Casual in southernmost Texas.

Eared Trogon *Euptilotis neoxenus* L 14" (36 cm)

Range: Casual in mountain streamside woodlands of southeastern Arizona. Wary. Larger and thicker-bodied than Elegant Trogon; bill is black or gray; lacks white breast band and barring on undertail. **Calls** include a loud upslurred squeal ending in a *chuck* note; also a loud, hard cackling. Male's **song** is a long, quavering series of whistled notes that increase in volume.

Broad-tailed Hummingbird

Calliope Hummingbird

♂

♀

Rufous Hummingbird

♀

♂

immature ♂

green-flecked ♂

♂

Allen's Hummingbird

Broad-tailed ♀   Rufous ♀   Allen's ♀   Calliope ♀

Eared Trogon

Elegant Trogan

♀

♂

♀

♂

♂

♀

Kingfishers (Family Alcedinidae)

Stocky and short-legged, with a large head, a large bill, and, in two North American species, a ragged crest. Look for kingfishers near woodland streams and ponds and in coastal areas. They hover over water or watch from low perches, then plunge headfirst to catch a fish. With strong bill and feet they also dig nest burrows in stream banks.

Belted Kingfisher *Ceryle alcyon L 13" (33 cm)*
The only kingfisher in most of North America. Both **male** and **female** have slate blue breast band, white belly and undertail coverts. Female has rust belly band and flanks, may be confused with female Ringed Kingfisher; note white belly and smaller size. Juvenile resembles adult but has rust spotting in breast band. **Call** is a loud, dry rattle. **Range:** Common and conspicuous along rivers and brooks, ponds and lakes, estuaries. Generally solitary. Rare in winter north into summer range.

Ringed Kingfisher *Ceryle torquata L 16" (41 cm)*
Larger than Belted Kingfisher; generally frequents larger rivers and ponds, perches on higher branches than Belted. Rufous underwing coverts of **female** distinctive in flight; white in **male.** Male is rust below with white undertail coverts. Female has slate blue breast, narrow white band, rust belly and undertail coverts. Juveniles resemble adult female, but juvenile male's breast is largely rust. **Calls** include a harsh rattle, lower and slower than in Belted Kingfisher, and single *chack* notes, given chiefly in flight. **Range:** Resident in lower Rio Grande Valley; casual elsewhere in southern Texas.

Green Kingfisher *Chloroceryle americana L 8¾" (22 cm)*
Smallest of our kingfishers; crest inconspicuous. **Male** is green above, with white collar; white below, with dark green spotting. **Female** has a band of green spots. Juvenile resembles adult female. One **call,** a faint but sharp *tick tick,* often ends in a short rattle; another, a squeaky *cheep,* is given in flight. Often perches on low, sheltered branches. Flight is direct and very fast; white outer tail feathers conspicuous in flight. **Range:** Uncommon and often hard to see. Resident of lower Rio Grande Valley; rarer on Edwards Plateau. Casual wanderer along the Texas coast; also to Big Bend region. In southeastern Arizona, a few pairs are resident along San Pedro River; also occasionally seen on Santa Cruz River near Nogales.

Belted Kingfisher

♀

♂

♂

Ringed Kingfisher

♂

♀

Green Kingfisher

♂

♀

Woodpeckers (Family Picidae)

Strong claws, short legs, and stiff tail feathers enable woodpeckers to climb tree trunks. Sharp bill is used to chisel out insect food and nest holes, and to drum a territorial signal to rivals.

Red-headed Woodpecker Melanerpes erythrocephalus
L 9¼" (24 cm) Entire head, neck, and throat are bright red in **adults,** contrasting with blue-black back and snowy white underparts. **Juvenile** is brownish; acquires red head during gradual winter molt. Distinctive white inner wing patches and white rump are visible in all ages in perched and flying birds. In breeding season utters a loud *queark,* similar to Red-bellied Woodpecker (next page) but harsher and sharper; common **call** a gutteral rattle. Inhabits a variety of open and densely wooded habitats; often seen fly-catching. **Range:** Now vagrant in New England, chiefly in fall; no longer breeds there, due in part to habitat loss and competition with Starlings for nest holes. Casual outside mapped range in west.

Acorn Woodpecker Melanerpes formicivorus
L 9" (23 cm) Black chin, yellowish throat, white cheeks and forehead, red cap. **Female** has smaller bill than **male,** less red on crown. In flight, white rump and small white patches on outer wings are conspicuous. Most frequent **call,** *waka,* usually repeated several times. Common in oak woods or pine forests where oak trees are abundant. Sociable; generally found in small, noisy colonies. Eats chiefly acorns and other nuts in winter, insects in summer. In the fall, is sometimes seen drilling small holes in a tree trunk and pounding a nut into each hole for a winter food supply. Colonies use the same "granary tree" year after year.

White-headed Woodpecker Picoides albolarvatus
L 9¼" (24 cm) Head and throat white. **Male** has a red patch on back of head. Body is black except for white wing patches. Juveniles have a variable patch of pale red on crown. **Calls** include a sharp *pee-dink* or *pee-dee-dink.* **Range:** Nests in coniferous mountain forests, especially ponderosa and sugar pine; feeds primarily on seeds from their cones; also pries away loose bark in search of insects and larvae. Casual at lower altitudes in winter. Fairly common over most of range; rare and local in the north.

Lewis's Woodpecker Melanerpes lewis L 10¾" (27 cm)
Greenish-black head and back; gray collar and breast; dark red face, pinkish belly. In flight, darkness, large size, and slow, steady wingbeats give it a crowlike appearance. **Juvenile** lacks collar and red face; belly may be only faintly pink; acquires more adultlike plumage from late fall through winter. Main food, insects, mostly caught in the air; also eats fruit, nuts. Stores acorns, which it first shells, in tree bark crevices. Generally silent. **Range:** Uncommon to fairly common in open woodlands of interior; rare on coast. Often gregarious; fall and winter movements unpredictable. Largely eliminated in coastal northwest; accidental in east.

Red-headed Woodpecker

juvenile

adults

♂

♀

♂

Acorn Woodpecker

White-headed Woodpecker

♂

♀

juvenile

Lewis's Woodpecker

adults

Golden-fronted Woodpecker *Melanerpes aurifrons*

L 9¾" (25 cm) Black-and-white barred back, white rump, usually an all-black tail; golden orange nape, paler in **females;** yellow feathering above bill. **Male** has a small red cap. Yellow tinge
on belly not easily seen. Juvenile has streaked breast, brownish
crown. In flight, all plumages show white wing patches, white
rump as in Red-bellied and Gila Woodpeckers; unlike them,
Golden-fronted shows black, not barred, tail. **Calls,** a rolling
churr-churr and cackling *kek-kek,* are slightly louder and raspier
than in Red-bellied. **Range:** Fairly common in dry woodlands,
pecan groves, mesquite brushlands.

Red-bellied Woodpecker *Melanerpes carolinus*

L 9¼" (24 cm) Black-and-white barred back; white uppertail
coverts; central tail feathers barred; small reddish patch or tinge
on belly. Crown and nape are red in **males. Females** have red
nape only. **Call,** a rolling *churr* or *chiv-chiv,* is slightly softer than
that of Golden-fronted. **Range:** Red-bellied Woodpeckers are
common in open woodlands, suburbs, parks. Are extending
breeding range northward. Rare to Maine and Maritimes.

Gila Woodpecker *Melanerpes uropygialis* L 9¼" (24 cm)

Black-and-white barred back and rump; central tail feathers
barred. **Male** has a small red cap. **Calls,** a rolling *churr* and a loud,
sharp, high-pitched *yip,* often given in a series. **Range:** Inhabits
towns, scrub desert, cactus country, streamside woods.

Northern Flicker *Colaptes auratus* L 12½" (32 cm)

Two distinct groups occur: "Yellow-shafted Flicker" in the east
and far north, and "Red-shafted Flicker" in the west. These flick-
ers have brown, barred back; spotted underparts, with black crescent bib. White rump is conspicuous in flight; no white wing
patches. Intergrades are regularly seen in the Great Plains.
"Yellow-shafted Flicker" has yellow wing lining and undertail
color, gray crown, and tan face with red crescent on nape. **"Red-
shafted Flicker"** has brown crown and gray face, with no red
crescent. "Yellow-shafted" male has a black moustachial stripe
(red stripe in "Red-shafted" male); females lack these stripes. **Call**
heard on the breeding ground is a long, loud series of *wick-er*
notes; a single, loud *klee-yer* is given year-round. **Range:** Common in open woodlands, suburban areas. "Yellow-shafted" is
rare in the west in fall and winter.

Gilded Flicker *Colaptes chrysoides* L 11½" (29 cm)

Restored to full species status from Northern Flicker. Gilded
Flicker's head pattern more like "Red-shafted" Northern, but
underwings and base of tail yellow; crown more cinnamon. Note
also smaller size; larger black chest patch; paler back with narrower black bars; more crescent-shaped markings below. Female
lacks red moustachial stripe. **Calls** are like Northern's. **Range:**
Inhabits low desert woodlands; favors saguaro. Hybrids with
"Red-shafted" are noted in cottonwoods at middle elevations in
southern Arizona and along the lower Colorado River.

Golden-fronted Woodpecker

♂

♀

Red-bellied Woodpecker

♂

♀

♂

Gila Woodpecker

♂

♀

"Yellow-shafted" ♂

Northern Flicker

"Red-shafted" ♂

♂

Gilded Flicker

"Yellow-shafted" ♂

Gilded Flicker ♂

"Red-shafted" ♂

Sapsuckers

These woodpeckers drill evenly spaced rows of holes in trees, then visit these "wells" for sap and the insects it attracts. All four species have a white rump, white wing patches, and at least some yellow on the belly. Calls include plaintive mews. Red-breasted and Red-naped Sapsuckers were formerly considered subspecies of Yellow-bellied.

Williamson's Sapsucker *Sphyrapicus thyroideus*

L 9" (23 cm) **Male** has black back, white rump, large white wing patch; black head with narrow white stripes, bright red chin and throat. Breast is black, belly yellow, flanks barred with black and white. **Female**'s head is brown; back, wings, and sides barred with dark brown and white; rump white; lacks white wing patch and red chin; breast has large dark patch; belly variably yellow. Juveniles resemble adults but are duller; attain adultlike plumage by November. Juvenile male has white throat; juvenile female lacks black breast patch. **Range:** Fairly common in dry, piney forests of the western mountains; moves south or to lower elevations in winter. Accidental in eastern North America.

Red-breasted Sapsucker *Sphyrapicus ruber*

L 8½" (22 cm) Red head, nape, and breast; large white wing patch; white rump. Back is black, lightly spotted with yellow in northern subspecies, *S. r. ruber;* more heavily marked with white in southern *daggetti.* Belly is yellow in *ruber; daggetti* has paler belly, duller head with longer white moustachial stripe. In both races, briefly held juvenile plumage is brownish, showing little or no red. **Range:** Common in coniferous or mixed forests in coastal ranges, usually at lower elevations and in moister forests than Williamson's Sapsucker. Most migrate south or move to lower elevations in winter. Red-breasted frequently hybridizes with Red-naped Sapsucker.

Yellow-bellied Sapsucker *Sphyrapicus varius*

L 8½" (22 cm) Red forecrown on black-and-white head; chin and throat red in **male,** white in **female.** Back is blackish, with white rump, large white wing patch. Underparts yellowish, paler in female. **Juvenile** retains largely brownish plumage until late in the winter. **Range:** Common in deciduous forests. Highly migratory; rare to very rare in the west during fall and winter. Has hybridized with Red-naped Sapsucker.

Red-naped Sapsucker *Sphyrapicus nuchalis*

L 8½" (22 cm) Very similar to Yellow-bellied, but has variable red patch on back of head; spotting on back more clearly organized into two rows. On **male,** extensive red on throat penetrates the surrounding black "frame"; on **female,** throat is partly red to almost entirely red on some birds. Juvenile is brownish overall; resembles adult by first fall except for lack of black chest. **Range:** Common in deciduous forests.

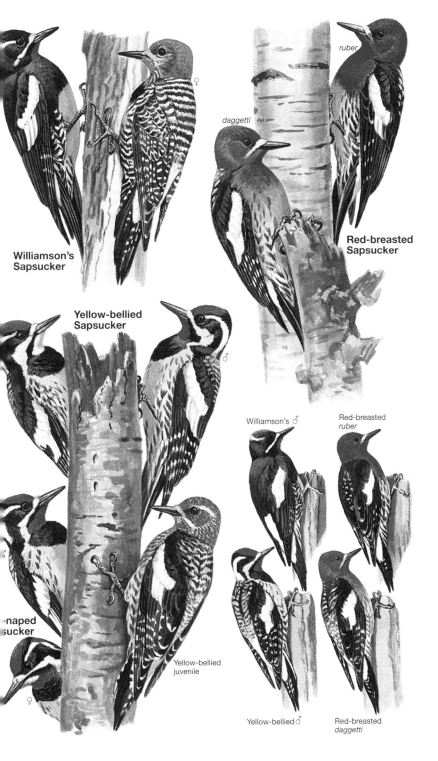

Williamson's Sapsucker

♀

ruber

daggetti

Red-breasted Sapsucker

Yellow-bellied Sapsucker

♂

naped
sucker

♀

Williamson's ♂

Red-breasted *ruber*

Yellow-bellied juvenile

Yellow-bellied ♂

Red-breasted *daggetti*

Ladder-backed Woodpecker *Picoides scalaris*

L 7¼" (18 cm) Black-and-white barred back, spotted sides; face and underparts slightly buffy or grayish; face marked with black lines. **Male** has red crown. In California, Ladder-backed may be confused with Nuttall's Woodpecker. Ladder-backed shows less black on face; white barring on back is more pronounced and extends to nape; is buffy-tinged rather than white below; white outer tail feathers are evenly barred rather than spotted. **Call** is a crisp *pik,* very similar to Downy Woodpecker's call and different from Nuttall's rattled *prrrt;* also gives a descending whinny. **Range:** Common in dry brushlands, mesquite and cactus country; often seen in towns and rural areas. Feeds on beetle larvae from small trees; also eats cactus fruits and forages on the ground for insects. May hybridize with Nuttall's where ranges overlap.

Red-cockaded Woodpecker *Picoides borealis* **E**

L 8½" (22 cm) Black-and-white barred back, black cap, and large white cheek patch identify this woodpecker more readily than the red tufts, usually invisible, on the **male**'s head. Similar Hairy and Downy Woodpeckers (next page) have solid white or gray-brown backs. Voices differ, too: Red-cockaded Woodpecker's raspy *sripp* and high-pitched *tsick* are much more buzzy. Juvenile lacks red tufts but may show some red on crown. Red-cockaded inhabits open, mature pine or pine-oak woodlands. Bores nest hole only in a large living pine afflicted with heartwood disease, then drills small holes around the nest opening. Pine pitch oozing down the trunk from these holes may repel predators; also makes the tree a distinctive signpost. Endangered: Populations continue to decline. Almost eliminated from Virginia and Kentucky, and has disappeared from Tennessee in the last five years.

Nuttall's Woodpecker *Picoides nuttallii* *L 7½" (19 cm)*

Closely resembles Ladder-backed Woodpecker. Nuttall's shows more black on face; white bars on back are narrower, with more extensive solid black just below the nape. White outer tail feathers are sparsely spotted rather than barred. **Call** is a low, rattled *prrrt,* much lower than Ladder-backed's *pik;* also gives a series of loud, spaced, descending notes. Nuttall's prefers less arid habitat than Ladder-backed; usually seen in chaparral mixed with scrub oak and in wooded canyons, streamside trees. Forages on tree trunks, generally probing crevices and chipping away loose bark rather than drilling. **Range:** Accidental to western Nevada.

Strickland's Woodpecker *Picoides stricklandi*

L 7½" (19 cm) Solid brown back distinguishes this species from all other woodpeckers. **Female** lacks red patch on back of head. Compare with female sapsuckers (preceding page), especially Williamson's, and with Northern Flicker (page 276). **Call** is a sharp *peek,* similar to call of Hairy Woodpecker but hoarser. **Range:** Uncommon resident in foothills and mountains; generally found in oak or pine-oak forests or canyons.

Ladder-backed Woodpecker

Red-cockaded Woodpecker

Nuttall's Woodpecker

Strickland's Woodpecker

Ladder-backed ♂   Nuttall's ♂   Strickland's ♂   Red-cockaded ♂

Downy Woodpecker *Picoides pubescens* *L 6¾" (17 cm)*
White back generally identifies both Downy and similar Hairy Woodpecker. Downy is much smaller, with a smaller bill; outer tail feathers generally have faint dark bars or spots. Birds in the Pacific northwest have pale gray-brown back and underparts. Rocky Mountain birds have less white spotting on wings. Downy's **call,** *pik,* and whinny are softer and higher pitched than Hairy Woodpecker's. **Range:** Common; active, and somewhat unwary; often seen in suburbs, parklands, and orchards, as well as in forests. A familiar visitor to feeders.

Hairy Woodpecker *Picoides villosus* *L 9¼" (24 cm)*
White back generally identifies both Hairy and similar Downy Woodpecker. Hairy is much larger, with a larger bill; outer tail feathers are entirely white. Birds in the Pacific northwest have pale gray-brown back and underparts. Rocky Mountain birds have less white spotting on wings. **Juveniles,** particularly in the Maritime Provinces, have some barring on back and flanks; sides may be streaked. Juveniles on the Queen Charlotte Islands have heavily barred outer tail feathers. In young males, the forehead is spotted with white; crown streaked with red or orange. Hairy's **calls** include a loud, sharp *pee*k and a slurred whinny. **Range:** Fairly common; inhabits both open and dense forests. Uncommon to rare in the south and Florida.

Three-toed Woodpecker *Picoides tridactylus*
L 8¾" (22 cm) Black-and-white barring down center of back distinguishes most races of Three-toed Woodpecker from similar Black-backed. Both have heavily barred sides. **Male's** yellow cap is usually more extensive in Three-toed but less solid. Density of barring on back is intermediate in northwestern race, *P. t. fasciatus.* In Rocky Mountain race, *dorsalis,* back is almost entirely white. Back is much darker in eastern race, *bacatus;* thinner submoustachial stripe helps distinguish it from Black-backed. **Range:** Three-toed is found in coniferous forests, especially in burned-over areas. Scarcer than Black-backed in the east.

Black-backed Woodpecker *Picoides arcticus*
L 9½" (24 cm) Solid black back, heavily barred sides. **Male** has a solid yellow cap. Compare especially with eastern race of Three-toed Woodpecker, *P. t. bacatus,* which has a darker back than other Three-toeds. Black-backed Woodpecker is larger; has longer, stouter bill; and lacks white streak behind the eye. **Call** note is a single, sharp *pik,* lower pitched than call of Three-toed. **Range:** Black-backed inhabits coniferous forests; often found in burned-over areas. Forages on dead conifers, flaking away large patches of loose bark rather than drilling into it, in search of larvae and insects. Casual south of mapped range in the east.

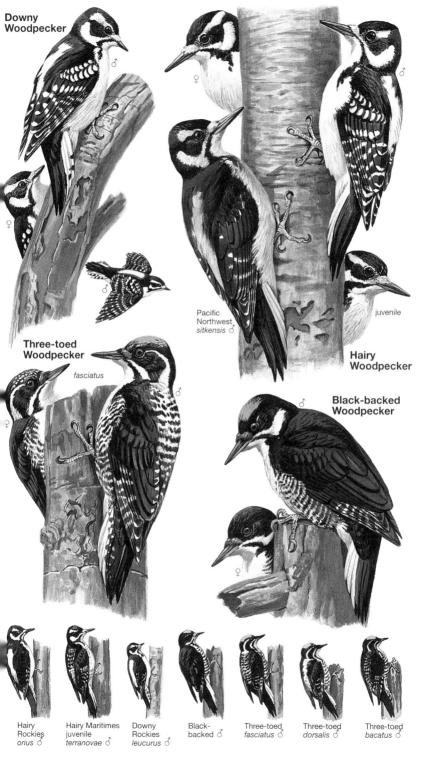

Downy Woodpecker

♀

♂

♀

♂

Pacific
Northwest
sitkensis ♂

juvenile

**Hairy
Woodpecker**

**Three-toed
Woodpecker**

fasciatus

♀

♂

**Black-backed
Woodpecker**

♂

♀

Hairy
Rockies
orius ♂

Hairy Maritimes
juvenile
terranovae ♂

Downy
Rockies
leucurus ♂

Black-
backed ♂

Three-toed
fasciatus ♂

Three-toed
dorsalis ♂

Three-toed
bacatus ♂

Ivory-billed Woodpecker *Campephilus principalis* **E**

L 19½" (50 cm) **Range:** Formerly found north to the Ohio River, near its confluence with the Mississippi. Thought now to be extinct in North America; last definite records from U.S. were in 1943 at the Singer Tract, near Tallulah in northeast Louisiana. Probably valid sightings were recorded in Florida into the 1950s; into the late 1980s in Cuba (subspecies *C. p. bairdii*), but now probably extinct there as well. Unconfirmed sightings in recent decades in Georgia, Florida, Louisiana, and Texas undoubtedly have been smaller Pileated Woodpecker. Note especially Ivory-billed Woodpeckers's black chin and ivory bill and the extensive white wing patches visible in perched birds. **Females** have black rather than red crests. Compare also the black-and-white wing patterns of Ivory-billed and Pileated Woodpeckers in flight. Distinctive **call** note sounds like a toy trumpet: a high-pitched, nasal *yank,* given singly or in a short series, like a loud version of the call of eastern White-breasted Nuthatch. Once our largest woodpecker, Ivory-billed required large tracts of old-growth river forest; dead and dying trees supplied nesting sites and food: the larvae of wood-boring beetles. Destruction of habitat in the last half of the 19th and early 20th centuries led to the probable extinction of this never common species.

Pileated Woodpecker *Dryocopus pileatus*

L 16½" (42 cm) Perched bird is almost entirely black on back and wings, lacking Ivory-billed Woodpecker's large white wing patches. White chin and dark bill also distinguish Pileated Woodpecker, along with smaller size. Compare also the wing patterns of the two species in flight; also note Pileated's deep, slow, crowlike wingbeats. This is the largest woodpecker now seen in North America. **Female**'s red cap is less extensive than in **male.** Juvenile plumage, held briefly, resembles adult but is duller and browner overall. Generally shy. **Call** is a loud *wuck* note or series of notes, given all year, often in flight; similar call of Northern Flicker is given only in the breeding season. **Range:** Prefers dense, mature forest. In woodlots and parklands as well as deep woods, listen for its loud, resonant, territorial drumming, given by both sexes but less frequently by females; look for the long rectangular or oval holes it excavates. Carpenter ants in fallen trees and stumps are its major food. Common in southeast; uncommon and local elsewhere.

Ivory-billed Woodpecker

Pileated Woodpecker

Tyrant Flycatchers (Family Tyrannidae)

A typical flycatcher darts out from a fixed perch to catch insects. Most have a large head, bristly "whiskers," and a broad-based, flat bill.

Greater Pewee *Contopus pertinax* L 8" (20 cm)
Slender crest often visible. Upper mandible is dark, lower mandible orange. Worn **summer** birds are grayish-olive above, yellowish-white below. Fall and **winter** birds are slightly greener above, yellower below, but underparts always show less contrast than in similar Olive-sided Flycatcher. Note also longer tail; unlike *Empidonax* flycatchers, most pewees do not flick their tails. **Song,** a whistled *ho-say ma-re-ah;* **call** is a repeated *pip.* **Range:** Fairly common in mountain pine-oak woodlands. Very rare in winter in southern Arizona, southern and central California.

Olive-sided Flycatcher *Contopus cooperi* L 7½" (19 cm)
Large and proportionately short-tailed. Brownish-olive above; white tufts on sides of rump distinctive but often not visible. Throat, center of breast, and belly dull white. Sides and flanks brownish-olive and streaked. Bill is mostly black; center and sometimes base of lower mandible dull orange. Distinctive **song,** a clear *quick-three-beers,* the second note higher; typical **call,** a repeated *pip.* **Range:** Fairly common in coniferous forests, bogs. Casual in winter on coastal slope of southern California.

Eastern Wood-Pewee *Contopus virens* L 6¼" (16 cm)
Plumage generally dark grayish-olive above, with dull white throat, darker breast; underparts whitish or pale yellow. Bill of **adult** has black upper mandible, dull orange lower mandible. **Juvenile** and **immature** may have all-dark bill. Distinctive **song** is a clear, slow, plaintive *pee-a-wee,* the second note lower; this phrase often alternates with a downslurred *pee-yer.* **Calls** include a loud *chip* and clear, whistled, rising *pweee* notes; often given together, *chip pweee.* **Range:** Common in a variety of woodland habitats. Casual in the west. No winter records in U.S.

Western Wood-Pewee *Contopus sordidulus*
L 6¼" (16 cm) Plumage variable; slightly darker, less greenish, than Eastern Wood-Pewee; base of lower mandible usually shows some yellow-orange. Identification very difficult; best done by range and voice. **Calls** include a harsh, slightly descending *peeer* and clear whistles suggestive of Eastern's *pee-yer.* **Song,** heard chiefly on breeding grounds, has three-note *tswee-tee-teet* phrases mixed with the *peeer* note. **Range:** Common in open woodlands. Casual in east. No winter records in U.S.

Cuban Pewee *Contopus caribaeus* L 6" (15 cm)
Range: West Indian species; accidental in south Florida. Short primary projection makes species look like *Empidonax,* but Cuban does minimal tail flicking. Note expansion of partial eye ring only behind eye; dull wing bars; faint "vest." **Call** a clear, steady *dee-dee-dee,* also a soft *dep* note.

Greater Pewee

winter

summer

Olive-sided Flycatcher

Eastern Wood-Pewee

immature

juvenile

Cuban Pewee

Western Wood-Pewee

Empidonax Flycatchers

All empids are drab, with pale eye rings and wing bars. From spring to summer, plumages grow duller from wear. Some species molt before fall migration, acquiring fresh plumage in late summer. Identification depends on voice, habitat, behavior, and subtle differences in size, bill shape, primary projection, and tail length. Most flip their tails up.

Acadian Flycatcher *Empidonax virescens L 5¾" (15 cm)*
Olive above, with yellow eye ring, two buffy or whitish wing bars; very long primary projection. Bill long and broad-based, with mostly yellowish lower mandible. Most birds show pale grayish throat, pale olive wash across upper breast, white lower breast, and yellow belly and undertail coverts. Molts before migration; **fall** birds have buffy wing bars. Juvenile is brownish-olive above, edged with buff. **Call** is a soft *peace,* extended in **song** to an emphatic *pee-tsup,* accented on first syllable. On breeding grounds, also gives a flicker-like *ti ti ti ti ti.* **Range:** Found in woodlands, swamps. Range is expanding in the northeast.

Yellow-bellied Flycatcher *Empidonax flaviventris*
L 5½" (14 cm) Proportionately short-tailed and big-headed. Olive above, yellow below. Broad yellow eye ring. Lower mandible entirely pale orange. Shows a more extensive olive wash across breast than Acadian Flycatcher; lacks pale area between olive and yellow belly. Also, throat is yellow, rather than whitish; bill smaller. Molts after migration; worn **fall** migrants slightly grayer above, duller below. **Song** is a liquid *je-bunk;* also a plaintive, rising *per-wee.* **Call,** a sharp, whistled *chiu* that sounds somewhat like Acadian. **Range:** Found in bogs, swamps, damp coniferous woods.

Alder Flycatcher *Empidonax alnorum L 5¾" (15 cm)*
Very similar to Willow Flycatcher, but bill is slightly shorter, eye ring usually more prominent, back greener. Distinguished from eastern race of Willow by darker head; from western races by well defined tertial edges, bolder wing bars, long primary projection. Best identified by voice. **Call,** a loud *pip,* similar to Hammond's Flycatcher but louder. Distinctive **song,** a falling, wheezy *weeb-ew.* On breeding grounds, also gives a descending *wheer.* **Range:** Common in brushy habitats near bogs, birch and alder thickets.

Willow Flycatcher *Empidonax traillii L 5¾" (15 cm)*
Lacks prominent eye ring. Color ranges from pale gray head, greenish back, of nominate eastern race to darker-headed, browner *E. t. brewsteri* in the northwest. Great Basin race, *adastus* (not illustrated), is paler than *brewsteri;* endangered southwestern *extimus* (**E**) even paler. Western races have duller wing bars, blended tertial edges, and shorter primary projection. Distinguished from pewees (preceding page) by shorter wings and upward flicks of tail. **Call** is a liquid *wit.* **Songs,** a sneezy *fitz-bew;* on breeding grounds, also a rising *brreet;* often sings in spring migration. **Range:** Found in brushy habitats in wet areas; also in pastures, mountain meadows. Very rare migrant in southeast.

Acadian Flycatcher

1st fall

worn summer adult

spring

Yellow-bellied Flycatcher

der ycatcher

worn fall adult

1st fall

worn fall adult

spring

spring

Willow Flycatcher

spring *extimus*

spring *brewsteri*

1st fall *traillii*

worn fall adult *traillii*

spring *traillii*

Least Flycatcher *Empidonax minimus L 5¼" (13 cm)*
Smallest eastern empid. Large-headed; bold white eye ring; rather
short primary projection. Throat whitish; breast washed with
gray; belly and undertail coverts pale yellow. Underparts are usually paler than similar Hammond's Flycatcher. Bill short, triangular; lower mandible mostly pale. Molt occurs after fall
migration. **Immature** has more buffy wing bars. **Song,** a dry *che-
bek* accented on the second syllable, is usually delivered in a rapid
series; **call,** a sharp *whit,* is sometimes also given in a series.
Range: Inhabits deciduous woods, orchards, parks. Common in
east, rare migrant through most of west.

Hammond's Flycatcher *Empidonax hammondii*
L 5½" (14 cm) A small empid, fairly large-headed and short-
tailed. White eye ring, usually expanded in a "teardrop" at rear.
Grayish head and throat; grayish-olive back; gray or olive wash
on breast and sides; belly tinged with pale yellow. Molt occurs
before migration; **fall** birds are much brighter olive above and
on sides of breast, yellower below. Medium length, slightly
notched tail is edged with gray. Bill is slightly shorter, thinner,
and usually somewhat darker than in similar Dusky Flycatcher;
primary projection is longer. **Call** note is a sharp *peek.* **Song**
resembles Dusky's but is hoarser and lower pitched, especially
on the second note. **Range:** Nests chiefly in coniferous forests.
Most Hammond's Flycatchers migrate earlier in spring and later
in fall than Dusky. Casual in the east.

Gray Flycatcher *Empidonax wrightii L 6" (15 cm)*
Gray above, with a slight olive tinge in fresh fall plumage; whitish
below, belly washed with pale yellow by late fall. Head is proportionately small and rounded; white eye ring inconspicuous
on pale gray face. Long bill; on most birds, lower mandible mostly
pinkish-orange at base, sharply divided from dark tip; on a few,
entire lower mandible is pinkish-orange. Short primary projection. Long tail, with thin whitish outer edge. Perched bird dips
its tail down slowly, like a phoebe. Juvenile is brownish-gray
above, with pale, buffy wing bars; underparts are tinged brown-
ish-buff. **Song** is a vigorous *chi-wip* or *chi-bit,* followed by a liquid *whilp,* trailing off in a gurgle. **Call,** a loud *wit.* **Range**: Fairly
common in dry habitat of Great Basin, in pine or piñon-juniper.
Regular migrant on California coast. Accidental in the east.

Dusky Flycatcher *Empidonax oberholseri L 5¾" (15 cm)*
Grayish-olive above; yellowish below, with whitish throat, pale
olive wash on upper breast. White eye ring. Bill partly dark,
orange at base of lower mandible blending into dark tip. Bill and
tail slightly longer than Hammond's Flycatcher. Short primary
projection. Molt occurs after fall migration; fresh late-fall birds
are quite yellow below. **Calls** include a *wit* note, softer than Gray
Flycatcher; a mournful *deehic,* heard on breeding grounds. **Song**
has several phrases: A clear *sillit;* an upslurred *ggrrreep;* another
high *sillit,* often omitted; and a clear, high *pweet.* **Range:**Breeds
in open woodlands and brush of mountainsides.

Least Flycatcher

1st fall

worn fall adult

spring

Hammond's Flycatcher

fall

spring

Gray Flycatcher

winter

spring

Dusky Flycatcher

1st fall

worn fall adult

winter

spring

Pacific-slope Flycatcher *Empidonax difficilis*

L 5½" (14 cm) Formerly considered same species as Cordilleran; known together as Western Flycatcher. Brownish-green above; yellowish below with brownish tinge on breast. Broad pale eye ring, broken above, expanded behind eye; lower mandible entirely orange. Tail longer, wing tip slightly shorter than Yellow-bellied; wings and back slightly browner; less contrast in wing bars and tertial edges. Pacific-slope molts after arrival on winter grounds, so **fall** migrant **adults** appear more worn than spring birds. **Immature** birds duller; wing bars buffy; variably whitish below, compare with Least Flycatcher (preceding page). Channel Islands race *E. d. insulicola* is slightly duller; some think it might be a separate species. **Call** is a sharp *seet;* male gives upslurred *psee-yeet* note. **Song,** a complex series of notes, including call notes. **Range:** Common in moist woodlands, coniferous forests, shady canyons. Winters in lowlands of western Mexico. Common migrant through southwest lowlands east to southeast Arizona. Accidental in eastern North America.

Cordilleran Flycatcher *Empidonax occidentalis*

L 5¾" (15 cm) Formerly considered same species as Pacific-slope Flycatcher. Nearly identical but slightly larger, darker, greener above; more olive and yellow below. Separable in field only by male's **call,** a two-note *pit peet. Seet* note seems sharper in Cordilleran than in Pacific-coast Flycatcher. **Range:** Breeds in coniferous forests and canyons in mountains of the west. Rare in lowlands in migration, even within breeding range. Casual on the Great Plains. Winters in mountains of Mexico.

Buff-breasted Flycatcher *Empidonax fulvifrons*

L 5" (13 cm) Smallest *Empidonax* flycatcher. Brownish above; breast cinnamon buff, paler on worn summer birds. Whitish eye ring; pale wing bars; small bill, with lower mandible entirely pale orange. Molts before migration. **Call** note is a soft *pwit.* Typical **song,** a quick *chicky-whew* or *chee-lick.* **Range:** Small colonies nest in dry woodlands of canyon floors. Very local in Huachuca and Chiricahua Mountains, Arizona; now casual in New Mexico, but recorded recently in Peloncillo Mountains. Formerly more widespread as a breeder.

Northern Beardless-Tyrannulet *Camptostoma imberbe*

L 4½" (11 cm) Grayish-olive above and on breast; dull white or pale yellow below. Indistinct whitish eyebrow; small, slightly curved bill. Crown is darker than nape in many birds and often raised in a bushy crest. Distinguished from similar Ruby-crowned Kinglet (page 338) by buffy wing bars and lack of bold eye ring. Difficult to spot; most easily located by voice. **Song** on breeding grounds is a descending series of loud, clear *peer* notes; **call,** an innocuous, whistled *pee-yerp.* **Range:** Rather uncommon in U.S. Often found near streams in sycamore, mesquite, and cottonwood groves.

Pacific-slope Flycatcher

pale 1st fall

1st fall

worn fall adult

spring

spring

Yellow-bellied Flycatcher for comparison

spring

Cordilleran Flycatcher

spring

worn summer adult

Buff-breasted Flycatcher

fresh

worn adult

Northern Beardless-Tyrannulet

fresh

Eastern Phoebe *Sayornis phoebe L 7" (18 cm)*
Brownish-gray above, darkest on head, wings, tail. Underparts mostly white with pale olive wash on sides and breast; **fresh fall** birds are washed with yellow below. Molts before migration. All phoebes are distinguished from pewees (page 286) by their habit of pumping down and spreading their tails; Eastern Phoebe also by all-dark bill, lack of distinct wing bars. Also compare lack of eye rings and wing bars with *Empidonax* flycatchers (preceding pages). Juvenile plumage, held only briefly, is browner above, with two buff wing bars, cinnamon rump. Distinctive **song,** a harsh, emphatic *fee-be,* accented on first syllable. Typical **call** note is a sharp *chip.* **Range:** Common in woodlands, farmlands, suburbs; often nests under bridges, in eaves and rafters. Rare late fall migrant and winter visitor in the southwest and on the west coast.

Black Phoebe *Sayornis nigricans L 6¾" (17 cm)*
Black head, upperparts, breast; white belly and undertail coverts. **Juvenile** plumage, held briefly, is browner, with two cinnamon wing bars, cinnamon rump. Four-syllable **song,** a rising *pee-wee* followed by a descending *pee-wee. Calls* include a loud *tseee* and a sharper *tsip,* slightly more plaintive than Eastern Phoebe's call. **Range:** Common in woodlands, parks, suburbs; prefers to nest near water.

Say's Phoebe *Sayornis saya L 7½" (19 cm)*
Grayish-brown above, darkest on head, wings, and tail; breast and throat are pale grayish-brown; belly and undertail coverts tawny. Juvenile plumage, held briefly, is browner above; shows two cinnamon wing bars. **Song** is a fast *pit-tse-ar,* often given in fluttering flight. Typical **call** is a thin, plaintive, whistled *pee-ee,* slightly downslurred. **Range:** Fairly common in dry, open areas, canyons, cliffs; perches on bushes, boulders, fences. Highly migratory; casual in eastern North America.

Vermilion Flycatcher *Pyrocephalus rubinus L 6" (15 cm)*
Adult male strikingly red and brown. **Adult female** grayish-brown above, with blackish tail; throat and breast white, with dusky streaking; belly and undertail coverts are peach; note also whitish eyebrow and forehead. **Juvenile** resembles adult female but is spotted rather than streaked below; belly white, often with yellowish tinge. **Immature male** begins to resemble adult by midwinter. Male in breeding season **sings** during fluttery display flight a soft, tinkling *pit-a-see pit-a-see;* also sings while perched. Typical **call** note is a sharp, thin *pseep.* Frequently pumps and spreads its tail. **Range:** Fairly common and approachable; found in streamside shrubs, bottomlands, and near small wooded ponds. Rare winter visitor to coastal southern California and the Gulf coast. Casual elsewhere in eastern North America, primarily in the fall.

Eastern Phoebe

worn summer adult

fresh fall

Black Phoebe

juvenile

Say's Phoebe

Vermilion Flycatcher

immature ♀

♀

immature ♂

adult ♂

juvenile

Brown-crested Flycatcher *Myiarchus tyrannulus*
L 8¾" (22 cm) Brownish-olive above; as in all *Myiarchus* fly-catchers, shows a bushy crest; bill is longer, thicker, broader than Ash-throated Flycatcher. Throat and breast are pale gray; belly slightly paler yellow than in Great Crested Flycatcher. Dusky tail feathers show reddish on outer two-thirds of inner webs. Texas race *M. t. cooperi* is smaller than southwestern *magister.* **Song** is a clear musical whistle, a rolling *whit-will-do.* **Call** is a sharp *whit.* **Range:** Fairly common in saguaro desert, river groves, lower mountain woodlands. Casual in Louisiana and Florida.

Great Crested Flycatcher *Myiarchus crinitus*
L 8" (20 cm) Dark olive above. Gray throat and breast; bright lemon yellow belly and undertail coverts. Note broad, sharply contrasting edge to inner tertial. Outer tail feathers show entirely reddish inner webs. Distinctive **call,** a loud whistled *wheep.* **Range:** Common in a wide variety of open woods; feeds high in the canopy. Very rare on California coast during fall migration.

Nutting's Flycatcher *Myiarchus nuttingi*
L 7¼" (18 cm) **Range**: Tropical species; found from northwest Mexico to Costa Rica; three certain winter records from south-eastern Arizona and coastal southern California. Similar to Ash-throated Flycatcher but belly yellower; slightly more olive above; rufous primary edges blend to yellow-cinnamon secondary edges. Dark on outer webs of outer tail feathers does not extend across tip as in Ash-throated; orange, not flesh-colored, mouth lining. **Call,** a rather sharp *wheep,* different from Ash-throated.

Ash-throated Flycatcher *Myiarchus cinerascens*
L 8½" (22 cm) Grayish-brown above; throat and breast pale gray; underparts paler than in Brown-crested. Tail shows rufous on inner webs with dark tips. As in all *Myiarchus* flycatchers, brief **juvenile** plumage shows mostly reddish tail. Distinctive **call,** heard year-round, is a rough *prrrt.* **Song,** heard on breeding grounds, is a series of burry *ka-brick's.* **Range:** Common in a wide variety of habitats. Very rare fall and winter visitor to east.

La Sagra's Flycatcher *Myiarchus sagrae* L 8" (20 cm)
Range: West Indian species from Bahamas, Cuba, and Caymans. Casual visitor, mainly in winter and spring, to south Florida; acci-dental in Alabama. Grayish-brown upperparts, mainly white underparts suggestive of Ash-throated Flycatcher, but bill longer; inner tertial edge stronger; rufous on outer tail less extensive. Dis-tinctive **call,** a rather high pitched *wink,* is often doubled.

Dusky-capped Flycatcher *Myiarchus tuberculifer*
L 7¼" (18 cm) Smaller, bill larger, belly and undertail coverts usually brighter yellow than in Ash-throated Flycatcher; tail shows less rufous. Secondaries have rufous edges, unlike other *Myiarchus.* **Call** is a mournful, descending *peeur.* **Range:** Fairly common in wooded mountain ranges. Casual in west Texas. Very rare in late fall and winter in southern and central California.

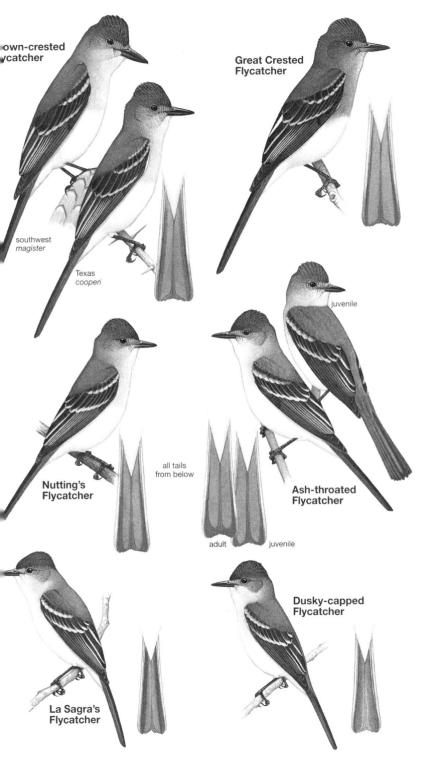

own-crested
ycatcher

Great Crested
Flycatcher

southwest
magister

Texas
cooperi

juvenile

Nutting's
Flycatcher

all tails
from below

Ash-throated
Flycatcher

adult   juvenile

La Sagra's
Flycatcher

Dusky-capped
Flycatcher

Western Kingbird *Tyrannus verticalis* L 8¾" (22 cm)
Black tail, with white edges on outer feathers. Bill much shorter than in Tropical and Couch's Kingbirds. Upperparts ashy-gray, paler than in Cassin's Kingbird, tinged with olive on back; dark wings contrast with paler back. Throat and breast pale gray; belly bright lemon yellow. Orange-red crown patch is usually concealed. Juvenile has slightly more olive on back and buffy edges on wing coverts, brownish tinge on breast, paler yellow belly. Common **call** is a sharp *whit*. **Range:** Common in dry, open country; perches on fences, telephone lines. Regular straggler in fall and early winter along the east coast from the Maritime Provinces south; winters in small numbers in southern Florida.

Cassin's Kingbird *Tyrannus vociferans* L 9" (23 cm)
Dark brown tail; narrow buffy tips and lack of white edges on outer tail feathers help distinguish this species from Western Kingbird. Bill is much shorter than in Tropical and Couch's Kingbirds. Upperparts darker gray than in Western, washed with olive on back; paler wings contrast with darker back. White chin contrasts with dark gray head and breast. Belly dull yellow. Orange-red crown patch is usually concealed. Juvenile is duller, slightly browner above, with bold buffy edges on wing coverts; paler below. Most common **call,** given year-round, is a short, loud *chi-bew,* accented on second syllable. **Range:** Fairly common in varied habitats; usually prefers denser foliage and hillier country than does Western Kingbird.

Tropical Kingbird *Tyrannus melancholicus* L 9¼" (24 cm)
Almost identical to Couch's Kingbird. Bill is thinner and longer; back slightly grayer, less green; at close range, tips of individual primaries are unevenly staggered on adults. Distinctive **call** is a rapid, twittering *pip-pip-pip-pip.* Distinguished from Western and Cassin's Kingbirds by larger bill, darker ear patch, and slightly notched brown tail. **Range:** Uncommon and local in southeastern Arizona and Rio Grande Valley, Texas; found in lowlands near water; often nests in cottonwoods. Rare but regular during fall and winter along the west coast to British Columbia.

Couch's Kingbird *Tyrannus couchii* L 9¼" (24 cm)
Almost identical to Tropical Kingbird. Bill is thicker; back slightly greener, less gray; at close range, tips of individual primaries are evenly spaced on adults. Distinctive **calls,** a shrill, rolling *breeeer;* and a more common *kip,* similar to call of Western Kingbird, given singly or in a series. Distinguished from Western and Cassin's Kingbirds by larger bill, darker ear patch, slightly notched brown tail. Juvenile is duller overall, with buffy edges on wing coverts. **Range:** Common in the lower Rio Grande Valley in summer; uncommon in winter. Found in groves and shrubs. Casual on Gulf coast in fall and winter.

Western Kingbird

Cassin's Kingbird

Tropical Kingbird

Couch's Kingbird

tails from above

Western   Cassin's   Couch's   Tropical

Fork-tailed Flycatcher *Tyrannus savana* *L 14½" (37 cm)*
Range: Tropical species; casual vagrant along Atlantic coast and in Texas; accidental elsewhere. Extremely long black tail flutters in flight. Black cap, white underparts, white wing linings distinguish it from Scissor-tailed Flycatcher (next page). Many sightings are of immatures, which resemble **adult** but have a much shorter tail.

Eastern Kingbird *Tyrannus tyrannus* *L 8½" (22 cm)*
Black head, slate gray back; tail has a broad white terminal band. Underparts are white, with a pale gray wash across the breast. Orange-red crown patch is seldom visible. **Juvenile** brownish-gray above, darker on breast. **Call** is a harsh *dzeet* note, also given in a series. **Range:** Common and conspicuous in woodland clearings, farms, orchards; often seen near water.

Loggerhead Kingbird *Tyrannus caudifasciatus*
L 9" (23 cm) **Range:** West Indian species; perhaps only four records (all in winter) in southernmost Florida, the last in 1976. Blackish head; back washed with olive; bill long and thick; all wing coverts have distinct whitish edges; tail is tipped with buffy-white. Yellow crown patch seldom visible. Underparts white, with pale yellowish wash on belly and undertail coverts. Distinguished from Gray Kingbird by head-and-back contrast; bill much larger than in Eastern Kingbird. Unlike other kingbirds, flight is not graceful, but undulating, with noisy wing flaps. Prefers wooded habitat; feeds in canopy, or sits on low perch; often picks insects off surface. **Call** is a loud, rolling, chattering *teeerrp.*

Gray Kingbird *Tyrannus dominicensis* *L 9" (23 cm)*
Pale gray above, with blackish mask. Red crown patch seldom visible. Bill long and thick. Underparts mostly white, with pale yellowish wash on belly and undertail coverts. Forked tail with no white terminal band. Juvenile plumage, held well into fall, is browner above. **Song** is a buzzy *pecheer-ry,* accented on second syllable. **Range:** Common on the Florida Keys, local in mangroves on the mainland. Casual wanderer north along the Atlantic coast to the Maritimes, inland to Michigan and Ontario, and along the Gulf coast to southeastern Texas.

Thick-billed Kingbird *Tyrannus crassirostris*
L 9½" (24 cm) Large, with very large bill. **Adult** is dusky-brown above, with a slightly darker head and seldom-seen yellow crown patch; whitish underparts washed with pale gray on breast, pale yellow on belly and undertail coverts. Yellow is brighter and more extensive in fresh fall adult and in **first-fall** birds, which have buffy edgings on wing coverts. Fall birds resemble Tropical Kingbird (preceding page), but have heavier bill and darker head. Common **call** is a loud, high, whistled *puareet.* **Range:** Perches high in sycamores of lowland streamsides. Common in Guadalupe Canyon, uncommon elsewhere in southeastern Arizona. Casual during fall and winter west to southern California and in summer to western Texas (Big Bend). Accidental to British Columbia.

Fork-tailed Flycatcher

adult

Eastern Kingbird

juvenile

Loggerhead Kingbird

Gray Kingbird

1st fall

Thick-billed Kingbird

worn summer adult

Scissor-tailed Flycatcher *Tyrannus forficatus*
L 13" (33 cm) Pearl gray above; whitish and salmon pink below. Has very long outer tail feathers, white with black tips; also salmon pink wing linings with reddish axillaries. **Male**'s tail is longer than female's; **juvenile** is paler overall, with shorter tail. **Calls** similar to Western Kingbird. **Range:** Common; found in semi-open country. Very rare to casual wanderer in much of North America.

Piratic Flycatcher *Legatus leucophaius L 6" (15 cm)*
Range: Widespread tropical species. Accidental in U.S. on Dry Tortugas, Florida; on an oil rig in the Gulf of Mexico (Texas); Big Bend, Texas; and southeast New Mexico. Dark olive-brown above; blurry olive streaking below. Distinct head pattern; dark malar streak; pale throat; stubby black bill. Black tail can show rufous edges. Often perches out in the open.

Variegated Flycatcher *Empidonomus varius*
L 7¼" (18 cm) **Range:** South American species; accidental in North America; three records in east. Similar to Piratic, but larger, longer bill has pale base; less distinct malar streak; more distinct streaking on upperparts, edging on wing coverts, and rufous edge on uppertail coverts and tail. Tends to perch lower than Piratic. Compare both to larger Sulphur-bellied Flycatcher. **Call** a high, thin *pseee*.

Great Kiskadee *Pitangus sulphuratus L 9¾" (25 cm)*
Yellow crown patch on black-and-white head is often concealed. Brown above, with reddish-brown wings and tail. Found chiefly in wet woodlands or near watercourses; as well as fly-catching, dives for fish. **Calls** include a slow, deliberate *kis-ka-dee*, and a loud *kreah*, given all year. **Range:** Fairly common. Casual vagrant in southeastern Arizona and on Gulf coast to Louisiana.

Sulphur-bellied Flycatcher *Myiodynastes luteiventris*
L 8½" (22 cm) Boldly streaked above and below. Upperparts often show an olive tinge; rump and tail rusty-red; underparts pale yellow. Loud **call** is an excited chatter, like the squeaking of a rubber duck. **Song** is a soft *tre-le-re-re*. **Range:** Fairly common in woodlands of mountain canyons, usually at elevations between 5,000 and 6,000 feet. Inconspicuous; often perches high in the canopy. Casual along the Gulf coast and in southern California.

Rose-throated Becard *Pachyramphus aglaiae*
L 7¼" (18 cm) Rosy throat distinctive in males; Arizona **adult males,** *P. a. albiventris* (shown), have blackish cap, pale gray underparts. **Females** have slate gray crown, browner back. **Immature male** shows partially pink throat; acquires full adult plumage after second summer. East Mexican race *gravis* (not shown), found in Texas, is darker overall. Foot-long nest is suspended from a tree limb in wooded canyon or bottomland. **Call,** thin, mournful *seeoo*, sometimes preceded by chatter. **Range:** Rare and local in southeast Arizona; casual along lower Rio Grande, Texas.

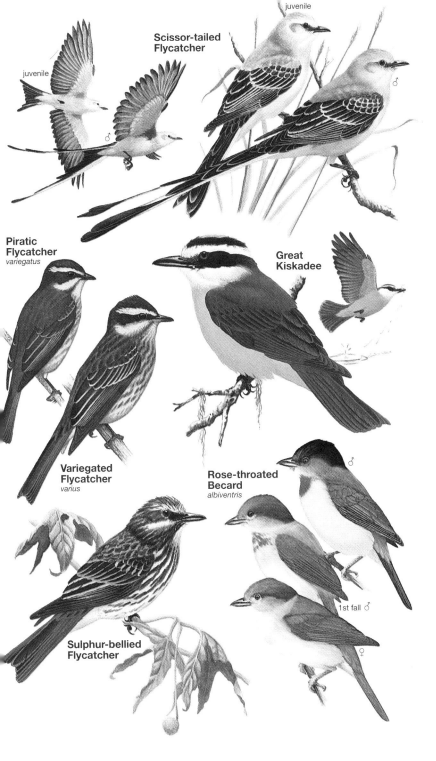

Scissor-tailed Flycatcher

juvenile

juvenile

♂

♂

Piratic Flycatcher
variegatus

Great Kiskadee

Variegated Flycatcher
varius

Rose-throated Becard
albiventris

♂

Sulphur-bellied Flycatcher

1st fall ♂

♀

Shrikes (Family Laniidae)

These masked hunters scan the countryside from lookout perches, then swoop down on insects, rodents, snakes, small birds. Known as "butcher-birds," they mostly impale their prey on thorns. Recent research indicates that this is to mark territory and attract mates.

Brown Shrike *Lanius cristatus L 7½" (19 cm)*
Range: Asian species; casual in Alaska where there are spring and fall records from western Aleutians, St. Lawrence Island, and Anchorage. Fall and winter records from California; late fall record from Nova Scotia. **Adult male** has distinct white border above black mask extending across forehead; warm brown upperparts, often brighter on rump and uppertail coverts; warm buff wash along sides and flanks. **Adult female** similar, but mask less solid; has some barring below. **Juveniles** are barred on sides and flanks; show distinct dark subterminal edges above; dark brown mask has short whitish border above and behind eye. Much juvenile plumage is retained into fall, some even into winter. Compare all ages and plumages to much larger, longer billed Northern Shrike. Old World Red-backed Shrike *(L. collurio)* and Isabelline Shrike *(L. isabellinus)* considered close relatives of Brown Shrike.

Loggerhead Shrike *Lanius ludovicianus L 9" (23 cm)*
Slightly smaller and darker than Northern Shrike. Head and back bluish-gray; underparts white, very faintly barred. Broad black mask extends above eye and thinly across top of bill. All-dark bill, shorter than in Northern Shrike, with smaller hook. Rump varies from gray to whitish. **Juvenile** is paler and barred overall, with brownish-gray upperparts; acquires adult plumage by first fall. Loggerheads hunt in open or brushy areas, diving from a low perch, then rising swiftly to the next lookout. Seen in flight, wings and tail are darker and white wing patches smaller than in Northern Mockingbird (page 354). **Song** is a medley of low warbles and harsh, squeaky notes; **calls** include a harsh *shack-shack.* **Range:** Fairly common over much of range; rare to very rare and declining in the eastern midwest and northeast.

Northern Shrike *Lanius excubitor L 10" (25 cm)*
Larger than Loggerhead Shrike, with paler head and back, lightly barred underparts; rump whitish. Mask is narrower than in Loggerhead, does not extend above eye; feathering above bill is white. Bill longer, with a more distinct hook. Often bobs its tail. **Juvenile** is brownish above and more heavily barred below than adult. **Immature** is grayer; retains barring on underparts until first spring. Northern Shrike's **song** and **calls** are similar to Loggerhead. **Range:** Uncommon; often perches high in tall trees. Southern range limit and numbers on wintering grounds vary unpredictably from year to year.

Brown Shrike
cristatus

juvenile

♀

♂

juvenile

**Loggerhead
Shrike**

Northern Mockingbird
for comparison

**Northern
Shrike**

adult

immature

juvenile

Vireos (Family Vireonidae)

Short, sturdy bills slightly hooked at the tip characterize these small songbirds. Vireos are closely related to shrikes. Some have "spectacles" and wing bars. Others have eyebrow stripes and no wing bars. They are generally chunkier and less active than warblers.

Black-capped Vireo *Vireo atricapillus* E

L 4½" (11 cm) Olive above, white below, with yellow flanks, yellowish wing bars. Hard to see, stays hidden in oak scrub, thickets. **Male**'s glossy black cap contrasts with broken white spectacles. Spectacles, smaller size, and secretive behavior distinguish **female** from Blue-headed Vireo (next page), which immature males are also thought to resemble; **immature females** are more buffy. Best located by **song,** a persistent string of varied, twittering, two- or three-note phrases. Common **call** note, *tsidik,* almost identical to Ruby-crowned Kinglet. **Range:** Endangered. Eliminated from Kansas in 1930s and now nearly gone from Oklahoma. Major factors are habitat destruction and brood parasitism by Brown-headed Cowbird.

White-eyed Vireo *Vireo griseus* L 5" (13 cm)

Grayish-olive above; white below, with pale yellow sides and flanks; two whitish wing bars; yellow spectacles. Distinctive white iris visible at close range. Juvenile is duller, with gray or brown iris. Subspecies on the Florida Keys, *V. g. maynardi,* is grayer above, with less yellow below; bill larger. South Texan race, *micrus,* is colored like *maynardi,* but smaller. Typical **song** is a loud, variable five-to-seven-note phrase usually beginning and ending with a sharp *chick;* also gives a chatter **call** suggestive of House Wren. **Range:** Casual vagrant to the west.

Thick-billed Vireo *Vireo crassirostris* L 5½" (14 cm)

Range: Caribbean species, accidental or casual visitor to southeast Florida from Bahamas. Most reports from south Florida are probably misidentified White-eyed Vireos. Larger than White-eyed, with larger, slightly stouter and grayer bill. Note overall browner color, lack of gray on nape, and broken spectacles. Iris darker than adult White-eyed; **song** similar but harsher; **call** notes slower and harsher.

Yellow-throated Vireo *Vireo flavifrons* L 5½" (14 cm)

Bright yellow spectacles, throat, and breast; white belly; two white wing bars. Upperparts olive, with contrasting gray rump. Compare with Pine Warbler, which has greenish-yellow rump, streaked sides, thinner bill, and less complete and distinct spectacles. **Song,** a slow repetition of buzzy, low-pitched two- or three-note phrases separated by long pauses, often contains a rising *three-eight.* **Calls** include a rapid, harsh series of *cheh* notes. **Range:** Fairly common in most of breeding range. Rare or casual in southernmost Florida in winter. Most reports are misidentified Pine Warblers or Yellow-breasted Chats (page 388). Very rare vagrant in the west.

Black-capped Vireo

adult ♀

adult ♂

immature ♀

White-eyed Vireo

Florida Keys
maynardi

Yellow-throated Vireo

Thick-billed Vireo
crassirostris

adult ♂ Pine Warbler
for comparison

Bell's Vireo *Vireo bellii L 4¾" (12 cm)*

Plumage variable. Endangered west coast race, *V. b. pusillus* (**E**), is grayish above, whitish below, with indistinct white spectacles; two whitish wing bars. Nominate eastern race is greenish above, yellowish below; often bobs tail. Southwestern *medius* and *arizonae*, are intermediate. Active, rather secretive. **Song,** a series of harsh, scolding notes. **Range:** Uncommon in moist woodlands, bottomlands, mesquite, and in east in shrubby areas on prairies.

Hutton's Vireo *Vireo huttoni L 5" (13 cm)*

Grayish-olive above, with pale area in lores; white eye ring broken above eye. Subspecies vary from paler, grayer southwestern *V. h. stephensi,* to greener coastal races such as *huttoni.* Separated from Ruby-crowned Kinglet by larger size, thicker bill, lack of dark area below lower wing bar. **Song,** a repeated or mixed rising *zu-wee* and descending *zoe zoo;* also a flat *chew.* **Calls** include a low *chit* and whining chatter; birds from interior southwest give a harsher *tchurr-ree.* **Range**: Fairly commmon in woodlands.

Gray Vireo *Vireo vicinior L 5½" (14 cm)*

White eye ring; wings brownish, with faint wing bars, the lower more prominent; long tail. Compare with smaller west coast race, *V. b. pusillus,* of Bell's Vireo. **Song** is a series of musical *chu-wee chu-weet* notes, faster and sweeter than Plumbeous. **Calls** include shrill, descending musical notes. **Range:** Found in semi-arid habitat. Sticks to undergrowth; flicks tail as it forages.

Blue-headed Vireo *Vireo solitarius L 5" (13 cm)*

Adult male's solid blue-gray hood contrasts with white spectacles and throat; hood of female and immatures partly gray. All ages have bright olive back; yellow-tinged wing bars and tertials; greenish-yellow edges to dark secondaries. Distinct white on outer tail; bright yellow sides and flanks, sometimes mixed with green. Larger Appalachian *V. s. alticola* has more slaty back; only flanks are yellow. **Song,** similar to Red-eyed Vireo, but slower. **Range:** Common in mixed woodlands. With Plumbeous, and Cassin's, formerly considered one species, Solitary Vireo.

Plumbeous Vireo *Vireo plumbeus L 5¼" (13 cm)*

Larger, bigger-billed than Cassin's Vireo, with sharper head and throat contrast, and gray upperparts. Pattern of tail feathers similar to Blue-headed Vireo. White wing bars and flight feather edges; yellow, if present, only on flanks. Sides of breast gray, sometimes tinged olive. Compare worn summer birds to shorter winged Gray Vireo. **Song** hoarser than Blue-headed. **Range:** Fairly common in varied woodland habitats.

Cassin's Vireo *Vireo cassinii L 5" (13 cm)*

Similar to Blue-headed, but slightly smaller and duller. Less contrast between head and throat; duller, whitish wing bars and tertial edges; less white in tail. Immature female can have entirely green head; compare to Hutton's Vireo. **Song** is hoarser than Blue-headed Vireo.

Ruby-crowned Kinglet for comparison

bellii

Bell's Vireo

west coast *pusillus*

west coast *huttoni*

Hutton's Vireo

southwest *stephensi*

Gray Vireo

Blue-headed Vireo

solitarius ♂

Plumbeous Vireo

Cassin's Vireo

♀

Yellow-green Vireo *Vireo flavoviridis* L 6" (15 cm)
Similar to Red-eyed Vireo, but bill longer; head pattern more blended. Strong yellow-green wash above extends onto sides of face; extensive yellow on sides, flanks, undertail; brightest in fall. **Song** a rapid but hesitant series of notes, suggesting House Sparrow. **Range:** Very rare but increasing in fall in coastal California, and very rare in summer in south Texas. Casual in spring on the upper Gulf coast. Restored to full species from Red-eyed Vireo.

Red-eyed Vireo *Vireo olivaceus* L 6" (15 cm)
Blue-gray crown; white eyebrow bordered above and below with black. Olive back, darker wings and tail; white underparts. Lacks wing bars. Ruby red iris visible at close range. **First-fall** bird has brown iris. Immatures and some fall adults have pale yellow on flanks and undertail coverts. Persistent **song**, sung all day, a variable series of deliberate, short phrases. **Calls** include a nasal, whining *quee*. **Range:** Common in eastern woodlands; rare migrant west of dashed line on map.

Black-whiskered Vireo *Vireo altiloquus* L 6¼" (16 cm)
Variable dark malar stripe, often hard to see. Bill larger and longer than in Red-eyed Vireo. Grayish-brown crown; white eyebrow bordered above and below with black; pattern more diffuse than in Red-eyed. Dull green above; whitish below, with variable pale yellowish wash on sides and flanks. **Song:** deliberate one- to four-note phrases, less varied and more emphatic than Red-eyed. **Range:** Common in summer in the mangrove swamps of Florida Keys and along Florida coasts. Casual along rest of Gulf coast.

Philadelphia Vireo *Vireo philadelphicus* L 5¼" (13 cm)
Breeding adult variably yellow below, palest on belly. Greenish above, with contrasting grayish cap, dull grayish-olive wing bar, dull white eyebrow, and dark eye line. First-fall birds and most **fall adults** are often brighter yellow below. Distinguished from Warbling Vireo by dark eye line extending through lores, darker cap, dark primary coverts, and yellow at center of throat and breast. **Song** resembles Red-eyed Vireo but is generally slower, thinner, and higher pitched. Similar Tennessee Warbler (page 368) has a thinner bill, white undertail coverts. **Range:** Uncommon; found in open woodlands, streamside willows and alders. Casual to mostly rare in west; chiefly occurs in fall.

Warbling Vireo *Vireo gilvus* L 5½" (14 cm)
Gray or olive-gray above; western birds, especially Pacific race *V. g. swainsoni*, are smaller than nominate, with slighter bill. Underparts white. Dusky post-ocular stripe; white eyebrow, without dark upper border; brown eye. Lacks wing bars. Smaller and paler than Red-eyed Vireo; crown does not contrast strongly with back. Birds in **fresh fall** plumage tend to be greener above, pale yellow on sides of flanks. **Song** of *gilvus* is delivered in long, melodious, warbling phrases; song of *swainsoni* less musical, with higher tones and break near beginning. **Range:** Common across most of North America in summer; found in deciduous woods.

Yellow-green Vireo

breeding

Red-eyed Vireo

1st fall

Black-whiskered Vireo

Florida
barbatulus

spring
gilvus

Philadelphia Vireo

fall

fall
gilvus

Warbling Vireo

spring

fall
swainsoni

Crows, Jays (Family Corvidae)

Harsh voice and aggressive manner draw attention to these large, often gregarious birds. Crows and ravens are somber in hue, jays and magpies more colorful. In most species, bristles cover nostrils. Powerful all-purpose bill efficiently handles a varied diet.

Blue Jay *Cyanocitta cristata* L 11" (28 cm)
Crested jay with black barring and white patches on blue wings and tail, black necklace on whitish underparts. Most common of varied **calls** is a piercing *jay jay jay;* also gives a musical *weedle-eedle* and mimics the call of Red-shouldered Hawk. Generally very noisy and bold. **Range:** Common in suburbs, parks, woodlands. Often migrates in large flocks. Casual fall and winter visitor to the west, especially the northwest.

Steller's Jay *Cyanocitta stelleri* L 11½" (29 cm)
Crested; dark blue and black overall. Some races, including nominate from coast to northern Rockies, are darker backed; have bluish streaks on forehead. Central and southern Rockies race, *C. s. macrolopha,* has long crest, paler back, white streaks on forehead, white mark over eye; largest race, *carlottae* (not shown), resident on the Queen Charlotte Islands off British Columbia, is almost entirely black above. Where ranges overlap in the eastern Rockies, Steller's Jay occasionally hybridizes with Blue Jay. **Calls** include a series of *shack* or *shooka* notes and other calls suggestive of Red-shouldered and Red-tailed Hawks. **Range:** Common in pine-oak woodlands and coniferous forests. Bold and aggressive; often scavenges at campgrounds and picnic areas. Casual winter visitor to lower elevations of the Great Basin, southern California, and southwestern deserts.

Gray Jay *Perisoreus canadensis* L 11½" (29 cm)
A fluffy, long-tailed jay with small bill, no crest. The three subspecies groups are shown here: Nominate *P. c. canadensis,* one of several races common in northern boreal forests, has a white collar and forehead, with brownish crown and nape; *capitalis,* in the southern Rockies, has a paler crown, head appears mostly white; *obscurus,* resident along the northwest coast from Washington to northernmost California, has a larger, darker cap extending to the crown, with underparts paler than in other races. **Juveniles** of all races are sooty-gray overall, with a faint white moustachial streak. Gray Jays are familiar camp and cabin visitors. **Call** notes include a whistled *wheeoo* and a low *chuck.*

Clark's Nutcracker *Nucifraga columbiana* L 12" (31 cm)
Chunky gray bird with black wings and black central tail feathers. White wing patches and white outer tail feathers are conspicuous in flight. Wingbeats are deep, slow, crowlike. Locally common in high coniferous forests at timberline. **Calls** include a very nasal, grating, drawn-out *kra-a-a.* **Range:** Every 10 to 20 years, Nutcrackers irrupt out of core range into desert and lowland areas of the west. Accidental to eastern North America.

Blue Jay

Steller's Jay

stelleri

southern
Rockies
macrolopha

**Gray
Jay**

juvenile

boreal
canadensis

southern
Rockies
capitalis

northwest
obscurus

**Clark's
Nutcracker**

Western Scrub-Jay *Aphelocoma californica*

L 11" (28 cm) Long tail; blue above; variable bluish band on chest. Coastal races, including nominate *A. c. californica,* deeper blue above; contrasting brown patch; distinct white eyebrow and blue breast band; undertail coverts geographically variable; may or may not be bluish. Tame and widespread; found in urban areas. Interior races (possibly a separate species) range from duller, slender-billed *nevadae* of Great Basin to bluer, stouter-billed *texana* (neither shown); *woodhouseii* is slender-billed, intermediate in color. Interior races shy; inhabit lower mountain woodland. All U.S. subspecies hold individual territories. **Calls** include raspy *shreep,* often in a short series. Western, Island, and Florida were formerly considered one species, Scrub Jay.

Island Scrub-Jay *Aphelocoma insularis L 12" (30 cm)*

Range: Restricted to Santa Cruz Island, California, where it is the only scrub-jay. Larger and much larger billed than Western; darker blue above; always shows rich blue undertail coverts. Birds hold individual territory; takes several years for young birds to acquire territory and breed.

Florida Scrub-Jay *Aphelocoma coerulescens* **T**

L 11" (28 cm) Restricted to Florida scrub region where population has declined some 90 percent in 20th century due to habitat destruction. Optimum habitat is transitional, produced by fire: consists of scrub, mainly oak, about ten feet high with small openings. Distinguished from other scrub-jays by whitish forehead and eyebrow; shorter, broader bill; paler back; distinct collar; indistinct streaking below; proportionately longer tail. Varied **calls** include raspy, hoarse notes. Has cooperative breeding system: Fledged young remain on territory and help rear nestlings.

Mexican Jay *Aphelocoma ultramarina L 11½" (29 cm)*

Blue above, with slight grayish cast on back, brownish patch on center of back. Lacks crest. Distinguished from scrub-jays by absence of white throat and white eyebrow and by chunkier shape; flight is more direct. Texas race, *A. u. couchii,* has richer blue head. Arizona **juvenile** *arizonae* retains pale bill past postjuvenile molt. **Calls** include a loud, ringing *week,* given singly or in a series. **Range:** Common in pine-oak canyons of the southwestern mountains, where it greatly outnumbers scrub-jays. Has cooperative breeding system similar to Florida Scrub-Jay.

Pinyon Jay *Gymnorhinus cyanocephalus L 10½" (27 cm)*

Blue overall; blue throat streaked with white; bill long and spiky; tail short. Immature is duller. Flight is direct, with rapid wingbeats, unlike scrub-jays' undulating flight. Typical flight **call** is a high-pitched, piercing *mew,* audible over long distances. Also gives a rolling series of *queh* notes. **Range:** Generally seen in large flocks, often numbering in the hundreds; nests in loose colonies. Common in piñon-juniper woodlands of interior mountains and high plateaus; also yellow pine woodlands. Casual to Plains states and coastal California.

interior juvenile
woodhouseii

**Western
Scrub-Jay**

interior
woodhouseii

coastal
californica

**Island
Scrub-Jay**

**Florida
Scrub-Jay**

**Mexican
Jay**

Texas
couchii

Arizona
arizonae

**Pinyon
Jay**

juvenile
arizonae

Brown Jay *Cyanocorax morio* L 16½" (42 cm)

Range: Tropical species; range extends to Texas, where it is resident but rare in woodlands and mesquite along the Rio Grande in vicinity of Falcon Dam. Very large jay with long, broad tail. Dark, sooty-brown overall except for pale belly. **Adult** has black bill. **Juvenile** has yellow bill and eye ring, turning black by second winter; in transition, many have blotchy yellow-and-black bills. A noisy species; its harsh scream is similar to the **call** of a Red-shouldered Hawk. Another call sounds like a hiccup.

Green Jay *Cyanocorax yncas* L 10½" (27 cm)

Range: Tropical species; range extends to southern Texas. Resident and locally common in brushy areas and streamside growth of the lower Rio Grande Valley. Green and blue plumage blends with dappled sun and shade in woodland habitat. Somewhat inquisitive. Gregarious and noisy; most common **call** is a series of raspy *cheh-cheh-cheh* notes.

Black-billed Magpie *Pica pica* L 19" (48 cm)

Readily identified as a magpie by black and white markings and unusually long tail with iridescent green highlights. White wing patches flash in flight. Black bill and range distinguish this species from look-alike Yellow-billed Magpie. Ranges almost overlap, and Black-billed Magpies casually stray south and east of normal range in winter. Gregarious and noisy; typical **calls** include a whining *mag* and a series of loud, harsh *chuck* notes. Calls and many behavior traits of North American race *P. p. hudsonia* differ markedly from those of the Old World races of magpie, whose calls are faster and lower pitched. **Range:** Common inhabitant of open woodlands and thickets in rangelands and foothills, especially along watercourses. Birds seen casually throughout the east may be escaped cage birds.

Yellow-billed Magpie *Pica nuttalli* L 16½" (42 cm)

Similar to Black-billed Magpie, but never occurs in Black-billed's normal range. Distinguished by its yellow bill and by a yellow patch of bare skin around the eye; extent of yellow variable, sometimes fully encircles eye; may be related to state of molt rather than individual variation, or may be a combination of both. **Calls** are similar to Black-billed; both species roost and feed in flocks, usually nest in loose colonies, but Yellow-billed Magpie's behavior is more colonial than Black-billed. **Range:** Prefers oaks, especially more open oak grassland, also orchards and parks. Common resident of rangelands and foothills of central and northern Central Valley, California, and coastal valleys south to Santa Barbara County. Not prone to wandering, but casual north almost to Oregon. Some authorities believe that Yellow-billed Magpie is more closely related to the North American race of Black-billed than either is to the Old World races of magpies.

juvenile

**Brown
Jay**

**Green
Jay**

**Black-billed
Magpie**

**Yellow-billed
Magpie**

Eurasian Jackdaw *Corvus monedula L 13" (33 cm)*

Range: Recent visitor to the northeast, perhaps arriving by ship; has nested in Pennsylvania; now almost eliminated. Small, black overall, with gray nape and ear patches, pale grayish eyes. Lively and inquisitive. **Calls** include a metallic *kow* and a softer *jack* note.

Tamaulipas Crow *Corvus imparatus L 14½" (37 cm)*

Range: First appeared in U.S. in late 1960s near Brownsville, Texas, where it has nested. Found at municipal dump. Present each winter since in varying numbers, declining over last decade. Smaller, glossier than American Crow. **Call,** a low, froglike croak.

American Crow *Corvus brachyrhynchos L 17½" (45 cm)*

Our largest crow. Long, heavy bill is noticeably smaller than in ravens. Fan-shaped tail distinguishes all crows from ravens in flight. Adult American Crow is readily identified by familiar *caw* **call** but juvenile's higher pitched, nasal *cah* begging call resembles the call of the similar Fish Crow. **Range:** Generally common throughout most of its range in a wide variety of habitats.

Northwestern Crow *Corvus caurinus L 16" (41 cm)*

Range: This species (not shown)inhabits northwestern coastal areas and islands, where it is a common scavenger along the shore. Closely resembles American Crow; very difficult to distinguish in the field. Northwestern Crow is slightly smaller; **call** is somewhat hoarser, lower. Best clue is range. Considered by some authorities to be a subspecies of American Crow.

Fish Crow *Corvus ossifragus L 15½" (39 cm)*

Smaller than similar American Crow, with proportionately longer tail, smaller head and bill, stiffer wingbeats. Best distinguished by voice: **Call,** a high, nasal *ca-hah,* the second note lower; also low, short *car* notes. **Range:** Favors tidewater marshes and low valleys along eastern river systems; less frequent inland, except along rivers. Often seen in winter in flocks with American Crows.

Chihuahuan Raven *Corvus cryptoleucus L 19½" (50 cm)*

Heavier bill and wedge-shaped tail distinguish both raven species from crows; but Chihuahuan's bill and wings are shorter, tail shorter and less wedge-shaped, than Common Raven. Common **call,** a drawn-out croak, usually slightly higher pitched than call of Common Raven; nasal bristles extend farther out on bill. Neck feathers white rather than grayish at base, but usually obscured. **Range:** Common in desert areas and scrubby grasslands.

Common Raven *Corvus corax L 24" (61 cm)*

Large, with long, heavy bill and long, wedge-shaped tail. Most common **call** is a low, drawn-out croak. Larger than Chihuahuan Raven; note thicker, shaggier throat feathers, and that nasal bristles do not extend as far out on larger bill. **Range:** Found in a variety of habitats, including mountains, deserts, coastal areas. Numerous in western and northern part of range; uncommon and local, but spreading, in Appalachians.

Eurasian
Jackdaw

Tamaulipas
Crow

American
Crow

Fish
Crow

Chihuahuan
Raven

Common
Raven

Larks (Family Alaudidae)

Ground dwellers of open fields, larks are slender-billed seed- and insect-eaters. They seldom alight on trees or bushes. On the ground, they walk rather than hop.

Sky Lark *Alauda arvensis* L 7¼" (18 cm)
Range: Nominate *A. a. arvensis,* a widespread European race introduced to Vancouver Island in the early 1900s, is resident there on open slopes and fields. The population on San Juan Islands is now extirpated. Plain brown bird with slender bill; slight crest is raised when bird is agitated. Upperparts heavily streaked; buffy-white underparts streaked on breast and throat. Dark eye prominent. Highly migratory Asian subspecies *pekinensis,* rare on western Aleutians and Pribilofs, is darker and more heavily streaked above; accidental in winter in Washington and northern California. All juveniles have a scaly brown mantle. In flight, Sky Larks show a conspicuous white trailing edge on the inner wing and white edges on tail. **Song** is a continuous outpouring of trills and warblings, delivered in high hovering or circling song flight. **Call,** a liquid *chirrup* with buzzy overtones.

Horned Lark *Eremophila alpestris* L 6¾-7¾" (17-20 cm)
Head pattern distinctive in all subspecies: black "horns," white or yellowish face and throat with broad black stripe under eye; black bib. **Female** duller overall than **male,** horns less prominent. Conspicuous in flight is the mostly black tail with white outer feathers, brown central feathers. Brief **juvenile** plumage has whitish markings above, streaks below; can be confused with Sprague's Pipit (page 362). Western subspecies vary widely in overall color; selected extremes are shown here: pale *E. a. enthymia;* dark *alpestris;* yellowish *sierrae* (and also *strigata*); streaked *insularis;* and reddish *rubea.* Three widespread races are found in the east: "Prairie Horned Lark," *praticola,* which breeds in south Canada and the eastern U.S., is pale, with white eyebrows and throat. "Northern Horned Lark," *alpestris,* is much darker, with a yellow throat. The central Arctic coast race, *hoyti,* is pale like *praticola,* but larger. Horned Lark's **calls** include a high *tsee-ee* or *tsee-titi.* **Song** is a weak twittering, delivered from the ground or in flight. **Range:** Widespread and common, Horned Lark prefers dirt fields, gravel ridges, shores. The flocks in winter in the eastern U.S. are mainly *alpestris.*

Sky Lark

pekinensis

arvensis

♂

tris ♂

alpestris ♀

juvenile *alpestris*

Horned Lark

sierrae ♂

enthymia ♂

ris ♂

rubea ♂

Swallows (Family Hirundinidae)

Slender bodies with long, pointed wings resemble swifts, but wrist angle is sharper and farther from the body; flight is more fluid. Adept aerialists, swallows dart to catch flying insects. Flocks perch in long rows on branches and wires.

Tree Swallow *Tachycineta bicolor L 5¾" (15 cm)*

Dark, glossy greenish-blue above, greener in fall plumage; white below. White cheek patch does not extend above eye as in Violet-green Swallow. **Juvenile** is gray-brown above; usually has more diffuse breast band than Bank Swallow (next page). **First-spring female** shows varying amount of adult color on crown and back. **Range:** Common in wooded habitat near water, and where dead trees provide nest holes. Also nests in fence posts, barn eaves, nest boxes. Migrates in huge flocks; goes north earlier in spring, lingers farther north in fall, than other swallows.

Bahama Swallow *Tachycineta cyaneoviridis*

L 5¾" (15 cm) **Range:** Endemic Bahamian species. Breeds in northern Bahamas and vicinity; casual visitor to the Florida Keys, especially Big Pine Key, and nearby mainland. Greenish above. Deeply forked tail and white underwing coverts separate this species from similar Tree Swallow. Immatures have shorter tail fork, dusky wash on breast and wing linings.

Violet-green Swallow *Tachycineta thalassina*

L 5¼" (13 cm) White on cheek extends above eye; white flank patches extend onto sides of rump; compare with similar Tree Swallow. May also be confused with White-throated Swift (page 262). Female is duller above than **male. Juvenile** is gray-brown above; white except on rump may be mottled or grayish. **Range:** Common in a variety of woodland habitats. Nests in hollow trees or rock crevices, often forming loose colonies. Casual in the east.

Purple Martin *Progne subis L 8" (20 cm)*

Male is dark, glossy, purplish-blue. **Female** and juvenile are gray below. **First-spring** males have some purple below. In flight, male especially resembles European Starling (page 358); but note forked tail, longer wings, and typical swallow flight, short glides alternating with rapid flapping. **Range:** Locally common where suitable nest sites are available. Declining over much of North America, especially in Pacific states. Very early spring migrant in south; winters in South America.

Common House-Martin *Delichon urbica L 5" (13 cm)*

Range: Old World species. Casual in spring in western Alaska; one record for Saint-Pierre, off Newfoundland. Deep, glossy blue above; mostly white below with white rump; underwing coverts pale smoky gray. Female slightly grayer below; juvenile duller. Soars for long periods. **Call** a rough scratchy *prrit,* somewhat similar to Rough-winged Swallow. One Alaska specimen of eastern race *D. u. lagopoda*; has more extensive white on rump.

Tree Swallow

spring adult ♀

1st spring ♀

juvenile

juvenile

fall adult ♂

spring ♂

Bahama Swallow

adults

♂ adults

juvenile

Violet-green Swallow

adult ♂

Common House-Martin
lagopoda

Purple Martin

♀

adult ♂

1st spring ♂

♀

adult ♂

Bank Swallow *Riparia riparia L 4¾" (12 cm)*
Our smallest swallow. Distinct brownish-gray breast band, often extending in a line down center of breast. Throat is white; white curves around rear border of ear patch. **Juvenile** has thin buffy wing bars; compare with juvenile Northern Rough-winged Swallow and juvenile Tree Swallow (preceding page). Locally common throughout most of range. Unlike Northern Rough-winged, wingbeats are shallow and rapid; also paler rump contrasts with wings. **Range:** Nests in large colonies, excavating nest burrows in steep riverbank cliffs, gravel pits, and highway cuts. Winters chiefly in South America; often migrates in large flocks.

Cliff Swallow *Petrochelidon pyrrhonota L 5½" (14 cm)*
Squarish tail and buffy rump distinguish this swallow from all others except Cave Swallow. Most Cliff Swallows have dark chestnut and blackish throat, pale forehead. A primarily southwestern race, *H. p. melanogaster,* has cinnamon forehead like Cave Swallow, but throat is dark chestnut. All **juveniles** are much duller and grayer than **adults;** throat is paler, forehead darker. **Range:** Locally common around bridges, rural settlements, in open country on cliffs. Range has expanded greatly in last two decades. Nests in colonies, building gourd-shaped mud nests.

Northern Rough-winged Swallow
Stelgidopteryx serripennis L 5" (13 cm) Brown above, whitish below, with gray-brown wash on chin, throat, and upper breast. Lacks Bank Swallow's distinct breast band; wings are longer, wingbeats deeper and slower. **Juvenile** has cinnamon wing bars. **Range:** Nests in single pairs in riverbanks, cliffs, culverts, and under bridges. Migrates singly or in small flocks.

Barn Swallow *Hirundo rustica L 6¾" (17 cm)*
Long, deeply forked tail. Throat is reddish-brown; underparts usually cinnamon or buffy. Two Eurasian, white-bellied races have occurred in west and north Alaska: *H. r. rustica,* which has a solid dark breast band, and *gutturalis,* with incomplete breast band, which also has been found on Queen Charlotte Islands. In all **juveniles,** tail is shorter but still noticeably forked; underparts pale. **Range:** Common; generally nests on or inside farm buildings, under bridges, and inside culverts, in pairs or small colonies.

Cave Swallow *Petrochelidon fulva L 5½" (14 cm)*
Squarish tail; buffy rump, richer color than Cliff Swallow; distinguished from most Cliffs by buffy throat color extending around nape; cinnamon forehead; but compare with southwestern form of Cliff that also has a cinnamon forehead. **Range:** Mexican and West Indian species: West Indies race, *P. f. fulva,* a local breeder in south Florida, is smaller than Mexican *pelodoma,* which is widespread in the southwest; *fulva* also has more buff below and darker rump. Nests in colonies in limestone caves, sinkholes, culverts, and under bridges, sometimes with Barn and Cliff Swallows. Very rare on east coast, mainly in fall; casual to south Arizona, south Louisiana, southeast California.

Bank Swallow

juvenile

southwestern *melanogaster*

Northern Rough-winged Swallow

juvenile

juvenile

Cliff Swallow

juvenile

juvenile

southwest *pelodoma*

Eurasian *rustica*

dark

juvenile

Barn Swallow

Cave Swallow

West Indies *fulva*

Babblers (Family Timaliidae)

Wrentit has recently been placed in an Old World family of which most species occur in southeast Asia.

Wrentit *Chamaea fasciata L 6½" (17 cm)*
Color varies from reddish-brown in northern populations to grayer in southern birds. Note distinct cream-colored eye and lightly streaked buffy breast; long, rounded tail usually cocked. Common in chaparral and coniferous brushland, Wrentits are usually heard before they are seen. Male's loud **song,** sung year-round, begins with a series of accelerating notes and runs into a descending trill: *pit-pit-pit-tr-r-r-r.* Female's song lacks trill.

Chickadees, Titmice (Family Paridae)

Small, hardy birds with short bills, short wings, and drab plumage. Active and agile, they often hang upside down from twigs to feed.

Bridled Titmouse *Baeolophus wollweberi L 5¼" (13 cm)*
Note distinct crest, black-and-white facial pattern, black throat. Most common **call** is a rapid, high-pitched variation of *chick-a-dee-dee,* similar to Juniper Titmouse. **Range:** Common resident of woodland stands of oak, juniper, and sycamore in the mountains of southern Arizona and New Mexico.

Oak Titmouse *Baeolophus inornatus L 5" (13 cm)*
Grayish-brown with a short crest. Northern race *B. i. inornatus* is slightly smaller, paler, and smaller billed than *affabilis* (shown here) from southwest California and northern Baja; birds from Little San Bernadino Mountains are paler, grayer than *affabilis.* **Song** variable, a repeated series of syllables made up of whistled, alternating, high and low notes. **Call,** a hoarse *tschick-a-dee.* **Range:** Common in warm, dry oak woodland. With Juniper Titmouse, formerly considered one species, Plain Titmouse.

Juniper Titmouse *Baeolophus griseus L 5¼" (13 cm)*
Similar to Oak Titmouse; ranges separate except on Modoc plateau in northern California. Slightly larger, paler, grayer than Oak; bill usually larger. **Song** variable; a rolling series of syllables given rapidly at a uniform pitch. **Call,** a hoarse *tschick-a dee* more like Bridled Titmouse than Oak's. **Range:** Uncommon to fairly common in juniper or piñon-juniper woodland.

Tufted Titmouse *Baeolophus bicolor L 6½" (17 cm)*
Most birds have gray crest and blackish forehead. In southern and western Texas, adult birds have whitish foreheads and blackish crests; formerly considered a separate species, **"Black-crested Titmouse."** In south-central Texas zone of overlap, birds show variable brown foreheads, dark gray crests. Active and noisy; typical **song** is a loud whistled *peter peter peter.* **Range:** Common in deciduous woodlands, mesquite, parks, suburbs, at feeders.

northern

southern

Wrentit

**Bridled
Titmouse**

**Oak
Titmouse**
affabilis

**Juniper
Titmouse**

**Tufted
Titmouse**

"Black-crested
Titmouse"

Black-capped Chickadee *Poecile atricapillus*

L 5¼" (13 cm) Black cap and bib; cheeks more extensively white than similar Carolina Chickadee. Note that Black-capped Chickadee's greater wing coverts and secondaries are broadly edged in white; tertials more boldly edged, with darker centers than Carolina's; flanks more olive, lower edge of black bib a bit more ragged. These differences are obscured in **worn summer** birds. Best distinction is voice. Black-capped's **call** is a lower, slower *chick-a-dee-dee-dee* than Carolina's; typical **song,** a clear, whistled *fee-bee* or *fee-bee-ee,* the first note higher in pitch. **Range:** Common in open woodlands, clearings, suburbs. Usually forages in thickets, low branches of trees. The usual ranges of Black-capped and Carolina barely overlap, but periodic fall and winter irruptions temporarily push Black-capped's range farther south. Where there is overlap, the two species may hybridize. In the Appalachians, Black-capped inhabits higher elevations.

Carolina Chickadee *Poecile carolinensis L 4¾" (12 cm)*

Very similar to Black-capped Chickadee: black cap and bib, white cheeks. Note that Carolina lacks broad white edgings on greater wing coverts; lower edge of black bib is usually neater, has less olive on flanks than Black-capped. Best distinction is voice. Carolina's **call** is a higher, faster version of *chick-a-dee-dee-dee* than Black-capped; typical **song** a four-note whistle, *fee-bee fee-bay.* **Range:** Common in open deciduous forests, woodland clearings and edges, suburban areas. Feeds in trees and thickets; seldom descends to ground. At northern edge, its range in some winters is invaded by Black-capped. Where ranges overlap, the two species may hybridize. In the Appalachians, Carolina prefers valleys and foothills.

Mexican Chickadee *Poecile sclateri L 5" (13 cm)*

The only breeding chickadee in its range. Extensive black bib is distinctive, along with dark gray flanks. Lacks white eyebrow of neighboring Mountain Chickadee. **Song** is a warbled whistle; call note, a husky buzz. **Range:** A Mexican species, fairly common resident in coniferous and pine-oak forests; found in U.S. only in Chiricahua Mountains of southeastern Arizona and Animas and Peloncillo Mountains of southwestern New Mexico.

Mountain Chickadee *Poecile gambeli L 5¼" (13 cm)*

White eyebrow and pale gray sides distinguish this species from other chickadees; lack of crest separates it from the Bridled Titmouse (preceding page). Birds of Rocky Mountain nominate race *P. g. gambeli* are tinged with buff on back, sides, flanks, and have broader eyebrows than *baileyae.* **Call** is a hoarse *chick-adee-adee-adee;* typical **song,** a three- or four-note descending whistle, *fee-bee-bay* or *fee-bee fee-bee.* **Range:** Common resident in coniferous and mixed woodlands. Some descend to lower elevations in winter.

fresh fall

**Black-capped
Chickadee**

worn summer

**Carolina
Chickadee**

**Mexican
Chickadee**

**Mountain
Chickadee**

Rockies *gambeli*

baileyae

Chestnut-backed Chickadee *Poecile rufescens*
L 4¾" (12 cm) Sooty-brown cap, white cheeks, black bib; back
and rump chestnut. Over most of its range, this species has bright
chestnut sides and flanks; *P. r. barlowi*, on central California coast
south of Golden Gate Bridge, shows almost no chestnut below.
Call is a hoarse, rapid *tseek-a-dee-dee*. **Range:** Found in coniferous forests, deciduous woodlands. Usually feeds high in trees.

Gray-headed Chickadee *Poecile cinctus* L 5½" (14 cm)
Gray-brown above, whitish below, with white cheek patch, black
bib, buffy sides and flanks. Distinguished from Boreal Chickadee
by more extensively white cheeks, longer tail, paler flanks, and
pale edges on wing coverts; also by **call,** a series of peevish *dee
deer* notes. **Range:** Rare; found in willows and spruces edging
tundra. Formerly called Siberian Tit.

Boreal Chickadee *Poecile hudsonicus* L 5½" (14 cm)
Gray-brown above, whitish below, with white cheeks, black bib,
brown sides and flanks. Distinguished from Gray-headed Chickadee by smaller cheek patch, shorter tail, all-gray wing coverts,
darker flanks; also by **call,** a nasal *tseek-a-day-day*. **Range:** Fairly
common in coniferous forests. In some winters, small numbers
wander hundreds of miles south of normal eastern range.

Verdins (Family Remizidae)

Small, spritely birds with finely pointed bills. They inhabit arid scrub
country, feed in brush chickadee-style, and build spherical nests.

Verdin *Auriparus flaviceps* L 4½" (11 cm)
Adult has dull gray plumage, chestnut shoulder patches, yellow
head and throat. **Juvenile** is brown-gray overall; shorter tail helps
separate it from Bushtit. Compare also with Lucy's Warbler(page
370). **Song,** a plaintive three-note whistle, the second note higher.
Calls include rapid *chip* notes. **Range:** Common in mesquite and
other dense thorny shrubs of the southwestern desert.

Bushtits (Family Aegithalidae)

Longer tail distinguishes these tiny birds from other chickadee-like
species. Usually feeds in large, busy, twittering flocks. Nest is an elaborate hanging structure.

Bushtit *Psaltriparus minimus* L 4½" (11 cm)
Gray above, paler below; fresh fall male may have pale pink flanks.
Coastal birds have brown crown; interior birds show brown ear
patch and gray cap, and have sharper, slower, twittering **calls.**
Juvenile male and some adult males in the southwest have a black
mask, and were formerly considered a separate species, the
"Black-eared Bushtit." Range: Common in woodlands, chap-
arral, parks, and gardens.

rufescens

Chestnut-backed Chickadee

coastal central California *barlowi*

Gray-headed Chickadee

Boreal Chickadee

Verdin

juvenile

Bushtit

interior ♂ *plumbeus*

interior ♀ *plumbeus*

"Black-eared Bushtit" juvenile ♂

coastal ♂

Creepers (Family Certhiidae)

Little tree-climbers whose curved bills dig insects and larvae from bark. Stiff tail feathers serve as props.

Brown Creeper *Certhia americana* L 5¼" (13 cm)
Camouflaged by streaked brown plumage, Creepers spiral upward from base of a tree, then fly to a lower place on another tree. **Call** is a soft, sibilant *see;* song, a high-pitched, variable *see see see titi see.* Fairly common but hard to spot. **Range:** Nests in coniferous, mixed, or swampy forests. Generally solitary, but sometimes seen in winter flocks of titmice and nuthatches.

Nuthatches (Family Sittidae)

These short-tailed acrobats climb up, down, and around tree trunks and branches. Winter flocks roam with chickadees and kinglets.

White-breasted Nuthatch *Sitta carolinensis*
L 5¾" (15 cm) Black cap tops all-white face and breast; extent of rust below is variable. **Females** in the northeast have gray crowns more consistently than in the south. Western birds have longer, thinner bills. Typical **song,** a rapid series of nasal whistles on one pitch. **Call** is usually a low-pitched, repeated, nasal *yank* in eastern nominate race; high-pitched in west coast *S. c. aculeata;* and higher pitched and given in a rapid series by Great Basin *tenuissima* and Rockies *nelsoni.* **Range:** Common; found in leafy trees in the east, oaks and conifers in the west.

Red-breasted Nuthatch *Sitta canadensis* L 4½" (11 cm)
Black cap and eye line, white eyebrow, rust underparts; **female** and juveniles have duller head, paler underparts. High-pitched, nasal **call** sounds like a toy tin horn. **Range:** Resident in northern and subalpine conifers; gleans small branches, outer twigs. Irruptive migrant; numbers and winter range vary yearly. In the east, resident range is expanding southward.

Pygmy Nuthatch *Sitta pygmaea* L 4¼" (11 cm)
Gray-brown cap; creamy-buff underparts. Pale nape spot visible at close range. Dark eye line bordering cap, most distinct in interior populations. Typical **calls,** a high, rapid *peep peep* and a piping *wee-bee;* grouped in three or more notes in coastal nominate race, *S. p. pygmaea.* **Range:** Favors yellow-pine forest, except for birds in coastal California pines. Roams in loose flocks.

Brown-headed Nuthatch *Sitta pusilla* L 4½" (11 cm)
Brown cap; dull buff underparts. Pale nape spot visible at close range. Narrow dark eye line borders cap. **Call** is a repeated double note like the squeak of a rubber duck. Feeding flocks also give twittering, chirping, and talky *bit bit bit* calls. **Range:** Fairly common; found in pine woodlands.

Brown Creeper

eastern
carolinensis

♀

**White-breasted
Nuthatch**

Great Basin
♂ *tenuissima*

**Red-
breasted
Nuthatch**

♀

♂

**Pygmy
Nuthatch**

**Brown-headed
Nuthatch**

Wrens (Family Troglodytidae)

Found throughout most of North America, wrens are chunky birds with slender, slightly curved bills. Tails are often uptilted. Loud song and vigorous territorial defense belie the small size of most species.

House Wren *Troglodytes aedon* L 4¾" (12 cm)

Brown above with faint eyebrow. Separated from Winter Wren by longer tail, less prominent barring on belly, and larger overall size. Western *T. a. parkmanii* breeds east to Ontario; grayer above, paler below. **Juvenile** shows a bright rufous rump and darker buff below. Birds from mountains of southeast Arizona, formerly known as **"Brown-throated Wren,"** have a slightly buffier throat and breast and a bolder eyebrow. Exuberant **song,** a cascade of bubbling whistled notes. **Range:** Common in shrubs, farms, gardens, parks. Winters rarely north into summer range.

Winter Wren *Troglodytes troglodytes* L 4" (10 cm)

Stubby tail; dark barring on belly. Widespread eastern subspecies *T. t. hiemalis* from the north breeds west to northeast British Columbia; similar *pullus* (not shown) breeds in the Appalachians. Western subspecies *pacificus* is richer buff on throat and breast, darker on back. Races from Bering Sea islands and Aleutians are larger, paler, and longer-billed. Eastern subspecies give a *kelp-kelp* **call** like Song Sparrow; all western races a *timp-timp* call like Wilson's Warbler. **Song,** a rapid series of melodious trills, is much faster in western birds. **Range:** Rather secretive, nests in dense brush, especially along stream banks, in moist coniferous woods; in winter may be found in any type of woodland. Winters casually into summer range.

Carolina Wren *Thryothorus ludovicianus* L 5½" (14 cm)

Deep rusty-brown above, warm buff below; white throat and prominent white eye stripe. Vivacious, melodious **song,** a loud, clear *teakettle tea-kettle teakettle* or *cheery cheery cheery.* Sings any time of day or year. **Range:** Common in the concealing underbrush of moist woodlands and swamps, wooded suburbs. Nonmigratory, but after mild winters resident populations expand north of mapped range. After harsh winters, range limits retract. Casual to Colorado and New Mexico.

Bewick's Wren *Thryomanes bewickii* L 5¼" (13 cm)

Long, sideways-flitting tail, edged with white spots; long white eyebrow. Subspecies differ mainly in dorsal color: Eastern *T. b. bewickii,* is bright reddish-brown above; south Texas *criptus* (not shown) duller, but still tinged red. Widespread *eremophilus* of the western interior is the grayest; western coastal races grow browner and darker as one travels north. Northwest *calaphonus* (not shown) is dark, richly colored, with a rufous cast. **Song** variable, a high, thin buzz and warble, similar to Song Sparrow. Calls include a flat, hollow *jip.* **Range:** Found in brushland, hedgerows, stream edges, open woods, clear-cuts in the east. Sharply declining east of the Rockies, especially east of the Mississippi.

southeast Arizona
"Brown-throated Wren"

**House
Wren**

*western
parkmanii*

juvenile

eastern
aedon

Aleutians

**Winter
Wren**

*western
pacificus*

**Carolina
Wren**

eastern
hiemalis

western interior
eremophilus

eastern
bewickii

Bewick's Wren

Cactus Wren *Campylorhynchus brunneicapillus*
L 8½" (22 cm) Large; dark crown, streaked back, heavily barred wings and tail, broad white eyebrow. Breast is densely spotted with black; threatened Californian subspecies, *C. b. sandiegense,* is less densely spotted. **Song,** heard all year, is a low-pitched, harsh, rapid *cha cha cha cha cha.* **Range:** Common in cactus country and arid hillsides and valleys. Bulky nests are tucked into the protective spines of cholla cactus or thorny bushes.

Rock Wren *Salpinctes obsoletus* L 6" (15 cm)
Dull gray-brown above with contrasting cinnamon rump, buffy tail tips, broad blackish tail band. Breast finely streaked. Frequently bobs its body, especially when alarmed. **Song** is a variable mix of buzzes and trills; **call,** a buzzy *tick-ear.* **Range:** Fairly common in arid and semiarid habitats, sunny talus slopes, scrublands, dry washes. Casual in fall and winter to the east.

Canyon Wren *Catherpes mexicanus* L 5¾" (15 cm)
White throat and breast, chestnut belly. Long bill aids in extracting insects from deep crevices. Loud silvery **song,** a decelerating, descending series of liquid *tee's* and *tew's.* Typical **call** is a sharp *jeet.* **Range:** Common in canyons and cliffs, often near water; may also build its cup nest in stone buildings, chimneys.

Marsh Wren *Cistothorus palustris* L 5" (13 cm)
Much plumage variation in eastern and western races. Where ranges overlap on Great Plains, eastern birds are darker, more richly colored, neck speckled black and white; western birds duller, brownish smudges on neck. Football-shaped nest attached to reeds above water. **Songs,** more liquid in the east; harsher and much more variable in the west. Alarm **call** a sharp *tsuk,* often doubled. **Range:** Common in reedy marshes, cattail swamps.

Sedge Wren *Cistothorus platensis* L 4½" (11 cm)
Crown and back streaked; eyebrow whitish, indistinct; underparts largely buff. **Song** begins with a few single notes followed by a weak staccato trill or chatter; **call** note, a rich *chip,* often doubled. Globular nest similar to that of Marsh Wren. **Range:** Found in wet meadows or sedge marshes. Generally common but local; uncommon to rare in the east. Rare and local in winter to New Mexico. Casual to California in late fall.

Dippers (Family Cinclidae)

Stocky, robust birds that lead an aquatic life, wading and even swimming underwater in clear, rushing mountain streams to feed.

American Dipper *Cinclus mexicanus* L 7½" (19 cm)
Adult sooty-gray; dark bill; tail and wings short. **Juvenile** has paler, mottled underparts, pale bill. **Song,** loud, musical, wren-like. **Range:** Found along mountain streams. Descends to lower elevations in winter; casual vagrant well outside mapped range.

Rock
Wren

Cactus
Wren

Canyon
Wren

Marsh
Wren

Sedge
Wren

juvenile

American
Dipper

Kinglets (Family Regulidae)

Small, active birds that often hover on rapidly beating wings to feed.

Golden-crowned Kinglet *Regulus satrapa* L 4" (10 cm)
Orange crown patch of **male** is bordered in yellow and black;
female's crown is yellow. Head pattern and paler underparts are
unlike Ruby-crowned Kinglet. **Call** is a series of high, thin *tsee*
notes. **Song,** almost inaudibly high, is a series of *tsee* notes accelerating into a trill. **Range:** Common in coniferous woodlands.

Ruby-crowned Kinglet *Regulus calendula* L 4¼" (11 cm)
Male's red crown patch seldom visible; dusky underparts. Compare carefully with Golden-crowned Kinglet. Active; flicks wings
rapidly. **Calls** include a scolding *je-ditt.* **Song,** several high, thin
tsee notes followed by descending *tew* notes, ends with warbled
three-note phrases. **Range:** Common in woodlands, thickets.

Old World Warblers, Gnatcatchers
(Family Sylviidae)

Old World Warblers are a large, diverse group. Sexes differ little,
except in genus *Sylvia.* Gnatcatchers are found only in the New World.

Blue-gray Gnatcatcher *Polioptila caerulea*
L 4¼" (11 cm) **Male** is blue-gray above, **female** grayer; long tail
black above with white outer feathers. Male has black line on sides
of crown in **breeding** plumage only. **Call,** a querulous *pwee.*
Active; favors woodlands, thickets, chaparral.

Black-capped Gnatcatcher *Polioptila nigriceps*
L 4¼" (11 cm) **Range**: West Mexican species, very rare, mostly
spring and summer in southeastern Arizona. Separated from
Blue-gray and Black-tailed Gnatcatcher by more graduated white
outer tail feathers, longer bill; **breeding male**'s black cap extends
below eye. **Female** and winter male best identified by tail shape
and pattern. **Calls** like California Gnatcatcher or Bewick's Wren.

Black-tailed Gnatcatcher *Polioptila melanura*
L 4" (10 cm) White terminal spots on graduated tail feathers;
short bill. **Breeding male** has glossy black cap, contrasting with
eye ring. **Female** washed with brown. **Calls** include rasping *cheeh*
and hissing *ssheh;* **song** a rapid series of *jee* notes. Desert resident; partial to washes.

California Gnatcatcher *Polioptila californica* **T**
L 4¼" (11 cm) Similar to Black-tailed, but is darker with less white
in outer tail feathers, less distinct eye ring. **Call,** a rising and
falling *zeeer;* **song,** a series of *jzer* or *zew* notes. **Range:** Local resident in sage scrub of southwest California. Northern nominate
race now threatened, due to habitat destruction.

Golden-crowned Kinglet

♀

♂

Ruby-crowned Kinglet

♀

♂

♀

breeding ♂

Blue-gray Gnatcatcher

♀

breeding ♂

Black-capped Gnatcatcher

♀

breeding ♂

Black-tailed Gnatcatcher

♀

California Gnatcatcher

breeding ♂

Lanceolated Warbler *Locustella lanceolata*

L 4½" (11 cm) **Range:** Mainly Asian species. Many occurred in spring and summer of 1984 on Aleutian island of Attu. Accidental in fall in California. Resembles Middendorff's Grasshopper-Warbler but smaller; less broadly streaked above, including crown and rump, but streaks extend to feather tips; clear brown fringe on tertials. Breast, undertail coverts, and flanks are streaked. Highly secretive. Walks and runs; flicks its wings. Distinctive **call,** a metallic *rink-tink-tink,* delivered infrequently; also an explosive *pwit* and excited *chack* when disturbed. **Song,** a thin, insect-like reeling sound, like a fishing line makes.

Middendorff's Grasshopper-Warbler

Locustella ochotensis L 6" (15 cm) **Range:** East Asian species, casual migrant mainly on westernmost Aleutians in fall; also two spring to summer records. Recorded also on St. Lawrence and Nunivak Islands and Pribilofs. Big, chunky warbler with whitish-tipped, wedge-shaped tail; hefty bill. Indistinct dark markings above; yellowish-buff below with a faintly streaked breast, rustier above. By late spring, the underparts are mostly whitish and lack streaking. Like all *Locustella* warblers, is very secretive.

Dusky Warbler *Phylloscopus fuscatus L 5½" (14 cm)*

Range: Asian species, casual on islands off western Alaska, and in fall off south coastal Alaska and in California. Dusky-brown upperparts and lack of wing bar distinguish this species from Arctic Warbler; tail slightly rounded; bill shorter, thinner. Usually has dark, slender legs; distinct eyebrow; dull white in front of eye; broad dark brown eye line; whitish eye ring. Underparts creamy white, with buffy brown wash on flanks and undertail coverts. **Calls** include a hard, sharp *tschick,* not unlike *chip* note of Lincoln's Sparrow. Constantly flicks wings.

Arctic Warbler *Phylloscopus borealis L 5" (13 cm)*

Long, yellowish-white eyebrow, often curving upward behind eye; straw-colored legs and feet. Broad, dark eye line, mottled ear patches. Has square tail, olive upperparts, and pale wing bar on tips of greater coverts; faint second wing bar. Brownish-olive on sides and flanks; long primary projection. Stout bill is thicker, straighter than Orange-crowned Warbler (page 368); lacks streaking below. Larger specimens taken in the western Aleutians with larger bills are either of nominate race *P. t. borealis,* with paler underparts, or yellower *xanthrodyas* (not shown). Alaskan race, *kennicotti,* is smaller, with smaller bill than either of the Asian races. Arctic Warbler's **song** is a long, loud, series of toneless buzzy notes. **Calls** include a buzzy *dzik.* **Range:** Fairly common in western and central Alaska; two fall records for coastal California; nests on grassy tundra or in willow thickets.

Lanceolated Warbler

adult

Middendorff's Grasshopper-Warbler

spring

fall

Dusky Warbler

fall
kennicotti

spring
kennicotti

Arctic Warbler

borealis

Old World Flycatchers (Family Muscicapidae)

Short-legged birds that perch upright and obtain insects primarily through fly-catching, often returning to the same perch. May flick wings or tail. Species of genus *Ficedula* nest in cavities; genus *Muscicapa* build exposed nests. Not related to New World flycatchers.

Narcissus Flycatcher *Ficedula narcissina*
L 5¼" (13 cm) **Range:** East Asian species; two spring records of males on Attu in the western Aleutians. **Adult male** overall black and yellow-orange; most orange on eyebrow and throat. Has yellow rump; white patch on inner secondary coverts. **First-spring male** similar, but duller. **Female** drab; brownish-olive above, with green on rump; contrasting reddish-tinged uppertail coverts and tail; whitish throat; brownish mottling on breast. First-fall male similar to female.

Siberian Flycatcher *Muscicapa sibirica L 5¼" (13 cm)*
Range: Asian species; casual to western Aleutians; one spring record for Pribilofs; one fall record for Bermuda. Dark grayish-brown upperparts and wash on sides and flanks; center of breast diffusely streaked. Whitish half-collar; brownish supraloral spot; short bill; long primary projection; dark centers on undertail coverts may be concealed. Northern nominate race, *M. s. sibirica*, is darker and more diffusely streaked than southern races.

Red-breasted Flycatcher *Ficedula parva*
L 5¼" (13 cm) **Range:** Eurasian species; casual in late spring to western Aleutians; one spring record on St. Lawrence Island. Distinct white oval patches at base of outer tail feathers visible in flight, barely visible on folded tail from below; prominent eye ring. On Asian subspecies, *F. p. albicilla*, felt by some to be a separate species, reddish-orange only on throat of **breeding adult male;** full reddish throat acquired by second spring. **Females** and immature males have whitish throats; grayish wash on breast; solid black uppertail coverts. Perches low; often drops to ground to catch prey, then returns to perch. Frequently flicks tail up while giving rattled *trrt* **call;** also a metallic *tic* and harsh *ze-it.*

Gray-spotted Flycatcher *Muscicapa griseisticta*
L 6" (15 cm) **Range:** East Asian species; casual to western Aleutians in spring. Larger and smaller headed than Siberian; primary projection longer. Note distinctive, but variable, streaking below; paler supraloral spot; more distinct submoustachial stripe usually shows some markings; undertail coverts white.

Asian Brown Flycatcher *Muscicapa dauurica*
L 5¼" (13 cm) **Range:** Asian species; two spring records for Attu Island, Aleutians, and St. Lawrence Island. Grayish-brown above; largely whitish below; grayish wash across chest or, rarely, some diffuse streaks. Bill larger than Siberian or Gray-spotted, extensively flesh-colored at base of lower mandible; primary projection shorter; supraloral area paler.

Narcissus Flycatcher

spring ♀

1st spring ♂

adult ♂

♀

♀

breeding adult ♂

Siberian Flycatcher

spring

1st fall

1st fall

Red-breasted Flycatcher
albicilla

spring ♀

Gray-spotted Flycatcher

spring

1st fall

spring

Asian Brown Flycatcher

1st fall

Thrushes (Family Turdidae)

Eloquent songsters of many habitats, including woodlands and open areas. With narrow, notched bills, they feed on insects and fruit.

Siberian Rubythroat *Luscinia calliope* L 6" (15 cm)
Range: Asian species; rare spring and fall migrant on western Aleutians, very rare on Pribilofs, casual on St. Lawrence Island. **Male** has a ruby red throat and broad, white submoustachial stripe. **Females** have white throats, often with some pink on adults and buffy on immatures; compare with smaller Bluethroat, which has rufous tail patches, dark breast band, paler underparts.

Bluethroat *Luscinia svecica* L 5½" (14 cm)
Colorful throat pattern distinguishes **breeding male** from all other birds. In all plumages, rufous patches at base of tail are conspicuous in flight, which is low off the ground. In **female** and immature, note dark breast band. Bluethroat runs along the ground, usually with tail cocked. Generally furtive, but in courtship males sing from high perches and in elaborate display flight. Varied, melodious **song** often begins with a crisp, metallic *ting ting ting;* **call,** *tchak,* often given in a series. **Range:** Uncommon; nests on the tundra in thickets near water. Regular migrant on St. Lawrence Island; casual on western Aleutians.

Red-flanked Bluetail *Tarsiger cyanurus* L 5½" (14 cm)
Range: Primarily Asian species; casual to western Aleutians, mainly in spring; one spring record for Pribilofs and one late fall record for Farallons, off California. Note bluish tail, often flicked down; orangish flanks. **Adult male** has bright blue upperparts, but much individual variation; brightest birds may be several years old. Immature males closely resemble **females** until second fall. Rather secretive. **Calls** include a *hueet* and dry *keck-keck.*

Northern Wheatear *Oenanthe oenanthe* L 5¾" (15 cm)
Tail pattern distinctive: white rump, white tail with dark central feathers and dark terminal band. Greenland race, *O. o. leucorhea,* averages a little larger and is richer buff below; western birds are whitish with a buff tinge. **Males** in fall and winter resemble females. Active; bob their tails. **Calls** include *chak* and whistled *wheet,* often combined. **Song** a scratchy warbling mixed with call notes, often given in flight with tail spread. **Range:** Prefers open, stony habitats; sits on posts. Fairly common; very rare along Atlantic coast during fall migration; casual elsewhere.

Stonechat *Saxicola torquata* L 5¼" (13 cm)
Range: Eurasian species; casual from scattered locations in Alaska; accidental in fall from New Brunswick. All records from the eastern *maura* group of races, known as "Siberian Stonechat." Compact body; pale spot on inner coverts; paler rump. **Adult male** has black head; orange-buff wash on breast; extensive white on sides of neck, belly, and rump. **Female** and **immature male** have pale throat; pale buffy rump. Favors open country.

Siberian Rubythroat

adult ♂

1st fall ♂

pink-throated adult ♀

♀

Bluethroat

1st fall ♀

♀

♀

breeding ♂

winter adult ♂

♀

Red-flanked Bluetail

♀

adult ♂

spring ♀ *oenanthe*

breeding adult ♂ *oenanthe*

fall adult ♂ *oenanthe*

Northern Wheatear

♀

1st fall *leucorhoa*

breeding adult ♂ *leucorhoa*

1st fall

spring ♂

spring ♀

fall adult ♂

Stonechat *maura* group

Eastern Bluebird *Sialia sialis* L 7" (18 cm)
Chestnut throat, sides of neck, breast, sides and flanks; contrasting white belly, white undertail coverts. **Male** is uniformly deep blue above; **female** grayer. The subspecies resident in the mountains of southeastern Arizona, *S. s. fulva,* is paler overall. All forms distinguished from Western Bluebird by chestnut on throat and sides of neck and by white, not grayish, belly and undertail. **Call** note is a musical, rising *chur-lee,* extended in **song** to *chur chur-lee chur-lee.* **Range:** Found in open woodlands, farmlands, orchards. Nests in holes in trees and posts; also in nest boxes. Serious decline in recent decades was due largely to competition with Starling and House Sparrow for nesting sites. The provision of specially designed boxes by concerned conservationists has resulted in a promising comeback.

Western Bluebird *Sialia mexicana* L 7" (18 cm)
Male's upperparts and throat are deep purple-blue; breast, sides, and flanks chestnut; belly and undertail coverts grayish. Most birds show some chestnut on shoulders and upper back. **Female** duller, brownish-gray above; breast and flanks tinged with chestnut, throat pale gray. **Call** note is a mellow *few,* extended in brief **song** to *few few fawee.* **Range:** Nests in holes in trees, posts; also in nest boxes. Common in woodlands, farmlands, orchards; in desert areas during winter, found in mesquite-mistletoe groves.

Mountain Bluebird *Sialia currucoides* L 7¼" (18 cm)
Male is sky blue above, paler below, with whitish belly and undertail coverts. **Female** is brownish-gray overall, with white belly and undertail coverts; white edges on coverts give folded wing a scalloped look. In fresh fall plumage, female's throat and breast are tinged with red-orange; brownish rear flank contrasting with white undertail coverts distinguishes her from female Eastern Bluebird, which has reddish flank. Note also longer, thinner bill and longer primary tip projection of Mountain Bluebird. **Call** is a thin *few;* **song,** a low, warbled *tru-lee.* More often than other bluebirds, hovers above prey, chiefly insects, before dropping to catch them; also catches insects in flight. **Range:** Nests in tree cavities, buildings. Inhabits open rangelands, meadows, generally at elevations above 5,000 feet; in winter, found primarily in open lowlands, desert. Highly migratory; casual in the east during migration and winter.

Townsend's Solitaire *Myadestes townsendi*
L 8½" (22 cm) Large and slender; gray overall, with bold white eye ring. Buff wing patches and white outer tail feathers are most conspicuous in flight. **Call** note is a high-pitched *eek;* **song,** heard all year, a loud, complex, melodious warbling. Often seen on a high perch, from which it sometimes fly-catches. **Range:** Nests on the ground. Fairly common in coniferous forests on high mountain slopes; in winter, also in wooded valleys, canyons, wherever juniper berries are available. Highly migratory; casual in fall and winter in eastern North America.

Eastern Bluebird
sialis

juvenile

♂

southwestern
♂ *fulva*

Western Bluebird

♀

♂

♀

♂

Mountain Bluebird

juvenile

Townsend's Solitaire

Wood Thrush *Hylocichla mustelina L 7¾" (20 cm)*
Reddish-brown above, brightest on crown and nape; rump and tail brownish-olive. White eye ring conspicuous on streaked face. Large dark spots on whitish throat, breast, and sides. Loud, liquid **song** of three- to five-note phrases, each phrase usually ending with a complex trill. **Calls** include a rapid *pit pit pit*. **Range:** Common in moist deciduous or mixed woods. Casual in the west.

Veery *Catharus fuscescens L 7" (18 cm)*
Reddish-brown above, white below, with gray flanks, grayish face, incomplete and indistinct gray eye ring. Upperparts duller, breast more spotted in more westerly *C. f. salicicola* than in eastern *fuscescens*. **Song** is a descending series of *veer* notes; **call** a sharp, descending, whistled *veer*. **Range:** Fairly common; found in dense, moist woodlands, streamside thickets.

Gray-cheeked Thrush *Catharus minimus L 7¼" (18 cm)*
Gray-brown above, with faint, incomplete eye ring. Dark spots on breast, which is usually less buffy than Swainson's; flanks brownish-gray. Breeding *C. m. minimus* on Newfoundland can be warmer colored above, more like Bicknell's. Thin, nasal **song** is somewhat like Veery's, but first and last phrases drop, middle one rises; **call,** a sharp *pheu* similar to Veery's, but higher pitched, not descending. **Range:** Favors coniferous or mixed woodlands.

Bicknell's Thrush *Catharus bicknelli L 6¼" (16 cm)*
Identification of Bicknell's Thrush when not singing is difficult due to variation within Gray-cheeked, of which it formerly was considered a subspecies. Bicknell's is smaller, warmer brown above, especially on tail; lower mandible has more yellow. **Song** usually comes in three parts, the first and last rising.

Swainson's Thrush *Catharus ustulatus L 7" (18 cm)*
Brownish above, with buffy lores and bold buffy eye ring; bright buffy breast with dark spots; brownish-gray sides and flanks. Pacific coast forms such as *C. u. ustulatus* are reddish-brown above, less distinctly spotted below; distinguished from *C. f. salicicola* race of Veery by face pattern, buffy-brown sides and flanks, and voice. **Song** is an ascending spiral of varied whistles; common **call,** a liquid *whit* in Pacific coast races, a sharper *quirk* in others; at night a peeping *queep* is heard. **Range:** Fairly common; found in moist woods and swamps.

Hermit Thrush *Catharus guttatus L 6¾" (17 cm)*
Complete, often whitish eye ring; reddish tail. Upperparts vary from rich brown to gray-brown. Eastern races such as widespread *C. g. faxoni* have buff-brown flanks. Larger, paler western mountain races, such as *auduboni,* and smaller, darker north Pacific coast races, such as *guttatus,* have grayish flanks. **Song** is a serene series of clear, flutelike notes, the similar phrases repeated at different pitches. **Calls** include a deeper *chuck,* often doubled, and a whiny, upslurred *wee*. **Range:** Fairly common; found in coniferous or mixed woodlands, thickets.

**Wood
Thrush**

Veery

western
salicicola

eastern
fuscescens

1st fall
aliciae

aliciae

**Bicknell's
Thrush**

**Gray-cheeked
Thrush**

minimus

juvenile
faxoni

cific coast
ulatus

Alaska
incanus

faxoni

**Hermit
Thrush**

**Swainson's
Thrush**

auduboni

ainsoni

guttatus

Varied Thrush *Ixoreus naevius* L 9½" (24 cm)

Male has grayish-blue nape and back, orange eyebrow; underparts orange with black breast band; buffy orange bar on underwing prominent in flight. **Female** distinguished from American Robin (next page) by orange eyebrow and wing bar, dusky breast band, and unmarked throat. **Juvenile** resembles female but has white belly, scalier looking throat and breast. In a very rare variant morph, all orange color is replaced by white. **Call** is a soft, low *tschook;* **song,** a slow series of variously pitched notes, rapidly trilled. **Range:** Common in dense, moist woodlands, especially coniferous forests. Generally feeds in trees. Very rare in winter as far east as New England and south to Virginia. Numbers vary from year to year in southern part of mapped winter range.

Eyebrowed Thrush *Turdus obscurus* L 8½" (22 cm)

Range: Asian species. Regular spring migrant on the Aleutians, casual in fall; casual on St. Lawrence Island and in northern Alaska. Brownish-olive above, with distinct white eyebrow. Belly is white, sides pale buffy orange. **Male** has dark gray throat and breast; **female**'s throat is white and streaked; browner head shows little contrast with rest of upperparts. Wing linings pale gray. Flight **call** is a high, piercing, drawn-out *dzee.*

Dusky Thrush *Turdus naumanni* L 9½" (24 cm)

Range: Asian species. Casual spring migrant on westernmost Aleutians; accidental on St. Lawrence Island, Point Barrow, and in winter in southeast Alaska, coastal British Columbia. White eyebrow conspicuous on blackish head. Upperparts strongly patterned; rump rust-colored; wings extensively rust, underwing almost entirely rufous. Below, white edgings give a scaly look to dark breast and sides. Note also distinctive white crescent across breast. Female and immatures average duller overall. **Call** is a series of *shack* notes; also a shrill, wheezy *shrree* similar to European Starling.

Fieldfare *Turdus pilaris* L 10" (25 cm)

Range: Eurasian species. Breeds from Greenland to Siberia. Casual vagrant to Alaska and northeastern North America. Accidental to Ontario and Minnesota. Gray head and rump contrast with purplish-brown upper back, blackish tail. Below, dark arrowhead-shaped spots pattern the buffy breast and extend along sides. White wing linings flash in flight. **Song** is a noisy twittering; **call** note is a series of *shack* notes, like Dusky Thrush; also gives a thin *seeh.*

Redwing *Turdus iliacus* L 8¼" (21 cm)

Range: Eurasian species; casual visitor to Newfoundland, mainly in winter; accidental on Long Island, New York. Distinctive whitish to buffy eyebrow; boldly streaked below, with rusty red flanks; rusty red wing linings visible in flight. **Call** is a thin, penetrating *seeeh,* usually heard in flight; also a hard *kuk* note.

juvenile

**Varied
Thrush**

♀

♂

♀

♂

**Eyebrowed
Thrush**

**Dusky
Thrush**

Fieldfare

Redwing

American Robin *Turdus migratorius L 10" (25 cm)*
Gray-brown above, with darker head and tail; bill yellow; under-parts brick red; lower belly white. Most western birds paler and duller overall than eastern nominate *T. m. migratorius* (shown here), which breeds to western Alaska; in most, tail has white cor-ners, visible in flight. Northwestern race, *caurinus,* is equally dark but lacks white tail spots; breeds north to southeast Alaska. **Juve-nile**'s underparts are tinged with cinnamon, heavily spotted with brown. Loud, liquid **song,** is a variable *cheerily cheer-up cheerio.* **Calls** include a rapid *tut tut tut;* a high, thin *ssip* in flight. **Range:** Common, widespread. Often seen on lawns, head cocked as it searches for earthworms; also eats insects, berries. Nests in shrubs, trees, on sheltered windowsills, eaves. In winter, found in moist woodlands, swamps, suburbs, parks. Numbers vary greatly from winter to winter.

White-throated Robin *Turdus assimilis L 9½" (24 cm)*
Range: Tropical species; casual to southernmost Texas in winter. Distinct white collar in front; white throat with dark brown streak-ing; head and upperparts brownish; often shows yellow orbital ring; underparts mostly gray. Compare to Clay-colored Robin's less marked throat; lack of collar; overall tawnier color; more extensively yellow bill. **Call** a nasal *rreeuh,* often doubled.

Rufous-backed Robin *Turdus rufopalliatus L 9¼" (24 cm)*
Range: West Mexican species, very rare winter visitor to south-ern Arizona, casual from southern and southwestern Texas to southern California. Distinguished from American Robin by reddish-brown back and wing coverts, uniformly gray head with no white around eye, and more extensively streaked throat. **Calls** include a plaintive, drawn-out, whistled *teeeuu,* a clucking series of *chuk* notes, and in flight, a high, thin *ssi.* Somewhat secretive; found in treetops and dense shrubbery.

Clay-colored Robin *Turdus grayi L 9" (23 cm)*
Range: Species from east Mexico to north Colombia; rare visi-tor and very rare breeder in southernmost Texas. Brownish-olive above; tawny-buff below; pale buffy throat is lightly streaked with olive. Lacks white around eye conspicuous in American Robin. **Calls** include a slurred *reeeur-ee,* a clucking note, and in flight a high, thin *ssi;* **song** resembles American Robin's but is slower, clearer, much less varied. Rather secretive; forages in dense thickets, streamside brush, woodlands. Will come to feeders.

Aztec Thrush *Ridgwayia pinicola L 9¼" (24 cm)*
Range: Mexican species, rare and irregular to southeast Arizona, casual to southwest Texas and central Texas coast. **Male** is very dark brown above, with white patches on wings, white uppertail coverts; tail broadly tipped with white; breast is dark; belly and undertail coverts white. **Female** is browner, more streaked on throat and breast. **Juvenile** is heavily streaked above with creamy-white; underparts whitish and heavily scaled with brown. **Calls,** a quavering *wheeerr,* a metallic *wheer,* and a clear *sweee-uh.*

juvenile

American
Robin

Rufous-backed
Robin

White-throated
Robin

Clay-colored
Robin

juvenile Aztec
Thrush

Mockingbirds, Thrashers
(Family Mimidae)

Notable singers, unequaled in North America for the rich variety and volume of their song. Some mimic the songs of other species.

Gray Catbird *Dumetella carolinensis* L 8½" (22 cm)
Plain dark gray with a black cap and a long, black tail, often cocked; undertail coverts chestnut. **Song** is a variable mixture of melodious, nasal, and squeaky notes interspersed with catlike *mew* notes; some individuals are good mimics. Most readily identified by harsh, downslurred *mew* **call**; also gives a low *quirt*, and a clucking noise. **Range:** Generally common but tends to stay hidden in low, dense thickets in woodlands and residential areas.

Northern Mockingbird *Mimus polyglottos* L 10" (25 cm)
White outer tail feathers and white wing patches flash conspicuously in flight and in territorial and courtship displays. **Song** is a mixture of original and imitative phrases, each repeated several times. Often sings at night. Imitates other species' songs and calls. Both sexes sing in fall, claiming feeding territories. **Call** is a loud, sharp *check*. Aggressive territorial defense; may attack any intruder. **Range:** Found in a variety of habitats, including towns. Casual well north of mapped range, as far as Alaska.

Bahama Mockingbird *Mimus gundlachii* L 11" (28 cm)
Range: Caribbean species; very rare on Dry Tortugas, Florida Keys, and southern Florida mainland. Larger and browner than Northern Mockingbird, with streaking on neck and flanks; white on tail is restricted to tip. Lacks white patches on wings; flight is more direct. **Song,** richly varied but not known to include imitations; **call** slightly harsher, more downslurred than Northern.

Brown Thrasher *Toxostoma rufum* L 11½" (29 cm)
Reddish-brown above, heavily streaked below. Distinguished from Long-billed Thrasher by shorter bill, redder head, and yellow eyes. Immature's eyes may be gray or brown. Compare also with Wood Thrush (page 348). **Sings** a long series of varied melodious phrases, each phrase usually given only two or three times. Seldom imitates other birds. **Calls** include a sharp *spuck* and a low *churr*. **Range:** Common in hedgerows, brush, and woodland edges, often close to human habitation. Rare in migration and winter in west and Maritimes. Casual to Newfoundland.

Long-billed Thrasher *Toxostoma longirostre*
L 11½" (29 cm) Closely resembles Brown Thrasher but much grayer above, with longer, more strongly curved bill; also has darker malar stripe, blacker streaking below, shorter primary projection. **Song** is very much like Brown's; sings from a high, open perch, especially in breeding season. Gives *tsuck* **call** like Brown; other calls, a mellow *kleak,* and a loud, whistled *cheeooep*. **Range:** Inhabits dense bottomland thickets and woodland edges. Very rare in west Texas; accidental in New Mexico and Colorado.

Gray
Catbird

juvenile

Northern
Mockingbird

Bahama
Mockingbird

Brown
Thrasher

Long-billed
Thrasher

Sage Thrasher *Oreoscoptes montanus L 8½" (22 cm)*
Yellow eye, white wing bars, white-cornered tail. Grayish above, boldly streaked below. **Worn** late-summer birds show much less streaking, can resemble Bendire's Thrasher. Juvenile has streaked head and back. **Song** is a long series of warbled phrases. **Calls** include a *chuck* and a high *churr*. **Range:** Found in sagebrush plains. Casual vagrant to eastern North America.

Bendire's Thrasher *Toxostoma bendirei L 9¾" (25 cm)*
Breast mottled; bill shorter and usually less curved than in Curve-billed Thrasher; base of lower mandible pale. White tail tips are similar to *T.c.oberholseri* race of Curve-billed. Distinctive arrow-head-shaped spots on breast are not present in worn summer plumage. **Song** is a sustained, melodic warbling, each phrase repeated one to three times. **Range:** Fairly common; found in open farmlands, grasslands, brushy desert. Casual to southern California coast in late summer, fall, and winter.

Curve-billed Thrasher *Toxostoma curvirostre*
L 11"(28 cm) Breast mottled; bill all-dark, longer, heavier, and us-ually more strongly curved than in Bendire's Thrasher. Breast spots indistinct in the westernmost race, *T.c.palmeri*. Race from extreme southeastern Arizona to south Texas, *oberholseri*, shows clearer spotting below; has pale wing bars; conspicuous white tips on tail. **Juveniles** and early-winter adults have darker spotting. Dis-tinctive **call,** a sharp *whit-wheet,* is sometimes three-noted. **Song,** elaborate, melodic, includes low trills and warbles. **Range:** Com-mon in canyons, semiarid brushlands. Casual (*palmeri*) in south-eastern California, the Great Plains, and upper midwest.

California Thrasher *Toxostoma redivivum L 12" (31 cm)*
Dark above, with pale eyebrow, dark eye, dark cheeks. Pale throat contrasts with dark breast; belly and undertail coverts tawny buff. Darker overall than Crissal Thrasher. **Calls** are a low, flat *chuck* and *chur-erp.* **Song** is loud and sustained, with mostly gut-tural phrases, often repeated once or twice. Imitates other species and sounds. **Range:** Common in chaparral-covered foothills.

Crissal Thrasher *Toxostoma crissale L 11½" (29 cm)*
Large and slender, with a distinctive chestnut undertail patch and a dark malar streak. **Song** is varied and musical, its cadence more leisurely than in Curve-billed Thrasher. **Calls** include a repeated *chideery* and a whistled *toit-toit-toit.* **Range:** Very secretive, hid-ing in underbrush. Found mainly in dense mesquite and willows along streams and washes; sometimes on lower mountain slopes.

Le Conte's Thrasher *Toxostoma lecontei L 11" (28 cm)*
Palest of the thrashers, with pale grayish-brown upperparts, darker tail; tawny undertail coverts. Bill and eye are dark. **Song,** heard chiefly at dawn and dusk, is loud, melodious. **Calls** include an ascending, whistled *tweeep.* **Range:** Prefers arid, sparsely veg-etated habitats. Uncommon over most of range.

Sage Thrasher

worn adult

Bendire's Thrasher

worn

fresh

Bendire's

Curve-billed *palmeri*

oberholseri

juvenile *palmeri*

Curve-billed Thrasher

oberholseri

palmeri

California Thrasher

Le Conte's Thrasher

Crissal Thrasher

Bulbuls (Family Pycnonotidae)

Noisy, active Old World family of the tropics and subtropics.

Red-whiskered Bulbul *Pycnonotus jocosus* *L 7" (18 cm)*
Range: Asian and African species. Escaped cage birds first noted in early 1960s in Miami, Florida; now established as a small population in suburbs and parklands south of Miami. Some also in Los Angeles area. Red ear spot and undertail coverts distinctive. **Juvenile** lacks ear patch; undertail coverts are paler.

Starlings (Family Sturnidae)

Chunky, dark, glossy birds, usually gregarious and bold. Four species of this widespread Old World family are found in North America.

Crested Myna *Acridotheres cristatellus* *L 9¾" (25 cm)*
Range: Asian species, introduced in Vancouver, British Columbia, in the 1890s. Now uncommon and declining. From populations in the thousands in the 1920s, numbers have decreased to perhaps fewer than a hundred birds. A major factor may be competition from European Starlings. Identified by bushy crest on forehead, yellow bill and legs, white wing patch.

Common Myna *Acridotheres tristis* *L 10" (25 cm)*
Range: Southern Asian species; introduced elsewhere, including Hawaii, where it is common. Established in south Florida; now is more widespread and numerous than Hill Myna. Dark brown, with black head and white undertail coverts; yellow bill and skin around eye; white tail tip, patch at base of primaries, and wing linings distinctive in flight. Juveniles have more brownish heads. **Calls** include gurglings, whistles, and screeches. Found in urban areas; also in open country in native range.

Hill Myna *Gracula religiosa* *L 10½" (27 cm)*
Range: Asian species, fine mimic, popular as a cage bird. A small number of escaped birds, first noted in 1960s, persists but is very local in Miami. Glossy black; orange-red bill; yellow wattles and legs; white wing patch.

European Starling *Sturnus vulgaris* *L 8½" (22 cm)*
Adult in **breeding** plumage is iridescent black, with a yellow bill with blue base in male, pink in female. In fresh **fall** plumage, feathers are tipped with white and buff, giving a speckled appearance; bill brownish. In flight, note short, square tail, stocky body, and short, broad-based, pointed wings that appear pale gray from below. **Juvenile** is gray-brown, with brown bill. **Call** notes include squeaks, warbles, chirps, and twittering; also imitates songs of other species. **Range:** A Eurasian species introduced in New York in 1890-91, it soon spread across the continent. Abundant, bold, aggressive, it often competes successfully with native species for nest holes. Outside nesting season, usually seen in large flocks.

Red-whiskered Bulbul

juvenile

Crested Myna

Common Myna

Hill Myna

fall

European Starling

winter

Brown-headed Cowbird for comparison

breeding ♂

juvenile

Accentors (Family Prunellidae)

Small Eurasian family, most species found in mountainous country. One species strays to North America.

Siberian Accentor *Prunella montanella* L 5½" (14 cm)
Range: Casual mainly fall and winter to Alaska and Pacific northwest. Bright tawny buff below; back and flanks are streaked. Dark crown, with broad gray median stripe. Note buffy eyebrow that broadens behind head; dark cheek patch with buff spots below; gray patch on side of neck. **Call** is a high, thin series of *see* notes.

Wagtails, Pipits (Family Motacillidae)

Ground dwellers with slender bills. Most species pump their tails up and down as they walk. Wagtail flight is strongly undulating.

Yellow Wagtail *Motacilla flava* L 6½" (17 cm)
Grayish-olive above, yellow below; tail shorter than other wagtails. In **breeding** plumage, Alaska race, *M. f. tschutschensis,* has a speckled breast band. Asian *simillima,* seen regularly on Aleutians and Pribilofs, is greener above, yellower below. **Females** duller, **immatures** whitish below. **Call,** a loud *tsweep,* is similar to Eastern Kingbird's. **Range:** Generally common on Alaska breeding grounds; casual fall migrant on California coast.

Gray Wagtail *Motacilla cinerea* L 7¾" (20 cm)
Range: Eurasian species. Very rare spring migrant on western Aleutians; casual on Pribilofs and St. Lawrence Island; accidental to California. Gray above, with greenish-yellow rump, yellow below; whitish tertial edges, but lacks wing bars. **Breeding male** has black throat. **Female** and winter birds have whitish throat, paler below. Distinctly longer tail and flesh-colored legs separate Gray from Yellow Wagtail. **Call,** a metallic *chink-chink.*

White Wagtail *Motacilla alba* L 7¼" (18 cm)
Breeding adult has black nape, gray back. Face and underparts white; eye line, throat, bib, and usually chin, are black. In flight, shows mostly dark wings. Juvenile and immature very similar to young Black-backed Wagtails. Immature separated with difficulty by dark bases to median coverts. **Calls** include a two-note *chizzik;* and a whistled *chee-wee,* given on the ground. Bobs its head as it walks, often wags its tail. **Range:** Casual on west coast.

Black-backed Wagtail *Motacilla lugens* L 7¼" (18 cm)
Range: Asian coastal species. Regular migrant and has bred on western Aleutians; rare on Bering Sea islands; casual on west coast. Similar to closely related White Wagtail in all plumages and vocalizations. **Breeding adult** has blacker back, usually a white chin. In flight, shows mostly white wings. Juvenile is brownish above, with two faint wing bars. **Immature** more closely resembles **winter adult** but retains most juvenile flight feathers.

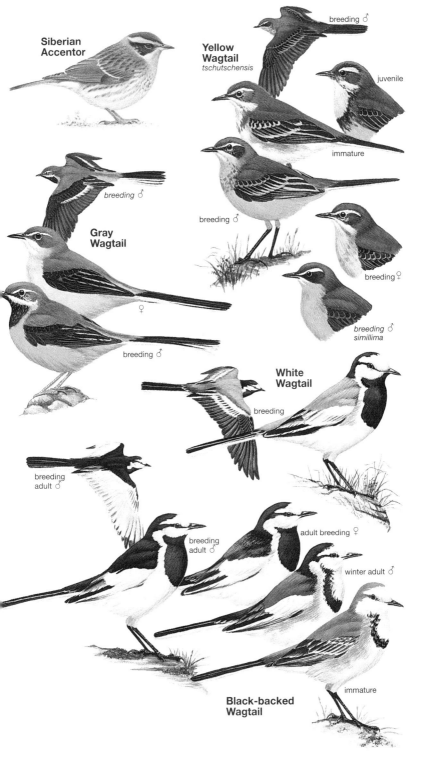

Siberian Accentor

Yellow Wagtail
tschutschensis

breeding ♂

juvenile

immature

breeding ♂

breeding ♀

Gray Wagtail

breeding ♂

♀

breeding ♂

breeding ♂
simillima

White Wagtail

breeding

breeding adult ♂

breeding adult ♂

adult breeding ♀

winter adult ♂

immature

Black-backed Wagtail

American Pipit *Anthus rubescens L 6½" (17 cm)*
Breeding birds are grayish above. Faintly streaked below, except
for the *A. r. alticola* race (not shown), from the Rockies and California's high mountains, which has richly colored underparts
with fewer or no streaks. In **winter** American Pipit becomes
browner above and more streaked below. Bill mostly dark; legs
dark or tinged with pink. Tail has white outer feathers. An Asian
subspecies, *japonicus,* rare in western Alaska, is more boldly
streaked below, with pink legs, white wing bars; casual in fall in
coastal California. **Call,** given in flight, is a sharp *pip-pit;* **song,**
a rapid series of *chee* or *cheedle* notes. **Range:** Common and
widespread; nests on tundra in the north, mountaintops farther
south. Winter flocks are found in fields and on beaches.

Sprague's Pipit *Anthus spragueii L 6½" (17 cm)*
Dark eye prominent in pale buff face. Pale edges on rounded back
feathers give a scaly look; rump is streaked. Underparts whitish,
with a buffy wash and short, dark streaks on the breast. Legs pinkish. Outer tail feathers are more extensively white than in American Pipit. **Call** is a loud, squeaky *squeet,* usually given two or
more times. **Song,** given continuously in high flight, is a descending series of musical *tzee* and *tzee-a* notes. Uncommon, secretive, and somewhat solitary. Does not pump tail. **Range:** Nests
in grassy fields. Very rare in fall and winter to California; accidental in eastern North America.

Olive-backed Pipit *Anthus hodgsoni L 6" (15 cm)*
Range: Asian species. Casual migrant on St. Lawrence Island and
Pribilofs; rare on western Aleutians; accidental to California and
Nevada. Grayish-olive back, faintly streaked. Eyebrow orange-
buff in front of eye, white behind. Broken white stripe borders
dark ear spot. Throat and breast rich buff, with rather large black
spots on breast. Belly pure white; legs pink. **Call** is a buzzy *tsee.*

Pechora Pipit *Anthus gustavi L 5½" (14 cm)*
Range: Asian species. Casual in spring on the western Aleutians;
accidental to St. Lawrence Island. Shows distinct primary projection. Resembles immature Red-throated Pipit, but compare
Pechora Pipit's richly patterned back plumage, extending onto
the nape; black centers with dull rufous edges contrast with white
lines, or "braces," on the sides. Also a yellowish wash across the
breast contrasts with the whitish belly. Quite secretive. **Call** is a
hard *pwit* or *pit,* but Pechora is often silent when flushed.

Red-throated Pipit *Anthus cervinus L 6" (15 cm)*
Note unpatterned nape. Pinkish-red head and breast are distinctive in **breeding male,** less extensive in **breeding female** and
fall adults. Fall **immatures** and some breeding females show no
red. **Call,** given in flight, is a high, piercing *tseee,* dropping in pitch
at the end. Loud, varied **song** is delivered from the ground or in
song flight. **Range:** Regular migrant on islands in Bering Sea;
rare migrant along California coast; casual inland.

American Pipit

breeding *rubescens*

winter *rubescens*

winter *japonicus*

Sprague's Pipit

Olive-backed Pipit

yunnanensis

Pechora Pipit

breeding ♀

Red-throated Pipit

immature

breeding ♂

Waxwings (Family Bombycillidae)

Red, waxy tips on secondary wing feathers are often indistinct and sometimes absent altogether. All waxwings have sleek crests, silky plumage, and yellow-tipped tails. Where berries are ripening, waxwings come to feast in amiable, noisy flocks.

Bohemian Waxwing *Bombycilla garrulus* L 8¼" (21 cm)
Larger and grayer than Cedar Waxwing; underparts gray; undertail coverts cinnamon. White and yellow spots on wings. In flight, white wing patch at base of primaries is conspicuous. **Juvenile** browner above, streaked below, with pale throat. Distinctive **call**, a buzzy twittering, lower and harsher than call of Cedar Waxwing. **Range:** Nests in open coniferous or mixed woodlands; often seen perched on top of a black spruce. Winter range varies widely and unpredictably; large flocks visit scattered locations, feeding on berries, small fruits. Also eat insects, flower petals, sap. Irregular winter wanderer to the northeast, usually in small numbers; annual in Maine, Maritimes, and Newfoundland. Individuals are sometimes seen in flocks of Cedar Waxwings.

Cedar Waxwing *Bombycilla cedrorum* L 7¼" 8 cm)
Smaller and browner than Bohemian Waxwing; belly pale yellow; undertail coverts white. Lacks yellow spots on wings. **Juvenile** is streaked; lacks white wing patches of juvenile Bohemian. Since this species usually nests late in summer, juvenile plumage is seen well into fall. **Call** is a soft, high-pitched, trilled whistle. **Range:** Found in open habitats where berries are available; also eats insects, flower petals, sap. Highly gregarious in migration and winter.

Silky-flycatchers (Family Ptilogonatidae)

This New World tropical family of slender, crested birds is closely related to the waxwings. The family's common name describes their soft, sleek plumage and agility in catching insects on the wing.

Phainopepla *Phainopepla nitens* L 7¾" (20 cm)
Male is shiny black; white wing patch conspicuous in flight. In both sexes, note distinct crest, long tail, red eyes. Juvenile resembles **adult female;** but has browner eyes; both have gray wing patches. Young males acquire patchy black in fall. Distinctive **call** note is a querulous, low-pitched, whistled *wurp?* **Song** is a brief warble, seldom heard. Flight is fluttery but direct, and often very high. **Range:** Phainopeplas nest in early spring in mesquite brushlands, feeding chiefly on insects, mistletoe berries. In late spring they move into cooler, wetter habitat and raise a second brood. Rare postbreeding wanderers north and east of mapped range. Accidental in eastern North America.

juvenile

**Bohemian
Waxwing**

juvenile

**Cedar
Waxwing**

Phainopepla

Wood-Warblers (Family Parulidae)

A New World family. About half of its numerous species occur in North America.

Prothonotary Warbler *Protonotaria citrea*
L 5½" (14 cm) Large, plump, short-tailed, and very long-billed. Eyes are large, dark, and prominent. **Male**'s head and underparts golden yellow, fading to white undertail coverts; wings blue-gray, without wing bars; blue-gray tail has large white patches. **Female** duller, head less golden. **Song** is a series of loud, ringing *zweet* notes; gives a dry *chip* note and buzzy flight **call. Range:** Fairly common. The only eastern warbler that nests in tree or other cavities and crannies; usually selects a low site along streams or surrounded by sluggish or stagnant water. Casual to rare vagrant across most of the continent during migration, especially in fall.

Blue-winged Warbler *Vermivora pinus* L 4¾" (12 cm)
Male has bright yellow crown and underparts, white or yellowish-white undertail coverts, black eye line, blue-gray wings with two white wing bars. **Female** duller overall. In both sexes, bill is long and slender; extensive white on tail is visible from below. Main **song** is a wheezy *beee-bzzz*, the second note lower; alternate song is longer and more complex. **Range:** Locally common; inhabits brushy meadows, second-growth woodlands; nests on the ground. Very rare vagrant to western U.S., but increasing. Blue-winged prefers a greater diversity of habitat than Golden-winged Warbler. Range is expanding at northern edge; gradually replacing Golden-winged. Hybridizes with Golden-winged where ranges overlap. Hybrids may vary considerably from parent species in amount of black on head and throat, amount of yellow below, and size and color of wing bars. Some variations are shown here of the two main types, the more frequent **"Brewster's Warbler"** and the rare **"Lawrence's Warbler"** backcross (produced by crossing a first-generation hybrid with one of the parent species).

Golden-winged Warbler *Vermivora chrysoptera*
L 4¾" (12 cm) **Male** has black throat; black ear patch bordered in white; yellow crown and wing patch. **Female** similar but duller. In both sexes, extensive white on tail is conspicuous from below; underparts are grayish-white; bill long and slender. Main **song** is a soft *bee-bz-bz-bz;* also gives an alternate song similar to Blue-winged Warbler. **Range:** Prefers overgrown pastures, briery woodland borders; nests on the ground. Uncommon to rare and declining. Very rare vagrant to western U.S. Found farther north and at higher elevations in the Appalachians than Blue-winged. Songs of hybrids of these two species (see above) usually sound like one of the parent species.

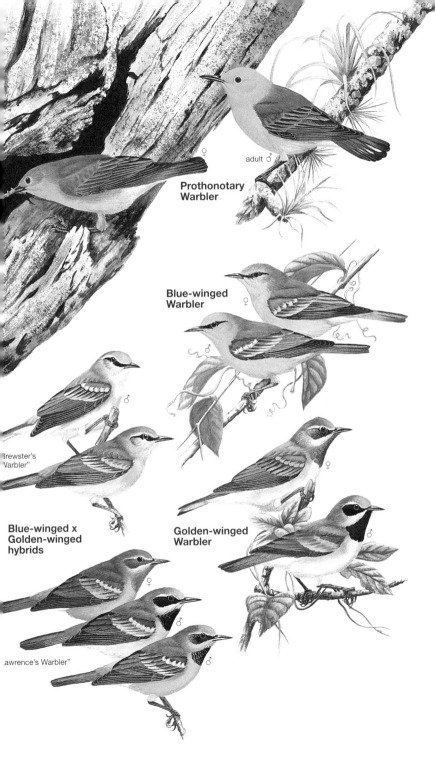

Prothonotary Warbler

♀

adult ♂

Blue-winged Warbler

♀

♂

"Brewster's Warbler"

♂

Blue-winged x Golden-winged hybrids

Golden-winged Warbler

♀

♂

"Lawrence's Warbler"

♀

♂

♂

Tennessee Warbler *Vermivora peregrina* L 4¾" (12 cm)

Plump, short-tailed, with long, straight bill. **Male** in spring is green above with gray crown, bold white eyebrow; white below. **Female** is tinged with yellow or olive overall, especially in fresh fall plumage. Adult male in fall resembles spring adult female but shows more yellow below. Immature also yellowish below; resembles young Orange-crowned, but is greener above and has a shorter tail and usually white undertail coverts. Spring male may be confused with Warbling and Red-eyed Vireos (page 310); note especially Tennessee Warbler's slimmer bill, greener back. Distinctive two- or three-part **song;** in three-part version, several rapid two-syllable notes are followed by a few higher single notes, ending with a staccato trill. **Range:** Fairly common. Found in coniferous and mixed woodlands in summer, mixed open woodlands and brushy areas during fall migration. Nests on the ground; generally feeds high in trees. Very rare in winter in coastal California.

Orange-crowned Warbler *Vermivora celata*

L 5" (13 cm) Olive above, paler below. Yellow undertail coverts and faint, blurred streaks on sides of breast distinguish this species from the similar Tennessee Warbler. Note also that Orange-crowned's bill is thinner and slightly downcurved; tail is longer. Plumage varies from the smaller, brighter, yellower birds of western U.S., such as *V. c. lutescens,* to the duller *orestera* (not shown) of the Great Basin and Rockies; to the dullest, *celata,* which breeds across Alaska and Canada and winters primarily in southeastern U.S.; *celata* is the latest fall migrant of the warblers. Tawny-orange crown, absent in some **females** and immatures, is seldom discernible in the field. Immature *celata* can be particularly drab. Young birds are similar to immature Tennessees but show yellow undertail coverts and grayer upperparts. **Song** is a high-pitched staccato trill, faster in *lutescens;* **call** note, a sharp *chip.* **Range:** Inhabits open, brushy woodlands, forest edges, thickets. Nests on the ground; generally feeds in low branches, often in dead leaf clumps. Common in the west; rarer in the east.

Bachman's Warbler *Vermivora bachmanii* **E**

L 4¾" (12 cm) Probably extinct; the last definite record was in 1962 near Charleston, South Carolina. **Range:** Bachman's once bred in canebrakes and wet woodlands; was known very locally in the southeastern U.S., from southeast Missouri and Logan County in south Kentucky east to South Carolina, but was probably never numerous. Wintered in Cuba and on Isle of Pines. Bill is very thin, long, somewhat downcurved; undertail coverts white in both sexes. **Male** has yellow forehead, chin, and shoulders; black crown and bib. **Immature male** has less black on crown and throat, less yellow on shoulders, and more white on lower belly. **Female** drabber, crown gray, throat and breast gray or yellow. Distinctive **song,** typically a rapid series of buzzes on one pitch; similar to Blue-winged Warbler's alternate song.

fall

fall

breeding ♀

breeding ♂

Tennessee Warbler

♀

celata

♂

Orange-crowned Warbler

lutescens ♂

adult ♀

1st spring ♂

adult ♂

Bachman's Warbler

Nashville Warbler *Vermivora ruficapilla L 4¾" (12 cm)*

Bold white eye ring, gray head, olive upperparts. White area between yellow belly and yellow undertail is more prominent in longer-tailed western race *V. r. ridgwayi* (not shown), which often wags its tail. **Female** is duller than **male. Song** of eastern *ruficapilla* is a series of high *see-weet* notes and a lower short trill; **call,** a dull *chink*. In *ridgwayi*, song is sweeter, call sharper. **Range:** Common; found in second-growth woodlands, spruce bogs.

Virginia's Warbler *Vermivora virginiae L 4¾" (12 cm)*

Bold white eye ring; gray head and back, greenish-yellow rump. Yellow patch on breast, yellow undertail coverts. Female is duller overall. Fall **immature** is browner; little or no yellow on breast. **Song,** a rapid series of thin notes, often ending with lower notes; **call,** a sharp *chink*. Often wags its tail. **Range:** Common in mountain brushlands. Rare to coastal California. Casual in the east.

Colima Warbler *Vermivora crissalis L 5¾" (15 cm)*

Range: Mexican species; range extends to oak woodlands of Chisos Mountains, Big Bend National Park, Texas. Larger and browner than Virginia's Warbler; rufous crown patch usually visible. **Song,** a trill similar to Orange-crowned Warbler.

Lucy's Warbler *Vermivora luciae L 4¼" (11 cm)*

Pale gray above, whitish below, short-tailed. **Male**'s reddish crown, patch, and rump distinctive. Female and **immatures** duller. Lively **song,** a short trill followed by lower, whistled notes. **Call** is a sharp *chink*. Fairly common in mesquite and cottonwoods along watercourses; nests in tree cavities.

Crescent-chested Warbler *Parula superciliosa*
L 4¼" (11 cm) **Range:** Resident from northern Nicaragua to northern Mexico; casual to southeast Arizona; one sighting for Chisos Mountains, Texas. Bluish-gray head with broad white eyebrow; green back; no wing bars or white in tail. Chestnut crescent distinct on **adult male;** reduced on female and immature male; absent or an orange wash on **immature female.**

Northern Parula *Parula americana L 4½" (11 cm)*

Short-tailed warbler, gray-blue above with yellowish-green upper back, two bold white wing bars. Throat and breast bright yellow, belly white. In **adult male,** reddish and black bands cross breast. In female and immature male, bands are fainter or absent. One **song** is a rising buzzy trill, ending with an abrupt *zip* in eastern birds; no clear final note in more westerly birds. **Range:** Common in coniferous or mixed woods, especially near water. Rare vagrant throughout the west in migration.

Tropical Parula *Parula pitiayumi L 4½" (11 cm)*

Range: Uncommon in south Texas. Dark mask and lack of distinct white eye ring distinguish Tropical from Northern Parula. Also yellow of throat extends farther onto sides of face; **male** has more blended orange breast band. **Song** like Northern Parula.

Nashville Warbler
ruficapilla

ture

♂

Virginia's Warbler

immature ♂

Colima Warbler

♂

immature ♀

Lucy's Warbler

♂

Crescent-chested Warbler

immature ♀

adult ♂

immature ♀

adult ♂

Northern Parula

♀

adult ♂

Tropical Parula

Chestnut-sided Warbler *Dendroica pensylvanica*

L 5" (13 cm) **Breeding male** has yellow crown, black eye line, black whisker stripe; extensive chestnut on sides; **female** has greenish crown, less chestnut. Fall adults and **immatures** are lime green above, with white eye ring, whitish underparts, yellowish wing bars. **Song** is a whistled *please please pleased to meetcha;* **call,** a *chip* note like Yellow Warbler. Chestnut-sided often cocks its tail. **Range:** Fairly common in second-growth deciduous woodlands. Rare migrant in west; casual in winter.

Cape May Warbler *Dendroica tigrina L 5" (13 cm)*

Most plumages have yellow on face, the color usually extending to sides of neck. Note also short tail; yellow or greenish rump; thin bill, slightly downcurved. **Breeding male**'s chestnut ear patch and striped underparts distinctive; wing patch white. **Female** drabber, grayer, with two narrow white wing bars. **Immature male**'s ear patch is less distinct. **Immature female** can be extremely drab, with gray face and only a tinge of yellow below and on rump; always has greenish edges on flight feathers. One **song** is a high, thin *seet seet seet seet;* **call,** a very high, thin *sip.* **Range:** Cape May Warbler shows aggressive behavior. Breeds in black spruce forests, where often uncommon except during spruce budworm outbreaks. Rare west to Texas in migration; very rare to casual throughout the west. Winters chiefly in the West Indies; a few birds winter in southernmost Florida.

Magnolia Warbler *Dendroica magnolia L 5" (13 cm)*

Male is blackish above, with white eyebrow, white wing patch, yellow rump; broad white tail patches. Underparts yellow, streaked on breast and sides; undertail coverts white; undertail white except for black band at tip. Female has two wing bars; some **first-spring females** have dull white eye ring; often confused with rare Kirtland's Warbler (page 378). **Fall adults** and **immatures** are drabber, with grayish-olive upperparts; white eye ring; faint gray band across breast. Compare immature Prairie Warbler (page 378). Magnolia Warbler does not bob tail. **Song** is a short, whistled *weety-weety-weeteo.* **Range:** Fairly common to common in moist coniferous forests. Casual in winter in southern Florida. Rare throughout the west in migration.

Yellow-rumped Warbler *Dendroica coronata*

L 5½" (14 cm) Yellow rump, yellow patch on side, yellow crown patch, white tail patches. In northern and eastern birds, **"Myrtle Warbler,"** note white eyebrow, white throat and sides of neck, contrasting cheek patch. Western birds, **"Audubon's Warbler,"** have yellow throat, except for a few immature females. Some males in the mountains of the southwest show more black. All **females** and fall males are duller than **breeding males** but show same basic pattern. **Song,** a slow warble, usually rising or falling at the end in "Audubon's," a musical trill in one song of "Myrtle." **Call** note of "Myrtle" is lower, flatter. **Range:** Abundant in coniferous or mixed woodlands. "Myrtle" is fairly common in winter on west coast; "Audubon's" is casual in the east.

Chestnut-sided Warbler

breeding adult ♀

immature ♀

breeding adult ♂

...reeding ♀

Magnolia Warbler

breeding adult ♂

1st spring ♀

Cape May Warbler

breeding adult ♂

immature ♀

immature ♂

immature ♀

fall adult ♂

"Myrtle Warbler"

"Audubon's Warbler"

breeding ♀

southwest breeding ♂

breeding ♂

Yellow-rumped Warbler

fall ♀

fall ♀

breeding ♂

Black-and-white Warbler *Mniotilta varia* L 5¼" (13 cm)

The only warbler that regularly creeps along branches and up and down tree trunks like a nuthatch. Boldly striped on head, most of body, and undertail coverts. **Male**'s throat and cheeks are black in breeding plumage; in winter, chin is white. **Female** and **immatures** have pale cheeks; female diffusely streaked on buffy flanks; buffy wash particularly bright on immatures. **Song** is a long series of high, thin *wee-see* notes. **Calls** include a sharp *chip* and high *seep-seep*. **Range:** Common in mixed woodlands.

Black-throated Blue Warbler *Dendroica caerulescens*

L 5¼" (13 cm) **Male**'s black throat, cheeks, and sides separate blue upperparts, white underparts. Bold white patch at base of primaries. Appalachian males south of Susquehanna drainage average darker above; back largely black in the case of *D. c. cairnsi* in southern Appalachians. **Female**'s pale eyebrow is distinct on dark face; upperparts brownish-olive; underparts buffy; wing patch smaller, occasionally absent on immature females. Typical **song** is a slow series of four or five wheezy notes, the last note higher: *zwee zwee zwee zweeee* or a slower *zur zurr zreee*. **Call** is a single sharp *dit*, like the call of a Dark-eyed Junco. **Range:** Inhabits deciduous forests; usually seen in lower or mid-level branches. Rare fall vagrant in the west. A few birds winter in south Florida; most migrate to the West Indies.

Cerulean Warbler *Dendroica cerulea* L 4¾" (12 cm)

Small and short-tailed; two wide white wing bars. **Adult male** is bluish above with dark streaks; white below, with dark breast band and dark blue-gray streaking on sides. **Female** has greenish mantle, blue-green or bluish crown; pale eyebrow broadens behind the eye; breast and throat are pale yellowish. Immature male is like female, but shows some bluish and dark streaks above. **Song** is a short, fast, accelerating series of buzzy notes on one pitch, ending with a long, single buzz note. **Range:** Sharply declining in the heart of its range. Found in tall trees in swamps, bottomlands, mixed woodlands near water. Fall migration begins from the second week of July. Range is expanding in northeast.

Blackburnian Warbler *Dendroica fusca* L 5" (13 cm)

Fiery orange throat, broad white wing patch, triangular ear patch, conspicuous in **adult male. Female** and immature male have paler throat, **immature female** paler still; note also the two white wing bars, streaked back, and bold yellow or buffy eyebrow, broader behind the eye, that curls around onto side of neck. Orange or yellow forehead stripe and white in outer tail feathers are distinct in all males, less so in females. One **song,** a short series of high notes followed by a squeaky, ascending trill, ends on a very high note. **Range:** Fairly common in coniferous or mixed forests of northern breeding range, pine-oak woodlands in the Appalachians. Generally stays in the upper branches. Vagrants are seen rarely in coastal California in fall migration; casually elsewhere west of dashed line on map in spring and fall.

Black-and-white Warbler

immature ♀

breeding adult ♂

♀

♀

Black-throated Blue Warbler

♂

Appalachians ♂
cairnsi

Cerulean Warbler

immature ♀

adult ♂

♀

breeding ♀

fall adult ♂

breeding adult ♂

immature ♀

Blackburnian Warbler

Black-throated Gray Warbler *Dendroica nigrescens*
L 5" (13 cm) **Adult** plumage is basically the same year-round: black-and-white head; gray back streaked with black; white underparts, sides streaked with black; small yellow spot between eye and bill. Lacks central crown stripe of the Black-and-white Warbler (preceding page); undertail coverts are white. Immature male resembles adult male; immature female is brownish-gray above, throat white. Varied **songs** include a buzzy *weezy weezy weezy weezy-weet.* **Range:** Inhabits woodlands, brushlands, chaparral. Rare in winter in lower Rio Grande Valley, Texas; casual otherwise in eastern North America. Very rare during migration and in winter along the Gulf coast.

Townsend's Warbler *Dendroica townsendi* L 5" (13 cm)
Dark crown, dark ear patch bordered in yellow. Olive above, streaked with black; yellow breast, white belly, yellowish black-streaked sides. **Adult male**'s throat and upper breast are black; **female** and immature male have streaked lower throat. **Immature female** is duller, lacks streaking on back; streaking on underparts is diffuse. Variable **song,** a series of hoarse *zee* notes. Occasionally hybridizes with Hermit Warbler; **hybrids** usually have yellowish, streaked underparts of Townsend's, yellow head of Hermit. **Range:** Found in coniferous forests. Casual in the east.

Hermit Warbler *Dendroica occidentalis* L 5½" (14 cm)
Yellow head, with dark markings extending from nape onto crown. **Male** has black chin and throat; in **female** and **immatures,** chin is yellowish, throat shows less or no dark color. Immature female is more olive above. **Song** is a high *seezle seezle seezle seezle zeet-zeet.* **Range:** Fairly common in mountain forests; nests in tall conifers. During migration, also seen in lowlands. Casual in the east.

Black-throated Green Warbler *Dendroica virens*
L 5" (13 cm) Bright olive green upperparts; yellow face with greenish ear patch. Underparts are white, tinged with yellow on sides of vent and often on breast. **Male** has black throat and upper breast and black-streaked sides. **Female** and **immatures** show much less black below; immature female generally has dark streaking only on sides. One **song** is a hoarse *zeee zeee zee-zo-zee;* the other, often written as *trees, trees, whispering trees.* **Range:** Fairly common in coniferous or mixed forests in summer.

Golden-cheeked Warbler *Dendroica chrysoparia* **E**
L 5½" (14 cm) Dark eye line, unmarked yellow ear patches, and lack of any yellow on underparts distinguish this species from similar Black-throated Green Warbler. **Male** black above, with black crown, black bib, black-streaked sides. **Female** and immature male duller, upperparts olive with dark streaks; chin yellowish or white; sides of throat streaked. **Immature female** shows less black on underparts. **Song,** *bzzzz layzee dayzee,* ends on a high note. **Range:** Endangered; local in mixed cedar-oak woodland of the Edwards Plateau in central Texas.

Black-throated Gray Warbler

♀

adult ♂

adult ♀

Townsend's Warbler

adult ♂

Townsend's x Hermit hybrid

adult ♂

adult ♀

adult ♂

Hermit Warbler

lt ♀

Black-throated Green Warbler

adult ♂

Golden-cheeked Warbler

adult ♀

adult ♂

immature females

Golden-cheeked

Black-throated Green

Townsend's

Hermit

Grace's Warbler *Dendroica graciae L 5" (13 cm)*

Black-streaked gray back; throat and upper breast bright yellow; rest of underparts white, with black streaks on sides. Short-billed; yellow eyebrow becomees white behind eye. **Female** slightly duller and browner above. Grace's Warbler's **song** is a rapid, accelerating trill. **Range:** Inhabits coniferous or mixed forests of southwestern mountains, especially yellow pines. Usually forages high in the trees. Casual to southern California.

Yellow-throated Warbler *Dendroica dominica*

L 5½" (14 cm) Plain gray back; large, white patch on each side of head. **Male** has black crown and face; in female, black is less extensive. Throat and upper breast bright yellow; rest of underparts white, with black streaks on sides; bold white eyebrow sometimes tinged with yellow. Eastern races *D. d. dominica*, and *stoddardi* (not shown) of eastern Gulf coast, have yellow supraloral area, unlike more westerly *albilora; stoddardi* and birds from Delmarva Peninsula, have very long bills. **Song** is a series of clear, downslurred whistles ending with a rising note. **Range:** Fairly common in live oak and pine woodlands, cypress, sycamores. Usually forages high in the trees, creeping methodically along the branches. Very rare northward to southern Ontario in spring and Newfoundland in fall. Casual in west during migration.

Kirtland's Warbler *Dendroica kirtlandii* **E**

L 5¾" (15 cm) Blue-gray above, strongly black-streaked on back; yellow below, streaked on sides; white eye ring, broken at front and rear; two whitish wing bars, thin and indistinct. Often confused with first-spring female Magnolia Warbler (page 372). **Adult female** is slightly duller; **immature female** brownish above. Kirtland's Warbler constantly wags its tail. **Song** is loud and lively, a variable series of low, sharp notes followed by slurred whistles. **Range:** An endangered species, Kirtland's current breeding adult population was estimated at around 1,600 in the annual survey of June 1998. Nests in northern Michigan, where controlled plantings and fires help produce the required habitat: thickets of young jack pines. Very rare in summer outside Michigan, with records from southern Ontario and especially Wisconsin. Very rarely seen in migration. Winters in the Bahamas.

Prairie Warbler *Dendroica discolor L 4¾" (12 cm)*

Olive above, with faint chestnut streaks on back; bright yellow eyebrow, yellow patch below eye; bright yellow below, streaked with black on sides of neck and body. Two indistinct wing bars. **Female** and immature male are slightly duller. **Immature female** is duller still, grayish-olive above; lack of complete eye ring or gray breast band distinguish her from fall Magnolia Warbler (page 372). Distinctive **song,** a rising series of buzzy *zee* notes. **Range:** Generally common in open woodlands, scrublands, scrub-grown fields, mangrove swamps. Usually forages in lower branches and brush, twitching its tail. Casual in the west, except in coastal California, where it is rare in fall. Also rare in fall to Maritimes and Newfoundland. Declining in upper midwest.

Yellow-throated Warbler

yellow-lored *dominica* ♂

white-lored *albilora* ♂

♀

Grace's Warbler

♂

immature ♀

Kirtland's Warbler

♀

♂

♀

Prairie Warbler

♂

immature ♀

Bay-breasted Warbler *Dendroica castanea*

L 5½" (14 cm) **Breeding male** has chestnut crown, throat, and sides; black face; creamy patch at each side of neck; two white wing bars. **Female** is duller. **Fall adults** and **immatures** resemble Blackpoll Warbler and Pine Warbler. Bay-breasted is brighter green above, wing bars are thicker; underparts show little or no streaking and little yellow; flanks usually show some buff or bay color; legs usually entirely dark; undertail coverts are buffy or whitish. Short tail projection past undertail coverts for both Bay-breasted and Blackpoll. **Song** consists of high-pitched double notes. **Range:** Common to abundant; nests in coniferous forests. Migrates earlier in fall than Blackpoll. Very rare in the west.

Blackpoll Warbler *Dendroica striata* L 5½" (14 cm)

Solid black cap, white cheeks, and white underparts identify **breeding male;** back and sides boldly streaked with black. Compare with Black-and-white Warbler (page 374). **Female** is duller overall, variably greenish above and pale yellow below; some are gray; note streaking. **Fall adults** and immatures resemble Bay-breasted and Pine Warblers. Blackpoll is mostly pale greenish-yellow below, with dusky streaking on sides; legs pale on front and back, dark on sides; undertail coverts long and usually white. **Song** is a series of high *tseet* notes. **Range:** Common; nests in coniferous forests. Migrates later in fall than Bay-breasted Warbler. Rare migrant over much of west. Very rare in fall in most of south because much migration is off east coast.

Pine Warbler *Dendroica pinus* L 5½" (14 cm)

Relatively large bill; long tail projection past undertail coverts; throat color extends onto sides of neck, setting off dark cheek patch. **Male** is greenish-olive above, without streaking; throat and breast yellow, with dark streaks on sides of breast; belly and undertail coverts white. **Female** is duller. **Immatures** are brownish or brownish-olive above, with whitish wing bars and brownish tertial edges; male is dull yellow below, female largely white; both have brown wash on flanks. **Song** is a twittering musical trill, varying in speed. **Range:** Common in pines in summer; also in mixed woodlands in winter. Casual to very rare in the west; rare to Newfoundland in fall.

Palm Warbler *Dendroica palmarum* L 5½" (14 cm)

Upperparts olive. **Breeding adult** of eastern race, *D. p. hypochrysea,* has chestnut cap, yellow eyebrow, and entirely yellow underparts, with chestnut streaking on sides of breast. Fall adults and immatures lack chestnut cap and streaking; yellow is duller. Western nominate race *palmarum* has whitish belly and darker streaks on sides of breast; less chestnut. **Fall adults** and immatures are drab. **Song** is a rapid, buzzy trill. **Range:** Fairly common; nests in brush at edge of spruce bogs. During migration and winter, found in woodland borders, open brushy areas, marshes. Habitually wags its tail as it forages. Regular on west coast in fall and winter (*palmarum*); *hypochrysea* casual to California.

Bay-breasted Warbler

fall ♂

immature ♀

breeding ♀

breeding adult ♂

Blackpoll Warbler

fall

breeding ♀

breeding ♂

Pine Warbler

adult ♀

adult ♂

immature ♀

immature ♂

Palm Warbler

eastern breeding *hypochrysea*

western breeding *palmarum*

western fall *palmarum*

Yellow Warbler *Dendroica petechia L 5" (13 cm)*
Plump, short-tailed, yellow overall; dark eye prominent in uniformly yellow face; reddish streaks below are distinct in **male**, faint or absent in **female**. Back, wings, and tail yellowish-olive, with yellow wing markings and tail spots. Northern races are greener above. Immature male resembles adult female; **immature female** is much duller in most races, almost gray in a few. Often bobs its tail. **Song,** rapid, variable, is sometimes written *sweet sweet sweet I'm so sweet.* **Range:** Favors wet habitats, especially willows and alders; open woodlands, gardens, orchards.

Mourning Warbler *Oporornis philadelphia L 5¼" (13 cm)*
Lack of bold white eye ring distinguishes **adult male** from Connecticut Warbler. **Adult female** and especially **immatures** may show a thin, nearly complete eye ring, but compare with Connecticut. Immatures generally have more yellow on throat than MacGillivray's; compare also with female Common Yellowthroat (page 388). Immature males often show a little black on breast. Mourning Warblers hop rather than walk. **Call** is a flat, hollow *chip.* **Song** usually has two parts: a series of slurred two-note phrases followed by two or more lower phrases. **Range:** Fairly common in dense undergrowth, thickets, moist woods; nests on the ground. Most spring migration is west of the Appalachians.

MacGillivray's Warbler *Oporornis tolmiei L 5¼" (13 cm)*
Bold white crescents above and below eye distinguish all plumages from male Mourning and all Connecticut Warblers. Crescents may be very hard to distinguish from the thin, nearly complete eye ring on female and immature Mourning Warblers. **Immature** MacGillivray's Warblers generally have grayer throat than immature Mournings and a fairly distinct breast band above yellow belly. Field identification is often difficult. MacGillivray's hops rather than walks. **Call** is a sharp, harsh *tsik.* **Song** has two parts: a buzzy trill ending in a downslur. **Range:** Fairly common; found in dense undergrowth; nests on the ground.

Connecticut Warbler *Oporornis agilis L 5¾" (15 cm)*
Large eye with bold white eye ring conspicuous on **male**'s gray hood and **female**'s brown or gray-brown hood. Eye ring is sometimes slightly broken on one side only. **Immature** has a brownish hood and brownish breast band. A large, stocky warbler, noticeably larger than Mourning and MacGillivray's Warblers. Like Mourning, long undertail coverts give Connecticut a short-tailed, plump appearance. Walks rather than hops. Loud, accelerating **song** repeats a brief series of explosive *beech-er* or *whip-ity* notes. **Range:** Uncommon; found in spruce bogs, moist woodlands; nests on the ground; generally feeds on the ground or on low limbs. Spring migration is almost entirely west of the Appalachians. Fall migrants uncommon in the east.

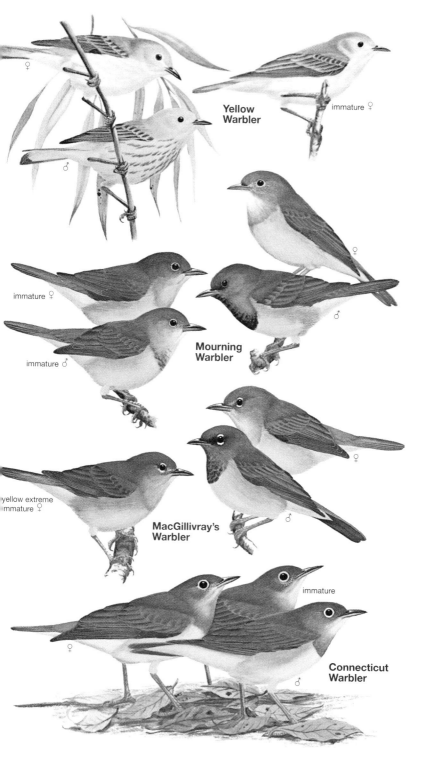

♀

Yellow
Warbler

immature ♀

♂

♀

immature ♀

♂

immature ♂

Mourning
Warbler

♀

yellow extreme
immature ♀

MacGillivray's
Warbler

♂

immature

♀

Connecticut
Warbler

♂

Kentucky Warbler *Oporornis formosus* L 5¼" (13 cm)
A short-tailed, long-legged warbler. Bold yellow spectacles separate black crown from black on face and sides of neck; underparts are entirely yellow, upperparts bright olive. Black areas are
duller on **female,** olive on immature female. **Song** is a series of
rolling musical notes, *churry churry churry,* much like the
song of the Carolina Wren. **Call** is a low, sharp *chuck.* **Range:**
Common in rich, moist woodlands; nests and feeds on the
ground in dense undergrowth. Very rare vagrant to California
and the southwest.

Canada Warbler *Wilsonia canadensis* L 5¼" (13 cm)
Black necklace on bright yellow breast identifies **male;** note also
bold yellow spectacles. In **females,** necklace is dusky and indistinct. Male is blue-gray above, females duller. All birds have white
undertail coverts. **Song** begins with one or more short, sharp
chip notes and continues as a rich and highly variable warble.
Range: Common in dense woodlands and brush. Usually forages in undergrowth or low branches, but also seen fly-
catching. Winters in South America. Casual vagrant in the west;
very rare in fall along California coast and in Newfoundland.

Wilson's Warbler *Wilsonia pusilla* L 4¾" (12 cm)
Olive above; yellow below, with yellow lores. Long tail is all-dark
above and below, and often cocked. **Male** has black cap; in
females, cap is blackish or absent, forehead yellowish. Yellow
lores and lack of white in tail help distinguish female from female
Hooded Warbler. Color of underparts varies geographically from
bright yellow in the Pacific states (shown) to greenish-yellow in
the east. **Song** is a rapid, variable series of *chee* notes; common
call, a sharp *chimp.* **Range:** Fairly common, much more numerous in the west than in the east; nests in dense, moist woodlands,
bogs, willow thickets, streamside tangles.

Hooded Warbler *Wilsonia citrina* L 5¼" (13 cm)
All ages have dark lores, unlike Wilson's Warbler; also bigger bill
and larger eye. Extensive black hood identifies **male. Adult
female** shows blackish or olive crown and sides of neck; sometimes has black throat or black spots on breast; **immature female**
lacks black. Note that in both sexes tail is white below; seen from
above, white outer tail feathers are conspicuous as the bird flicks
its tail open. **Song,** loud, musical, whistled variations of *ta-wit
ta-wit ta-wit tee-yo.* **Call** is a flat, metallic chink. **Range:** Fairly
common in swamps, moist woodlands; generally stays hidden
in dense undergrowth and low branches. Rare migrant in the
southwest and California, where it has nested; also has nested in
Colorado; casual in other western states. Rare in fall to the Maritimes; casual to Newfoundland.

Kentucky Warbler

♂

♀

Canada Warbler

immature ♀

adult ♂

Wilson's Warbler

♀

♂

Hooded Warbler

adult ♀

adult ♂

immature ♀

Worm-eating Warbler *Helmitheros vermivorus*

L 5¼" (13 cm) Bold, dark stripes on rich buffy head; upperparts brownish-olive; underparts buffy; long, spikelike bill. **Song** is a series of sharp, dry *chip* notes, like Chipping Sparrow's song but faster. Common **call**, *zeep-zeep*. **Range:** Found chiefly in dense undergrowth on wooded slopes. Often feeds in clusters of dead leaves. Casual vagrant in California and the southwest.

Swainson's Warbler *Limnothlypis swainsonii*

L 5½" (14 cm) Pale eyebrow, conspicuous between brown crown and dark eye line. Brown-olive above, grayish below. Bill very long and spiky. Uncommon and secretive. **Song** is a series of slurred whistles like beginning of song of Louisiana Waterthrush; often ends with a rising *tee-oh*. **Calls** include a loud, dry *chip*. **Range:** Found in undergrowth in swamps, canebrakes; rare and local in mountain laurel and rhododendron. Walks or shuffles on the ground and shivers while picking up dead leaves.

Ovenbird *Seiurus aurocapillus L 6" (15 cm)*

Russet crown bordered by dark stripes; bold white eye ring. Olive above; white below, with bold streaks of dark spots; pinkish legs. Generally seen on the ground; walks, with tail cocked, rather than hops. Typical **song** is a loud *teacher teacher teacher,* rising in volume. **Range**: A plump warbler, common in mature forests. Rare in the west. Rare in winter along Gulf and Atlantic coasts to North Carolina.

Louisiana Waterthrush *Seiurus motacilla L 6" (15 cm)*

Distinguished from Northern Waterthrush by contrast between white underparts and salmon-buff flanks; bicolored eyebrow, pale buff in front of eye, white and much broader behind eye; larger bill; bubblegum pink legs. A ground dweller; walks, rather than hops, bobbing its tail constantly but usually slowly. **Call** note, a sharp *chink*, is slightly flatter than that of Northern Waterthrush. **Song** begins with three or four shrill, slurred notes followed by a brief, rapid jumble. **Range:** Uncommon; found along mountain streams in dense woodlands, also near ponds and in swamps. Casual in west.

Northern Waterthrush *Seiurus noveboracensis*

L 5¾" (15 cm) Distinguished from Louisiana Waterthrush by lack of contrast in color between flanks and rest of underparts; buffy eyebrow, of even width throughout or slightly narrowing behind eye; smaller bill; drabber leg color. Some birds are whiter below, with whiter eyebrow. A ground dweller; walks, rather than hops, bobbing its tail constantly and usually rapidly. **Call** note, a metallic *chink*, is slightly sharper than that of Louisiana Waterthrush. **Song** begins with loud, emphatic notes and ends in lower notes, delivered more rapidly. **Range:** Found chiefly in woodland bogs, swamps, and thickets. Rare to uncommon migrant in California and the southwest.

Worm-eating Warbler

Swainson's Warbler

Ovenbird

Louisiana Waterthrush

Northern Waterthrush

paler

Common Yellowthroat *Geothlypis trichas* L 5" (13 cm)
Adult male's broad black mask is bordered above by gray or white, below by bright yellow throat and breast; undertail coverts yellow. **Female** lacks black mask; has whitish eye ring. Races vary geographically in color of mask border and extent of yellow below. Southwestern race, *G. t. chryseola*, is brightest below and shows the most yellow. **Immatures** are duller and browner over-all. Often cocks tail. Variable **song;** one version is a loud, rolling *wichity wichity wichity wich.* **Calls** include a raspy *chuck.* **Range:** Common; stays low in grassy fields, shrubs, marshes.

Gray-crowned Yellowthroat *Geothlypis poliocephala*
L 5½" (13 cm) **Range:** Tropical species; former resident of Brownsville area, south Texas; population eliminated in early 20th century. Recently, several certain records in the lower Rio Grande Valley; other reports uncertain. Large, with a long, grad-uated tail; thick, bicolored bill with curved culmen; split white eye ring; lores blackish in **males,** slaty gray in **females. Song,** a rich, varied warble; **call** a rising *chee dee.* Favors grassland with scattered bushes.

Fan-tailed Warbler *Euthlypis lachrymosa*
L 5¾" (15 cm) **Range:** Tropical species; casual, mainly late spring, to southeast Arizona. Large, with long, graduated, white-tipped tail held partly open and pumped sideways or up and down. Head pattern distinct with broken white eye ring; white lore spot; yel-low crown patch. Note tawny wash on breast. **Song** of rich, loud slurred notes; **call** a penetrating *schree.* Found low in canyons or ravines; often walks or shuffles on ground; secretive.

Golden-crowned Warbler *Basileuterus culicivorus*
L 5" (13 cm) **Range:** Tropical species, casual in south Texas, chiefly in winter. Resembles Orange-crowned Warbler (page 368) but crown shows a distinct yellow or buffy-orange central stripe, bordered in black; note also yellowish-green eyebrow. **Call,** a rapidly repeated *tuck.*

Rufous-capped Warbler *Basileuterus rufifrons*
L 5¼" (13 cm) **Range:** Casual from Mexico to Edward's Plateau and Big Bend, Texas; also southeast Arizona. Rufous crown, bold white eyebrow, throat extensively bright yellow. Long tail, often cocked. **Song** begins with musical *chip* notes and accelerates into a series of dry, whistled warbles; **call,** a *tik,* often doubled or in a rapid series. Inhabits dense brush and woodlands of foothills or low mountains, generally staying low in the undergrowth.

Yellow-breasted Chat *Icteria virens* L 7½" (19 cm)
Our largest warbler. Long-tailed, thick-billed, white spectacles. Lores black in **males,** gray in **females.** Unmusical **song,** a jum-ble of harsh, chattering clucks, rattles, clear whistles, and squawks, sometimes given in hovering display flight. **Range:** Inhabits dense thickets and brush. Rather shy. Regular straggler in fall to Maritimes and Newfoundland; rare in winter on the east coast.

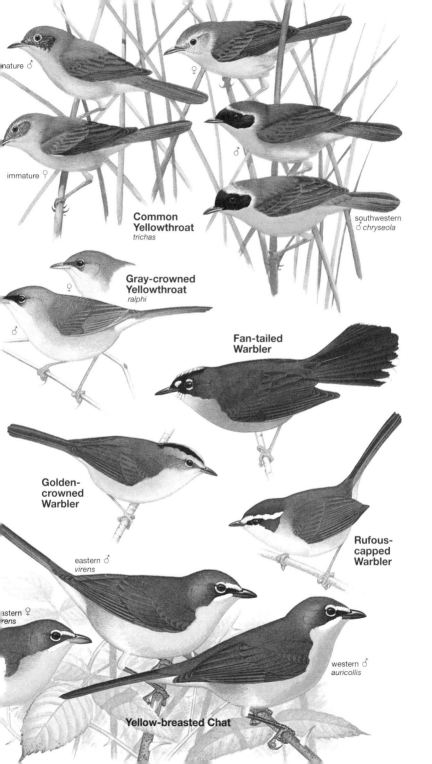

Common Yellowthroat
trichas

nature ♂

immature ♀

♀

♂

southwestern ♂ *chryseola*

Gray-crowned Yellowthroat
ralphi

♀

♂

Fan-tailed Warbler

Golden-crowned Warbler

Rufous-capped Warbler

eastern ♂ *virens*

eastern ♀ *virens*

western ♂ *auricollis*

Yellow-breasted Chat

American Redstart *Setophaga ruticilla L 5¼" (13 cm)*
Male glossy black, with bright orange patches on sides, wings, tail; belly and undertail coverts white. **Female** is gray-olive above, white below with yellow patches. Immature male resembles female; by **first spring,** lores are usually black, breast has some black spotting; adult male plumage is acquired by second fall. Like redstarts of the genus *Myioborus,* often fans its tail and spreads its wings when perched. Variable **song,** a series of high, thin notes usually followed by a wheezy, downslurred note. **Range:** Common in second-growth woodlands. Rare to uncommon migrant in California and the southwest.

Slate-throated Redstart *Myioborus miniatus L 6" (15 cm)*
Range: Middle and South American species, accidental in southeast Arizona, southeast New Mexico, and west Texas. Head, throat, and back are slate black, breast dark red. Chestnut crown patch visible only at close range. Lacks white wing patch of similar Painted Redstart; white on outer tail feathers less extensive; tail strongly graduated. **Call,** a *chip* note, very different from Painted Redstart. Found in pine-oak canyons, forests.

Painted Redstart *Myioborus pictus L 5¾" (15 cm)*
Bright red lower breast and belly; black head and upperparts; bold white wing patch. White outer tail feathers conspicuous as the bird fans its tail. **Juvenile** acquires full adult plumage by end of summer. **Song** is a series of rich, liquid warbles; **call,** a clear, whistled *chee.* **Range:** Found in pine-oak canyons. Very rare visitor to southern California; a scattering of records elsewhere.

Red-faced Warbler *Cardellina rubrifrons L 5½" (14 cm)*
Adult's red-black-and-white head pattern distinctive; back and tail gray, rump and underparts white. Juvenile is duller, face pinkish. **Song** is a series of varied, ringing *zweet* notes. **Range:** A warbler of high mountains, generally found above 6,000 feet. Fairly common, especially in fir and spruce mixed with oaks. Nests on the ground. Casual to southern California and west Texas.

Olive Warbler (Family Peucedramidae)

Recently placed in its own family because relationships are uncertain.

Olive Warbler *Peucedramus taeniatus L 5¼" (13 cm)*
Dark face patch broadens behind eye. Long, thin bill; two broad white wing bars; outer tail feathers extensively white. **Adult male**'s head, throat, and nape tawny-brown. **Female** has olive crown, yellow face; pale yellow throat and breast. Juveniles and **first-fall** birds resemble female but are paler or whitish below; crown is gray. Young male acquires adult plumage by second fall. Typical **song** is a loud *peeta peeta peeta,* similar to call of Tufted Titmouse; **call,** a soft, whistled *phew.* **Range:** Favors open coniferous forests at elevations above 7,000 feet. Nests and forages high in trees. A few remain on breeding grounds in winter.

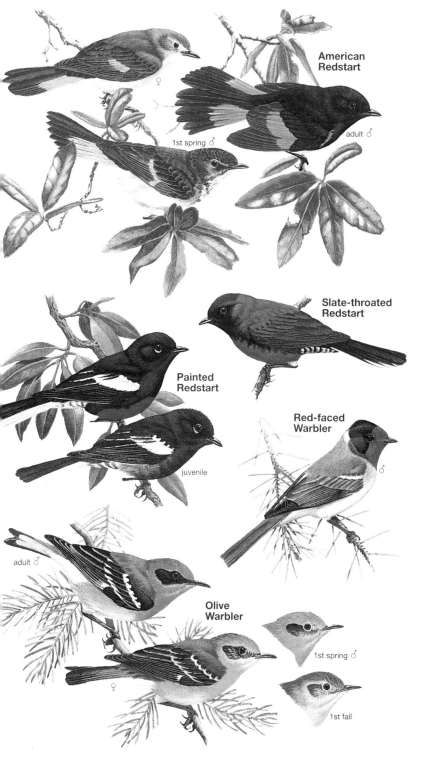

American
Redstart

1st spring ♂

adult ♂

Slate-throated
Redstart

Painted
Redstart

juvenile

Red-faced
Warbler

♂

adult ♂

Olive
Warbler

♀

1st spring ♂

1st fall

Tanagers (Family Thraupidae)

Brightly colored, mostly fruit-eating, tropical birds, related to warblers. Only a few species of this large family reach North America.

Summer Tanager *Piranga rubra* L 7¾" (20 cm)
Adult male is rosy red year-round. **First-spring male** usually has red head. Some **females** show overall reddish wash; most have a mustard tone, lack olive of female Scarlet Tanager; bill larger. Western birds are larger, paler; females generally grayer above. **Song** is robinlike; **call**, a staccato *ki-ti-tuck*. **Range:** Common in pine-oak woods in the east, cottonwood groves in the west. Rare north of summer range. Rare in winter in coastal California.

Hepatic Tanager *Piranga flava* L 8" (20 cm)
Large grayish cheek patch and gray wash on flanks set off brighter throat, breast, and cap in both sexes. **Adult male** plumage is acquired by second fall; dull red plumage retained year-round. Juvenile resembles yellow-and-gray **female** but is heavily streaked overall. **Song** is robinlike. *Chip* note, a single low *chuck*. Inhabits its mixed mountain forests.

Scarlet Tanager *Piranga olivacea* L 7" (18 cm)
Breeding male bright red and black. In late summer, becomes splotchy green-and-red as he molts to yellow-green winter plumage. **Female** has uniformly olive head, back, and rump; whitish wing linings; bill smaller than in Summer Tanager. **Immature male** resembles adult male, but note brownish primaries and secondaries. Some immatures show faint wing bars. Robinlike **song** of raspy notes, *querit queer query querit queer,* is heard in deciduous forests in summer. **Call** is a hoarse *chip-burr.* **Range:** Very rare vagrant in the west.

Western Tanager *Piranga ludoviciana* L 7¼" (18 cm)
Conspicuous wing bars, often paler and thinner in **female,** upper bar yellow in **male.** Male's red head becomes yellowish and finely streaked in **winter.** Note that female's grayish back contrasts with greenish-yellow nape and rump. Some females are duller below, grayer above. **Range:** Breeds in coniferous forests. Rare in winter north along coastal slope to central California. Rare in Gulf coast region, otherwise casual in eastern North America.

Flame-colored Tanager *Piranga bidentata*
L 7¼" (18 cm) **Range:** Resident from western Panama to northern Mexico; casual to mountains of southeast Arizona in spring and summer; accidental in Chisos Mountains, Texas. Has gray bill with visible "teeth"; blackish rear border to ear patch; streaked back; white wing bars and tertial tips; whitish tail corners. **Male** of nominate west Mexican race, *P. b. bidentata,* is flaming orange, eastern *sanguinolenta* male redder. **Female** and immatures are colored like female Western Tanager. **First-spring males** have brighter yellow head; some spotting. **Song** similar to Western and Scarlet Tanagers; **call** also, but huskier, a low-pitched *prreck.*

Hepatic Tanager

adult ♂

1st spring ♂

red morph ♀

Summer Tanager
rubra

♀

adult ♂

1st spring ♂

♀

1st fall ♂

Scarlet Tanager

fall adult ♂

breeding adult ♂

1st fall ♂

gray morph ♀

♀

winter adult ♂

Western Tanager

breeding adult ♂

1st spring ♂

Flame-colored Tanager
bidentata

♀

adult ♂

Stripe-headed Tanager *Spindalis zena* L 6¾" *(17 cm)*
Range: West Indian species; very rare visitor, except in summer, from Bahamas to southeast Florida and Florida Keys. **Males** are strikingly patterned: Most are black-backed (*S. z. zena*); a few records of *townsendi*, restricted to Grand Bahama and Abaco, show greenish-orange back; occasionally black with dull orange edgings. **Females** of both races are grayish-olive, with pale eyebrow, pale greater covert patch, and distinct white spot at base of primaries. **Call** is a thin, high *tsee,* given singly or in a series.

Bananaquits (Family Coerebidae)

Small species closely related to tanagers; feeds mainly on nectar.

Bananaquit *Coereba flaveola* L 4½" *(11 cm)*
Range: Tropical species; casual visitor from the Bahamas to southern Florida. Note thin, downcurved bill. **Adult** has conspicuous white eyebrow, yellow rump; underparts white, with yellow breast; small white wing patch. **Juvenile** is duller; eyebrow and yellowish rump less conspicuous.

Emberizids (Family Emberizidae)

Widespread species, all with conical bills. This large family includes the towhees, sparrows, longspurs, and *Emberiza* buntings.

White-collared Seedeater *Sporophila torqueola*
L 4½" *(11 cm)* Tiny, with thick, short, strongly curved bill; rounded tail. **Adult male** has black cap; white crescent below eye; incomplete buffy collar; white wing bars; white patch at base of primaries. **Females** are paler, lack cap and collar; wing bars duller. **Song** is pitched high, then low, a variable *sweet sweet sweet sweet cheer cheer cheer.* **Calls** include a distinct, high *wink.* In U.S. favors canes and river bottoms. **Range:** Tropical species; resident in south Texas along the Rio Grande Valley.

Black-faced Grassquit *Tiaris bicolor* L 4½" *(11 cm)*
Range: West Indian species; casual stray to south Florida. **Adult male** mostly black below, dark olive above; head is black. **Female** and immatures pale gray below, gray-olive above. **Song** is a buzzing *tik-zeee;* **call,** a lisping *tst.*

Yellow-faced Grassquit *Tiaris olivacea* L 4¼" *(11 cm)*
Range: Tropical species. Accidental in southern Florida and southernmost Texas. **Adult male** of mainland race, *T. o. pusilla,* shows extensive black on head, breast, and upper belly; golden-yellow subeyebrow, throat, and crescent below eye; olive above. **Adult female** and immature male have traces of same head pattern; olive above. Adult male of West Indian race, *olivacea,* shows less black. Female lacks black below. **Song** is thin, insectlike trills; **call,** a high-pitched *sik* or *tsi.*

Stripe-headed Tanager

♂ *zena*

♂ *townsendi*

♀ *townsendi*

♂ *townsendi*

White-collared Seedeater
sharpei

♀

1st winter ♂

adult ♂

Bananaquit
bahamensis

juvenile

adult

Black-faced Grassquit

♀

♂

t Indies
cea

Yellow-faced Grassquit

♂

♀

mainland
pusilla

adult ♂

Olive Sparrow *Arremonops rufivirgatus* L 6¼" (16 cm)

Range: Mexican species, common in southernmost Texas in dense undergrowth, brushy areas, live oak. Dull olive above, with brown stripe on each side of crown. Lacks reddish cap of similar Green-tailed Towhee. **Juveniles** are buffier, with pale wing bars; faintly streaked on neck and breast. **Calls** include a dry *chip* and a buzzy *speeee*. **Song** is an accelerating series of *chip* notes.

Green-tailed Towhee *Pipilo chlorurus* L 7¼" (18 cm)

Olive above with reddish crown, distinct white throat bordered by dark stripe and white stripe. **Juvenile** has two faint olive wing bars; plumage is streaked overall; upperparts tinged with olive; lacks reddish crown. Clear, whistled **song** begins with *weet-chur*, ends in raspy trill. **Calls** include a catlike *mew*. **Range:** Fairly common in dense brush, chaparral, on mountainsides and high plateaus. Casual in winter throughout the east.

California Towhee *Pipilo crissalis* L 9" (23 cm)

Brownish overall; crown slightly warmer brown than rest of upperparts. Buff throat is bordered by a distinct broken ring of dark brown spots; no dark spot on breast as in Canyon Towhee. Lores are same color as throat and contrast with cheek; undertail coverts warm cinnamon. **Juvenile** shows faint wing bars. **Call** is a sharp, metallic *chink* note; also gives some thin, lispy notes and an excited, squealing series of notes, often delivered as a duet by a pair. **Song,** accelerating *chink* notes with stutters in the middle, is heard mostly in late afternoon. **Range:** Resident in chaparral, parks, gardens. *P. c. eremophilus* (**T**) of Inyo County, California, is threatened. With Canyon Towhee, California was formerly considered one species, Brown Towhee.

Canyon Towhee *Pipilo fuscus* L 8" (20 cm)

Similar to California Towhee, with which it was formerly considered a single species. Canyon is paler, grayish rather than brown; shorter tailed; more contrast in reddish crown gives a capped appearance; crown is sometimes raised as short crest. Larger whitish belly patch with diffuse dark spot at junction with breast; paler throat bordered by finer streaks; lores the same color as cheek; distinct buffy eye ring. Juveniles are streaked below. **Call** is a shrill *chee-yep* or *chedep*. **Song,** more musical, less metallic, than California; opens with a call note, followed by sweet slurred notes. Also gives a duet of lisping and squealing notes, like California. **Range:** Favors arid, hilly country; desert canyons. Resident within range; no range overlap with California.

Abert's Towhee *Pipilo aberti* L 9½" (24 cm)

Black face; upperparts cinnamon-brown, underparts paler, with cinnamon undertail coverts. **Call** is a sharp *peek;* **song,** a series of *peek* notes. **Range:** Common within its range, but somewhat secretive. Inhabits desert woodlands, streamside thickets, at lower altitudes than similar Canyon Towhee. Also found in suburban yards and orchards.

juvenile

Olive Sparrow

spring

Green-tailed Towhee

fall

juvenile

juvenile

California Towhee

Canyon Towhee

Abert's Towhee

Eastern Towhee *Pipilo erythrophthalmus* L 7½" (19 cm)
Male's black upperparts and hood contrast with rufous sides and white underparts. Distinct white patch at base of primaries and distinct white tertial edges. White in outer tail feathers is conspicuous in flight, or seen from below when bird is perched. Most have red eyes. **Females** are similarly patterned, but black areas are replaced by brown. **Juveniles** are brownish and show distinct streaks below. The nominate race is largest and shows most extensive white in tail. Wing length, and the extent of white in wings and tail, declines from the northern part of the range to the Gulf coast, while the size of bill, legs, and feet increases. The subspecies from the Florida peninsula, *P. e. alleni*, is smaller in all measurements, paler, and duller; has less white in wings and tail; has straw-colored eyes. The *rileyi* race (not shown), from northernmost Florida to east-central North Carolina, shows intermediate characteristics, eyes being either red or straw-colored; eye color particularly variable in birds from southern Georgia and coastal South Carolina. Like other towhees, Eastern scratches with its feet together. Full **song** has three parts, often rendered as *drink your tea*, or shortened to two-parts: *drink tea*. Northeastern birds' **call** is a slightly upslurred *chwee*; in *alleni*, a clearer, even-pitch or upslurred *swee*. **Range:** Partial to second growth with dense shrubs and extensive leaf litter; southern races, especially *alleni*, favor coastal scrub or sand dune ridges and pinelands. Nominate race is partly migratory; casual west to Colorado and New Mexico. Has declined from the northeastern part of its range by as much as 90 percent in recent decades. Other races are largely resident. Eastern and Spotted Towhee have each been restored to full species status; formerly considered one species, Rufous-sided Towhee. The two interbreed along rivers in the Great Plains, particularly the Platte and its tributaries.

Spotted Towhee *Pipilo maculatus* L 7½" (19 cm)
Distinguished from similar Eastern Towhee by white spotting on back and scapulars; also on tips of median and greater coverts, which forms white wing bars. In general, **females** differ less from **males** than in Eastern, with *P. m. arcticus* from Great Plains showing the greatest difference. In both sexes the amount of white spotting above and white in tail shows marked geographical variation, with *arcticus* displaying most white. Races, principally *montanus*, from the Great Basin and Rockies show less white. The northwest coast's *oregonus* is darkest and shows least white of all the races. White increases southward to *megalonyx* of southern California and *falcinellus* (not shown) of the Central Valley region. **Song** and calls also show great geographical variation. Interior races give introductory notes, then a trill. Pacific coast birds sing a simple trill of variable speed. **Call** of *montanus* is a descending and raspy mewing. Great Plains *arcticus* and all coastal races give an upslurred, questioning *queee*. **Range:** Some populations are largely resident while others are migratory; *arcticus* is the most migratory and is casual in eastern North America.

Eastern Towhee
erythrophthalmus

juvenile

♀

Florida ♂ *alleni*

♂

Spotted Towhee

♀ *arcticus*

♂ *arcticus*

♂ *montanus*

♀ *oregonus*

♂ *oregonus*

♀ *montanus*

♀ *megalonyx*

juvenile *oregonus*

♂ *megalonyx*

Eastern

Spotted

rythrophthalmus

alleni

arcticus

montanus

megalonyx

oregonus

Bachman's Sparrow *Aimophila aestivalis* L 6" (15 cm)

A large sparrow with large bill, fairly flat forehead, and long, rounded, dark tail. **Adults** gray above, heavily streaked with chestnut or dark brown; sides of head buffy gray; a thin dark line extends back from eye. Breast and sides buff or gray; belly whitish. Subspecies range in overall brightness from the reddish *A. a. illinoensis* of the western part of range to the grayer and darker *aestivalis* of Florida. Birds from northeastern part of range are intermediate. **Juvenile** has a distinct eye ring; throat, breast, and sides are streaked. First-winter plumage usually retains some streaking. Quite secretive outside breeding season; best located and identified by **song:** one clear, whistled introductory note, followed by a variable trill or warble on a different pitch. Male sings from open perch; often heard in late summer. **Range:** Inhabits dry, open woods, especially pines; scrub palmetto. Northern range has markedly declined over last several decades.

Botteri's Sparrow *Aimophila botterii* L 6" (15 cm)

A large, plain sparrow with large bill, fairly flat forehead; tail long, rounded, dusky-brown, lacking white tips and central barring of the very similar Cassin's Sparrow. Best located and identified by **song:** several high sharp *tsip* or *che-lik* notes, often followed by a short, accelerating, rattly trill. Upperparts streaked with dull black, rust or brown, and gray; underparts unstreaked; throat and belly whitish, breast and sides grayish-buff. Subspecies *A. b. arizonae* of southeastern Arizona is redder above; *texana* (not shown) of extreme southern Texas is slightly grayer. **Juvenile**'s belly is buffy; breast broadly streaked, sides narrowly streaked. **Range:** Generally secretive; inhabits grasslands dotted with mesquite, cactus, brush. The *texana* form is declining because of habitat loss; now uncommon and local.

Cassin's Sparrow *Aimophila cassinii* L 6" (15 cm)

A large, drab sparrow, with large bill, fairly flat forehead. Long, rounded tail is dark gray-brown; distinctive white tips on outer feathers are most conspicuous in flight. In fresh fall plumage, shows bolder white wing bars than similar Botteri's Sparrow, and black-centered, white-fringed tertials. Best located and identified by **song,** often given in brief, fluttery song flight: typically a soft double whistle, a loud, sweet trill, a low whistle, and a final, slightly higher note; or a series of *chip*'s ending in a trill or warbles. Also gives a trill of *pit* notes. Gray upperparts are streaked with dull black, brown, and variable amount of rust; underparts are grayish-white, usually with a few short streaks on the flanks. **Juvenile** is streaked below; paler overall than juvenile Botteri's. **Range:** Secretive; inhabits arid grasslands with scattered shrubs, cactus, mesquite. Casual vagrant to the east and far west.

illinoensis

Bachman's Sparrow

juvenile
illinoensis

aestivalis

Botteri's Sparrow
arizonae

juvenile

Cassin's Sparrow

juvenile

Rufous-winged Sparrow *Aimophila carpalis*

L 5¾" (15 cm) Pale gray head marked with reddish eye line and black moustachial and malar stripe on side of face; two-tone bill, with pale lower mandible; sides of crown streaked with reddish-brown. Back is gray-brown, streaked with black; two whitish wing bars. Reddish lesser wing coverts distinctive but difficult to see. Underparts grayish-white, without streaking. Tail long, rounded. **Juvenile**'s facial stripes are less distinct; wing bars buffier; bill dark; breast and sides lightly streaked; plumage can be seen as late as November. Distinctive **call** note, a sharp, high *seep*. Variable **song,** several chip notes followed by an accelerating trill of *chip* or *sweet* notes. **Range:** Fairly common but local; found in flat areas of tall desert grass mixed with brush, cactus.

Rufous-crowned Sparrow *Aimophila ruficeps*

L 6" (15 cm) Gray head with dark reddish crown, distinct whitish eye ring, rufous line extending back from eye, single black malar stripe on each side of face. Gray-brown above, with reddish streaks; gray below; tail long, rounded. Subspecies range in overall color from paler, grayer *A. r. eremoeca,* found over most of eastern interior range, to widespread southwestern race *scottii,* which is paler and reddish. Pacific coastal races are slightly smaller and darker and show variable amounts of reddish above. **Juvenile** is buffier above; breast and crown streaked; may show two pale wing bars. Distinctive **call,** a sharp *dear,* usually given in a series; **song,** a rapid, bubbling series of *chip* notes. Locally common on rocky hillsides and steep brushy or grassy slopes

American Tree Sparrow *Spizella arborea* L 6¼" (16 cm)

Gray head and nape crowned with rufous; rufous stripe behind eye. Gray throat and breast, with dark central spot, rufous patches at sides of breast. Back and scapulars streaked with black and rufous. Tail notched; outer feathers thinly edged in white on outer webs. Underparts grayish-white with buffy sides. **Winter** birds are buffier; rufous color on crown sometimes forms a central stripe. **Juvenile** is streaked on head and underparts. Western populations are paler overall. American Tree Sparrow gives a musical *teedle-eet* **call;** also a thin *seet.* **Song** usually begins with several clear notes followed by a variable, rapid warble. **Range:** Fairly common. Uncommon to rare west of Rockies. Breeds along edge of tundra, in open areas with scattered trees, brush. Winters in weedy fields, marshes, groves of small trees.

Field Sparrow *Spizella pusilla* L 5¾" (15 cm)

Gray face with reddish crown, distinct whitish eye ring, bright pink bill. Back is streaked except on gray-brown rump. Breast and sides are buffy red; belly grayish-white; legs pink. **Juvenile** streaked below; wing bars buffy. Birds in westernmost part of range, such as *S. p. arenacea,* are paler and grayer; extremes are shown here. **Song** is a series of clear, plaintive whistles accelerating into a trill; *chip* note similar to Orange-crowned Warbler. **Range:** Fairly common in open, brushy woodlands, fields. Uncommon to rare in Maritimes; casual west of mapped range.

Rufous-winged Sparrow

juvenile

Rufous-crowned Sparrow

coastal

interior
eremoeca

coastal
juvenile

American Tree Sparrow

juvenile

breeding

winter

Field Sparrow

western
arenacea

eastern juvenile
pusilla

eastern
pusilla

Chipping Sparrow *Spizella passerina* L 5½" *(14 cm)*
Breeding adult identified by bright chestnut crown, distinct white eyebrow, and black line extending from bill through eye to ear; note also the gray nape and cheek; gray unstreaked rump; and two white wing bars. As in all sparrows of the genus *Spizella*, the tail is fairly long and notched. **Winter adult** has browner cheek, dark lores, and streaked crown showing some rufous color. **First-winter** bird is similar but averages less rufous on the crown; breast and sides are tinged with buff. In **juvenile** plumage, often held into October, the underparts are prominently streaked; crown usually lacks rufous; rump may show slight streaking. **Song** is a rapid trill of dry *chip* notes, all on one pitch. Flight **call**, also given perched, is a high, hard *seep* or *tsik*. **Range:** Widespread and common, Chipping Sparrows are found on lawns and in grassy fields, woodland edges, and pine-oak forests.

Clay-colored Sparrow *Spizella pallida* L 5½" *(14 cm)*
Brown crown with black streaks and a distinct buffy white or whitish central stripe. Broad, whitish eyebrow; pale lores; brown cheek outlined by dark postocular and moustachial stripes; conspicuous pale submoustachial stripe. Nape gray; back and scapulars are buffy brown, with dark streaks; rump is not streaked but color does not contrast with back as in Chipping Sparrow. Adult in fall and winter is buffier overall. **Juvenile** and **immature** birds are much buffier; gray nape and pale stripe on sides of throat stand out more; in juvenile, breast and sides are streaked. **Song** is a brief series of insectlike buzzes. Flight **call** is a thin *sip*. **Range:** Fairly common in brushy fields, groves, streamside thickets. Winters primarily from Mexico south, uncommonly in southern Texas. Rare in fall, casual in winter and spring on both coasts and in Arizona. Rare in winter in south Florida.

Brewer's Sparrow *Spizella breweri* L 5½" *(14 cm)*
Brown crown with fine black streaks. Lacks clear, pale central stripe of Clay-colored Sparrow, and head pattern lacks Clay-colored's strong contrast. Distinct whitish eye ring; grayish-white eyebrow; ear patch pale brown with darker borders; pale lores; dark malar stripe. Upperparts buffy brown and streaked; rump buffy brown, may be lightly streaked. **Juvenile** is buffier overall, lightly streaked on breast and sides. Immature, and fall and winter adult, are somewhat buffy below. **Song** is a series of varied bubbling notes and buzzy trills at different pitches. **Call** is a thin *sip*, like call of Clay-colored Sparrow. Common; breeds in mountain meadows, sagebrush flats. A separate subspecies, *S. b. taverneri* (not shown) of the alpine zone of the Canadian Rockies to east-central Alaska, has a slightly different song and larger bill. Juveniles are heavily streaked with blackish below. It is thought that this "Timberline Sparrow" may be a separate species.

breeding

**Chipping
Sparrow**

winter

juvenile

1st winter

immature

juvenile

breeding

**Clay-colored
Sparrow**

juvenile

**Brewer's
Sparrow**
breweri

Lark Sparrow *Chondestes grammacus* L 6½" (17 cm)
Head pattern distinctive in **adults;** whitish underparts are marked only with dark central breast spot. **Juvenile**'s colors are duller; breast, sides, and crown streaked. In all ages, white-cornered tail is conspicuous in flight. **Song** begins with two loud, clear notes, followed by a series of rich, melodious notes and trills and unmusical buzzes. **Call** is a sharp *tsip*, often a rapid series. **Range:** Found west of the Mississippi on prairies, roadsides, farms, open woodlands, mesas; gregarious. Formerly bred as far east as New York and Maryland; now rare in the east.

Black-chinned Sparrow *Spizella atrogularis*
L 5¾" (15 cm) Medium gray overall; back and scapulars rusty, with black streaks; bill bright pink; long tail. **Male** has black lores and chin; lower belly is whitish-gray; long tail is all-dark. **Female** has less or no black. **Juvenile** and winter birds lack any black on face. Juveniles resemble female but show light streaks below. Plaintive **song** begins with slow *sweet sweet sweet* and continues in a rapid trill. **Call** is a high, thin *seep.* **Range:** Inhabits brushy arid slopes in foothills and mountains. Rarely seen in migration.

Black-throated Sparrow *Amphispiza bilineata*
L 5½" (14 cm) Black lores and triangular black patch on throat and breast contrast with white eyebrow, white submoustachial stripe, white underparts. Upperparts plain brownish-gray. **Juvenile** plumage, often held well into fall, lacks black on throat, but note bold white eyebrow; breast and back finely streaked. In all ages, extent of white on tail is greater than in Sage Sparrow. **Song** is rapid, high-pitched: two clear notes followed by a trill; **calls** are faint, tinkling notes. **Range:** Fairly common in desert, especially on rocky slopes; casual to eastern U.S. in fall and winter.

Five-striped Sparrow *Aimophila quinquestriata*
L 6" (15 cm) Dark brown above; breast and sides gray; white throat bordered by black and white stripes. Dark central spot at base of breast. Juvenile lacks the streaks found on juveniles of other sparrows. **Range:** West Mexican species; range barely reaches southeastern Arizona. Highly specialized habitat: tall, dense shrubs on rocky, steep hillsides, canyon slopes. Very local; most often seen in breeding season; few winter records.

Sage Sparrow *Amphispiza belli* L 6¼" (16 cm)
White eye ring, white supraloral, broad white submoustachial stripe bordered by dark malar stripe. Back buffy brown with dusky streaks on interior (and palest) race *A. b. nevadensis.* Dark central breast spot, dusky streaking on sides. **Juvenile** is duller overall but more heavily streaked. California coastal race *belli* is much darker, lacks streaks on back, has stronger malar stripe. From a low perch, male **sings** a jumbled series of rising-and-falling phrases. Twittering **call** consists of thin, juncolike notes. Runs on ground with tail cocked. **Range:** Interior *nevadensis* and slightly darker *canescens* favor alkaline flats in sagebrush, saltbush. Coastal *belli* found in mountain chaparral.

Lark Sparrow

juvenile

Black-chinned Sparrow

breeding ♀

breeding ♂

juvenile

Black-throated Sparrow

juvenile

Five-striped Sparrow

coastal *belli*

Sage Sparrow

interior *nevadensis*

interior juvenile *nevadensis*

Grasshopper Sparrow *Ammodramus savannarum*

L 5" (13 cm) Buffy breast and sides, usually without obvious streaking. Small and chunky, with short tail, flat head. Dark crown has a pale central stripe; note also white eye ring and, on most birds, a yellow-orange spot in front of eye. Lacks broad buffy-orange eyebrow and pale blue-gray ear patch of Le Conte's Sparrow (next page). Compare also with female Orange Bishop (page 456) and Savannah Sparrow (page 412). **Juvenile**'s breast and sides are streaked with brown. **Fall** birds are buffier below but never as bright as Le Conte's. Subspecies vary in overall color from dark Florida race, *A. s. floridanus* (**E**), to reddish *ammolegus* of southeastern Arizona. Eastern *pratensis* is slightly more richly colored than western *perpallidus,* which spreads east through the Great Plains. Typical **song** is one or two high chip notes followed by a brief, grasshopperlike *buzz;* also sings a series of varied squeaky and buzzy notes. **Range:** Found in pastures, grasslands, palmetto scrub, old fields. Somewhat secretive; feeds and nests on the ground. Declining in east.

Baird's Sparrow *Ammodramus bairdii* *L 5½" (14 cm)*

Orange tinge to head (duller on worn summer birds), usually with less distinct median crown stripe than Savannah Sparrow (page 412); note especially the two isolated dark spots behind ear patch, and no postocular line. Widely spaced, short dark streaks on breast form a distinct necklace; also shows chestnut on scapulars. **Juvenile**'s head is paler, creamier; central crown stripe finely streaked; white fringes give a scaly appearance to upperparts; underparts more extensively streaked. Secretive, especially away from breeding grounds. **Song** consists of two or three high, thin notes, followed by a single warbled note and a low trill. **Range:** Uncommon, local, and declining. Found in grasslands, weedy fields. Accidental in eastern North America and California.

Henslow's Sparrow *Ammodramus henslowii*

L 5" (13 cm) Large flat head; large gray bill. Resembles Baird's Sparrow but head, nape, and most of central crown stripe are greenish; wings extensively dark chestnut. **Juvenile** is paler, yellower, with less streaking below; compare with adult Grasshopper Sparrow. Secretive, but after being flushed several times may perch in the open for a few minutes before dropping back into cover. Distinctive **song,** a short *se-lick,* accented on second syllable. **Range:** Uncommon, local, and declining; now occurs only casually in the northeast; found in wet shrubby fields, weedy meadows, reclaimed strip mines. In winter, found also in the understory of pine woods.

Grasshopper Sparrow

summer
perpallidus

floridanus

juvenile *pratensis*

fall *pratensis*

fall *ammolegus*

Orange Bishop ♀
for comparison

Baird's Sparrow

Henslow's Sparrow

juvenile

juvenile

Saltmarsh Sharp-tailed Sparrow

Ammodramus caudacutus L 5" (13 cm) Similar to Nelson's, but bill longer; flatter-headed; orange-buff face triangle contrasts strongly with paler, crisply streaked underparts. Also dark markings around eye and head are more sharply defined; eyebrow streaked with black behind eye. **Juvenile**'s crown is blacker than juvenile Nelson's; cheek darker; streaks below more widespread and distinct. **Song** softer, more complex than Nelson's, with which it hybridizes in Maine. With Nelson's Sharp-tailed Sparrow, formerly treated as one species, Sharp-tailed Sparrow

Le Conte's Sparrow *Ammodramus leconteii L 5" (13 cm)*

White central crown stripe, becoming orange on forehead, chestnut streaks on nape, and straw-colored back streaks distinguish Le Conte's from sharp-tailed sparrows. Bright, broad, buffy orange eyebrow, grayish ear patch, thinner bill, and orange-buff breast and sides separate it from Grasshopper Sparrow (preceding page). Sides of breast and flanks have dark streaks. **Juvenile** plumage, seen on breeding grounds and in migration, is buffy; crown stripe tawny; breast heavily streaked. **Song** is a short, high, insectlike buzz. **Range:** A bird of wet grassy fields, marsh edges. Fairly common but secretive; scurries through matted grasses like a mouse. Casual migrant in the northeast and in the west.

Nelson's Sharp-tailed Sparrow *Ammodramus nelsoni*

4¾" *(12 cm)* Distinguished from Le Conte's by gray median crown stripe; whitish or gray streaks on scapulars; gray, streakless nape; **juvenile** has fainter median crown stripe; duller nape; variably thicker eye line; less contrast above; lacks streaking across breast. Plumage variable: *A.n.nelsoni,* of interior has orange-buff triangle on face; streaked buffy breast contrasts with white belly; back strongly marked with black and white stripes; *subvirgatus* of the Maritimes and coastal Maine, is duller overall; has diffuse streaking below; grayer upperparts. In *alterus* (not shown) from James and Hudson Bays, brightness is intermediate, streaks blurred. **Song,** a wheezy *p-tssssshh-uk,* ends on a lower note.

Seaside Sparrow *Ammodramus maritimus L 6" (15 cm)*

Long, spikelike bill, thick-based and thin-tipped. Tail is short, pointed. Yellow supraloral patch. Dark malar stripe separates whitish throat and broad, pale stripe along cheek. Breast is white or buffy, with at least some streaking. **Juveniles** are duller, browner, than **adults.** Seaside Sparrows vary widely in overall color. Most races, like the widespread *A. m. maritimus,* are grayish-olive above. The greener *mirabilis* (**E**), formerly called Cape Sable Sparrow, inhabits a small area in southwest Florida. Gulf coast races such as *fisheri* have buffier breasts. The darkest race, *nigrescens,* formerly called "Dusky Seaside Sparrow," was found only near Titusville, Florida, and became extinct in June 1987. This subspecies was blackish above, heavily streaked below. Seaside Sparrow's **song** resembles that of Red-winged Blackbird but is buzzier. **Range:** Fairly common in grassy tidal marshes; accidental inland. Rare in Maine; very rare to the Maritimes.

Saltmarsh Sharp-tailed Sparrow

juvenile

Le Conte's Sparrow

juvenile

subvirgatus

nelsoni

nelsoni

Nelson's Sharp-tailed Sparrow

juvenile nelsoni

maritimus

fisheri

maritimus juvenile

nigrescens

mirabilis

Seaside Sparrow

Fox Sparrow *Passerella iliaca L 7" (18 cm)*

Highly variable. Most subspecies have reddish rump and tail; reddish in wings; underparts heavily marked with triangular spots merging into a larger spot on central breast. The brightest, *P. i. iliaca,* and slightly duller *zaboria* breed in the far north from Seward Peninsula, Alaska to Newfoundland; winter in southeastern U.S. Western mountain races have gray head and back, grayish-olive base to bill; range from small-billed Rockies *schistacea* to large-billed California *stephensi.* Dark coastal races, with browner rumps and tails, vary from sooty *fuliginosa* of the Pacific northwest to paler *unalaschcensis* of southwest Alaska. **Songs** are sweet, melodic in northern, reddish races; include harsher trills in other races. Large-billed Pacific races give a sharp *chink* call, like California Towhee; others give a *tschup* note, like Lincoln's Sparrow but louder. **Range:** Uncommon to common; found in undergrowth in coniferous or mixed woodlands, chaparral.

Lark Bunting *Calamospiza melanocorys L 7" (18 cm)*

Stocky, short-tailed with whitish wing patches; bill bluish-gray. **Breeding male** is mostly black. **Female** is streaked below, with buffy sides, brown primaries. **Winter male** is similar, but has black primaries; immature male darker, has some black around bill and chin. Distinctive **call** is a soft *hoo-ee.* **Song,** a varied series of rich whistles and trills. **Range:** Common; nests in dry plains and prairies, especially in sagebrush. Gregarious in migration and winter. In flight, looks short and round-winged, with shallow wingbeat. Rare in fall and winter to west coast; casual to Pacific northwest and in the east.

Savannah Sparrow *Passerculus sandwichensis*

L 5½" (14 cm) Highly variable. Eyebrow yellow or whitish; pale median crown stripe; strong postocular stripe. **Song** begins with two or three chip notes, followed by two buzzy trills. Distinctive flight **call,** a thin *seep.* Common in a variety of open habitats, marshes, grasslands. The numerous subspecies vary geographically; extremes are shown here. West coast races show increasingly darker color from north to south, with Alaskan and interior races paler, widespread *P. s. nevadensis* the palest; *beldingi* of southern California coastal marshes is darkest. The *rostratus* subspecies, **"Large-billled Sparrow,"** which winters in small numbers on the edge of Salton Sea, rarely in coastal California, is very dull with a large bill. Its song, markedly different from other Savannah Sparrows, has short, high introductory notes, followed by about three rich, buzzy *dzeeee's;* call a soft, metallic *zink.* In the east, the degree of darkness is reversed: Arctic races are darker than more southerly Canadian and U.S. races. Large, pale *princeps,* **"Ipswich Sparrow,"** breeds on Sable Island, Nova Scotia, winters on east coast beaches.

Fox Sparrow

iliaca

schistacea

stephensi

unalaschcensis

fuliginosa

Lark Bunting

breeding ♂

early spring ♂

winter ♂

♀

Savannah Sparrow

nevadensis

"Ipswich Sparrow" *princeps*

beldingi

"Large-billed Sparrow" *rostratus*

Lincoln's Sparrow *Melospiza lincolnii* L 5¾" (15 cm)

Buffy wash and fine streaks on breast and sides, contrasting with whitish, unstreaked belly. Note broad gray eyebrow, whitish chin and eye ring. Briefly held **juvenile** plumage is paler overall than juvenile Swamp Sparrow. Distinguished from juvenile Song Sparrow by shorter tail, slimmer bill and thinner malar stripe, often broken. Often raises slight crest when disturbed. Two **call** notes: a flat *tschup*, repeated in a series as an alarm call; and a sharp, buzzy *zeee*. Rich, loud **song,** a rapid, bubbling trill. Found in brushy bogs and mountain meadows; in winter prefers thickets.

Song Sparrow *Melospiza melodia* L 5¾-7½" (16-19 cm)

All *Melospiza* subspecies have long, rounded tail, pumped in flight. All show broad grayish eyebrow and broad, dark malar stripe bordering whitish throat. Highly variable. Upperparts are usually streaked. Underparts whitish, with streaking on sides and breast that often converges in a central spot. Legs and feet are pinkish. **Juvenile** is buffier overall, with finer streaking. Typical **song**: three or four short clear notes followed by a buzzy *tow-wee*, then a trill. Distinctive **call** note, a nasal, hollow *chimp.* The numerous subspecies vary geographically in size, bill shape, overall coloration, and streaking. *M. m. melodia* typifies eastern races; large Alaskan races, the largest resident on the Aleutians, reach an extreme in the gray-brown *maxima;* paler races such as *saltonis* inhabit southwestern deserts; *morphna* represents the darker, redder races of the Pacific northwest; *heermanni* is one of the blackish-streaked California races. **Range:** Generally common, Song Sparrows are found in brushy areas, especially dense streamside thickets.

Vesper Sparrow *Pooecetes gramineus* L 6¼" (16 cm)

White eye ring; dark ear patch bordered in white along lower and rear edges; white outer tail feathers. Lacks bold eyebrow of Savannah Sparrow (preceding page). Distinctive chestnut lesser coverts not easily seen. Eastern nominate race is slightly darker overall than the widespread subspecies, *P. g. confinis,* shown here. **Song** is rich and melodious, two long, slurred notes followed by two higher notes, then a series of short, descending trills. **Range:** Uncommon to fairly common in dry grasslands, farmlands, forest clearings, sagebrush; declining in the east.

Swamp Sparrow *Melospiza georgiana* L 5¾" (15 cm)

Gray face; rich rufous upperparts and wings; variable black streaks on back; white throat. **Breeding adult** has reddish crown, gray breast, whitish belly. **Winter adult** is buffier overall; crown is streaked, shows gray central stripe; sides are rich buff. Briefly held **juvenile** plumage is usually even buffier; darker overall than juvenile Lincoln's or Song Sparrow; wings and tail redder. **Immature** resembles winter adult. Typical **song** is a slow, musical trill, all on one pitch. Two **call** notes: a prolonged *zeee,* softer than Lincoln's Sparrow, and a metallic *chip.* **Range:** Nests in dense, tall vegetation in marshes, bogs. Winters in marshes, brushy fields. Generally rare in the west.

Lincoln's Sparrow

juvenile

melodia

juvenile *melodia*

Song Sparrow

heermanni

maxima

morphna

saltonis

Vesper Sparrow

breeding

Swamp Sparrow

winter adult

juvenile

immature

Harris's Sparrow *Zonotrichia querula* L 7½" (19 cm)
A large sparrow with black crown, face, and bib; pink bill. **Winter adult**'s crown is blackish; cheeks buffy; throat may be all-black or show white flecks or partial white band. **Immature** resembles winter adult but shows less black; white throat is bordered by dark malar stripe. **Song** is a series of long, clear, quavering whistles, often beginning with two notes on one pitch followed by two notes on another pitch. **Calls** include a loud *wink* and a drawn-out *tseep.* **Range:** Fairly common; nests in stunted boreal forest; winters in open woodlands, brushlands. Rare to casual in winter in rest of North America outside mapped range.

White-throated Sparrow *Zonotrichia albicollis*
L 6¾" (17 cm) Conspicuous and strongly outlined white throat; mostly dark bill; dark crown stripes and eye line. Broad eyebrow is yellow in front of eye; remainder is either white or tan. Upperparts rusty-brown; underparts grayish, sometimes with diffuse streaking. **Juvenile**'s eyebrow and throat are grayish, breast and sides heavily streaked. **Song** is a thin whistle, generally two single notes followed by three triple notes: *pure sweet Canada Canada Canada,* often heard in winter. **Calls** include a sharp *pink* and a drawn-out, lisping *tseep.* **Range:** Common in woodland undergrowth, brush, gardens. Generally rare in the west.

White-crowned Sparrow *Zonotrichia leucophrys*
L 7" (18 cm) Black-and-white striped crown; pink, orange, or yellowish bill; whitish throat; underparts mostly gray. **Juvenile**'s head is brown and buff, underparts streaked. **Immature** has tan and brownish head stripes; compare with immature Golden-crowned Sparrow. Nominate race *Z. l. leucophrys,* mainly found in the east Canadian tundra, and *oriantha* (not shown) of the High Sierra, southern Cascades, and Rockies, have a black supraloral area and large, dark pink bill; *gambelii,* ranging from Alaska to Hudson Bay, has a whitish supraloral and a smaller, orange-yellow bill; in coastal *nuttalli* and *pugetensis,* (not shown) breast and back are browner, bill dull yellow, supraloral pale. **Song,** often heard in winter, is usually one or more thin, whistled notes followed by a twittering trill; *leucophrys* and *gambelii* give a more mournful song with no trill at end. **Calls** include a loud *pink* and sharp *tseep.* **Range:** Generally common in woodlands, grasslands, roadside hedges.

Golden-crowned Sparrow *Zonotrichia atricapilla*
L 7" (18 cm) Yellow patch tops black crown; back brownish, streaked with dark brown; breast, sides and flanks grayish-brown. Bill is dusky above, pale below. Yellow is less distinct on **immature**'s brown crown. Briefly held **juvenile** plumage has dark streaks on breast and sides. **Winter adults** are duller overall; amount of black on crown varies. **Song** is a series of three or more plaintive, whistled notes: *oh dear me.* **Calls** include a soft *tseep* and a flat *tsick.* **Range:** Fairly common in stunted boreal bogs and in open areas near tree line, especially in willows. Winters in dense woodlands, tangles, and brush; casual in east.

breeding

winter adult

Harris's Sparrow

winter adult

immature

White-throated Sparrow

tan-striped morph

white-striped morph

juvenile

adult *gambelii*

juvenile *gambelii*

adult *nuttalli*

adult *leucophrys*

White-crowned Sparrow

Immature *leucophrys*

Golden-crowned Sparrow

juvenile

immature

breeding

winter adult

Dark-eyed Junco *Junco hyemalis L 6¼" (16 cm)*

Variable; most races have a gray or brown head and breast sharply set off from white belly. White outer tail feathers are conspicuous in flight. **Male** of the widespread **"Slate-colored Junco"** group of subspecies has a dark gray hood; upperparts are entirely gray or have varying amount of brown at center of back. **Female** is brownish-gray overall. **Juveniles** of all races are streaked. "Slate-colored" winters mostly in eastern North America; uncommon in the west. Male **"Oregon Junco"** of the west has slaty to blackish hood, rufous-brown to buffy brown back and sides; females have duller hood color. Of the seven subspecies in the "Oregon" group, the more southerly races are paler. "Oregon" types winter mainly in the west; very rare during winter in the east. **"Pink-sided Junco,"** *J. h. mearnsi,* breeding in the central Rockies, has broad, bright pinkish-cinnamon sides, blue-gray hood and blackish lores. The **"White-winged Junco"** race, *aikeni,* breeding in the Black Hills area, is mostly pale gray above, usually with two thin, white wing bars; also larger, with more white on tail. In the **"Gray-headed Junco"** of the southern Rockies, the pale gray hood is barely darker than the underparts; back is rufous. In much of Arizona and New Mexico, resident "Gray-headed," *dorsalis,* has an even paler throat and a large, bicolored bill, black above, bluish below. Intergrades between some races are frequent. Dark-eyed Junco's **song** is a musical trill on one pitch, often heard in winter. Varied **calls** include a sharp *dit* and, in flight, a rapid twittering. Songs and calls of "Gray-headed" *dorsalis* are more suggestive of Yellow-eyed Junco. **Range:** Breeds in coniferous or mixed woodlands. In migration and winter, found in a wide variety of habitats.

Yellow-eyed Junco *Junco phaeonotus L 6¼" (16 cm)*

Bright yellow eyes, set off by black lores. Pale gray above, with a bright rufous back and rufous-edged greater wing coverts and tertials; underparts paler gray. **Juveniles** are similar to juveniles of gray-headed races of Dark-eyed Junco; eye is brown, becoming pale before changing to yellow of adult; look for rufous on wings. **Song** is a variable series of clear, thin whistles and trills. **Calls** include a high, thin *seep,* similar to call of Chipping Sparrow. **Range:** Yellow-eyed Junco is found on coniferous and pine-oak slopes, generally above 6,000 feet. Resident within its range. Some move to lower altitude in winter.

"Oregon"
thurberi

♀

♂

"Slate-colored"
hyemalis

♀

♂

juvenile

"White-winged"
aikeni

♂

**Dark-eyed
Junco**

"Slate-colored" ♂

"Pink-sided"
mearnsi

♂

"Gray-headed"
races

caniceps ♂

dorsalis ♂

**Yellow-eyed
Junco**

juvenile

Chestnut-collared Longspur *Calcarius ornatus*

L 6" (15 cm) White tail marked with blackish triangle. Very short primary projection; primary tips barely extend to base of tail. **Breeding adult male**'s black-and-white head, buffy face, and black underparts are distinctive; a few have chestnut on underparts. Lower belly and undertail coverts whitish. Upperparts black, buff, and brown, with chestnut collar, whitish wing bars. **Winter males** are paler; feathers edged in buff and brown, obscuring black underparts. Male has small white patch on shoulder, often hidden; compare with Smith's Longspur (next page). Breeding adult female resembles **winter female** but is darker, usually shows some chestnut on nape. Juvenile's pale feather fringes give upperparts a scaled look; tail pattern and bill shape distinguish juvenile from juvenile McCown's Longspur. Fall and winter birds have grayish, not pinkish, bills. **Song,** heard only on breeding grounds, is a pleasant rapid warble, given in song flight or from a low perch. Distinctive **call,** a two-syllable *kittle,* repeated one or more times. Also gives a soft, high-pitched rattle and a short *buzz* call. **Range:** Fairly common; nests in moist upland prairies. Somewhat shy; generally found in dense grass; gregarious in fall and winter. Casual during migration to eastern North America and Pacific northwest; more regularly to California.

McCown's Longspur *Calcarius mccownii* *L 6" (15 cm)*

White tail marked by dark inverted T-shape. Note also that bill is stouter and thicker based than bills of other longspurs. Primary projection slightly longer than in Chestnut-collared Longspur; in perched bird, wings extend almost to tip of short tail. **Breeding adult male** has black crown, black malar stripe, black crescent on breast; gray sides. Upperparts streaked with buff and brown, with gray nape, gray rump; chestnut median coverts form contrasting crescent. **Breeding adult female** has streaked crown; may lack black on breast and show less chestnut on wing. In **winter adults,** bill is pinkish with dark tip; feathers are edged with buff and brown. Winter adult female is paler than female Chestnut-collared, with fewer streaks on underparts and a broader buffy eyebrow. Some winter males have gray on rump; variable blackish on breast; retain chestnut median coverts. **Juvenile** is streaked below; pale fringes on feathers give upperparts a scaled look; paler overall than juvenile Chestnut-collared. **Song,** heard only on breeding grounds, is a series of exuberant warbles and twitters, generally given in song flight. **Calls** include a dry rattle, a little softer and more abrupt than Lapland Longspur; also gives single finchlike notes. **Range:** Locally fairly common but range has shrunk significantly since the 19th century. Nests in dry shortgrass plains; in winter, also found in plowed fields, dry lake beds, often amid large flocks of Horned Larks. Look for McCown's chunkier, shorter tailed shape, slightly darker plumage, mostly white tail, thicker bill, and undulating flight. Very rare visitor to interior California, Nevada. Casual in coastal California and southern Oregon; accidental to the east coast.

Chestnut-collared Longspur

breeding males

winter ♂

winter ♀

McCown's Longspur

breeding ♂

breeding ♀

winter ♀

winter ♂

juvenile

Smith's Longspur *Calcarius pictus* L 6¼" (16 cm)

Outer two feathers on each side of tail are almost entirely white. Bill is thinner than in other longspurs. Note long primary projection, a bit shorter than Lapland, but much longer than Chestnut-collared or McCown's (preceding page); shows rusty edges to greater coverts and tertials. **Breeding adult male** has black-and-white head, rich buff nape and underparts; white patch on shoulder, often obscured. **Breeding adult female** and all **winter** plumages are duller, crown streaked, chin paler. Dusky ear patch bordered by pale buff eyebrow; pale area on side of neck often breaks through dark rear edge of ear patch. Underparts are pale buff with thin reddish-brown streaks on breast and sides. Females have much less white on lesser coverts than males. Typical **call** is a dry, ticking rattle, harder and sharper than call of Lapland and McCown's Longspurs. **Song,** heard in spring migration and on the breeding grounds, is delivered only from the ground or a perch. It consists of rapid, melodious warbles, ending with a vigorous *wee-chew.* **Range:** Generally uncommon and secretive, especially in migration and winter. Nests on open tundra and damp, tussocky meadows. Winters in open, grassy areas; sometimes seen with Lapland Longspurs. Regular spring migrant in the midwest, east to western Indiana. Casual vagrant to east coast from Massachusetts to South Carolina, and to California.

Lapland Longspur *Calcarius lapponicus* L 6¼" (16 cm)

Outer two feathers on each side of tail are partly white, partly dark. Note also, especially in winter plumages, the reddish edges on the greater covert; and on the tertials, which are also indented. **Breeding adult male**'s head and breast are black and well outlined: a broad white or buffy stripe extends back from eye and down to sides of breast; nape is reddish-brown. **Breeding adult female** and all **winter** plumages are duller; note bold dark triangle outlining plain buffy ear patch; dark streaks (female) or patch (male) on upper breast; dark streaks on side. On all winter birds, note broad buffy eyebrow and buffier underparts; belly and undertail are white, unlike Smith's Longspur; also compare head and wing patterns. **Juvenile** is yellowish and heavily streaked above and on breast and sides. **Song,** heard only on the breeding grounds, is a rapid warbling, frequently given in short flights. **Calls** include a musical *tee-lee-oo* or *tee-dle* and, in flight, a dry rattle distinctively mixed with whistled *tew* notes. **Range:** Fairly common, Lapland Longspurs breed on Arctic tundra, winter in grassy fields, grain stubble, and on shores. Often found amid flocks of Horned Larks and Snow Buntings; look for Lapland's darker overall coloring and smaller size.

Smith's
Longspur

breeding ♂

breeding ♀

winter ♂

breeding ♂

breeding ♀

Lapland
Longspur

winter ♂

winter ♀

juvenile

buffy fall ♀

Snow Bunting *Plectrophenax nivalis* L 6¾" (17 cm)

Black-and-white breeding plumage acquired by end of spring, largely by wear. Bill is black in summer, orange-yellow in winter. In all seasons, note long black-and-white wings. **Males** usually show more white overall than **females**, especially in the wings. **Juvenile** is grayish and streaked, with buffy eye ring; very similar to juvenile McKay's Bunting. First-winter plumage, acquired before migration, is darker overall than adult. **Calls** include a sharp, whistled *tew,* a short buzz, and a musical rattle or twitter. **Song,** heard only on the breeding grounds, is a loud, high-pitched musical warbling. **Range:** Fairly common; breeds on tundra, rocky shores, talus slopes. During migration and winter, found on shores, especially sand dunes and beaches, and in weedy fields, grain stubble, along roadsides, often in large flocks that may include Lapland Longspurs and Horned Larks.

McKay's Bunting *Plectrophenax hyperboreus*

L 6¾" (17 cm) **Adult breeding** plumage mostly white, with less black on wings and tail than Snow Bunting; **female** shows a white panel on greater coverts. **Winter** plumage is edged with rust or tawny-brown, but male is whiter overall than Snow Bunting; female very similar to male Snow Bunting. Juvenile is buffy-gray and streaked, with gray head, prominent buffy eye ring; very similar to juvenile Snow Bunting. **Calls** and **song** similar to Snow Bunting. **Range:** McKay's is known to breed only on Hall and St. Matthew Islands in the Bering Sea. A few sometimes present in late spring on St. Lawrence Island; summer rarely on Pribilofs. Rare to uncommon in winter along west coast of Alaska; casual in winter southward in interior of Alaska and on Aleutians. Some authorities think McKay's may be a subspecies of Snow Bunting.

Yellow-breasted Bunting *Emberiza aureola*

L 6" (15 cm) **Range:** Mainly Asian species; casual to Alaska, mostly on western Aleutians. Has the white outer tail feathers characteristic of most *Emberiza* buntings. **Breeding male** has rufous-brown upperparts, bright yellow underparts, white patch on lesser and median wing coverts. East Asian race, *E. a. ornata,* which reaches Alaska, has black on forehead and base of breast band. Winter adult male usually shows features of breeding plumage. **Female** and immatures have striking head pattern with median crown stripe; ear patches with dark border and pale spot in rear; yellowish underparts with sparse streaking; unmarked belly. **Call** is a *tzip,* similar to Little Bunting.

Gray Bunting *Emberiza variabilis* L 6¾" (17 cm)

Range: Asian species, accidental spring vagrant on western Aleutians. A large, heavy-billed bunting; shows no white in tail. **Breeding male** is gray overall, prominently streaked with blackish above. Winter males are a bit browner above, paler below. **Adult female** is brown; chestnut rump is conspicuous in flight. **Immature male** resembles adult female above but is mostly gray below with some gray on the head; immature plumage is largely held through first spring. **Call** is a sharp *zhii.*

breeding ♂

breeding ♂

winter ♀

Snow Bunting

winter ♂

breeding ♀

juvenile

winter ♀

winter ♂

McKay's Bunting

breeding ♀

breeding ♂

breeding ♂

winter ♂

Yellow-breasted Bunting

♀

Gray Bunting

breeding ♂

♀

breeding ♂

immature ♂

Reed Bunting *Emberiza schoeniclus*

L 6" (15 cm) **Range:** Eurasian species, casual vagrant on westernmost Aleutians in late spring. All records are of pale east Asian *E. s. pyrrhulina,* which resembles Pallas's Bunting in female and winter plumages. Reed Bunting has solid chestnut lesser wing coverts. Note also heavy, gray bill with curved culmen; cinnamon wing bars; dark lateral crown stripes, paler median crown stripe. **Breeding male** has black head and throat, a broad white submoustachial stripe, and white nape; upperparts streaked black and rust, rump gray. Underparts white with thin reddish streaks along sides and flanks. **Female** has pale brownish rump, broad buffy-white eyebrow; compare with female Pallas's. **Fall male** resembles female Reed, but shows black on throat and a more distinct collar. Active and conspicuous, Reed Bunting often flicks its tail, showing white outer tail feathers. **Calls,** a *seeoo,* falling in pitch; flight note a hoarse *brzee.*

Pallas's Bunting *Emberiza pallasi L 5" (13 cm)*

Range: Asian species, accidental spring vagrant at Point Barrow, Alaska; St. Lawrence Island; western Aleutians. Compare with Reed Bunting. Note Pallas's smaller size, smaller two-toned bill with straighter culmen (except **breeding male,** which has black bill); grayish lesser wing coverts; less rufous wing bars; shorter tail. **Female** has more indistinct eyebrow and lateral crown stripes than female Reed; lacks median crown stripe. **Call,** a *cheeep,* recalling Eurasian Tree Sparrow, very unlike Reed's call.

Little Bunting *Emberiza pusilla L 5" (13 cm)*

Range: Eurasian species, accidental fall vagrant on western Aleutians; St. Lawrence Island; off northwest Alaska; and in southern California. Small, short-legged, short-tailed, with a small triangular bill, bold creamy white eye ring, chestnut ear patch, and two thin pale wing bars. Underparts whitish and heavily streaked; outer tail feathers white. In **breeding plumage,** shows chestnut crown stripe bordered by black stripes. Many **males** have chestnut on chin. **Immatures** and winter adults have chestnut crown, tipped and streaked with buff and black; compare especially with female Rustic and Reed Buntings. **Call** note is a sharp *tsick.*

Rustic Bunting *Emberiza rustica L 5¾" (15 cm)*

Range: Eurasian species; uncommon spring migrant on western and central Aleutians, rare in fall; very rare on other islands in Bering Sea; casual elsewhere along west coast. Has a slight crest, whitish nape spot, and prominent pale line extending back from eye. **Male** has black head; upperparts bright chestnut with buff and blackish streaks on back; outer tail feathers white. Underparts are white, with chestnut breast band and streaks on sides. **Female** and fall and winter males have brownish head pattern, with pale spot at rear of ear patch. Female may be confused with Little Bunting; note Rustic's larger size, heavier bill with pink lower mandible, diffuse rusty streaking below, and lack of eye ring. **Call** note is a hard, sharp *jit* or *tsip.* **Song,** a soft, bubbling warble.

Reed Bunting
pyrrhulina

fall adult ♂

♀

breeding ♂

Little Bunting

immature

breeding ♂

♀

breeding ♂

Pallas's Bunting

Rustic Bunting

♀

breeding ♂

Cardinals (Family Cardinalidae)

In North America, these seedeaters include Northern Cardinal, certain grosbeaks, the *Passerina* and other buntings, and Dickcissel.

Rose-breasted Grosbeak Pheucticus ludovicianus

L 8" (20 cm) Large size; very large, triangular bill; upper mandible paler than Black-headed Grosbeak. **Breeding male** has rose red breast, white underparts, white wing bars, white rump. Rose red wing linings show in flight. Brown-tipped **winter** plumage is acquired before migration. **Female**'s streaked plumage and yellow wing linings resemble female Black-headed, but underparts are more heavily and extensively streaked. Similar **first-fall male** is buffier above, with buffy wash across breast; often has a few red feathers on breast; red wing linings distinctive. Rich, warbled **songs** of both species are nearly identical. Rose-breasted's **call,** a sharp *eek,* is squeakier than Black-headed's. **Range:** Common in wooded habitat along watercourses. Rare throughout west in migration. Very rare in winter on southern California coast.

Black-headed Grosbeak Pheucticus melanocephalus

L 8¼" (21 cm) Large, with a very large, triangular bill, upper mandible darker than in Rose-breasted Grosbeak. **Male** has cinnamon underparts, all-black head. In flight, both sexes show yellow wing linings. **Female** plumage is generally buffier above and below than female Rose-breasted, with less streaking below. **First-fall male** Black-headed is rich buff below, with little or no streaking. **Songs** and **calls** of the two species are nearly identical, but Black-headed's call is lower pitched. **Range:** Common in open woodlands, forest edges. Casual during migration and winter to the midwest and east. Black-headed hybridizes occasionally with Rose-breasted in range of overlap in the Great Plains.

Crimson-collared Grosbeak Rhodothraupis celaeno

L 8½" (22 cm) **Range:** Endemic to northeast Mexico; casual to south Texas, mainly in winter. Stubby, mostly black bill; long tail; black on head variable. **Adult male** has pinkish-red rear collar; pinkish-red below, mottled with black; blackish above. **Adult female** is olive above; has thin yellowish wing bars; yellow-green rear collar; yellowish-olive underparts; wing panel on primaries and secondaries. Immatures show less black than female; male shows some red and black patches by second spring. Skulks on or near ground; often raises rear crown feathers. **Song,** a variable warble; **call** a penetrating, rising and falling *seeiyu.*

Yellow Grosbeak Pheucticus chrysopeplus L 9¼" (24 cm)

Range: Mexican species, casual early-summer vagrant to southeastern Arizona, chiefly in open woodlands and river courses of low mountains. **Male** distinguished by large size, massive bill, yellow plumage. **Females** similar to male but duller; crown streaked; immature male has yellower head than female; like adult male by second spring. Compare with Evening Grosbeak (page 454). **Call** and **song** are like Black-headed's.

Rose-breasted Grosbeak

breeding adult ♂

winter adult ♂

breeding adult ♂

1st fall ♂

♀

1st spring ♂

Black-headed Grosbeak

♀

breeding adult ♂

1st fall ♂

adult ♀

adult ♂

Crimson-collared Grosbeak

adult ♂

adult ♀

Yellow Grosbeak

Northern Cardinal *Cardinalis cardinalis* L 8¾" (22 cm)
Conspicuous crest; cone-shaped reddish bill. **Male** is red overall, with black face. **Female** is buffy brown or buffy olive, tinged
with red on wings, crest, tail. **Juvenile** browner overall, dusky
bill; juvenile female lacks red tones. Bill shape helps distinguish
female and juveniles from similar Pyrrhuloxia. **Song** is a loud,
liquid whistling with many variations, including *cue cue cue* and
cheer cheer cheer and *purty purty purty*. Both sexes sing almost
year-round. Common **call** is a sharp *chip*. **Range:** Abundant
throughout the east, inhabits woodland edges, swamps, streamside thickets, suburban gardens. Nonmigratory, but this species
has expanded its range northward during the 20th century.

Pyrrhuloxia *Cardinalis sinuatus* L 8¾" (22 cm)
Thick, strongly curved, pale bill helps distinguish this species
from female and juvenile Northern Cardinal. **Male** is gray overall, with red on face, crest, wings, tail, underparts. **Female** shows
little or no red. **Song** is a liquid whistle, thinner and shorter than
Northern Cardinal's; **call** is a sharper *chink*. **Range:** Fairly common in thorny brush, mesquite thickets, desert, woodland edges,
and ranchlands. Casual to southeastern California.

Dickcissel *Spiza americana* L 6¼" (16 cm)
Yellowish eyebrow, thick bill, and chestnut wing coverts are distinctive. **Breeding male** has black bib under white chin, bright
yellow breast. **Female** lacks black bib, but has some yellow on
breast; chestnut wing patch muted. **Winter adult male**'s bib is
less distinct. **Immatures** are duller overall than adults, breast and
flanks lightly streaked; female may show almost no yellow or
chestnut. The Dickcissel's common **call,** often given in flight, is
a distinctive electric-buzzer *bzrrrrt*. **Song,** a variable *dick dick
dickcissel*. **Range:** Breeds in open weedy meadows, grainfields,
prairies. Abundant and gregarious, especially in migration, but
numbers and distribution vary locally from year to year outside
core breeding range. Irregular east of the Appalachians; occasional breeding is reported outside mapped range. Rare migrant
to both coasts; more common in the east, where a few winter.

Blue Grosbeak *Guiraca caerulea* L 6¾" (17 cm)
Wide chestnut wing bars, large heavy bill, and larger overall size
distinguish **male** from male Indigo Bunting (next page). **Females**
of these two species also similar; compare bill shape, wing bars,
and overall size. Juvenile resembles female; in first fall, some
immatures are richer brown than female. **First-spring male**
shows some blue above and below; resembles adult male by second winter. In poor light, Blue Grosbeak resembles Brown-
headed Cowbird (page 440); note Blue Grosbeak's bill shape and
wing bars; also the habit of twitching and spreading its tail. Listen for distinctive **call,** a loud, explosive *chink*. **Song** is a series
of rich, rising and falling warbles. **Range:** Fairly common; found
in low, overgrown fields, streamsides, woodland edges, brushy
roadsides. Uncommon to rare in fall north to New England and
the Maritime Provinces.

Northern Cardinal

♂

♀

juvenile ♂

Pyrrhuloxia

♀

♂

Dickcissel

breeding ♂

breeding ♀

winter adult ♂

immature ♂

immature ♀

Blue Grosbeak

breeding adult ♂

♀

immature

1st spring ♂

Indigo Bunting *Passerina cyanea* L 5½" (14 cm)

Breeding male deep blue. Smaller than Blue Grosbeak (preceding page); bill much smaller; lacks wing bars. In **winter** plumage, blue is obscured by brown and buff edges. Female is brownish, with diffuse streaking on breast and flanks. Young birds resemble female. **Song,** a series of varied phrases, usually paired. **Range:** Common in woodland clearings, borders. Uncommon to rare to Maritimes, Newfoundland; rare to Pacific states.

Lazuli Bunting *Passerina amoena* L 5½" (14 cm)

Adult male bright turquoise above and on throat; cinnamon across breast; thick white wing bars. **Female** is grayish-brown above, rump grayish-blue; underparts white, with buffy wash on throat and breast. Juveniles resemble female but have distinct fine streaks across breast; **immature male** is mostly blue by first spring. Winter male's blue color is obscured by brown and buff edges. **Song** is a series of varied phrases, sometimes paired; faster and less strident than Indigo Bunting's song. **Range:** Found in open deciduous or mixed woodlands, chaparral, especially in brushy areas near water. Occasionally hybridizes with Indigo.

Painted Bunting *Passerina ciris* L 5½" (14 cm)

Adult male's gaudy colors are retained year-round. **Female** is bright green above, paler yellow-green below. **Juvenile** is much drabber; look for telltale hints of green above, yellow below. Fall molt in eastern nominate race takes place on breeding grounds; western *P. c. pallidior* molts on winter grounds. First-winter male resembles adult female; by spring, may show tinge of blue on head, red on breast. **Song** is a rapid series of varied phrases, thinner and sweeter than song of Lazuli Bunting. Distinctive **call** is a loud, rich *chip.* **Range:** Locally common in low thickets, streamside brush, woodland borders. Casual vagrant north on Atlantic coast to New York; west to midwest, California. Declining in east.

Varied Bunting *Passerina versicolor* L 5½" (14 cm)

Breeding male's plumage is colorful in good light; otherwise appears black. In **winter,** colors are edged with brown. **Female** is plain gray-brown or buffy-brown above, slightly paler below; resembles female Indigo Bunting but lacks streaks and all wing markings; note also that Varied Bunting's culmen is slightly more curved. First-spring male resembles female. **Song** is similar to song of Painted Bunting. **Range:** Locally common in thorny thickets in washes, canyons, often near water.

Blue Bunting *Cyanocompsa parellina* L 5½" (14 cm)

Range: Tropical species, very rare and irregular in southern Texas, mainly in winter. Smaller than Blue Grosbeak; lacks wing bars. Found in brushy fields, woodland edges. **Adult male** is blackish-blue overall, paler blue on crown, cheeks, shoulder, and rump. Immature male similar, but with brownish cast to wings. Contrasting colors and thick, strongly curved bill distinguish male from male Indigo Bunting. **Females** separated by female Blue Bunting's richer, uniform color, lack of streaking below.

Indigo Bunting

winter adult ♂

fall ♀

1st spring ♂

breeding adult ♂

Lazuli Bunting

breeding adult ♂

1st spring ♂

♀

juvenile

Painted Bunting

adult ♂

♀

Varied Bunting

breeding adult ♂

winter adult ♂

♀

Blue Bunting

adult ♂

♀

Blackbirds (Family Icteridae)

Strong, direct flight and pointed bills mark this diverse group. Species vary in plumage from iridescent black to yellow to brilliant orange.

Bobolink *Dolichonyx oryzivorus* L 7" (18 cm)

Breeding male entirely black below; hindneck is buff, fading to whitish by midsummer; scapulars and rump white. Male in **spring** migration shows pale edgings. **Breeding female** is buffy overall, with dark streaks on back, rump, and sides; head is striped with dark brown. Juvenile resembles female, but lacks streaking below; has indistinct spotting on throat and upper breast. All **fall** birds resemble female, but are rich yellow-buff below, especially, on average, the immatures. In all plumages, note sharply pointed tail feathers. Bobolinks nest primarily in hayfields, weedy meadows, where male's loud, bubbling *bob-o-link* **song,** often given in flight, is heard in spring and summer. Flight **call** heard year-round is a repeated, whistled *ink.* **Range:** Most birds migrate east of the Great Plains. Rare in fall on west coast.

Eastern Meadowlark *Sturnella magna* L 9½" (24 cm)

Black V-shaped breast band on yellow underparts is characteristic of both Meadowlark species after postjuvenile molt. In fresh **fall** plumage, birds are more richly colored overall, with partly veiled breast band and buffy flanks. On Eastern females, yellow does not reach submoustachial area, and barely does so on males. In widespread northern nominate race, dark centers are visible on central tail feathers, uppertail coverts, secondary coverts, and tertials. Southeastern *S. m. argutula* is smaller and darker, especially those from Florida. Southwestern *lilianae* is pale, like Western Meadowlark, but note more extensively white tail. South Texas birds, *hoopesi,* are intermediate in color. **Song** is a clear, whistled *see-you see-yeeer;* distinctive **call** a high, buzzy *drzzt,* given in a rapid series in flight. **Range:** Generally common in fields and meadows; has declined in the east in recent decades.

Western Meadowlark *Sturnella neglecta* L 9½" (24 cm)

Plumages similar to those of Eastern Meadowlark, but in **spring** and summer yellow extends well into the submoustachial area, especial in males; yellow often veiled in **fall.** Lack of dark centers to feathers of upperparts helps to separate from the more easterly races of Eastern, in areas where ranges overlap. Also, in fresh fall and winter plumage, upperparts, flanks, and undertail region are much paler. Distinguished from pale Eastern *S. m. lilianae* by mottled cheeks, more mottled postocular and lateral crown stripes, and less white in tail. Northwestern *S. n. confluenta* is darker above, and can show dark feather centers like Eastern. **Song** is a series of bubbling, flutelike notes of variable length, usually accelerating toward the end. Sharp *chuck* note; rattled flight **call** similar to Eastern, but lower pitched; also gives a whistled *wheet.* **Range:** Westerns are gregarious in winter; large flocks often gather along roadsides, while Easterns usually prefer taller cover. Eastern and Western Meadowlarks hybridize in midwest.

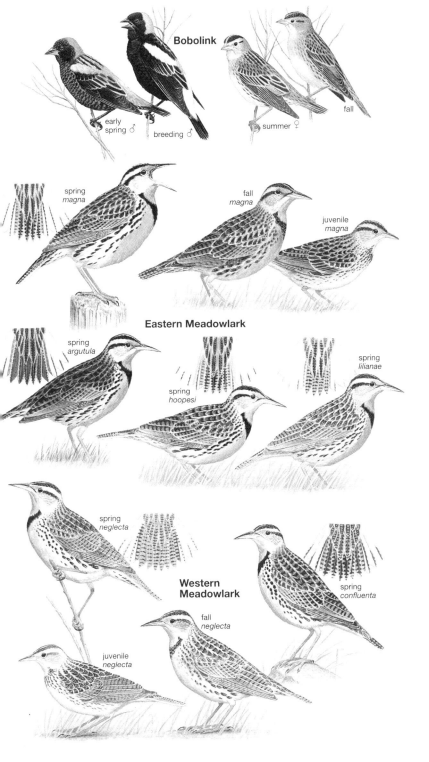

Bobolink

early spring ♂

breeding ♂

summer ♀

fall

spring
magna

fall
magna

juvenile
magna

Eastern Meadowlark

spring
argutula

spring
hoopesi

spring
lilianae

spring
neglecta

Western Meadowlark

spring
confluenta

fall
neglecta

juvenile
neglecta

Yellow-headed Blackbird

Xanthocephalus xanthocephalus L 9½" *(24 cm)* **Adult male**'s yellow head and breast and white wing patch contrast sharply with black body. **Adult female** is dusky brown, lacks wing patch; eyebrow, lower cheek, and throat are yellow or buffy yellow; belly streaked with white. **Juvenile** is dark brown with buffy edgings on back and wing; head mostly tawny. **First-winter male** resembles female but darker; wing coverts tipped with white; acquires adult plumage by following fall. **Song** begins with a harsh, rasping note, ends with a long, descending buzz. **Call** note is a hoarse *croak.* **Range:** Locally common throughout most of range; uncommon and very local in the midwest. Prefers freshwater marshes or reedy lakes; often seen foraging in nearby farmlands. Rare fall and winter visitor to the east coast. Casual in spring and fall as far north as southern Alaska.

Red-winged Blackbird *Agelaius phoeniceus*

L 8¾" *(22 cm)* More rounded wings and usually stouter bill than Tricolored Blackbird. Glossy black **male** has red shoulder patches broadly tipped with buffy-yellow. In perched birds, red patch may not be visible; only the buffy or whitish border shows. **Females** are dark brown above, heavily streaked below; sometimes show a red tinge on wing coverts or pinkish wash on chin and throat. **First-year male** plumage is distinguished from female Tricolored by reddish shoulder patch. Males in races of California's Central Valley and central coast region nearly or totally lack the buffy band behind red shoulder patch; known collectively as **"Bicolored Blackbird."** Females are darker bellied, more like female Tricolored; but note chestnut-buff edging on feathers of upperparts, except when worn away; more rounded wings; stouter bill, except for *A. p. aciculatus* of Kern Basin in south-central California, which has a bill like Tricolored. Red-winged Blackbird's **song** is a liquid, gurgling *konk-la-reee,* ending in a trill. Most common **call** is a *chack* note. **Range:** This abundant, aggressive species is often found in immense flocks in winter. Generally nests in thick vegetation of freshwater marshes, sloughs, dry fields; forages in surrounding fields, orchards, woodlands.

Tricolored Blackbird *Agelaius tricolor* L 8¾" *(22 cm)*

More pointed wings and bill than Red-winged Blackbird. Glossy black **male** has dark red shoulder patches, often hidden, broadly tipped with white; tips are buffy white in fresh fall plumage. **Females** usually lack any red on shoulder and never show pinkish on throat; plumage is sooty-brown and streaked overall; darker than female Red-winged Blackbird, particularly on belly; note more pointed wings and bill. In fresh fall plumage, all Tricolored Blackbirds have grayish-buff edging on feathers of upperparts, unlike chestnut-buff of Red-winged. Distinction between females is more difficult when feathers are worn. Tricolor's variety of **calls** are much like Red-winged's, but its harsh, braying *on-ke-kaaangh* **song** lacks Red-winged's liquid tones. **Range:** Gregarious; found year-round in large flocks in open country and dairy farms; nests in large colonies in marshes.

Yellow-headed Blackbird

♀

juvenile

spring adult ♂

1st winter ♂

spring adult ♂

Red-winged Blackbird

♀

immature ♀

1st year ♂

♀

"Bicolored Blackbird"

adult ♂

adult ♂

breeding ♂

Tricolored Blackbird

♀

Common Grackle *Quiscalus quiscula L 12½" (32 cm)*

Long, keel-shaped tail; pale yellow eyes. Plumage appears all-black at a distance. In good light, **males** show glossy purplish-blue head, neck, and breast. Widespread race *Q. q. versicolor,* called "Bronzed Grackle," occurs in most of New England and west of the Appalachians; it has a bronze back, blue head, and purple tail. Smaller "Purple Grackle," *quiscula* of the southeast, has a narrow bill, purple head, bottle green back, and blue tail. An intergrade population from the mid-Atlantic *(stonei)* shows variable head color and purplish back with iridescent bands of variable color. Females are smaller and duller than males. **Juveniles** are sooty-brown, with brown eyes. Common Grackle's **song** is a short, creaky *koguba-leek;* **call** note, a loud *chuck.* **Range:** Abundant and gregarious, roaming in mixed flocks in open fields, marshes, parks, suburban areas. Casual in Pacific states and Alaska, primarily in late spring.

Boat-tailed Grackle *Quiscalus major*

♂ *L 16½" (42 cm)* ♀ *L 14½" (37 cm)* Large grackle with a very long, keel-shaped tail; smaller overall size, duller eye color, and more rounded crown than Great-tailed Grackle. **Adult male** is iridescent blue-black. **Adult female** is tawny-brown with darker wings and tail. Eye color is mostly brown in nominate race of coastal Texas and Louisiana and *Q. m. westoni* of Florida; *alabamensis* of coastal Mississippi to northwest Florida and the largest race, *torreyi,* on the Atlantic coast, have a yellow iris. **Juvenile male** is black but lacks iridescence; **young female** shows a hint of spotting or streaking on breast. Juveniles resemble respective adults by mid-fall. **Calls** include a quiet chuck and a variety of rough squeaks, rattles, and other chatter. Most common **song** is a series of harsh *jeeb* notes. **Range:** This common, noisy grackle seldom strays beyond coastal saltwater marshes except in Florida, where it also inhabits inland lakes and streams. Nests in small colonies. Range is expanding northward on the Atlantic coast.

Great-tailed Grackle *Quiscalus mexicanus*

♂ *L 18" (46 cm)* ♀ *L 15" (38 cm)* A large grackle with very long, keel-shaped tail, golden yellow eyes. **Adult male** is iridescent black with purple sheen on head, back, and underparts. **Adult female**'s upperparts are brown; underparts cinnamon-buff on breast to grayish-brown on belly; shows less iridescence than male. **Juveniles** resemble adult female but are even less glossy and show some streaking on underparts. Juvenile males are like adult males by mid-fall. Females west of central Arizona are smaller and paler below than races to the east. In narrow zone of range overlap, Great-tailed Grackle is distinguished from Boat-tailed by bright yellow eyes, larger size, and flatter crown. Varied **calls** include clear whistles and loud *clack* notes. **Range:** Common, especially in open flatlands with scattered groves of trees and in marshes, wetlands. Casual far north of breeding range; rapidly expanding north and west.

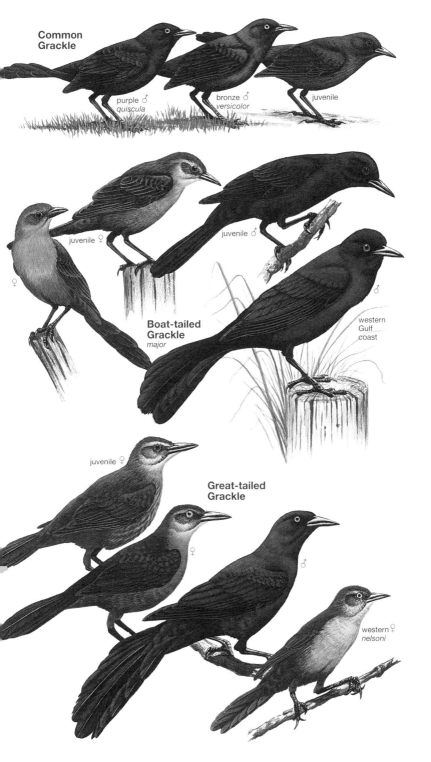

Common Grackle

purple ♂ *quiscula*   bronze ♂ *versicolor*   juvenile

juvenile ♀   juvenile ♂

♀

Boat-tailed Grackle *major*

western Gulf coast   ♂

juvenile ♀

Great-tailed Grackle

♀   ♂

western ♀ *nelsoni*

Rusty Blackbird *Euphagus carolinus* L 9" (23 cm)

Adults and fall immatures have yellow eyes. Fall adults and immatures are broadly tipped with rust; tertials and wing coverts edged with rust. **Fall female** has broad, buffy eyebrow, buffy underparts, gray rump. **Fall male** is darker; eyebrow fainter. The rusty feather tips wear off by spring, producing the dark **breeding** plumage. Juveniles resemble winter adults but have dark eyes. **Call** is a harsh *tschak;* **song,** a high, squeaky *koo-a-lee.* **Range:** Fairly common in wet woodlands, swamps; nests in shrubs or conifers near water. Gregarious in fall and winter. Rare in west.

Brewer's Blackbird *Euphagus cyanocephalus*

L 9" (23 cm) **Male** has yellow eyes; **female**'s are usually brown. Male is black year-round, with purplish gloss on head and neck, greenish gloss on body and wings. A few **fall males** show buffy feather edgings, but never on tertials or wing coverts, as in Rusty Blackbird; note also the shorter, thicker bill. Female and juveniles are gray-brown. Typical **call** is a harsh *check;* song, a wheezy *que-ee* or *k-seee.* **Range:** Common in open habitats; gregarious. Casual in winter northeast of mapped range.

Shiny Cowbird *Molothrus bonariensis* 7½" (19 cm)

Range: Mainly South American species, which spread through the West Indies, arriving in south Florida in 1985. Uncommon in coastal south Florida; rare to eastern Gulf coast; casual to Texas and North Carolina; accidental to Oklahoma, Maine, and New Brunswick. Sleeker, with longer tail, flatter head, and longer, more pointed bill than Brown-headed. **Male** blackish with purple gloss on head, breast, back. **Female** and juveniles resemble female Brown-headed except for shape, darker color, more prominent eyebrow. **Song,** whistled notes followed by trills.

Brown-headed Cowbird *Molothrus ater* L 7½" (19 cm)

Male's brown head contrasts with metallic green-black body. **Female** is gray-brown above, paler below. **Juvenile** is paler above, more heavily streaked below; pale edgings give its back a scaled look. Young males molting to adult plumage in late summer are a patchwork of buff, brown, and black. Southwestern birds are distinctly smaller than eastern; Rockies and Great Basin birds are larger. Male's **song** is a squeaky gurgling. **Calls** include a harsh rattle and squeaky whistles. Common; found in woodlands, farmlands, suburbs. Feeds with tail cocked up. All cowbirds lay their eggs in nests of other species.

Bronzed Cowbird *Molothrus aeneus* L 8¾" (22 cm)

Red eyes distinctive at close range. Bill larger than Brown-headed Cowbird. **Adult male** is black with bronze gloss; wings and tail blue-black; thick ruff on nape and back gives a hunchbacked look. **Adult female** of the Texas race, *M. a. aeneus,* is duller than the male; **juveniles** are dark brown. In southwestern *loyei,* female and juveniles are gray. **Call** is a harsh, guttural *chuck.* **Song** is wheezy and buzzy. **Range:** Locally common in open country, brushy areas, wooded mountain canyons; forages in flocks.

Rusty Blackbird

fall ♀

fall ♂

breeding ♀

breeding ♂

Brewer's Blackbird

fall variant ♂

♀

Shiny Cowbird

♀

♂

Brown-headed Cowbird

juvenile

♀

♂

Bronzed Cowbird
aeneus

southwestern
♀ *loyei*

juvenile

♂

♀

Orchard Oriole *Icterus spurius L 7¼" (18 cm)*

Adult male is chestnut overall, with black hood. During winter, **female** is olive above, yellowish below. **Immature male** resembles female; acquires black bib and, sometimes, traces of chestnut by first spring. Smaller size, lack of orange tones or whitish belly, and thinner, more curved bill distinguish female and immature male from Baltimore and Bullock's Orioles. Compare especially with *I. c. nelsoni* race of Hooded Oriole. Locally common in suburban shade trees, orchards. **Calls** include a sharp *chuck*. **Song** is a loud, rapid burst of whistled notes, downslurred at the end. **Range:** Rare vagrant to Arizona, California, the Maritimes.

Hooded Oriole *Icterus cucullatus L 8" (20 cm)*

Bill long and slightly curved. **Breeding male** is orange or orange-yellow; note black patch on throat. Western birds *(I. c. nelsoni)* are yellower; the two Texas races *(sennetti* is shown) are orange, with black on forehead. All **winter adult males** have buffy brown tips on back, forming a barred pattern; compare with Streak-backed Oriole (next page). Hooded **female** and **immature male** lack pale belly of Bullock's Oriole; bill is more curved. Compare *nelsoni* also with female and immature male Orchard Oriole, which are smaller, purer lemon yellow below, and have smaller bill. Immature male acquires black patch on throat by winter. **Calls** include a whistled, rising *wheet;* **song** is a series of whistles, trills, and rattles. Common in varied habitats, especially near palms. **Range:** Breeding has expanded northward on west coast.

Baltimore Oriole *Icterus galbula L 8¼" (22 cm)*

Adult male has black hood and back, bright orange rump and underparts; large orange patches on tail. **Adult females** are brownish-olive above and orange below, with varying amounts of black on head and throat; those with maximum black (shown) resemble first-spring males. Extent and intensity of color on underparts of **fall immatures** is highly variable; has distinctly contrasting wing bars and palish lores; no eye line or yellowish eyebrow. Common **call** is a rich *hew-li;* also gives a series of rattles. **Song** is a musical, irregular sequence of *hew-li* and other notes. **Range:** Common breeder in deciduous woodland over much of the east. Some winter in the south. Rare vagrant to west.

Bullock's Oriole *Icterus bullockii L 8¼" (22 cm)*

Formerly considered same species as Baltimore Oriole; some interbreeding on Great Plains. **Adult male** has less black on head than Baltimore: crown, eye line, throat patch; note bold white patch on wing and entirely orange outer tail feathers. **Females** and **immatures** have yellow throat and breast, unlike extensive orange of most Baltimores; note Bullock's dark eye line, less contrasting wing bars. Most birds show dark "teeth" intruding into white of median covert bar. By **first spring,** males have black lores and throat. **Song** made up of whistles and harsher notes; **call** a harsh *cheh* or series of same. **Range:** Breeds where shade trees grow. Small numbers winter in coastal California. Casual vagrant to the east, but most reports are dull, immature Baltimores.

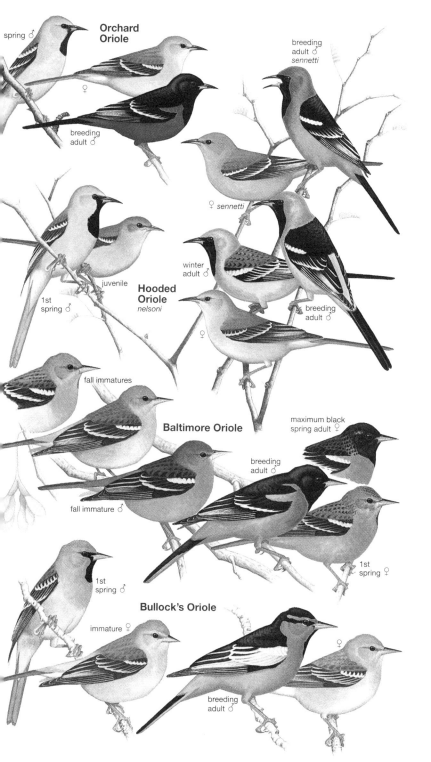

Orchard Oriole

spring ♂

♀

breeding adult ♂

breeding adult ♂ *sennetti*

♀ *sennetti*

1st spring ♂

juvenile

Hooded Oriole
nelsoni

winter adult ♂

♀

breeding adult ♂

fall immatures

Baltimore Oriole

maximum black spring adult ♀

breeding adult ♂

fall immature ♂

1st spring ♀

1st spring ♂

Bullock's Oriole

immature ♀

♀

breeding adult ♂

Black-vented Oriole *Icterus wagleri L 8½" (22 cm)*

Range: Resident from central Nicaragua to northern Mexico; accidental to south and west Texas, southeast Arizona. Long, narrow bill and long, graduated tail. **Adult** has solid black head, back, undertail coverts, tail, and wings, except for yellow shoulders; the border between breast and belly is chestnut. **Immature** has black lores and chin; streaked back. Juvenile lacks black bib. Black-vented Oriole's **call** is a nasal *nyeh,* often repeated.

Streak-backed Oriole *Icterus pustulatus L 8¼" (21 cm)*

Range: Mexican species, casual in fall and winter in southeastern Arizona, southern California. Distinguished from winter Hooded Oriole (preceding page) by broken streaks on upper back; deeper orange head; and much thicker based, straighter bill. **Female** is duller than **male. Immatures** resemble adult female, but immature female lacks black on throat. *Wheet* **call** is softer than Hooded Oriole's call and does not rise in pitch. Other calls resemble those of Baltimore Oriole.

Altamira Oriole *Icterus gularis L 10" (25 cm)*

Distinguished from Hooded Oriole (preceding page) by larger size, thicker based bill, and, in **adult,** by orange shoulder patch. Lower wing bar whitish. **Immatures** are duller than adults, shoulder patch yellow; like adults by second fall. **Calls** include a low, raspy *ike ike ike;* **song** is a series of clear, varied whistles. **Range:** Found in southernmost Texas in tall trees, willows, mesquite.

Audubon's Oriole *Icterus graduacauda L 9½" (24 cm)*

Range: Tropical species, resident but uncommon in southern Texas. **Male** has greenish-yellow back. Female is slightly duller. Rather secretive; often seen foraging on ground. **Song,** a series of soft, tentative, three-note warbles.

Spot-breasted Oriole *Icterus pectoralis L 9½" (24 cm)*

Adults have an orange or yellow-orange patch on shoulders; black lores and throat; dark spots on upper breast; extensive white on wings. **Juveniles** are yellower overall; **immatures** may lack breast spots. **Song** is a long, loud series of melodic whistles. **Range:** Middle American species, introduced and now established in southern Florida. Prefers suburban gardens. Florida population has declined over past two decades.

Scott's Oriole *Icterus parisorum L 9" (23 cm)*

Adult male's black hood extends to back and breast; rump, wing patch, and underparts bright lemon yellow. Adult female is olive and streaked above, dull greenish-yellow below; throat shows variable amount of black. **Immature male**'s head is mostly black by first spring. **Females** and immatures are larger, grayer and more streaked above, have straighter bill, than female Hooded Oriole (preceding page). Common **call** note is a harsh *shack;* **song,** a mixture of rich, whistled phrases. **Range:** Found in arid and semiarid habitats. Casual east to Minnesota, Wisconsin, Louisiana. A few winter in southern California.

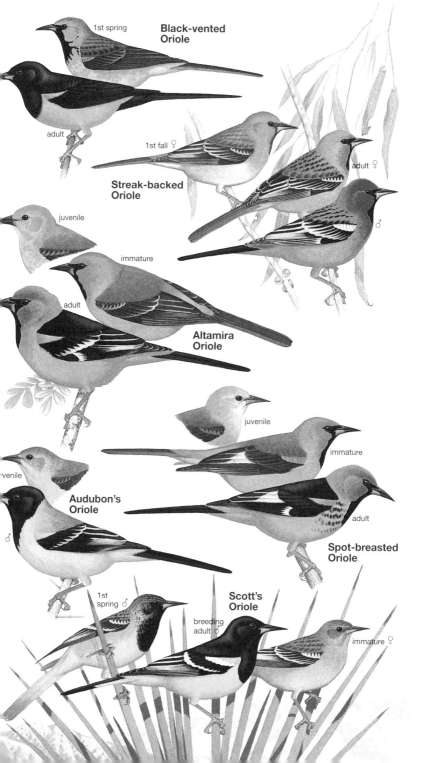

Black-vented Oriole

1st spring

adult

Streak-backed Oriole

1st fall ♀

adult ♀

♂

juvenile

immature

adult

Altamira Oriole

juvenile

immature

venile

adult

Audubon's Oriole

♂

Spot-breasted Oriole

1st spring ♂

Scott's Oriole

breeding adult ♂

immature ♀

Finches (Family Fringillidae)

Seedeaters with an undulating flight. Many nest in the far north; in fall, flocks of "winter finches" may roam south.

Oriental Greenfinch *Carduelis sinica* L 6" (15 cm)
Range: Asian species. Casual migrant, mainly in spring, on outer Aleutians; one Pribilofs record. **Adult male** has greenish face and rump, dark gray nape and crown, bright yellow wing patch and undertail coverts. **Adult female** is paler, with a brownish head. **Juvenile** has same yellow areas as adults but is streaked overall.

Brambling *Fringilla montifringilla* L 6¼" (16 cm)
Range: Eurasian species; fairly common but irregular migrant on Aleutians; rare on Pribilofs and St. Lawrence Island; casual in fall and winter in Canada and northern U.S. **Adult male** has tawny orange shoulders, spotted flanks; head and back fringed with buff in fresh fall plumage that wears down to black by spring. **Female** and juvenile have mottled crown, gray face, striped nape. Flight **call,** a nasal *check-check-check;* also gives a nasal *zwee.*

Common Chaffinch *Fringilla coelebs* L 6" (15 cm)
Range: Palearctic species; casual to northeastern North America; reports elsewhere are probably escaped cage birds. Has white patches on lesser coverts, base of primaries, wing bar; outer tail feathers white. **Male**'s crown and nape are blue-gray; shows pinkish below, pinkish-brown above. **Female**'s head is mostly gray with brown lateral stripes. **Call** a metallic *pink-pink;* also a *hweet.*

Gray-crowned Rosy-Finch *Leucosticte tephrocotis*
5¾" (15 cm) With Brown-capped and Black Rosy-Finches, restored to full species status from subspecies of Rosy Finch. All have yellow bill in **winter,** black by spring. Dark brown, with gray on head; pink on wings and underparts; underwings silvery. Female less pink, **juveniles** grayish. Western *L. t. littoralis,* **"Hepburn's Rosy-Finch,"** and much larger, darker Pribilofs *umbrina* and Aleutians *griseonucha* show more gray on face. **Call,** a high, chirping *chew,* often given in courtship flight. **Range:** Descends from higher elevations in winter. Some races are migratory.

Brown-capped Rosy-Finch *Leucosticte australis*
L 6" (15 cm) Plumages, behavior, and voice like Gray-crowned. Lacks gray head band of other North American Rosy-Finches. **Male** rich brown; darker crown; extensive pink on underparts **Female** much drabber.

Black Rosy-Finch *Leucosticte atrata* L 6" (15 cm)
Plumages, behavior, and voice like Gray-crowned. Darkest Rosy-Finch. **Male** is blackish; in fresh plumage, scaled with silver-gray; has gray head band; shows extensive pink. **Female** is blackish-gray with little pink. **Range:** Casual to California, Arizona.

Oriental Greenfinch

adult ♂

adult ♀

juvenile

Brambling

breeding ♂

fall ♂

♀

Common Chaffinch

♀

♂

Pribilofs winter ♂ *umbrina*

"Hepburn's" winter ♂ *littoralis*

Gray-crowned Rosy-Finch

juvenile

interior

breeding ♂

Brown-capped Rosy-Finch

breeding ♂

breeding ♀

Black Rosy-Finch

breeding ♀

breeding ♂

Purple Finch *Carpodacus purpureus L 6" (15 cm)*

Not purple, but rose red over most of **adult male**'s body, brightest on head and rump. Rose color is acquired in second fall. Back is streaked; tail strongly notched. Pacific coast race, *C. p. californicus*, is buffier below and more diffusely streaked than the widespread *purpureus*, especially in females. **Adult female** and immatures are heavily streaked below; closely resemble Cassin's Finch. Ear patch and whitish eyebrow and submoustachial stripe are slightly more distinct in Purple Finch; bill slightly stubbier and more curved; undertail coverts are often not streaked. Compare also with female House Finch. **Calls** include a musical *churlee* and, in flight, a sharp *pit*, a bit sharper in *californicus*. **Song** is a rich warbling, longer and more variable in *purpureus;* shorter than Cassin's song, lower and less strident than House Finch song. **Range:** Fairly common; found in coniferous or mixed woodland borders, suburbs, parks, orchards; in the Pacific states, inhabits coniferous forests, oak canyons, lower mountain slopes.

Cassin's Finch *Carpodacus cassinii L 6¼" (16 cm)*

Crimson of **adult male**'s cap ends sharply at brown-streaked nape. Throat and breast paler than Purple Finch; streaks on sides more distinct. Red hues begin to appear late in second summer. Tail strongly notched. Undertail coverts always distinctly streaked, unlike many Purples. **Adult female** and immatures otherwise closely resemble Purple Finch. Cassin's facial pattern is slightly less distinct; culmen is straighter and longer; has longer primary projection. In flight, Cassin's gives a dry *kee-up* or *tee-dee-yip* **call**. Lively **song,** a variable warbling, longer and more complex than song of Purple Finch, especially *californicus*. **Range:** Fairly common in upper mountain forests, evergreen woodlands. Casual in winter east of range and to west coast.

House Finch *Carpodacus mexicanus L 6" (15 cm)*

Male has brown cap; front of head, bib, and rump are typically red but can vary to orange or occasionally yellow. Bib is clearly set off from streaked underparts. Tail is squarish. **Adult female** and juveniles are brown-streaked overall; lack distinct ear patch and eyebrow of Purple and Cassin's Finches. Young males acquire adult coloring by first fall. Lively, high-pitched **song** consists chiefly of varied three-note phrases; includes strident notes, unlike Purple Finch's song; usually ends with a nasal *wheer*. **Calls** include a whistled *wheat*. **Range:** Abundant; found in semiarid lowlands and slopes up to about 6,000 feet. Introduced in the east in the 1940s, where its range is fast expanding; range has expanded rapidly also in the west; especially numerous in towns.

Common Rosefinch *Carpodacus erythrinus*

L 5¾" (15 cm) **Range:** Eurasian species; very rare migrant, chiefly in spring, on the western Aleutians and other western Alaska islands. Strongly curved culmen. Lacks distinct eyebrow. **Adult male**'s head, breast, and rump are red. **Female** and immatures are diffusely streaked above and below except on pale throat. **Call** is a soft, nasal *djuee.*

♀ *californicus*

Purple Finch

♀ *purpureus*

ific coast
lt ♂
ornicus

eastern adult ♂
purpureus

Cassin's Finch

adult ♀

adult ♂

typical ♂

House Finch

variant ♂

♀

Common Rosefinch

♀

adult ♂

Red Crossbill *Loxia curvirostra* L 6¼" (16 cm)
Bill with crossed tips identifies both crossbill species. Red Cross-bill's dark brown wings lack the bold white bars of White-winged Crossbill. Plumage highly variable. Most **males** are reddish over-all, brightest on crown and rump, but may be pale rose or scar-let or largely yellow; always have red or yellow on throat. Most **females** are yellowish-olive; may show patches of red; throat is always gray, except in a small northern subspecies where yellow extends to center, but not sides, of throat. **Juveniles** are boldly streaked; a few juveniles and a very few adult males show white wing bars, the upper bar thinner than the lower. Immatures are like the respective adult but juvenile wing is retained. All birds except adult males have olive edges on wings. Subspecies vary widely in size; extremes are shown here. All have large heads and short, notched tails. **Calls,** given chiefly in flight, vary from one subspecies to another. **Song** begins with several two-note phrases followed by a warbled trill. **Range:** Fairly common, Red Cross-bills inhabit coniferous woods. May nest at any time of year, especially in southern range. Highly irregular in their wander-ings, dependent upon cone crops. Any race may turn up almost anywhere. Irruptive migrant. Has bred as far south as Georgia.

White-winged Crossbill *Loxia leucoptera* L 6½" (17 cm)
All ages have black wings with white tips on the tertials, two bold, broad white wing bars. Upper wing bar is often hidden by scapu-lars. **Adult male** is bright pink overall, paler in winter. **Immature male** is largely yellow, with patches of red or pink. **Adult female** is mottled with yellowish-olive or grayish; rump pale yellow; underparts grayish-olive, with yellow wash on breast and sides. **Juvenile** is heavily streaked; wing bars thinner than in adults. White-winged Crossbill's distinctive flight **call,** is a rapid series of harsh *chet* notes. Variable **song,** often delivered in display flight, combines harsh rattles and musical warbles. **Range:** Inhabits coniferous woods. Highly irregular in its wanderings, dependent upon pine cone crops. Irruptive migrant.

Pine Grosbeak *Pinicola enucleator* L 9" (23 cm)
Large, plump, and long-tailed. Bill is dark, stubby, strongly curved. Two white wing bars, sometimes tinged with pink in adult male. **Male**'s gray plumage is tipped with red on head, back, and underparts, pinker in fresh fall plumage. **Female** and immatures are grayer overall; head, rump, and underparts vari-ably yellow or reddish; some females and immature males are russet. Typical flight **call** is a whistled *pui pui pui;* alarm call, a musical *chee-vli.* Location call shows considerable geographic variation. **Song** is a rather short, musical warble. **Range:** Fairly common; inhabits open coniferous woods. In winter, found also in deciduous woods, orchards, suburban shade trees. Usually unwary and approachable. Irruptive winter migrant in the east.

variant ♂

juvenile

Red Crossbill

northern *minor* ♀

typical ♀

typical ♂

southwestern *stricklandi* ♂

immature ♂

juvenile

White-winged Crossbill

♀

winter adult ♂

♀

adult ♂

russet variant

Pine Grosbeak

Pine Siskin *Carduelis pinus* L 5" (13 cm)

Prominent streaking; yellow at base of tail and in flight feathers conspicuous in flight; bill thinner than in other finches. **Juvenile**'s overall yellow tint is lost by late summer. **Calls** include a rising *tee-ee* and, in flight, a harsh, descending *chee.* **Song** is similar to that of American Goldfinch but much huskier. **Range:** Gregarious; may flock with goldfinches in winter. Found in coniferous and mixed woods in summer; forests, shrubs, and fields in winter. Winter range is erratic.

American Goldfinch *Carduelis tristis* L 5" (13 cm)

Breeding adult male is bright yellow with black cap; black wings have white bars, yellow shoulder patch; uppertail and undertail coverts white; tail black-and-white. **Female** is duller overall, olive above; lacks black cap and yellow shoulder patch. White undertail coverts distinguish female from most Lesser Goldfinches. **Winter adults** and immatures are either brownish or grayish above; male may show some black on forehead. **Juvenile** plumage, held into November, has cinnamon-buff wing markings and rump. **Song** is a lively series of trills, twitters, and *swee* notes. Distinctive flight **call,** *per-chik-o-ree.* **Range:** Common and gregarious; found in weedy fields, open second-growth woodlands, roadsides, especially in thistles, sunflowers.

Lesser Goldfinch *Carduelis psaltria* L 4½" (11 cm)

All birds have a white wing patch at base of primaries. Entire crown black on **adult male;** back varies from black in eastern part of range to greenish in western birds. Most **adult females** are dull yellow below; except for a few extremely pale birds, they lack the white undertail coverts typical of American Goldfinch. **Immature male** lacks full black cap. Juveniles resemble adult female. **Call,** a plaintive, kittenlike *tee-yee.* **Song** is somewhat similar to that of American Goldfinch. **Range:** Common in dry, brushy fields, woodland borders, gardens. Casual in Great Plains; accidental in the east.

Lawrence's Goldfinch *Carduelis lawrencei*

L 4¾" (12 cm) Wings extensively yellow; upperparts grayish in breeding plumage; large yellow patch on breast. **Male** has black face and yellowish tinge on back. **Winter** birds are browner above, duller below. **Juvenile** is faintly streaked, unlike other goldfinches. **Call** is a bell-like *tink-ul.* Mixes *tink* notes into jumbled, melodious **song.** Lawrence's and Lesser Goldfinches often mimic other species' songs. **Range:** Fairly common in spring and early summer; may sometimes flock with other goldfinches, but generally prefers drier interior foothills and mountain valleys; also western fringe of desert near watercourses. Erratic but usually uncommon at other seasons. Irregular fall movements to southwestern U.S. Casual as far east as western Texas.

Pine Siskin

juvenile

American Goldfinch

breeding ♀

breeding ♂

winter adult ♂

winter ♀

juvenile

Lesser Goldfinch

♀

ack-backed ♂

en-backed ♂

pale ♀

immature ♂

Lawrence's Goldfinch

winter ♀

winter ♂

breeding ♂

juvenile

Common Redpoll *Carduelis flammea L 5¼" (13 cm)*
Red or orange-red cap or "poll," black chin. Closely resembles
Hoary Redpoll, but usually has distinct streaks on flanks, rump,
undertail coverts; bill is slightly larger. **Male** usually has bright
rosy breast and sides. Both sexes paler, buffier in winter. **Juveniles** lack red cap until late-summer molt; males acquire pinkish breast by end of second summer. Extent of interbreeding
between Common and Hoary Redpolls is unknown, and taxo-
nomic status uncertain. When perched, Common gives a *swee-
ee-eet* **call;** flight call, a dry rattling. **Song** combines trills and
twittering. **Range:** Fairly common; breeds in subarctic forests
and tundra scrub. Unwary. Forms large winter flocks; frequents
brushy, weedy areas, also catkin-bearing trees like alder and birch.

Hoary Redpoll *Carduelis hornemanni L 5½" (14 cm)*
Closely resembles Common Redpoll but is usually frostier and
paler overall, with a slightly smaller bill. Streaking below and on
rump minimal or absent. **Male**'s breast is usually paler and pinker
than on Common; color does not extend to cheeks or sides. **Calls**
and **song** similar to Common. **Range:** Fairly common; nests on
or near the ground above Arctic tree line. *C. h. hornemanni,* of
Canadian Arctic islands and Greenland, is larger and paler than
more widespread *exilipes.* Rare sightings, especially of *exilipes,*
occur south of Canada in winter, almost always with Commons.

Evening Grosbeak *Coccothraustes vespertinus*
L 8" (20 cm) Stocky, noisy finch. Big bill pale yellow or greenish
by spring, whitish by fall; prominent white patch on inner wing.
Yellow forehead and eyebrow on **adult male;** dark brown and
yellow body. Grayish-tan **female** has thin, dark malar stripe,
white-tipped tail; second wing patch, on primaries, is conspicuous in flight. **Juveniles** have brown bills; female resembles adult
female; male yellower overall, wing and tail like adult male. Loud,
strident **call:** *clee-ip* or *peeer.* **Range:** Breeds in mixed woods; in
the west, mainly in mountains. In winter frequents woodlots,
shade trees, feeders; numbers and range limits vary greatly.

Hawfinch *Coccothraustes coccothraustes L 7" (18 cm)*
Range: Eurasian species. Rare spring stray on western Aleutians;
casual off other islands of western Alaska. Stocky; yellowish-
brown above; pinkish-brown below; has black throat and lores;
shows conspicuous white band on extended wing. Big bill is blue-
black in spring, yellowish in fall. Female resembles **male,** but is
duller; has grayish secondaries and inner primaries. Walks with
parrotlike waddle. **Call** is a loud, explosive *ptik.*

Eurasian Bullfinch *Pyrrhula pyrrhula L 6½" (17 cm)*
Range: Eurasian species. Casual migrant on Aleutians; casual in
winter on Alaskan mainland. Cheeks, breast, and belly intense
rosy red in **male,** brown in **female.** Black cap and face, gray back,
prominent whitish bar on wing, distinct white rump. In profile,
top of head and bill form unbroken curve. Juvenile resembles
female, but with brown cap. **Call** is a soft, piping *pheew.*

juvenile breeding ♀ breeding ♂ winter ♀

Common Redpoll
flammea

winter ♂

winter ♀ *exilipes*

winter ♂ *hornemanni*

Hoary Redpoll

winter ♂ *exilipes*

♂

♀

Evening Grosbeak

breeding ♂

juvenile ♂

breeding ♀

...wfinch

breeding ♂

♂

♀

Eurasian Bullfinch
cassinii

Old World Sparrows (Family Passeridae)

A large Old World family. Two species have become established in North America, with shorter legs, thicker bills than native sparrows.

House Sparrow *Passer domesticus* L 6¼" (16 cm)

Male in breeding plumage has gray crown, chestnut nape, black bib, black bill. Fresh **fall** plumage is edged with gray, obscuring these markings; bill becomes brownish. **Female** is best identified by the combination of streaked back, buffy eye stripe, and unstreaked breast. Juveniles resemble adult female. **Range:** Abundant and aggressive, House Sparrows are omnipresent in populated areas. Gregarious in winter. Also known as English Sparrow.

Eurasian Tree Sparrow *Passer montanus* L 6" (15 cm)

Range: Old World species, introduced and now locally common in parks, suburbs, and farmlands around St. Louis, Missouri, and in nearby Illinois. Accidental in Indiana, Wisconsin, Manitoba, Kentucky, Ontario. Gregarious all year. Brown crown, black ear patch, black throat distinguish **adult.** Compare with House Sparrow's gray crown and more extensively black throat. **Juvenile** has dark mottling on crown, dark gray throat and ear patch.

Estrildid Finches (Family Estrildidae)

Large, Old World family found from Africa to Australia and South Pacific islands. Most are small, with pointed tails. Related to weavers.

Nutmeg Mannikin *Lonchura punctulata*

L 4½" (11 cm) **Range:** Widespread southeast Asian species, now established in greater Los Angeles area. Small, with heavy bill, pointed tail. **Adults** are rich reddish-brown above; dark scaling on breast, sides, flanks; yellowish on uppertail coverts; bill black. **Juveniles** are tan; bill slate gray. **Song,** *tiks* and whistles, is nearly inaudible; **call,** a loud *kibee.* Favors grassy, weedy areas.

Weavers (Family Ploceidae)

Large, primarily African family of finchlike birds. Breeding males are often highly colored. Known for elaborate woven nests.

Orange Bishop *Euplectes franciscanus*

L 4" (10 cm) **Range:** Native to sub-Saharan Africa; widely introduced. Established since the early 1980s in greater Los Angeles area, where it favors weedy areas, especially river bottoms. **Breeding male** is bright orange-red with black cap, breast, and belly; long tail coverts obscure tail. **Females,** immatures, and winter birds are streaked above. Compare especially with Grasshopper Sparrow (page 408); note Orange Bishop's thicker, pinkish bill; short, blunt tail, often flicked open. Complex **song** high and buzzy. **Calls** include a sharp *tsip* and a mechanical *tsik tsik tsk.*

fall ♂

breeding ♂

House Sparrow

♀

Eurasian Tree Sparrow

juvenile

displaying

breeding ♂

Orange Bishop

Nutmeg Mannikin

ile

♀

Index

The main entry for each species is listed in **boldface** type and refers to the text page opposite the illustration.

A check-off box is provided next to each common-name entry so that you can use this index as a checklist of the species you have identified.

Library of Congress Cataloging-in-Publication Data
Field guide to the birds of North America.
    Includes index.
    1. Birds—North America—Identification I. National
Geographic Society (U.S.) II. Title: Birds of North America.
QL681.F53   1987
598.297   86-33249
ISBN 0-87044-692-4 (prev. ed.)   ISBN 0-7922-7451-2 (rev.)

Artists' Credits

Jonathan K. Alderfer: pages 11-Pacific Golden-Plover, Short-tailed Albatross, and Black-bellied Plover, 15, 27-heads, 29, 31-except Northern Fulmar, 35-Dark-rumped and Murphy's petrels, 37, 39-Wedge-tailed Shearwater, Bulwer's Petrel, left Short-tailed Shearwater, and heads, 41-top right comparison figures, 49, 139-Displaying male Sharp-tailed Grouse, Gunnison Sage-Grouse, Greater Sage-Grouse, 153, 169, 171-flying Black Turnstone, 181, 183, 225-flying winter Dovekie, 227-Long-billed Murrelet, 233-flying Rhinoceros Auklet, 237 (with Schmitt), 339-female Blue-gray Gnatcatcher tail, 359-Common Myna. **David Beadle:** pages 11-Least Flycatcher, 13-Acadian Flycatcher, 14, 19-Willow Flycatcher, 289-293, 311-Philadelphia and Warbling vireos, 335-western Winter Wren, 371-Crescent-chested Warbler, 381-fall male Bay-breasted Warbler, 391-Red-faced Warbler. **Peter Burke:** pages 6-Shiny Cowbird and Variegated Flycatcher, 12, 65-Glossy (except flying) and White-faced ibises, 287-Cuban Pewee and smaller Olive-sided Flycatcher, 297, 303-Piratic and Variegated flycatchers, 307-Thick-billed Vireo, 309-Gray Vireo, 353-White-throated Robin, 389-except Common Yellowthroat, 393, 395-adult male White-collared Seedeater and Yellow-faced Grassquit, 397, 399, 429-Crimson-collared Grosbeak, 441-Shiny Cowbird, 443, 445. **Marc R. Hanson:** pages 31-Northern Fulmar, 35-Mottled, Stejneger's, and Cook's petrels, 39-Flesh-footed, Sooty, and right Short-tailed shearwaters, 41-except top right comparison figures, 43, 45, 145-149. **Cynthia J. House:** pages 9, 11-American Black Duck, 67-except immature Whooper Swan, 69-73, 75-except flying Muscovy Duck, 77-except female American Black Duck, 79-95, 97-except Egyptian Goose, 98-101. **H. Jon Janosik:** pages 25, 27-except heads, 47, 51-55, 159. **Donald L. Malick:** pages 7-sapsuckers, 8, 17,

18-Red-cockaded Woodpecker, 103-105, 109-except Steller's Sea-Eagle and third year Bald Eagle, 111-except three flying juveniles, 113-perched figures, except adult Common Black-Hawk, 117, 119-except dark morph Ferruginous and adult and dark juvenile White-tailed hawks, 121-Crested Caracara and perched Aplomado Falcon, 123-all perched figures and upper flying American Kestrel, 125, 239, 249-257, 273-285. **Killian Mullarney:** pages 157, 179, 185, 188-Little Ringed Plover. **John P. O'Neill:** pages 271-trogons, 303-Rose-throated Becard, 321, 327-331. **Michael O'Brien:** page 33. **Kent Pendleton:** pages 107, 126-except Hook-billed Kite, 127-129, 131-except Chachalaca and flying Chukar, 133-143. **Diane Pierce:** pages 10-Lark and Chipping sparrows, 16-Indigo Bunting, 19-Seaside Sparrow, 57, 59, 61-except Little Egret, 63, 65-White, Scarlet, and flying Glossy ibises and Roseate Spoonbill, 151, 401-407, 409-except Orange Bishop, 411-Seaside Sparrow, 413, 415-except Vesper Sparrow, 417, 419-except flying Dark-eyed Junco, 421, 423, 425-except Yellow-breasted Bunting, 427, 429-except Crimson-collared Grosbeak, 431, 433, 447-except Common Chaffinch, 449-455. **John C. Pitcher:** pages 155, 161-except Common Redshank, 163, 165, 171-except flying Black Turnstone, 175, 177. **H. Douglas Pratt:** pages 2-3, 10-Northern Parula, 16-European Starling, 18-Bachman's Warbler, 235, 245, 247, 265-except immature Green Violet-ear, Lucifer Hummingbird, and Green-breasted Mango, 267-except Xantus's Hummingbird, 269-except wing figures, 271-hummingbirds, 287-except small Olive-sided Flycatcher and Cuban Pewee, 295, 299, 301, 303-except Piratic and Variegated flycatchers and Rose-throated Becard, 305-except Brown Shrike, 307-except Thick-billed Vireo, 309-except Gray Vireo, 311-except Philadelphia and Warbling vireos, 313, 315-except

Island Scrub-Jay and adult Mexican Jays, 317, 319, 323-except Common House-Martin, 325, 333, 335-except western Winter Wren, 337, 339-except female Blue-gray Gnatcatcher tail, 341-except Lanceolated Warbler, 347, 351-except Fieldfare and Red-wing, 353-except White-throated Robin, 355, 359-except Common Myna, 361-except Siberian Accentor, 363-American, tail of Sprague's, and Red-throated pipits, 365-369, 371-except Crescent-chested Warbler, 373-379, 381-except fall male Bay-breasted Warbler, 383-387, 389-Common Yellowthroat, 391-except Red-faced Warbler, 395- Bananaquit, Black-faced Grassquit, and female and first winter male White-collared Seedeater, 437, 439, 441-except Shiny Cowbird. **David Quinn:** pages 16-Redwing and Narcissus Flycatcher, 21, 23, 61-Little Egret, 161-Common Redshank, 187-Common Redshank, 305-Brown Shrike, 323-Common House-Martin, 341-Lanceolated Warbler, 343, 345, 351- Fieldfare and Redwing, 361-Siberian Accentor, 363-Sprague's (except tail), Olive-backed, and Pechora pipits, 425-Yel-low-breasted Bunting, 447-Common Chaffinch. **Chuck Ripper:** pages 225-except flying winter Dovekie, 227-except Long-billed Murrelet, 229, 231, 233-except flying Rhinoceros Auklet, 259, 261-except *arizonae* Whip-poor-will tail. **N. John Schmitt:** pages 6-Island Scrub-Jay, 7-Orange Bishop, 10-Common Black-Hawk,

13-House Sparrow, 67-immature Whooper Swan, 75-flying Muscovy Ducks, 77-female American Black Duck, 97-Egyptian Goose, 109-Steller's Sea-Eagle and third year Bald Eagle, 111- three flying juveniles, 113-adult Common Black-Hawk and all flight figures, 115, 119-dark morph Ferruginous and adult and dark juvenile White-tailed hawks, 121-Hobby and flying Aplomado Falcons, 123-all flight figures except upper American Kestrel, 126-Hook-billed Kite, 131-Chachalaca and fly-ing Chukar, 167- Little, Bristle-thighed, and Eurasian curlews, 186-Little Curlew, 237 (with Alderfer), 241, 243, 263, 315-Island Scrub-Jay and adult Mexican Jays, 357, 409-Orange Bishop, 411-except Seaside Sparrow, 415-Vesper Sparrow, 419-flying Dark-eyed Junco, 457. **Thomas R. Schultz:** pages 10-Western and California gulls, 11-Great Black-backed Gull wing, 16-Black-headed Gull, 173, 191-223, 349, 395-Stripe-headed Tanager, 435. **Daniel S. Smith:** pages 167-Eskimo, Long-billed, and Far Eastern curlews and Whimbrel, 186-except Little Curlew, 187-except Common Redshank, 188-except Little Ringed Plover, 189. **Patricia A. Topper:** cover. **Sophie Webb:** pages 261-*arizonae* Whip-poor-will tail, 265- immature Green Violet-ear, Green-breasted Mango and Lucifer Hummingbird, 267-Xantus's Hummingbird, 269-wing figures.

The world's largest nonprofit scientific and edu-cational organization, the National Geographic Society was founded in 1888 "for the increase and diffusion of geographic knowledge."

For more information about the National Geo-graphic Society and its educational programs and publications, please call 1-800-NGS-LINE (647-5463), or write to the following address:

National Geographic Society
1145 17th Street N.W.
Washington, D.C. 20036-4688 U.S.A.

Visit the Society's Web site at www.nationalgeographic.com.

Acknowledgments

The Book Division wishes to express its gratitude to Kimball L. Garrett (Los Angeles County Museum of Natural History) for his invaluable assistance throughout the preparation of this new edition.

We also thank the following individuals and organizations for their contributions: David Agro; Jon Barlow; Giff Beaton; Louis Bevier; Eirik A.T. Blom; Jack Bowling; Edward S. Brinkley; the Department of Ornithology at the British Museum, Tring; Dawn Burke; Richard Cannings; Steven W. Cardiff; Charles Carlson; Graham Chisholm; Carla Cicero; Rene Corado; Marian Cressman; Bruce Deuel; Donna L. Dittman; Peter J. Dunn; Cameron Eckert; Richard Erickson; Field Museum of Natural History, Chicago; Dr. Clemency Fisher; John W. Fitzpatrick; David Fix; Daniel D. Gibson; Jon S. Greenlaw; J.B. Hallett, Jr.; Robert Hamilton; Jo and Tom Heindel; Matt Heindel; Steve Heinl; Paul M. Hill; Chris Hobbs; Phill Holder; Steve N.G. Howell; Frank Iwen; Greg Jackson; Alvaro Jaramillo; Joseph R. Jehl, Jr.; Ned K. Johnson; Roy Jones; Colin Jones; Marianne G. Koszorus; Los Angeles County Museum of Natural History; Daniel Lane; Dr. Malcolm Largen; Greg Lasley; Nick Lethaby; Tony Leukering; Rich Levad; Liverpool Museum, England; Mark Lockwood; Tim Loseby; Aileen Lotz; Rich MacIntosh; Bruce Mactavish; Laura Martin; Terry McEneaney; Doug McRae; Dominic Mitchell; Steve Mlodinow; Museum of Vertebrate Zoology, University of California, Berkeley; Glen Murphy; Harry Nehls; Michael O'Brien; Jerry Oldenettel; Tony Parker; John Parmeter; Michael Patten; Brian Patteson; Mark Peck; Paul Prior; Peter Pyle; Dr. J.V. Remsen; Don Roberson; Mark Robins; Gary Rosenberg; Royal Ontario Museum; San Diego Natural History Museum; Larry Sansone; Rick Saval; N. John Schmitt; Brad Schram; Thomas Schulenberg; Scott Seltman; David Sibley; Ross Silcock; Mark Stackhouse; Rick Steenberg; Andrew Stepniewski; Doug Stotz; Sherman Suter; Thede Tobish; Charles Trost; Bill Tweit; Philip Unitt; T.R. Wahl; George Wallace; Western Foundation of Vertebrate Zoology; Mel White; David W. Willard; Jeff Wilson; Alan Wormington; Louise Zemaitis; Barry Zimmer; and Kevin Zimmer.

For the First and Second Editions

The following people contributed their time and knowlege to the production of the first and second editions: Thomas A. Allen, J. Phillip Angle, Stephen Bailey, Lawrence G. Balch, Dr. Richard C. Banks, John Barber, Jen and Des Bartlett, Louis Bevier, Daniel Boone, Danny Bystrak, Charles T. Clark, William S. Clark, Robert Dixon, Peter Dunne, Victor Emanuel, Kimball L. Garrett, Freida Gentry, Daniel D. Gibson, Peter Grant, John A. Gregoire, Dr. James L. Gulledge, Dr. George A. Hall, Rebecca Hyman, Lars Jonsson, Kenn Kaufman, Wayne Klockner, Lasse J. Laine, Greg W. Lasley, Paul E. Lehman, Guy McCaskie, Joseph Morlan, Killian Mullarney, Gerald Oreel, Dennis Paulson, Betsy Reeder, Dr. J. V. Remsen, Robert F. Ringler, Philip D. Round, John Rowlett, Richard A. Rowlett, Rose Ann Rowlett, Will Russell, Lawrence Sansone III, Robert T. Scholes, James Stasz, Thede Tobish, Dr. John Trochet, Laurel Tucker, Nigel Tucker, Arnoud van den Berg, Terence R. Wahl, Tony White, Hal Wierenga, Claudia P. Wilds, Alan Wormington, and Kevin Zimmer.

The National Museum of Natural History, Smithsonian Institution, Washington, D.C. was particularly helpful and important to this project. The following organizations also contributed their expertise: U.S. Fish and Wildlife Service's Patuxent Wildlife Research Center in Laurel, Maryland; the Museum of Natural Science, Louisiana State University, Baton Rouge; the Museum of Vertebrate Zoology, University of California at Berkeley; the Denver Museum of Natural History, Colorado; the Museum of Natural History, Santa Barbara, California; and the Natural History Museum, San Diego, California.

Published by the National Geographic Society
John M. Fahey, Jr. *President and Chief Executive Officer*
Gilbert M. Grosvenor *Chairman of the Board*
Nina D. Hoffman *Senior Vice President*

Prepared by the Book Division
William R. Gray *Vice President and Director*
Charles Kogod *Assistant Director*
Barbara A. Payne *Editorial Director and Managing Editor*
David Griffin *Design Director*

Consultants for the Third Edition

Jon L. Dunn, *Chief Consultant*
Jonathan K. Alderfer, *Art Consultant and General Consultant*
Paul E. Lehman, *Chief Map Consultant*

Staff for the Third Edition

Mary B. Dickinson, *Editor*
Lyle Rosbotham, *Art Director*
Carl Mehler, *Director of Maps*
Dale-Marie Herring, *Assistant Editor*
Gillian Carol Dean, *Designer*
Victoria Cooper, *Contributing Editor*
Paul E. Lehman, *Chief;* Jon L. Dunn, Shawneen E. Finnegan, Bruce G. Peterjohn, *Map Researchers*
Keith R. Moore, *Map Coordinator*
Michelle H. Picard, *Chief;* Sven M. Dolling, Lonnie Lanham, Scott Lockheed, Gregory Ugiansky, Martin Walz, *Map Production*
Catherine Herbert Howell, *Writer*
R. Gary Colbert, *Production Director*
Richard S. Wain, *Production Project Manager*
Peggy Candore, *Assistant to the Director*
Alexander L. Cohn, *Staff Assistant*
Mark A. Wentling, *Indexer*

Manufacturing and Quality Control

George V. White, *Director*
John T. Dunn, *Associate Director*
Vincent P. Ryan, *Manager*
James J. Sorensen, *Budget Analyst*

Consultants for the First and Second Editions

Jon L. Dunn, Eirik A. T. Blom, *Chief Consultants*
Dr. George E. Watson, *General Consultant*
Dr. John P. O'Neill, *Consultant on Songbirds*

Staff for the First and Second Editions

Shirley L. Scott, *Editor*
Lise M. Swinson, *Associate Editor*
Mary B. Dickinson, Catherine Herbert Howell, *Assistant Editors*
David M. Seager, *Art Director*
Thomas B. Allen, Wayne Barrett, Seymour L. Fishbein, Philip Kopper, Edward Lanouette, David F. Robinson, Robert D. Selim, Jonathan B. Tourtellot, *Writers*
Paul A. Dunn, Martha B. Hays, Feroline B. Higginson, Diane S. Marton, Maura J. Pollin, Penelope A. Timbers, L. Madison Washburn, Jayne Wise, *Researchers*
Charlotte J. Golin, *Design Assistant*
Georgina L. McCormack, Teresita Cóquia Sison, *Editorial Assistants*
Karen F. Edwards, *Traffic Manager*
Richard S. Wain, *Production Manager*
Leslie A. Adams, Andrea Crosman, *Production*
John T. Dunn, *Quality Control Director*
David V. Evans, *Engraving and Printing*
John D. Garst, Jr., Virginia L. Baza, Peter J. Balch, Joseph F. Ochlak, *Publications Art*
Teresa S. Purvis, *Index*
Contributions by Caroline Hottenstein, Robert M. Poole, Deborah Robertson, Margaret Sedeen

First Edition (1983) 295,000 copies
Second printing (1985) 30,000 copies
Second Edition (1987) 50,000 copies
Second printing (1988) 75,000 copies
Third printing (1989) 50,000 copies
Fourth printing (1991) 50,000 copies
Fifth printing (1992) 100,000 copies
Sixth printing (1994) 100,000 copies
Seventh printing (1995) 100,000 copies

Eighth printing (1996) 150,000 copies
Ninth printing (1998) 10,000 copies
Third Edition (1999) 250,000 copies
Second printing (2000) 100,000 copies
Third printing (2001) 120,000 copies

EXERCISE PHYSIOLOGY

Theory and Application to Fitness and Performance

NINTH EDITION

Scott K. Powers
University of Florida

Edward T. Howley
University of Tennessee, Knoxville

McGraw Hill Education

EXERCISE PHYSIOLOGY: THEORY AND APPLICATION TO FITNESS AND PERFORMANCE,
NINTH EDITION

1 2 3 4 5 6 7 8 9 0 DOW/DOW 1 0 9 8 7 6 5 4

ISBN 978-1-259-09500-9

MHID 1-259-09500-2